...alysis!! This is Buhiro Watsukino!

Beef
1%
(Brain)

Chicken
1%
(Heart)

Pork
98%
(Body)

Escargot 100% (High Quality)

I have trouble with my underwear ripping. Maybe it's because I've been consistently sitting since this series started, or perhaps it's the corrosive nature of Watsuki flatulence, but my underwear continues to self-destruct. Before long, I found myself down to only three pairs. I've never felt so forlorn.

For the last two decades, ever since junior high, I've worn boxers. Perhaps it's time that I took the next step and moved on to a truly manly undergarment, the *fundoshi* [traditional Japanese male loincloth]. I'm honestly considering this move. See my decision in the next volume!

—Nobuhiro Watsuki

Nobuhiro Watsuki earned international accolades for his first major manga series, **Rurouni Kenshin**, about a wandering swordsman in Meiji Era Japan. Serialized in Japan's *Weekly Shonen Jump* from 1994 to 1999, **Rurouni Kenshin**, available in North America from VIZ Media, quickly became a worldwide sensation, inspiring a spin-off short story ("Yahiko no Sakabatô"), an animated TV show and a series of novels. Watsuki's latest hit, **Buso Renkin**, began publication in *Weekly Shonen Jump* in June 2003, and is being adapted into an anime series.

BUSO RENKIN
VOL. 3
The SHONEN JUMP ADVANCED
Manga Edition

STORY AND ART BY
NOBUHIRO WATSUKI

English Adaptation/Lance Caselman
Translation/Toshifumi Yoshida
Touch-up Art & Lettering/James Gaubatz
Design/Yukiko Whitley
Editor/Urian Brown

Editor in Chief, Books/Alvin Lu
Editor in Chief, Magazines/Marc Weidenbaum
VP of Publishing Licensing/Rika Inouye
VP of Sales/Gonzalo Ferreyra
Sr. VP of Marketing/Liza Coppola
Publisher/Hyoe Narita

Printed in the U.S.A.

Published by VIZ Media, LLC
P.O. Box 77010
San Francisco, CA 94107

SHONEN JUMP ADVANCED Manga Edition
10 9 8 7 6 5 4 3 2
First printing, December 2006
Second printing, November 2007

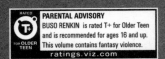

www.viz.com

RATED T+ FOR OLDER TEEN

PARENTAL ADVISORY
BUSO RENKIN is rated T+ for Older Teen and is recommended for ages 16 and up. This volume contains fantasy violence.
ratings.viz.com

SHONEN JUMP ADVANCED MANGA EDITION

Buso Renkin

ブソウレンキン

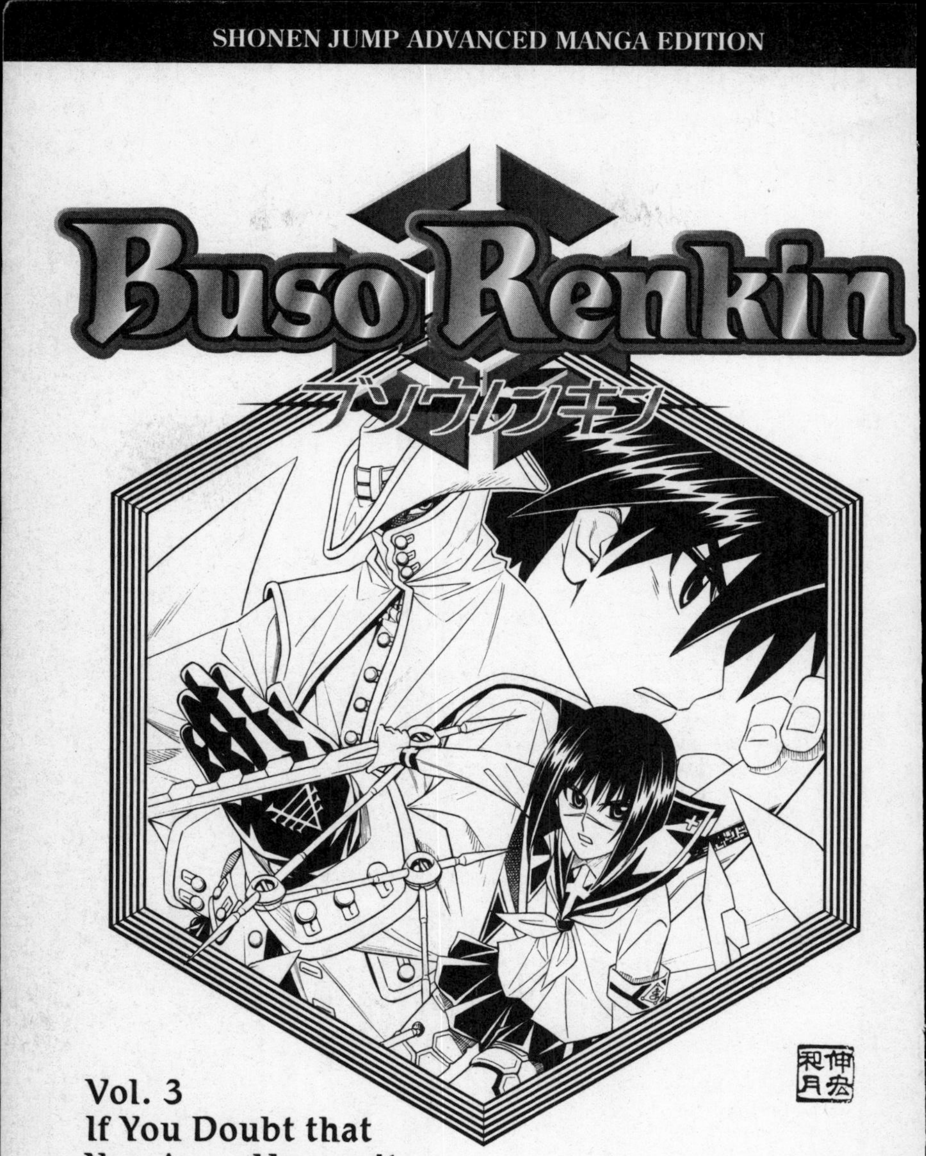
伸宏
和月

Vol. 3
If You Doubt that You Are a Hypocrite

STORY & ART BY
NOBUHIRO WATSUKI

Alchemy

An early scientific practice that combines elements of various disciplines that swept through all of Europe. Such studies were based on the transmutation of base metals into gold, and the preparation of the Elixir of Immortality, none of which succeeded. However, unknown to the public, two alchemic studies succeeded and achieved success of super-paranormal proportions—the homunculus and kakugane.

Kazuki Muto

Once killed by a homunculus but revived by Tokiko, who gave Kazuki the kakugane as a replacement for his heart. He is 16 years old—a year older than his sister, Mahiro. Kazuki's Buso Renkin is the Lance, named the Sunlight Heart.

CHARACTERS

Buso Renkin

Created from a super-paranormal alloy that uses the most advanced alchemic technology. It is activated by the deepest part of the human psyche, one's basic instincts. It can heighten one's ability to heal by arousing the survival instinct. It can also become a one-of-a-kind weapon by materializing the wielder's fighting instincts. The weapon that is formed is called the Buso Renkin. Each kakugane forms into a unique weapon.

Tokiko Tsumura

Selected from those who have knowledge of alchemy, she is an expert of the Buso Renkin, an "Alchemist Warrior." Her Buso Renkin is the Death Scythe, called the Valkyrie Skirt.

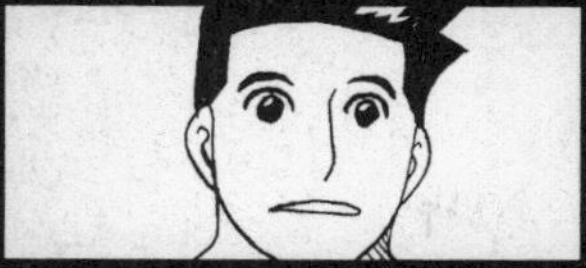

Masashi Daihama

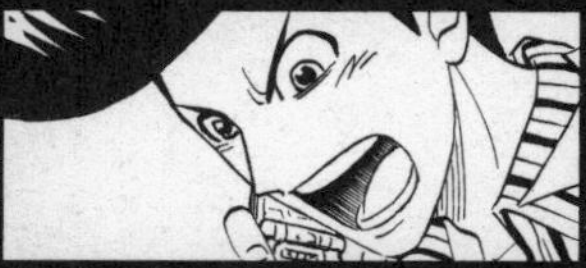

Hideyuki Okakura

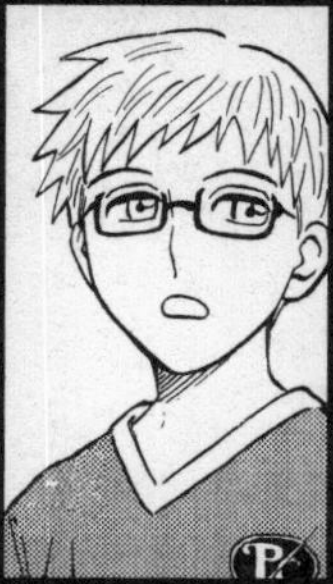

Kouji Rokumasu

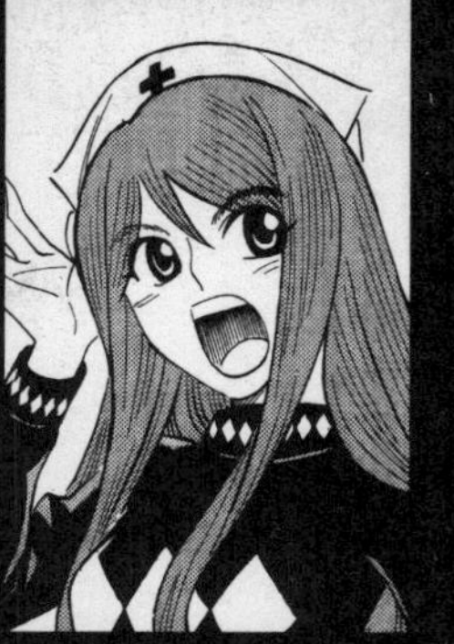

Mahiro Muto

S T O R Y

The homunculus is an artificial life form created by alchemy. Hidden in darkness, it feeds upon unsuspecting humans. The Alchemic Warrior Tokiko comes to Ginsei City and uses herself as a decoy to lure a homunculus out of hiding. High school student Kazuki Muto, unaware of Tokiko's ploy, tries to save her but is killed in the process. Tokiko revives Kazuki by giving him the kakugane, which becomes not only Kazuki's new lease on life but also gives him the power to fight the homunculus. Kazuki makes the decision to fight alongside Tokiko in order to save his friends.

Tokiko finds herself infected by the enemy Papillon Mask Creator with a parasitic core that turns the host into a homunculus. The two investigate the identity of the enemy, who is the only one that can provide the antidote. They find out that the Creator is Koushaku Chouno, who has used his ancestor's research into alchemy to create the homunculus, hoping to eventually cure his disease-ridden body by becoming a homunculus himself. Kazuki and Tokiko manage to defeat the homunculus Washino, but the parasite inside Tokiko progresses to the point of making her immobile. Leaving Tokiko in the care of his sister, Kazuki heads to Chouno's residence. Chouno becomes a homunculus using an incomplete parasite and proceeds to devour everyone around him. Kazuki faces off against Chouno with the aid of Tokiko's kakugane. After a great battle, Kazuki uses up the last of his strength and falls unconscious. Tokiko's superior, a Warrior Chief, appears on the scene and manages to deliver the antidote to Tokiko in time.

The Papillon Mask Creator

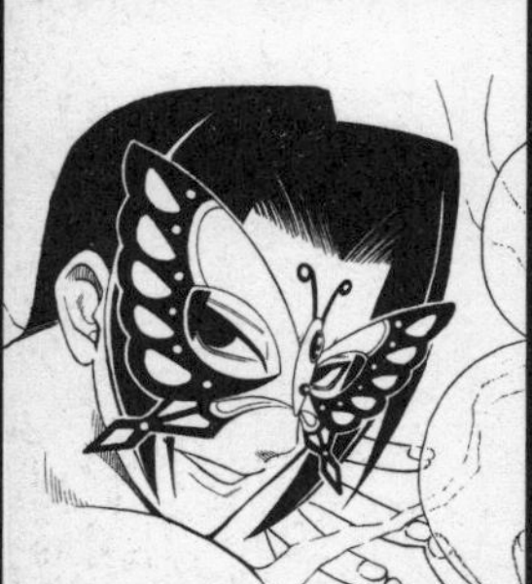

Homunculus

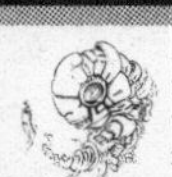

An artificial life form created though alchemic research. Once the homunculus core created from an organism's cell lodges itself in the brain, it will take control of the host's body. The core alters the compounds of the body, changing the host into a monster with the physical attributes of the sample organism. Should a human be the base sample, the host becomes a humanoid homunculus, allowing the host to retain the human psyche. A homunculus can only be destroyed by the power of alchemy.

Warrior Chief

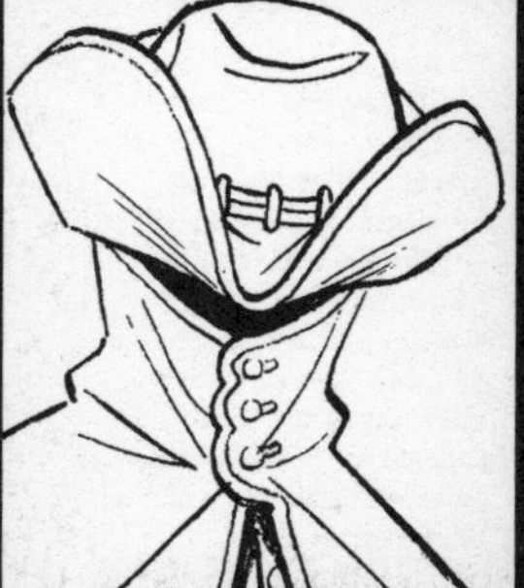

BUSO RENKIN
Volume 3: If You Doubt that You Are a Hypocrite

CONTENTS

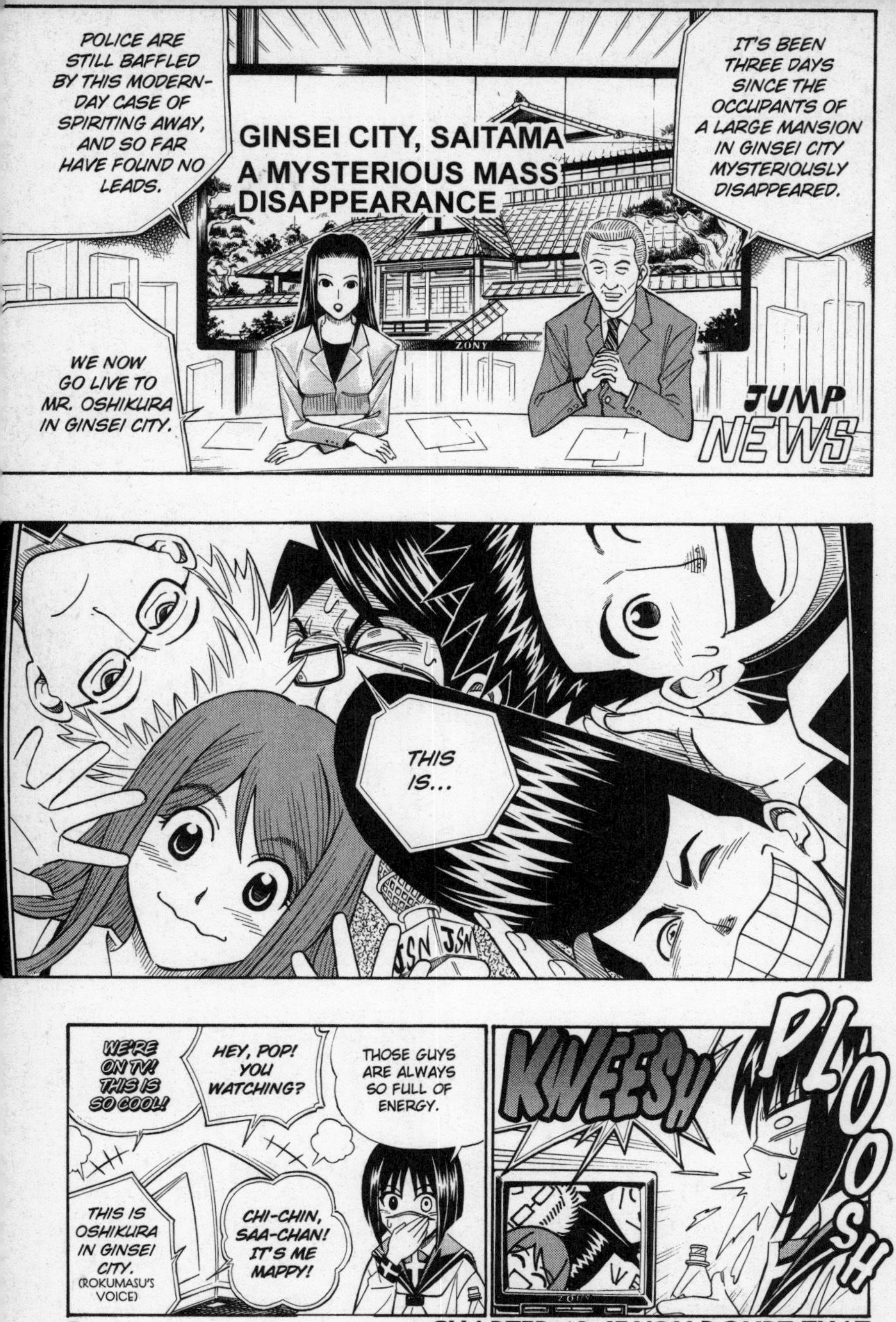
IT'S BEEN THREE DAYS SINCE THE OCCUPANTS OF A LARGE MANSION IN GINSEI CITY MYSTERIOUSLY DISAPPEARED.
GINSEI CITY, SAITAMA A MYSTERIOUS MASS DISAPPEARANCE
POLICE ARE STILL BAFFLED BY THIS MODERN-DAY CASE OF SPIRITING AWAY, AND SO FAR HAVE FOUND NO LEADS.
ZONY
JUMP NEWS
WE NOW GO LIVE TO MR. OSHIKURA IN GINSEI CITY.
THIS IS...
JSN
KWEESH
PLOOOSH
THOSE GUYS ARE ALWAYS SO FULL OF ENERGY.
HEY, POP! YOU WATCHING?
WE'RE ON TV! THIS IS SO COOL!
CHI-CHIN, SAA-CHAN! IT'S ME MAPPY!
THIS IS OSHIKURA IN GINSEI CITY. (ROKUMASU'S VOICE)

CHAPTER 18: IF YOU DOUBT THAT YOU ARE A HYPOCRITE

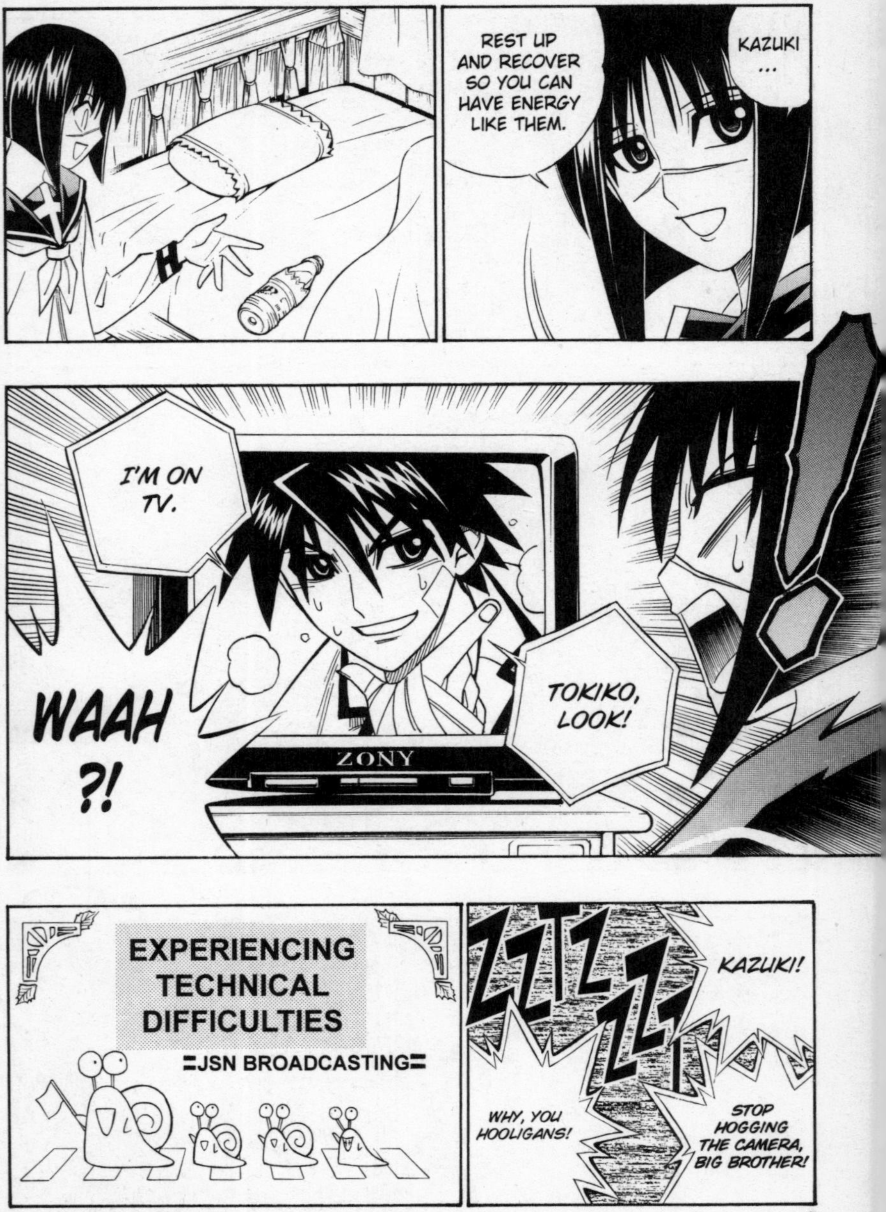
KAZUKI ...
REST UP AND RECOVER SO YOU CAN HAVE ENERGY LIKE THEM.
TOKIKO, LOOK!
I'M ON TV.
WAAH ?!
KAZUKI!
STOP HOGGING THE CAMERA, BIG BROTHER!
WHY, YOU HOOLIGANS!
ZZZZ
EXPERIENCING TECHNICAL DIFFICULTIES
=JSN BROADCASTING=

CHAPTER 18:

IF YOU DOUBT THAT YOU ARE A HYPOCRITE

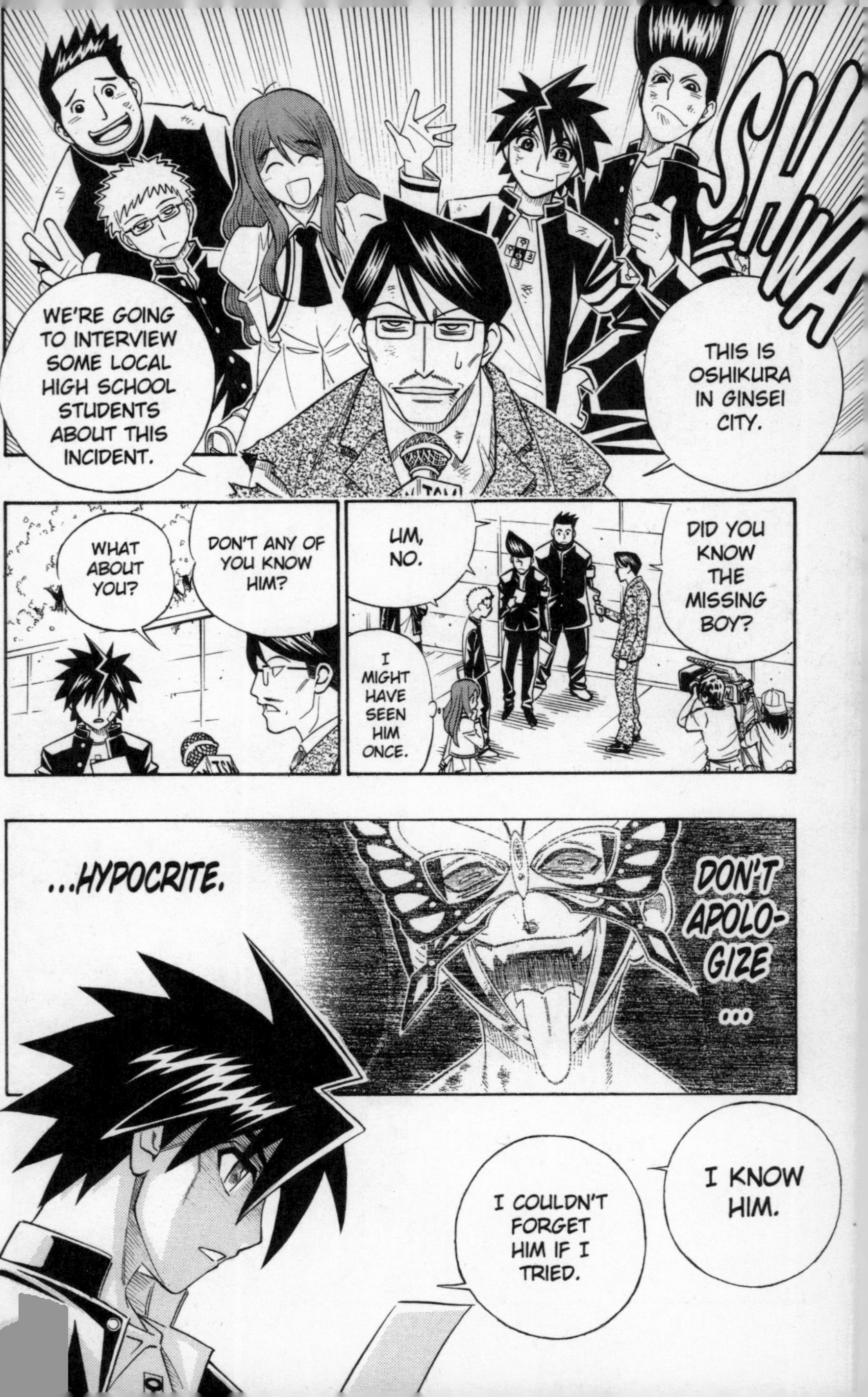
SHWA
THIS IS OSHIKURA IN GINSEI CITY.
WE'RE GOING TO INTERVIEW SOME LOCAL HIGH SCHOOL STUDENTS ABOUT THIS INCIDENT.
DID YOU KNOW THE MISSING BOY?
UM, NO.
I MIGHT HAVE SEEN HIM ONCE.
DON'T ANY OF YOU KNOW HIM?
WHAT ABOUT YOU?
DON'T APOLO-GIZE...
...HYPOCRITE.
I KNOW HIM.
I COULDN'T FORGET HIM IF I TRIED.

READ THIS WAY

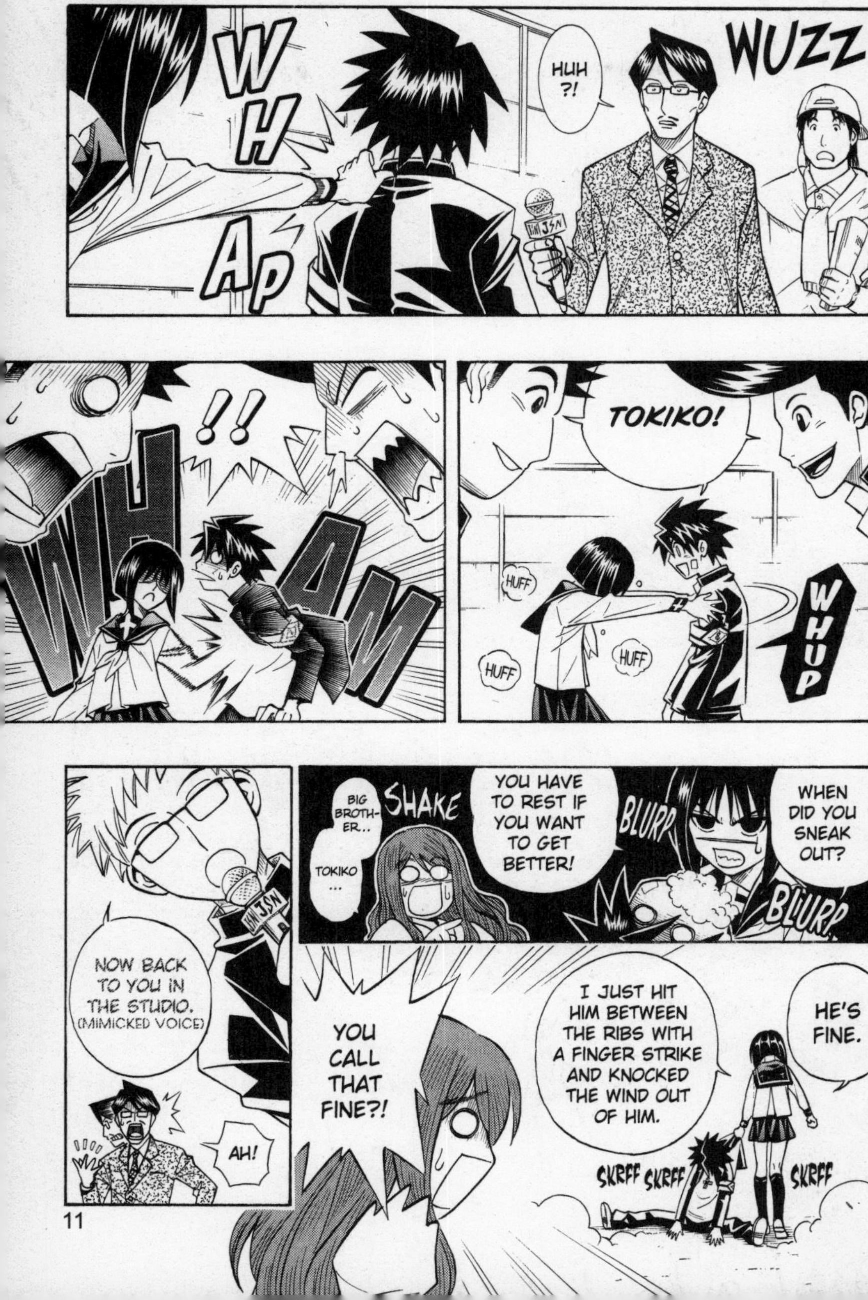
WUZZ
HUH ?!
WHAP
TOKIKO!
WHUP
HUFF
HUFF
HUFF
!!
WHAM
WHEN DID YOU SNEAK OUT?
BLURP
BLURP
YOU HAVE TO REST IF YOU WANT TO GET BETTER!
SHAKE
BIG BROTH-ER...
TOKIKO ...
HE'S FINE.
I JUST HIT HIM BETWEEN THE RIBS WITH A FINGER STRIKE AND KNOCKED THE WIND OUT OF HIM.
SKRFF
SKRFF
SKRFF
YOU CALL THAT FINE?!
NOW BACK TO YOU IN THE STUDIO. (MIMICKED VOICE)
AH!

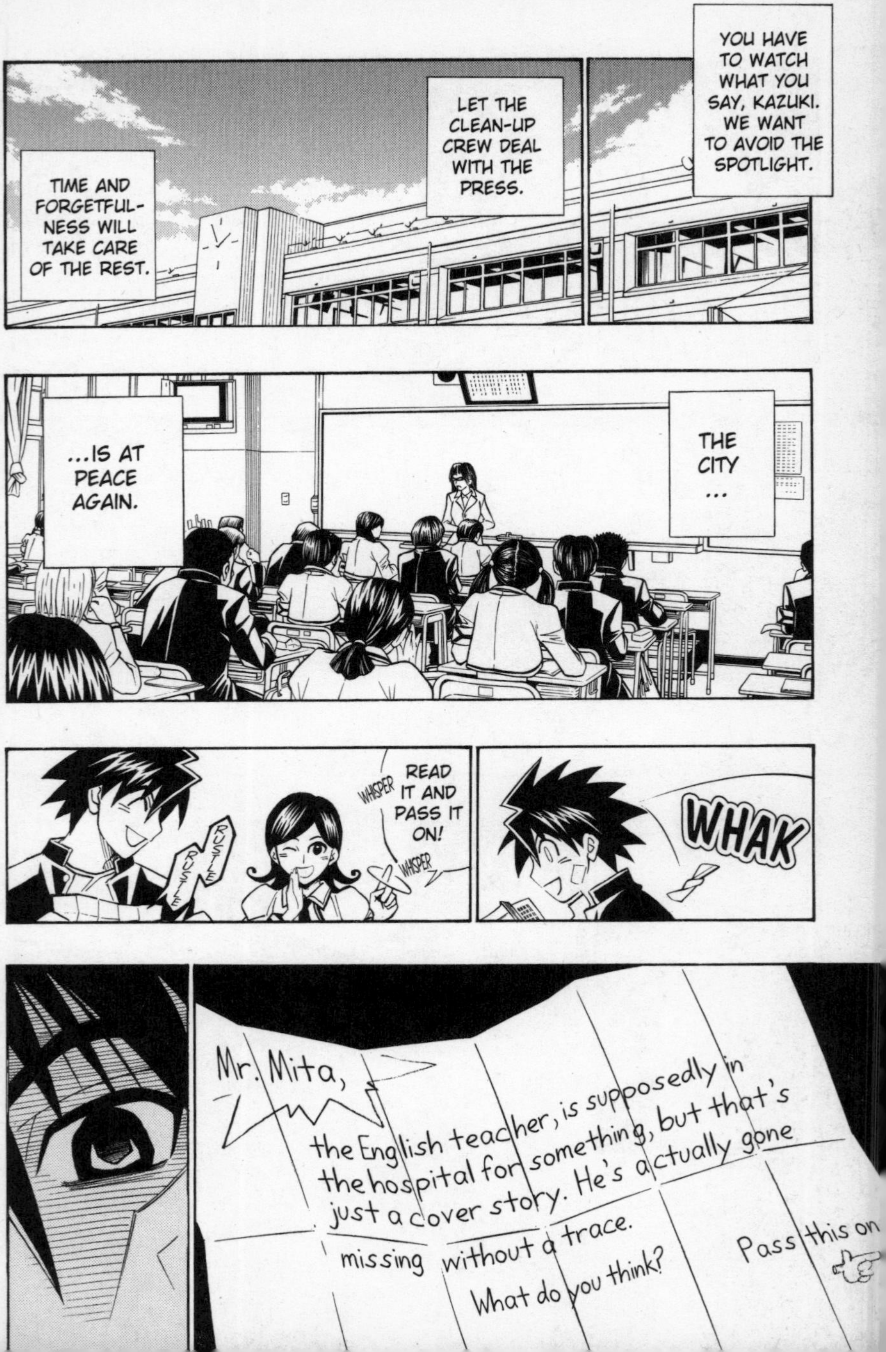
YOU HAVE TO WATCH WHAT YOU SAY, KAZUKI. WE WANT TO AVOID THE SPOTLIGHT.
LET THE CLEAN-UP CREW DEAL WITH THE PRESS.
TIME AND FORGETFUL-NESS WILL TAKE CARE OF THE REST.
THE CITY ...
...IS AT PEACE AGAIN.
WHAK
WHISPER
READ IT AND PASS IT ON!
WHISPER
RUSTLE
RUSTLE
Mr. Mita,
the English teacher, is supposedly in the hospital for something, but that's just a cover story. He's actually gone missing without a trace.
What do you think?
Pass this on

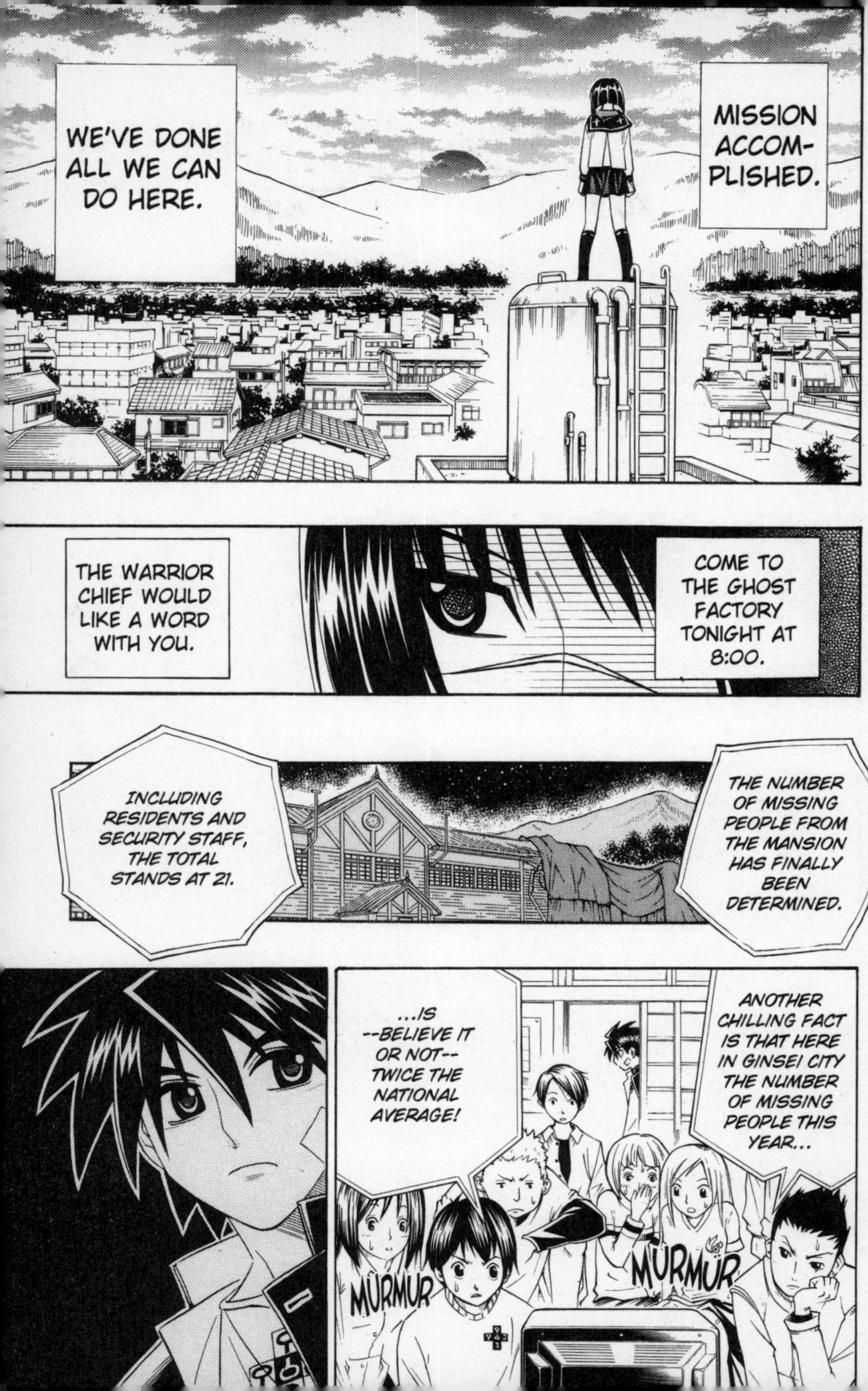
MISSION ACCOM-PLISHED.
WE'VE DONE ALL WE CAN DO HERE.
COME TO THE GHOST FACTORY TONIGHT AT 8:00.
THE WARRIOR CHIEF WOULD LIKE A WORD WITH YOU.
THE NUMBER OF MISSING PEOPLE FROM THE MANSION HAS FINALLY BEEN DETERMINED.
INCLUDING RESIDENTS AND SECURITY STAFF, THE TOTAL STANDS AT 21.
ANOTHER CHILLING FACT IS THAT HERE IN GINSEI CITY THE NUMBER OF MISSING PEOPLE THIS YEAR...
...IS --BELIEVE IT OR NOT-- TWICE THE NATIONAL AVERAGE!
MURMUR
MURMUR

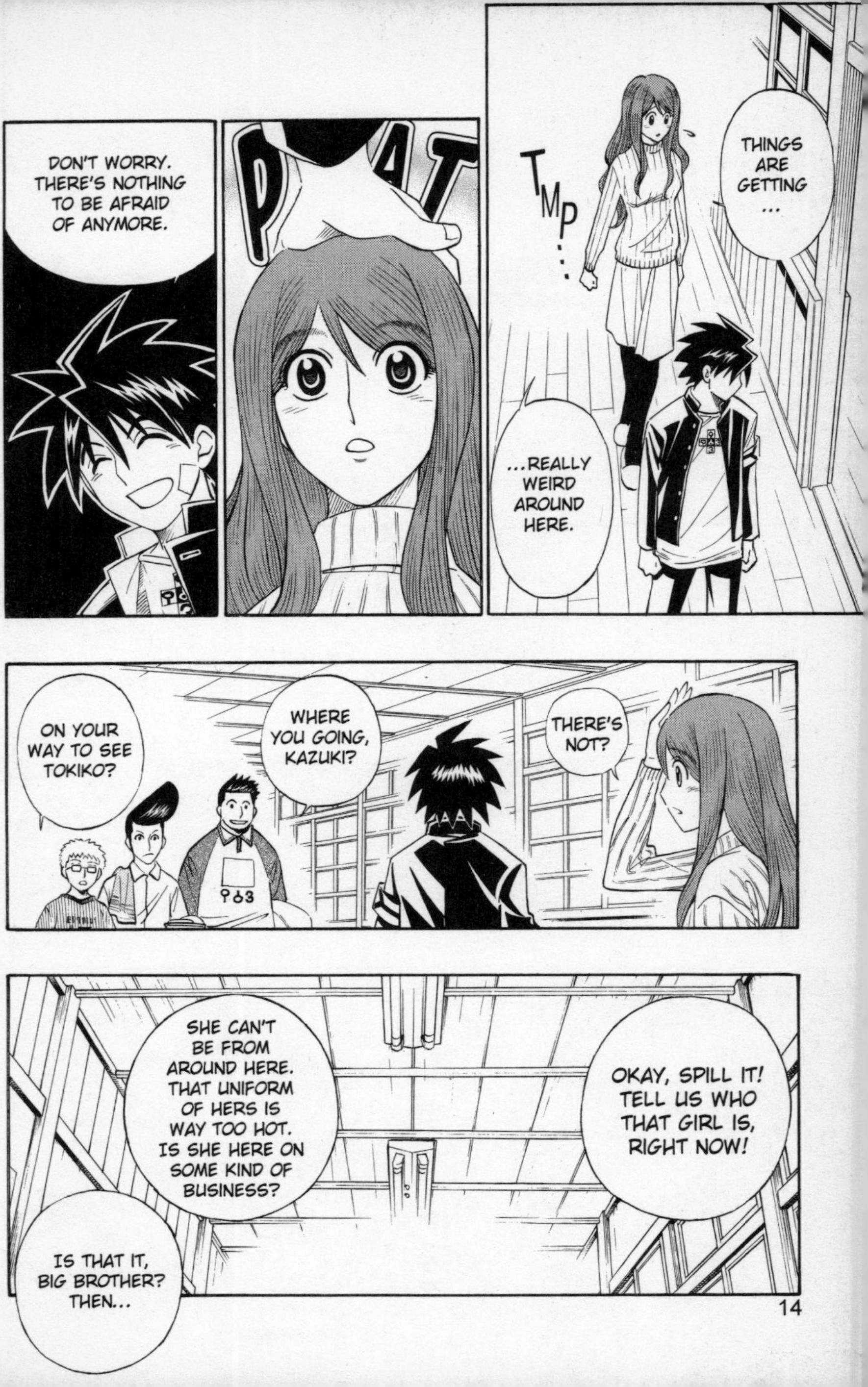
THINGS ARE GETTING ...
TMP...
...REALLY WEIRD AROUND HERE.
PAT
DON'T WORRY. THERE'S NOTHING TO BE AFRAID OF ANYMORE.
THERE'S NOT?
WHERE YOU GOING, KAZUKI?
ON YOUR WAY TO SEE TOKIKO?
OKAY, SPILL IT! TELL US WHO THAT GIRL IS, RIGHT NOW!
SHE CAN'T BE FROM AROUND HERE. THAT UNIFORM OF HERS IS WAY TOO HOT. IS SHE HERE ON SOME KIND OF BUSINESS?
IS THAT IT, BIG BROTHER? THEN...

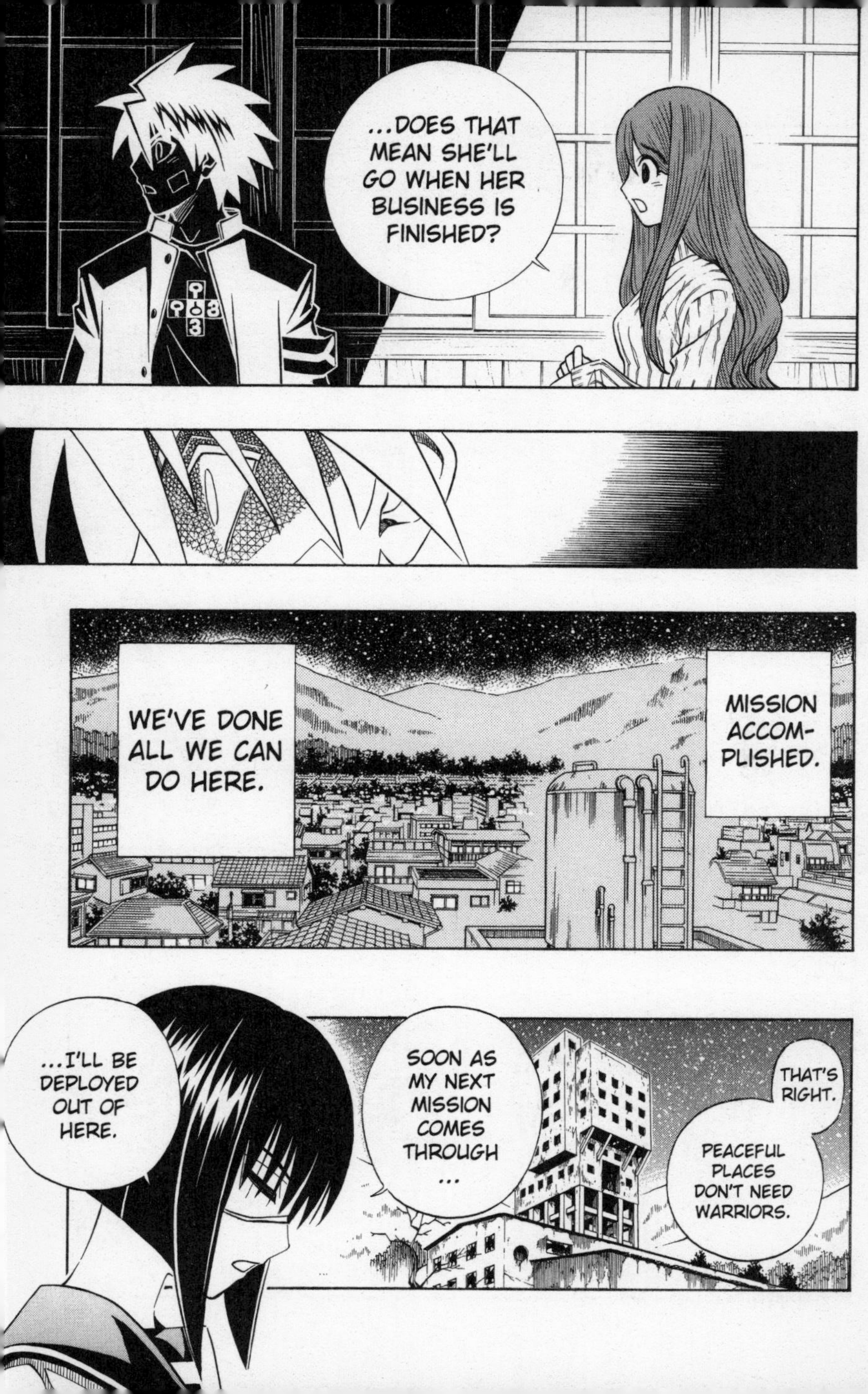
...DOES THAT MEAN SHE'LL GO WHEN HER BUSINESS IS FINISHED?
MISSION ACCOM-PLISHED.
WE'VE DONE ALL WE CAN DO HERE.
THAT'S RIGHT.
PEACEFUL PLACES DON'T NEED WARRIORS.
SOON AS MY NEXT MISSION COMES THROUGH ...
...I'LL BE DEPLOYED OUT OF HERE.

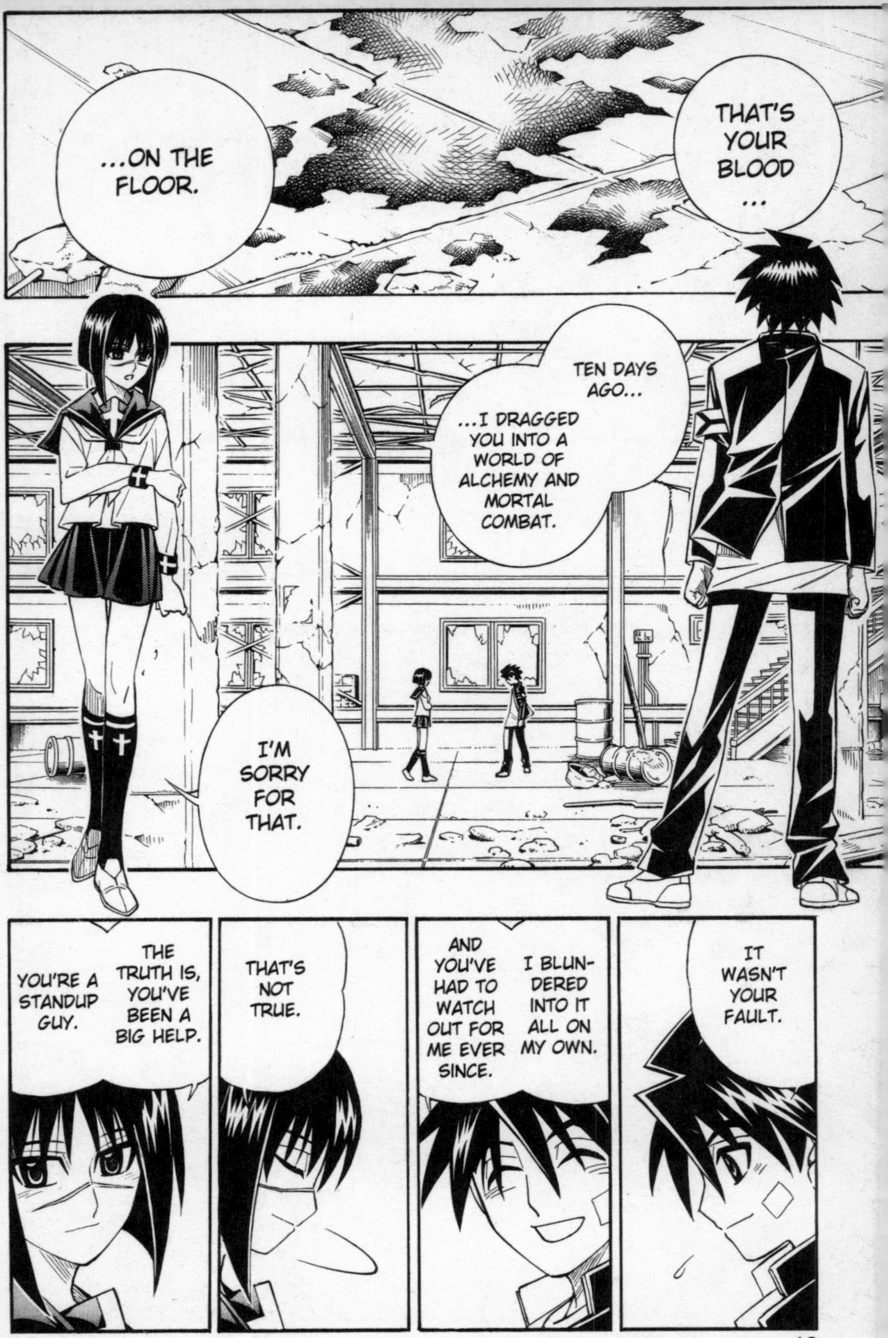
THAT'S YOUR BLOOD ...
...ON THE FLOOR.
TEN DAYS AGO...
...I DRAGGED YOU INTO A WORLD OF ALCHEMY AND MORTAL COMBAT.
I'M SORRY FOR THAT.
IT WASN'T YOUR FAULT.
I BLUNDERED INTO IT ALL ON MY OWN.
AND YOU'VE HAD TO WATCH OUT FOR ME EVER SINCE.
THAT'S NOT TRUE.
THE TRUTH IS, YOU'VE BEEN A BIG HELP.
YOU'RE A STANDUP GUY.

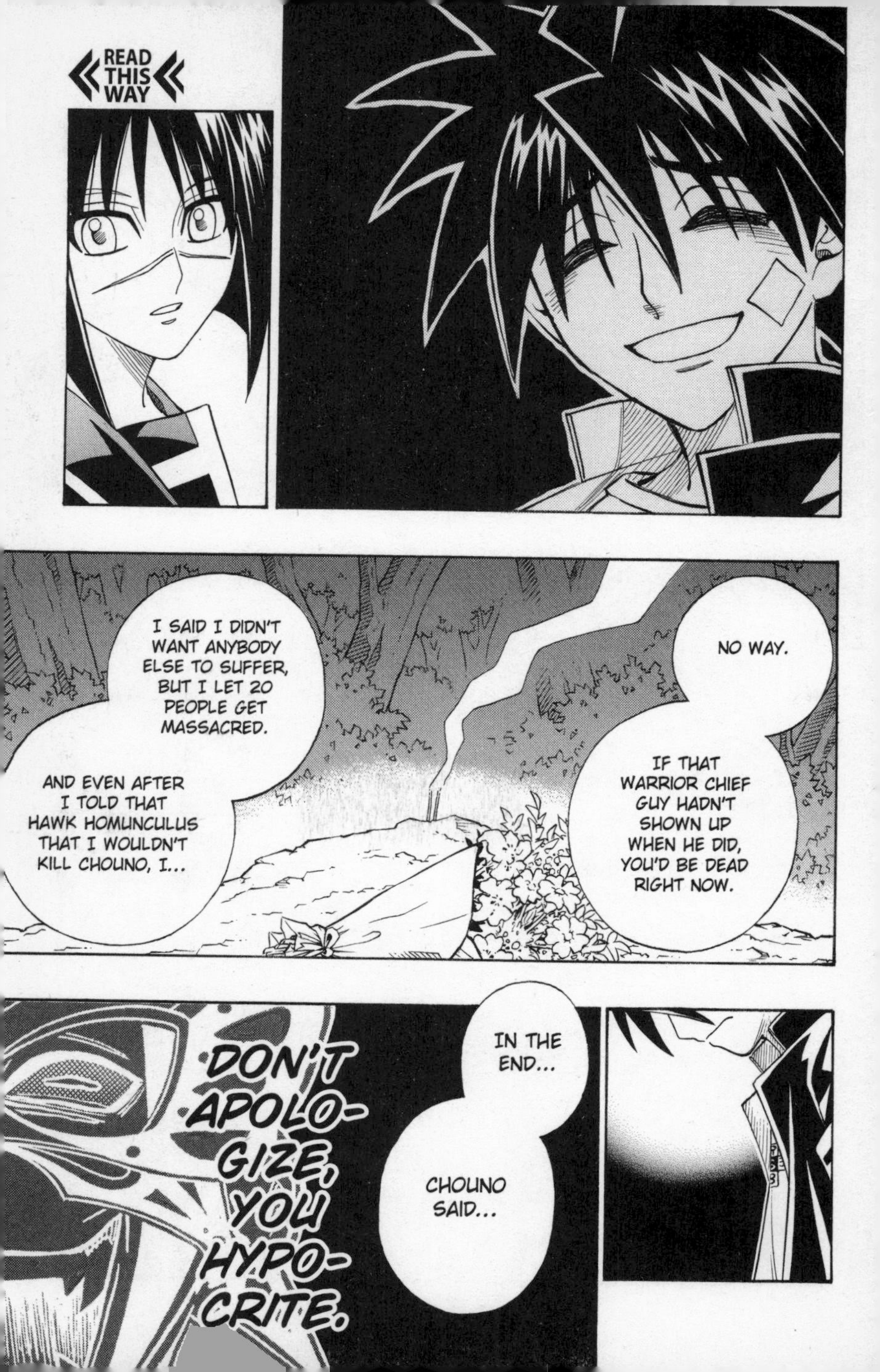
READ THIS WAY
NO WAY.
IF THAT WARRIOR CHIEF GUY HADN'T SHOWN UP WHEN HE DID, YOU'D BE DEAD RIGHT NOW.
I SAID I DIDN'T WANT ANYBODY ELSE TO SUFFER, BUT I LET 20 PEOPLE GET MASSACRED.
AND EVEN AFTER I TOLD THAT HAWK HOMUNCULUS THAT I WOULDN'T KILL CHOUNO, I...
IN THE END...
CHOUNO SAID...
DON'T APOLOGIZE, YOU HYPOCRITE.

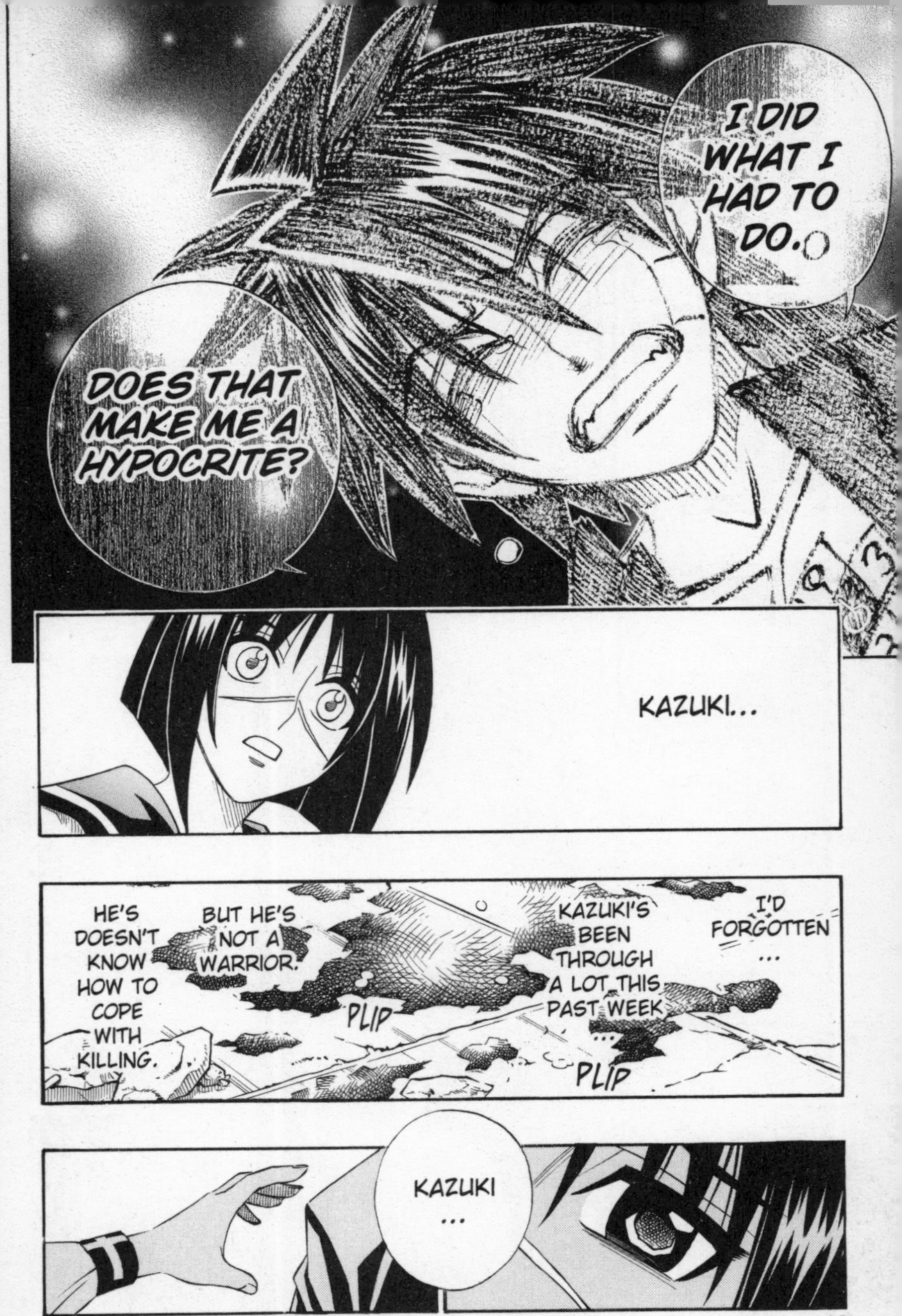
I DID WHAT I HAD TO DO.
DOES THAT MAKE ME A HYPOCRITE?
KAZUKI...
I'D FORGOTTEN ...
KAZUKI'S BEEN THROUGH A LOT THIS PAST WEEK ...
PLIP
BUT HE'S NOT A WARRIOR.
HE'S DOESN'T KNOW HOW TO COPE WITH KILLING.
PLIP
KAZUKI ...

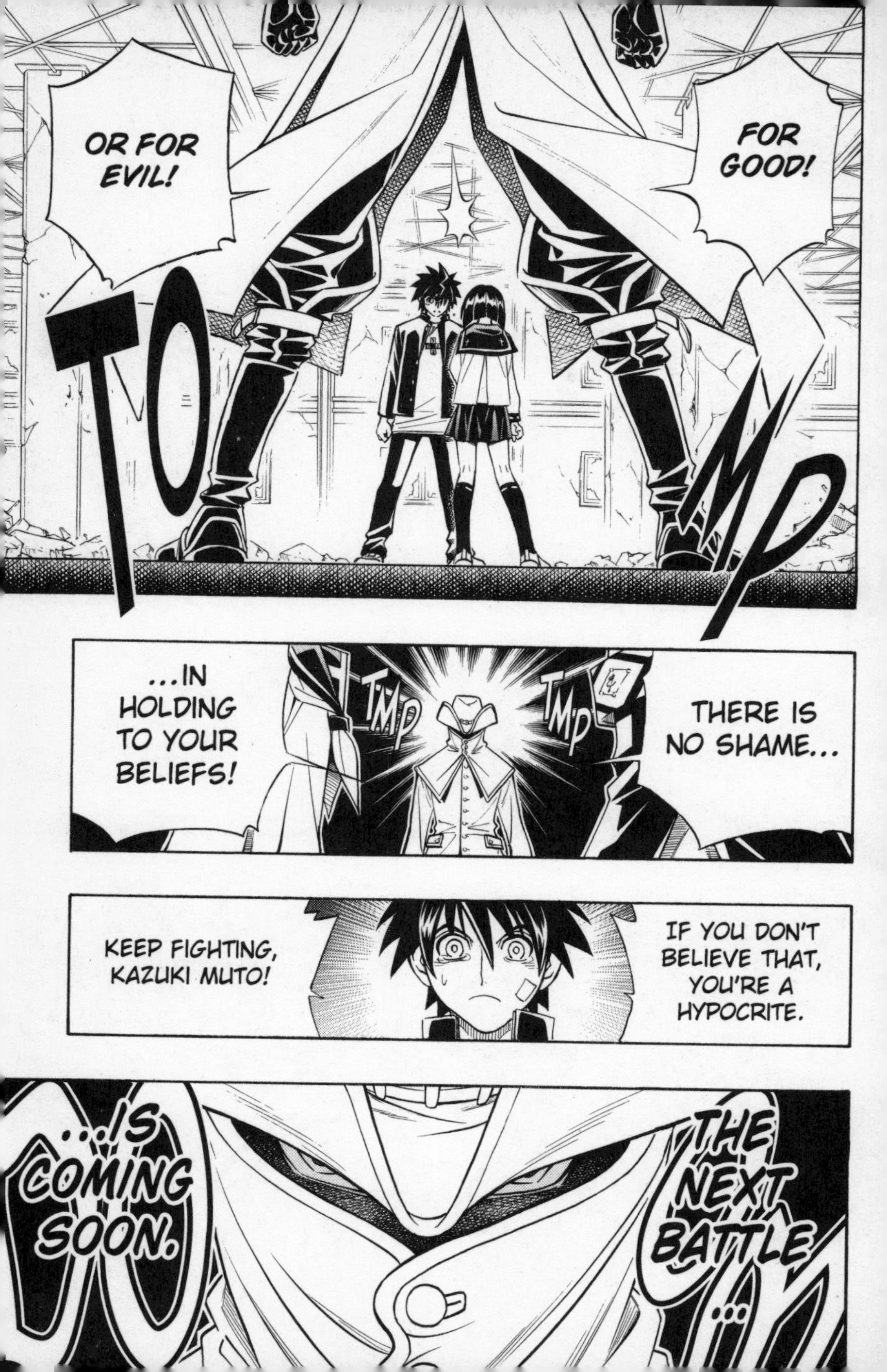
FOR GOOD!
OR FOR EVIL!
TOMP
THERE IS NO SHAME...
TMP
TMP
...IN HOLDING TO YOUR BELIEFS!
IF YOU DON'T BELIEVE THAT, YOU'RE A HYPOCRITE.
KEEP FIGHTING, KAZUKI MUTO!
THE NEXT BATTLE...
...IS COMING SOON.

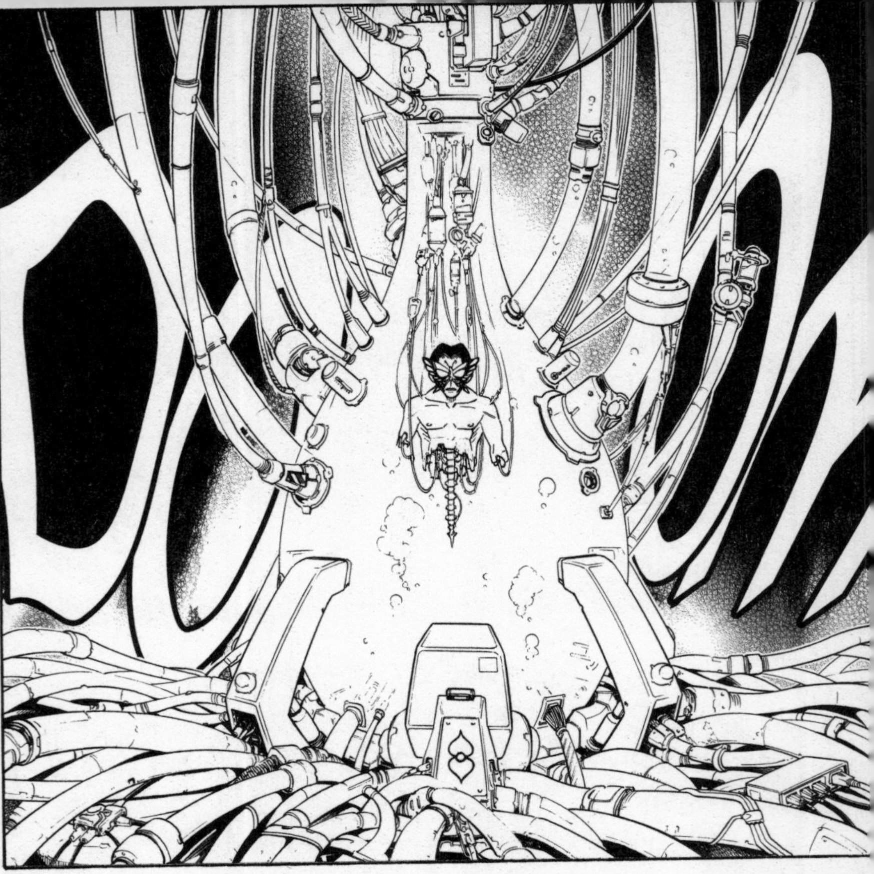

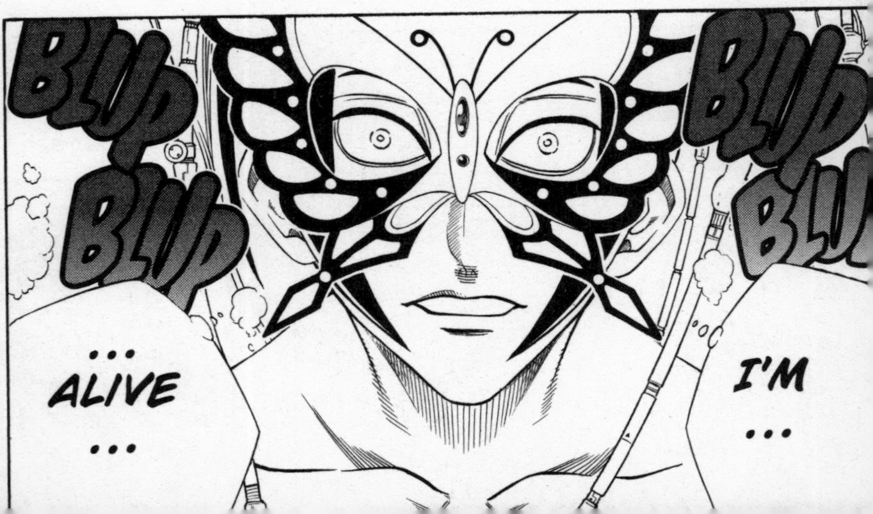
BLUP
BLU
I'M ...
BLUP
BLUP
... ALIVE ...

READ THIS WAY

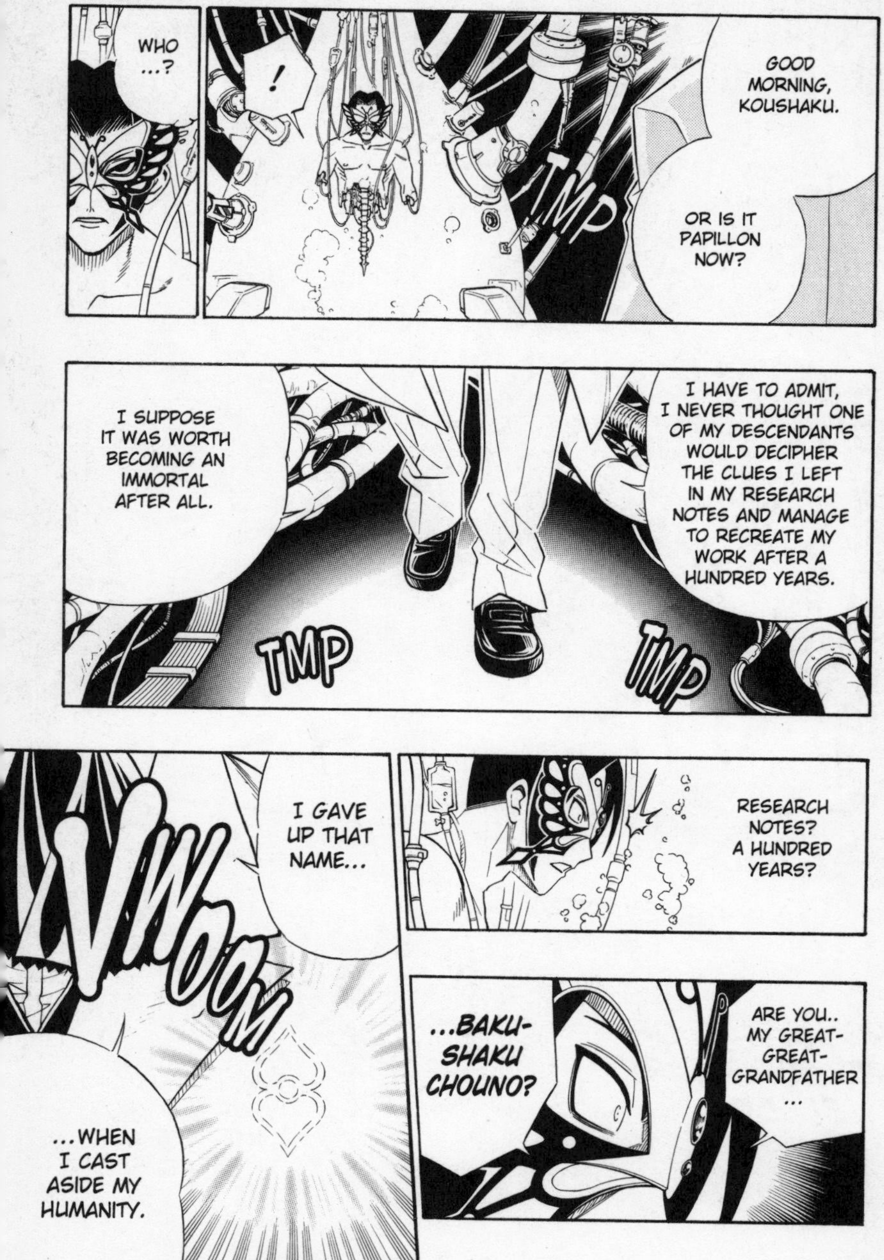
GOOD MORNING, KOUSHAKU.
OR IS IT PAPILLON NOW?
TMP
!
WHO ...?
I HAVE TO ADMIT, I NEVER THOUGHT ONE OF MY DESCENDANTS WOULD DECIPHER THE CLUES I LEFT IN MY RESEARCH NOTES AND MANAGE TO RECREATE MY WORK AFTER A HUNDRED YEARS.
I SUPPOSE IT WAS WORTH BECOMING AN IMMORTAL AFTER ALL.
TMP
TMP
RESEARCH NOTES? A HUNDRED YEARS?
ARE YOU.. MY GREAT-GREAT-GRANDFATHER ...
...BAKU-SHAKU CHOUNO?
I GAVE UP THAT NAME...
WHOOM
...WHEN I CAST ASIDE MY HUMANITY.

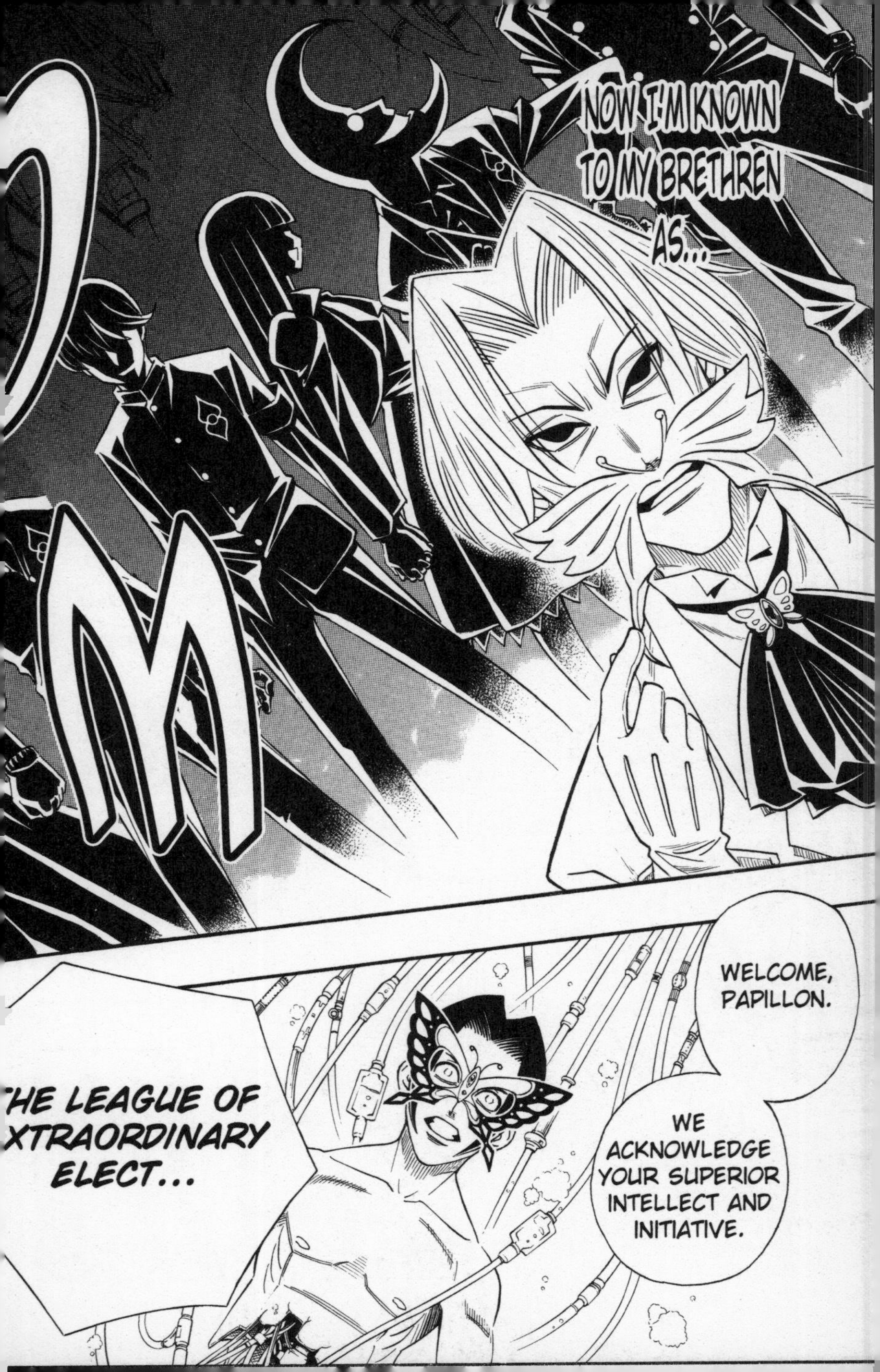
NOW I'M KNOWN TO MY BRETHREN AS...
WELCOME, PAPILLON.
WE ACKNOWLEDGE YOUR SUPERIOR INTELLECT AND INITIATIVE.
THE LEAGUE OF EXTRAORDINARY ELECT...

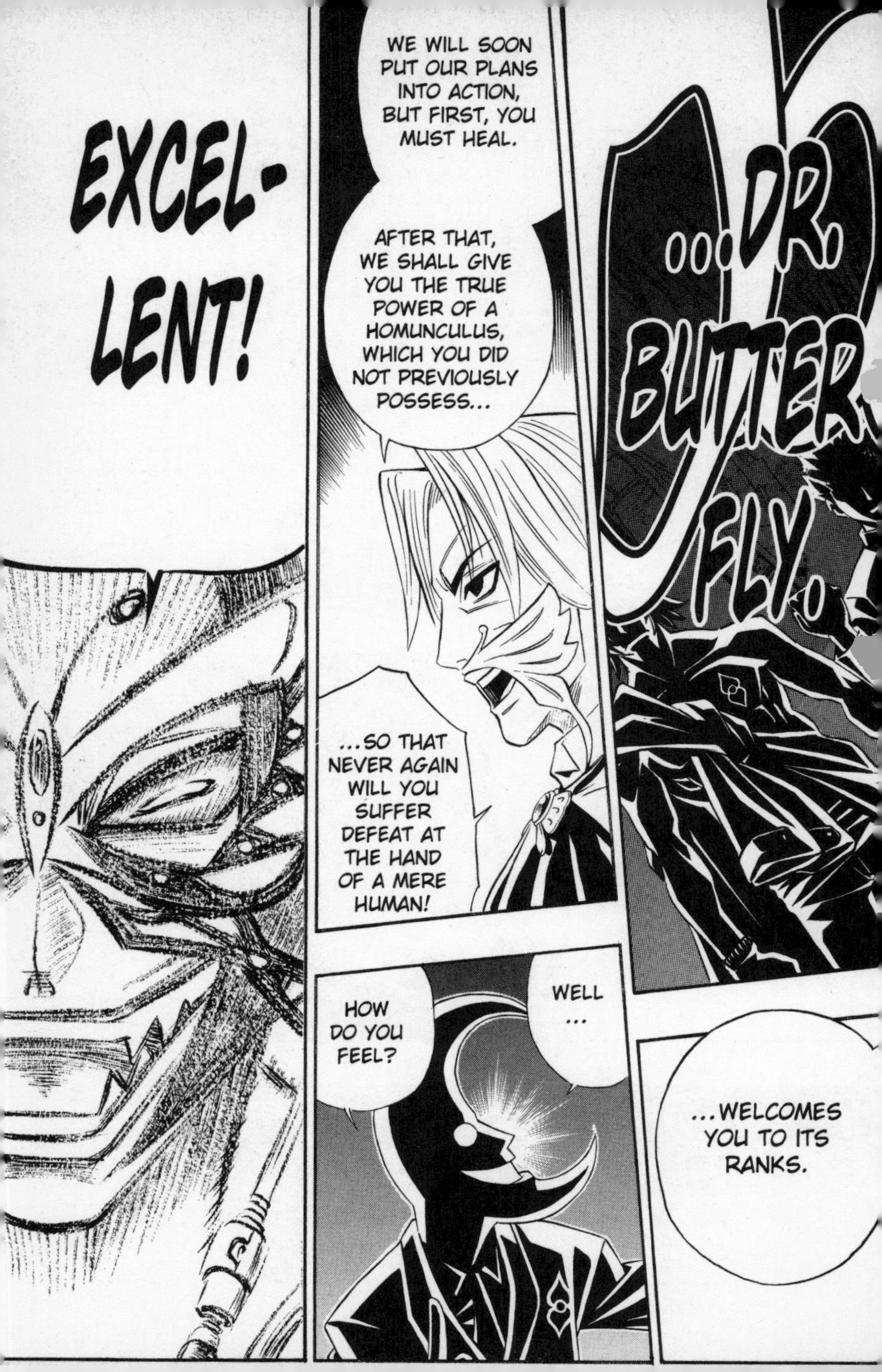
...DR. BUTTERFLY.
WE WILL SOON PUT OUR PLANS INTO ACTION, BUT FIRST, YOU MUST HEAL.
AFTER THAT, WE SHALL GIVE YOU THE TRUE POWER OF A HOMUNCULUS, WHICH YOU DID NOT PREVIOUSLY POSSESS...
...SO THAT NEVER AGAIN WILL YOU SUFFER DEFEAT AT THE HAND OF A MERE HUMAN!
...WELCOMES YOU TO ITS RANKS.
HOW DO YOU FEEL?
WELL ...
EXCEL-LENT!

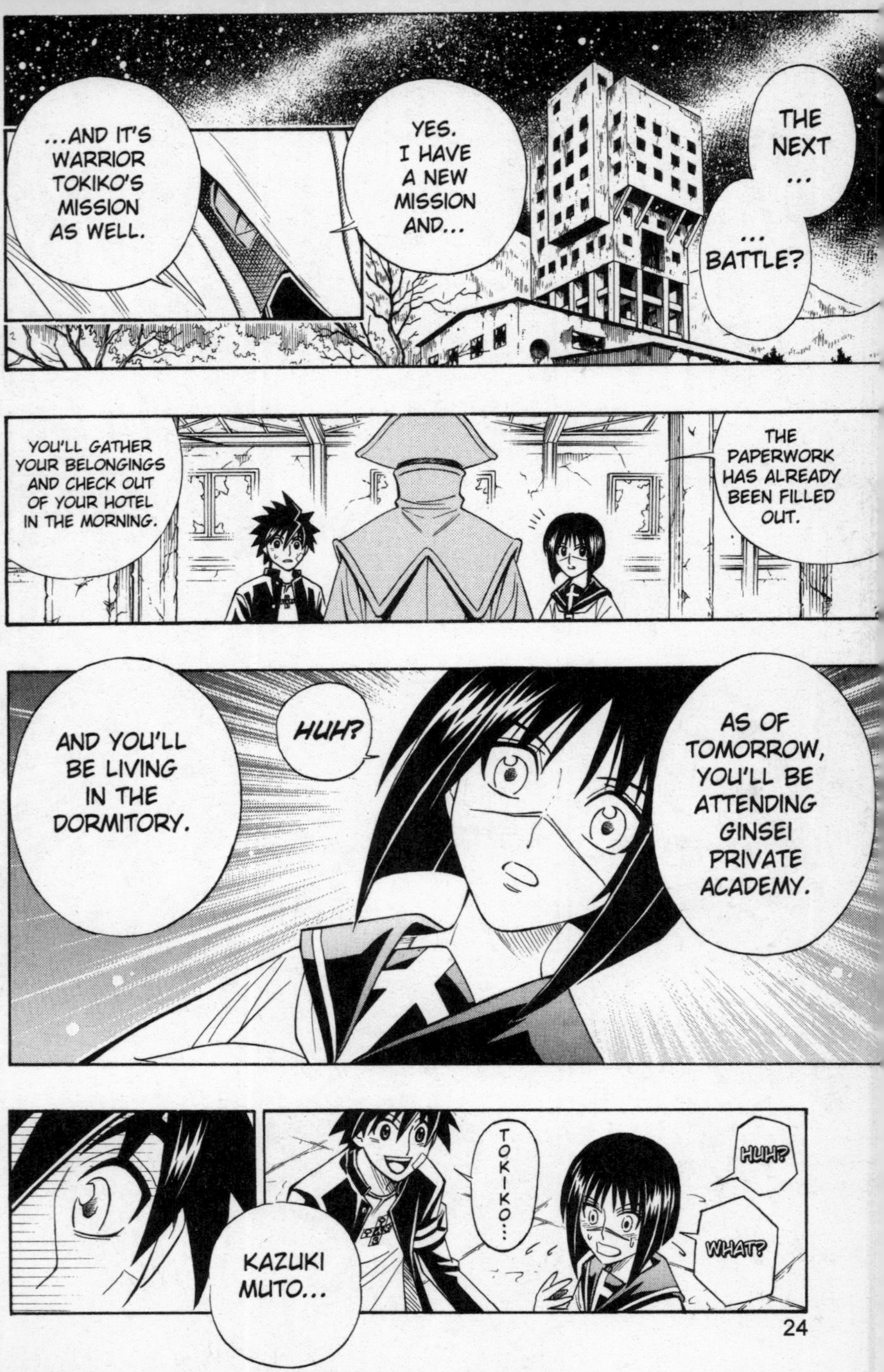
THE NEXT... ...BATTLE?
YES. I HAVE A NEW MISSION AND...
...AND IT'S WARRIOR TOKIKO'S MISSION AS WELL.
THE PAPERWORK HAS ALREADY BEEN FILLED OUT.
YOU'LL GATHER YOUR BELONGINGS AND CHECK OUT OF YOUR HOTEL IN THE MORNING.
AS OF TOMORROW, YOU'LL BE ATTENDING GINSEI PRIVATE ACADEMY.
HUH?
AND YOU'LL BE LIVING IN THE DORMITORY.
HUH?
WHAT?
TOKIKO...
KAZUKI MUTO...

READ THIS WAY

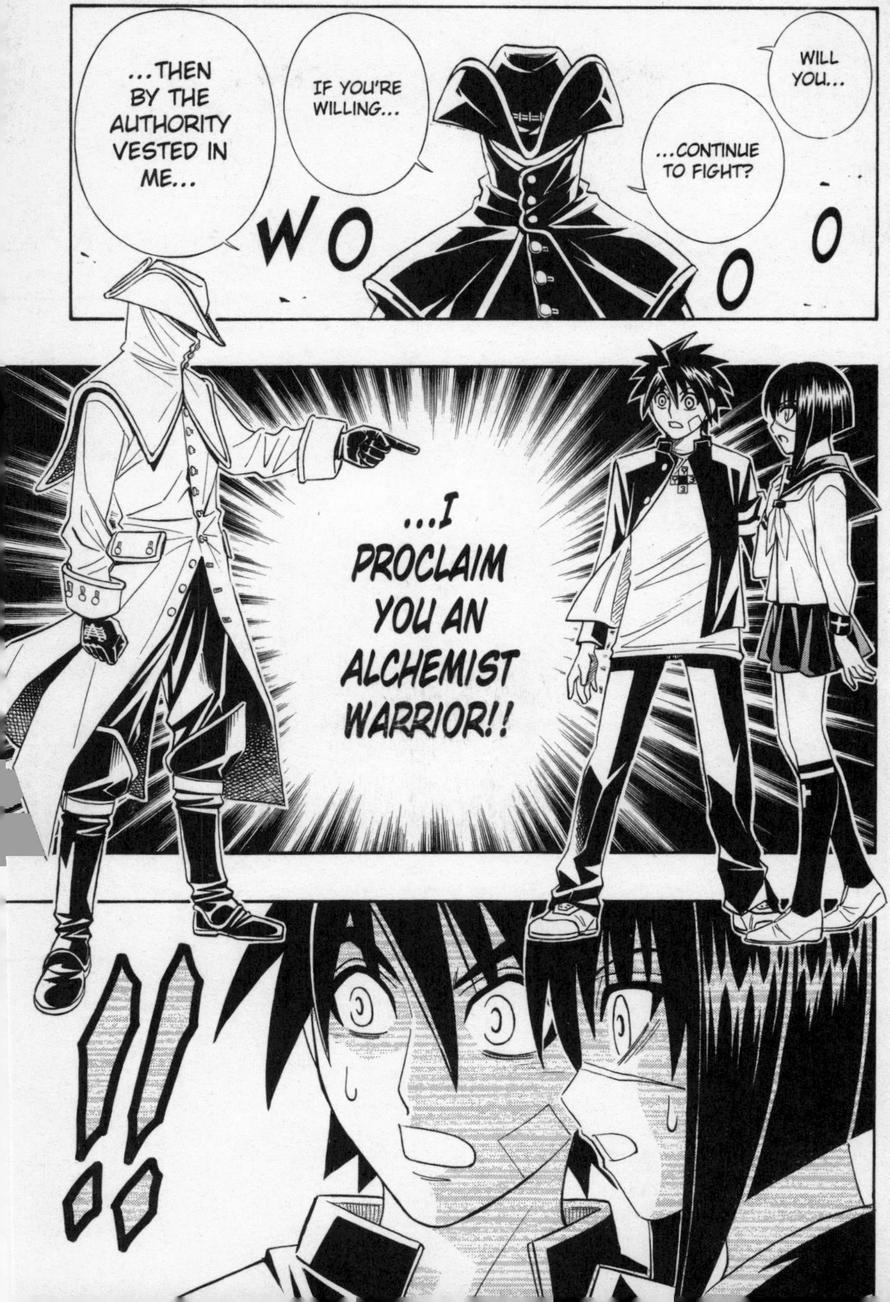
WILL YOU...
...CONTINUE TO FIGHT?
IF YOU'RE WILLING...
...THEN BY THE AUTHORITY VESTED IN ME...
WOOO
...I PROCLAIM YOU AN ALCHEMIST WARRIOR!!
!!

- Height: 185cm; Weight: 75kg
- Born: October 10; Libra; Age: 27
- Likes: Justice, smiles
- Dislikes: Evil, tears
- Hobby: Weekend carpentry
- Special Ability: He can get though any situation without revealing his real name.
- Affiliation: An organization (as yet unnamed) that directs the Alchemist Warriors. Rank of Warrior Chief.

Character File No. 14
CAPTAIN BRAVO

Author's Notes
- This character was created to be Kazuki and Tokiko's leader. In the early stages, before the series started, he was going to be Tokiko's older brother.
- He's named after an American toy--Matchbox's Mega Rig Mission Bravo. I know that "Captain" is English and "Bravo" is French, but just go with it.
- This character is virtually invincible. Captain Bravo fights the battles that Kazuki can't. He's a combination of Marcus and J. J. from my previous series Gun Blaze West. The design is a grown-up version of Viu.
- Captain Bravo is yet another version of the grown-up who watches over the children, and the person that a youth must surpass in order to become an adult--archetypes I've depicted in other series.
- His real name is a secret for now. I'm sure it will be revealed eventually.

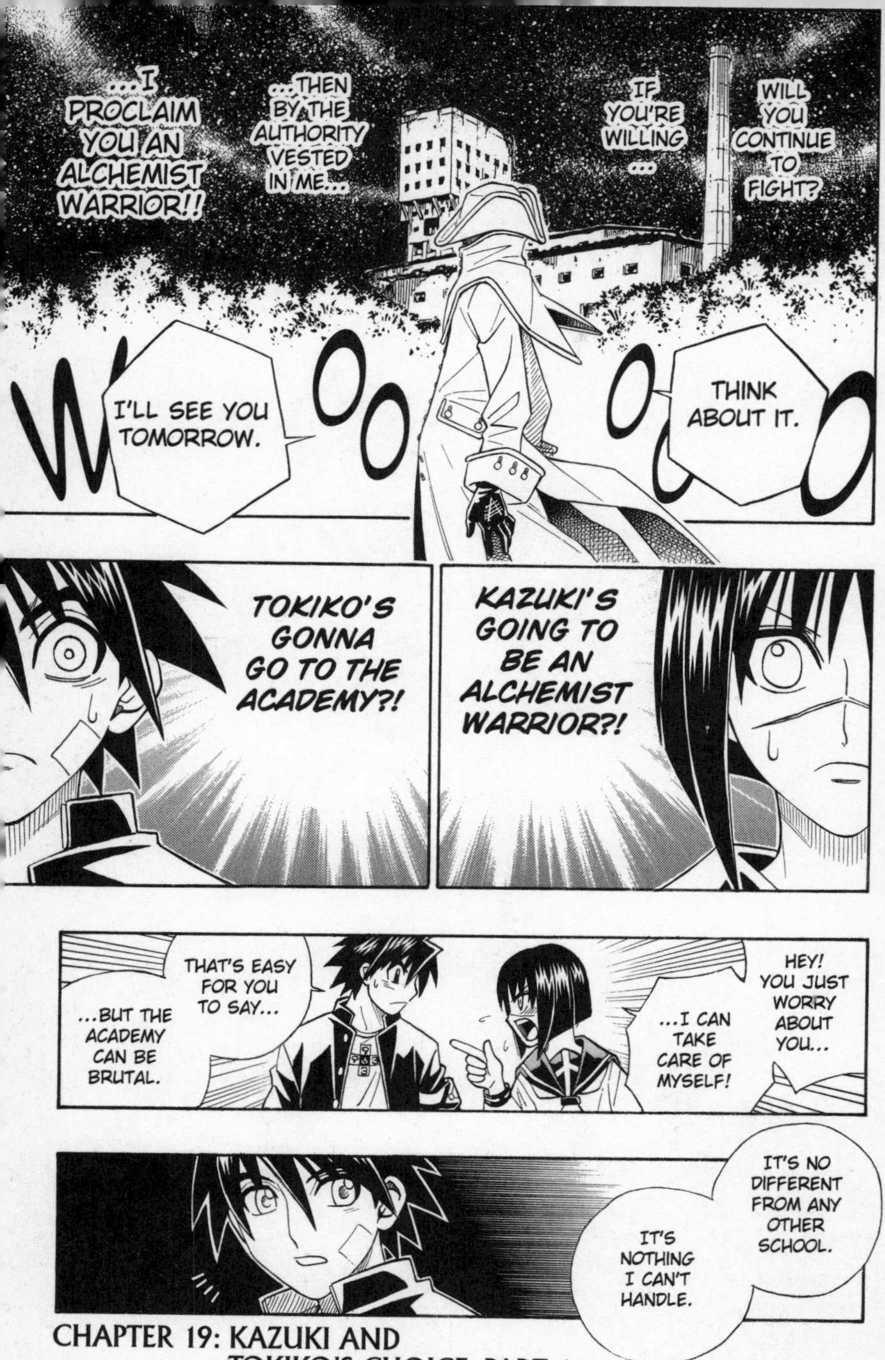
WILL YOU CONTINUE TO FIGHT?
IF YOU'RE WILLING...
...THEN BY THE AUTHORITY VESTED IN ME...
...I PROCLAIM YOU AN ALCHEMIST WARRIOR!!
THINK ABOUT IT.
I'LL SEE YOU TOMORROW.
KAZUKI'S GOING TO BE AN ALCHEMIST WARRIOR?!
TOKIKO'S GONNA GO TO THE ACADEMY?!
HEY! YOU JUST WORRY ABOUT YOU...
...I CAN TAKE CARE OF MYSELF!
THAT'S EASY FOR YOU TO SAY...
...BUT THE ACADEMY CAN BE BRUTAL.
IT'S NO DIFFERENT FROM ANY OTHER SCHOOL.
IT'S NOTHING I CAN'T HANDLE.

CHAPTER 19: KAZUKI AND TOKIKO'S CHOICE, PART 1

CHAPTER 19:
KAZUKI AND TOKIKO'S CHOICE, PART 1

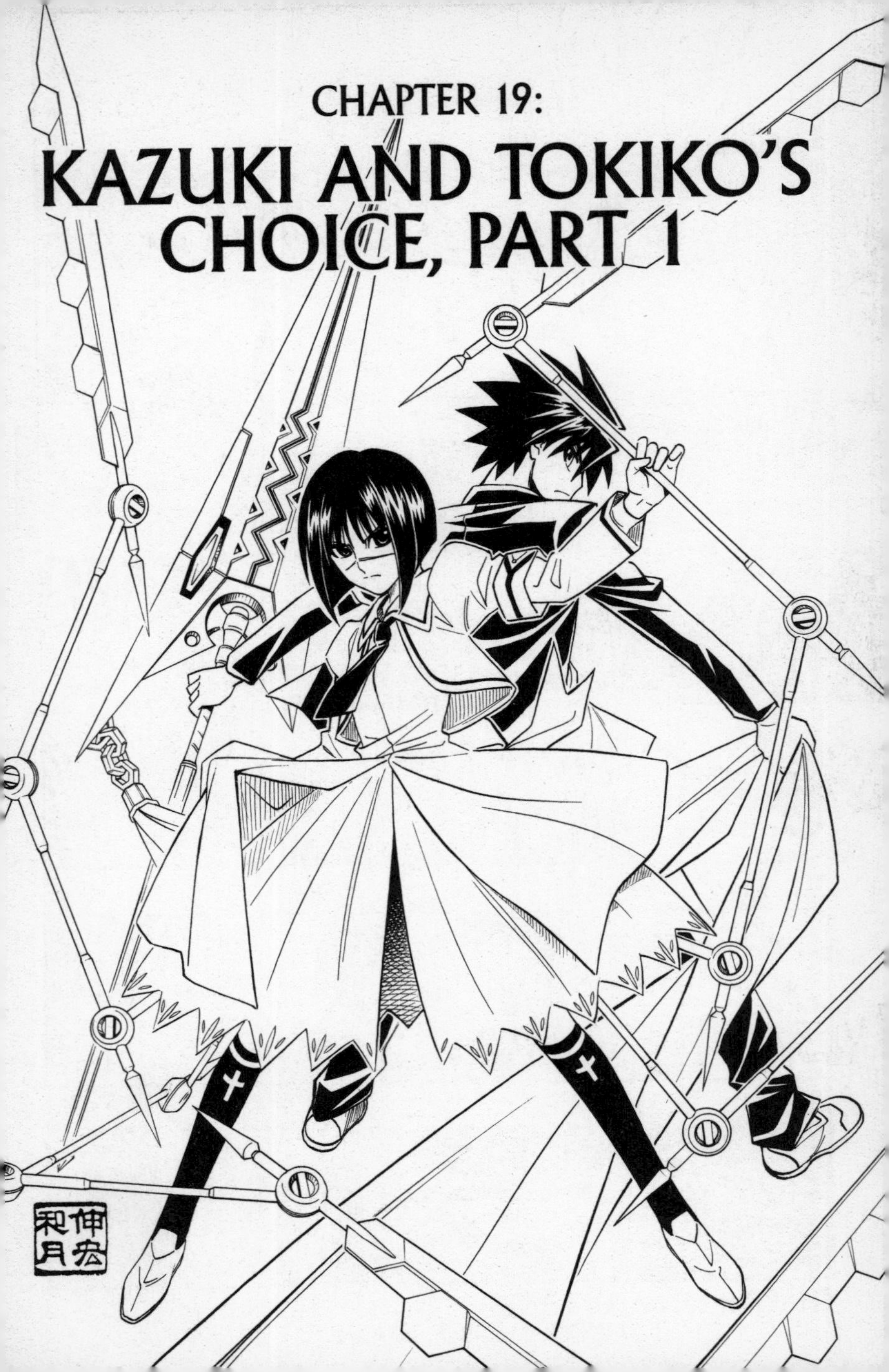
伸宏
和月

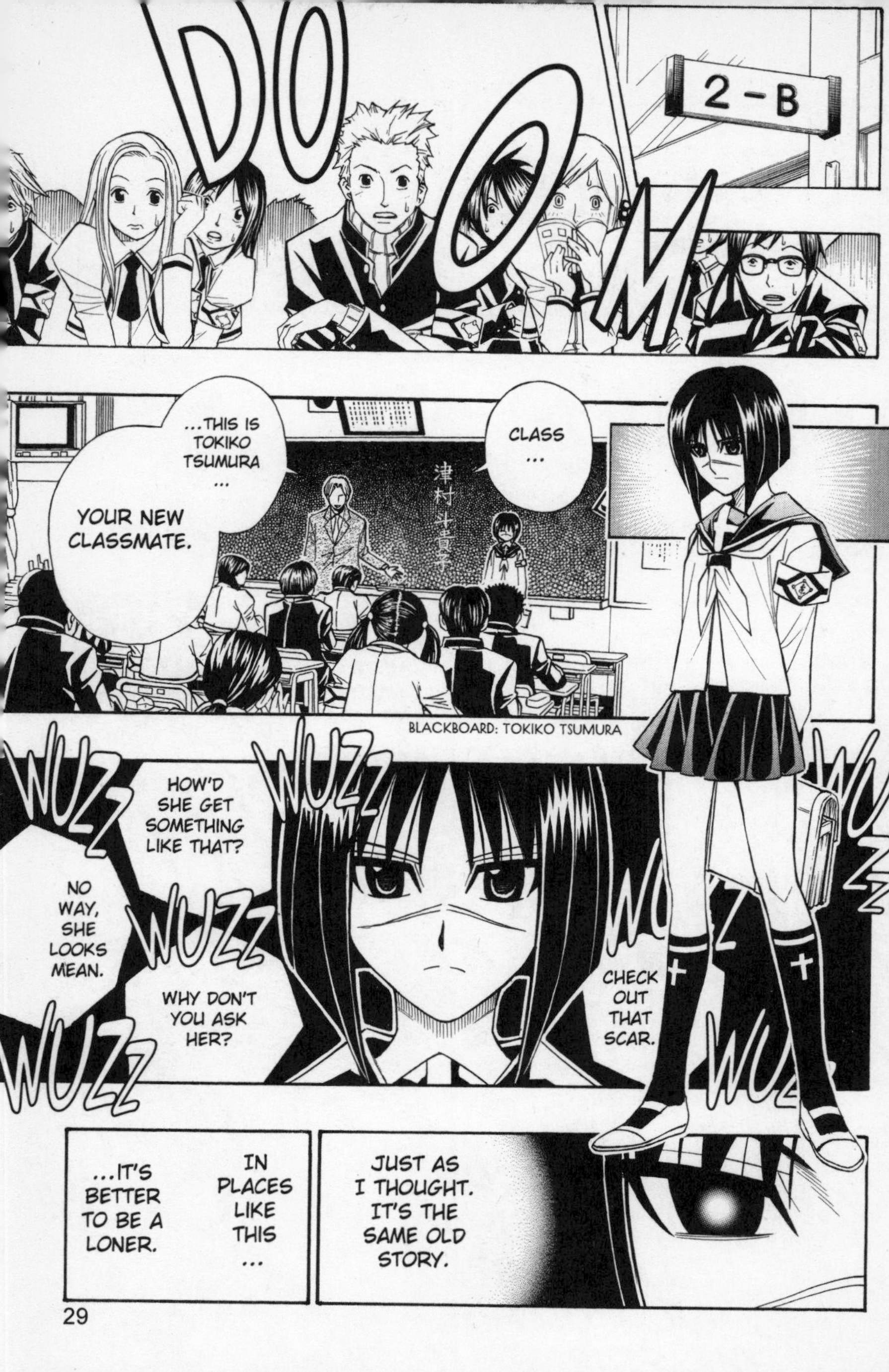
2-B
DOOOM
CLASS ...
...THIS IS TOKIKO TSUMURA ...
YOUR NEW CLASSMATE.
BLACKBOARD: TOKIKO TSUMURA
WUZZ
CHECK OUT THAT SCAR.
WUZZ
HOW'D SHE GET SOMETHING LIKE THAT?
WUZZ
NO WAY, SHE LOOKS MEAN.
WUZZ
WHY DON'T YOU ASK HER?
WUZZ
JUST AS I THOUGHT. IT'S THE SAME OLD STORY.
IN PLACES LIKE THIS ...
...IT'S BETTER TO BE A LONER.

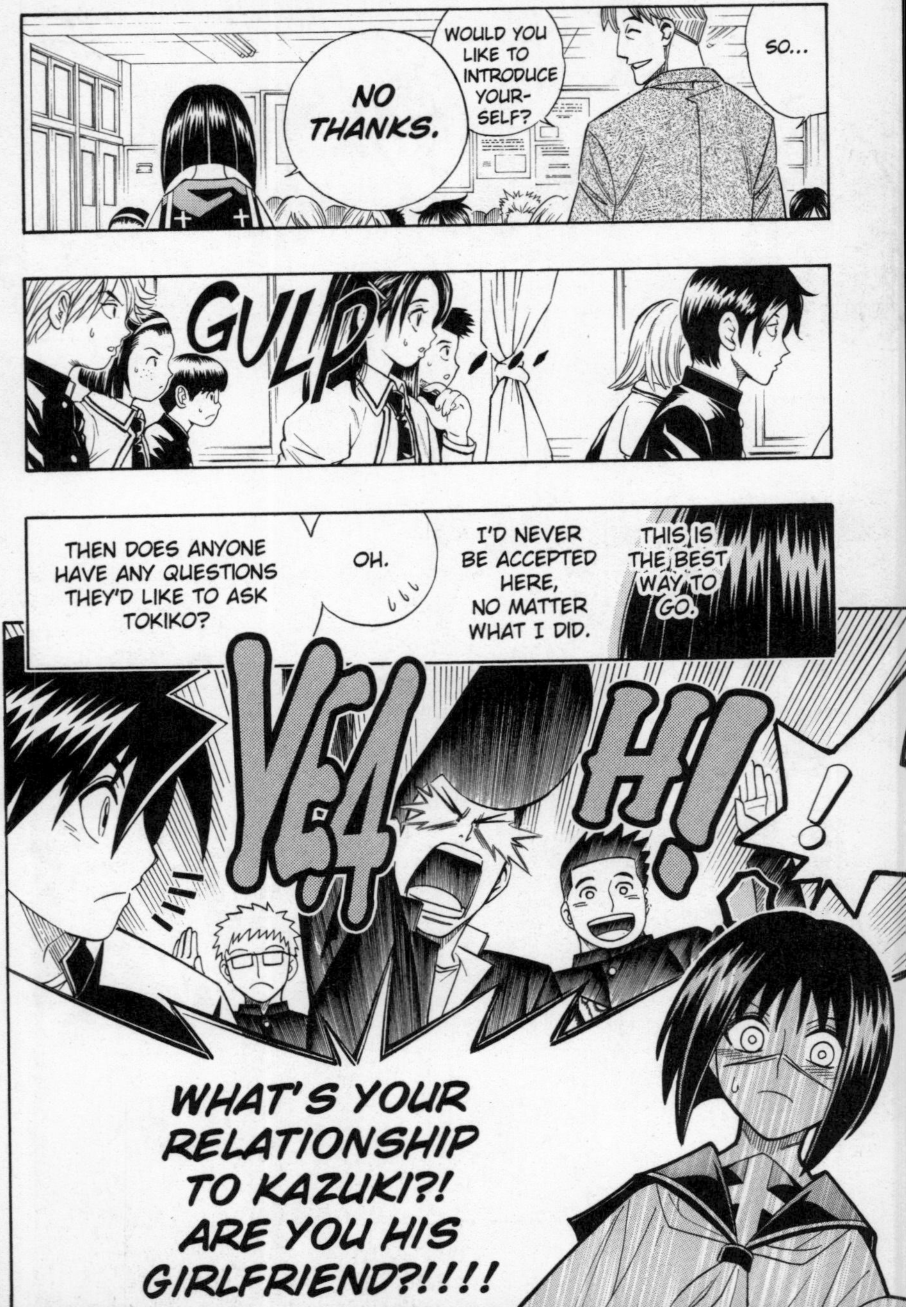
SO...
WOULD YOU LIKE TO INTRODUCE YOUR-SELF?
NO THANKS.
GULP
THIS IS THE BEST WAY TO GO.
I'D NEVER BE ACCEPTED HERE, NO MATTER WHAT I DID.
OH.
THEN DOES ANYONE HAVE ANY QUESTIONS THEY'D LIKE TO ASK TOKIKO?
YEAH!
WHAT'S YOUR RELATIONSHIP TO KAZUKI?! ARE YOU HIS GIRLFRIEND?!!!!

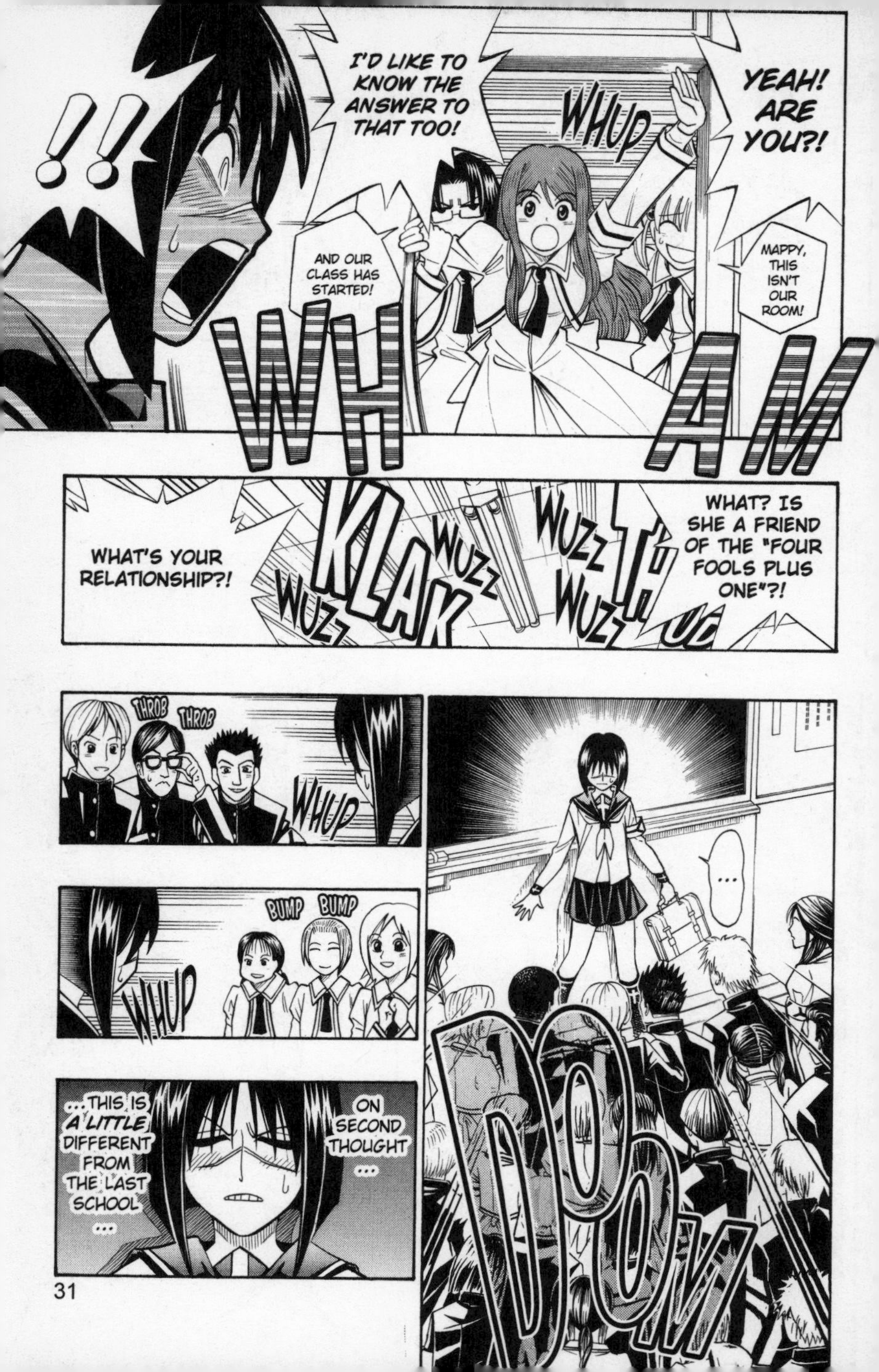
YEAH! ARE YOU?!
MAPPY, THIS ISN'T OUR ROOM!
WHUP
I'D LIKE TO KNOW THE ANSWER TO THAT TOO!
AND OUR CLASS HAS STARTED!
!!
WHAM
WHAT? IS SHE A FRIEND OF THE "FOUR FOOLS PLUS ONE"?!
WUZZ
WUZZ
KLAK
WUZZ
WUZZ
WHAT'S YOUR RELATIONSHIP?!
...
DOOM
THROB THROB
WHUP
BUMP BUMP
WHUP
ON SECOND THOUGHT...
...THIS IS A LITTLE DIFFERENT FROM THE LAST SCHOOL...

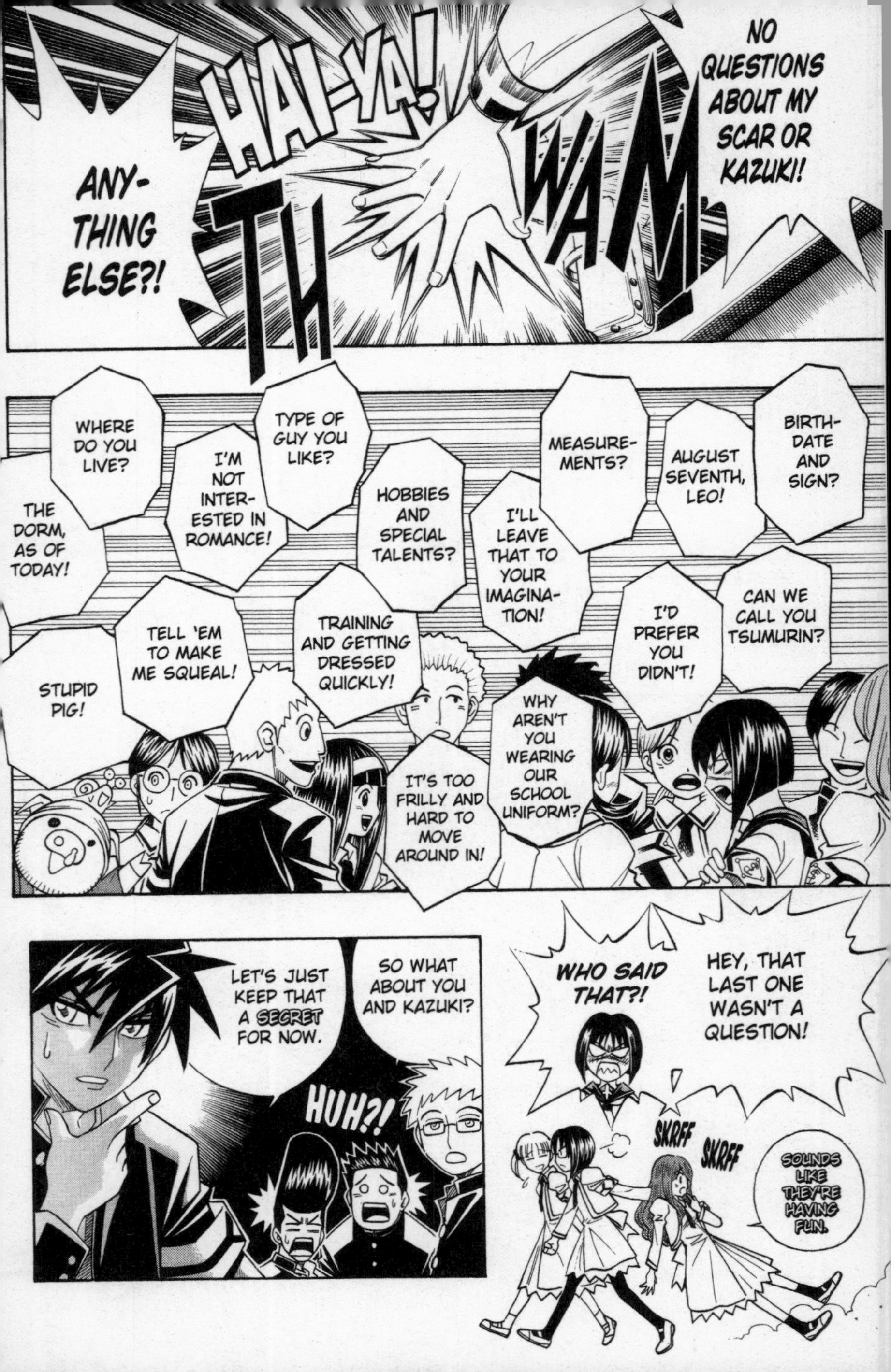
NO QUESTIONS ABOUT MY SCAR OR KAZUKI!
HAI-YA!
WAM
TH
ANY-THING ELSE?!
BIRTH-DATE AND SIGN?
AUGUST SEVENTH, LEO!
MEASURE-MENTS?
I'LL LEAVE THAT TO YOUR IMAGINA-TION!
HOBBIES AND SPECIAL TALENTS?
TRAINING AND GETTING DRESSED QUICKLY!
TYPE OF GUY YOU LIKE?
I'M NOT INTER-ESTED IN ROMANCE!
WHERE DO YOU LIVE?
THE DORM, AS OF TODAY!
CAN WE CALL YOU TSUMURIN?
I'D PREFER YOU DIDN'T!
WHY AREN'T YOU WEARING OUR SCHOOL UNIFORM?
IT'S TOO FRILLY AND HARD TO MOVE AROUND IN!
TELL 'EM TO MAKE ME SQUEAL!
STUPID PIG!
HEY, THAT LAST ONE WASN'T A QUESTION!
WHO SAID THAT?!
SKRFF
SKRFF
SOUNDS LIKE THEY'RE HAVING FUN.
SO WHAT ABOUT YOU AND KAZUKI?
LET'S JUST KEEP THAT A SECRET FOR NOW.
HUH?!

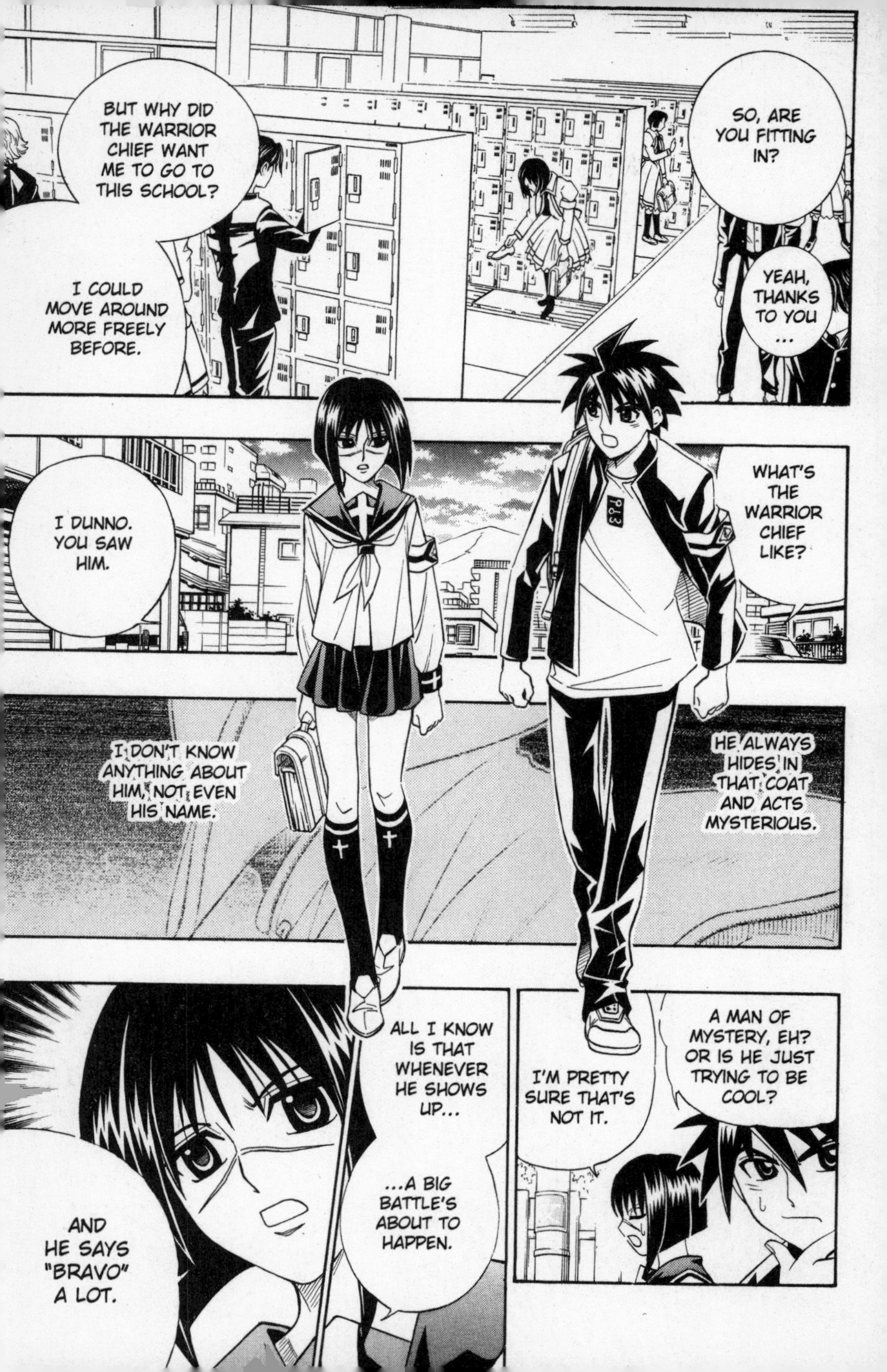
SO, ARE YOU FITTING IN?
YEAH, THANKS TO YOU ...
BUT WHY DID THE WARRIOR CHIEF WANT ME TO GO TO THIS SCHOOL?
I COULD MOVE AROUND MORE FREELY BEFORE.
WHAT'S THE WARRIOR CHIEF LIKE?
I DUNNO. YOU SAW HIM.
HE ALWAYS HIDES IN THAT COAT AND ACTS MYSTERIOUS.
I DON'T KNOW ANYTHING ABOUT HIM, NOT EVEN HIS NAME.
A MAN OF MYSTERY, EH? OR IS HE JUST TRYING TO BE COOL?
I'M PRETTY SURE THAT'S NOT IT.
ALL I KNOW IS THAT WHENEVER HE SHOWS UP...
...A BIG BATTLE'S ABOUT TO HAPPEN.
AND HE SAYS "BRAVO" A LOT.

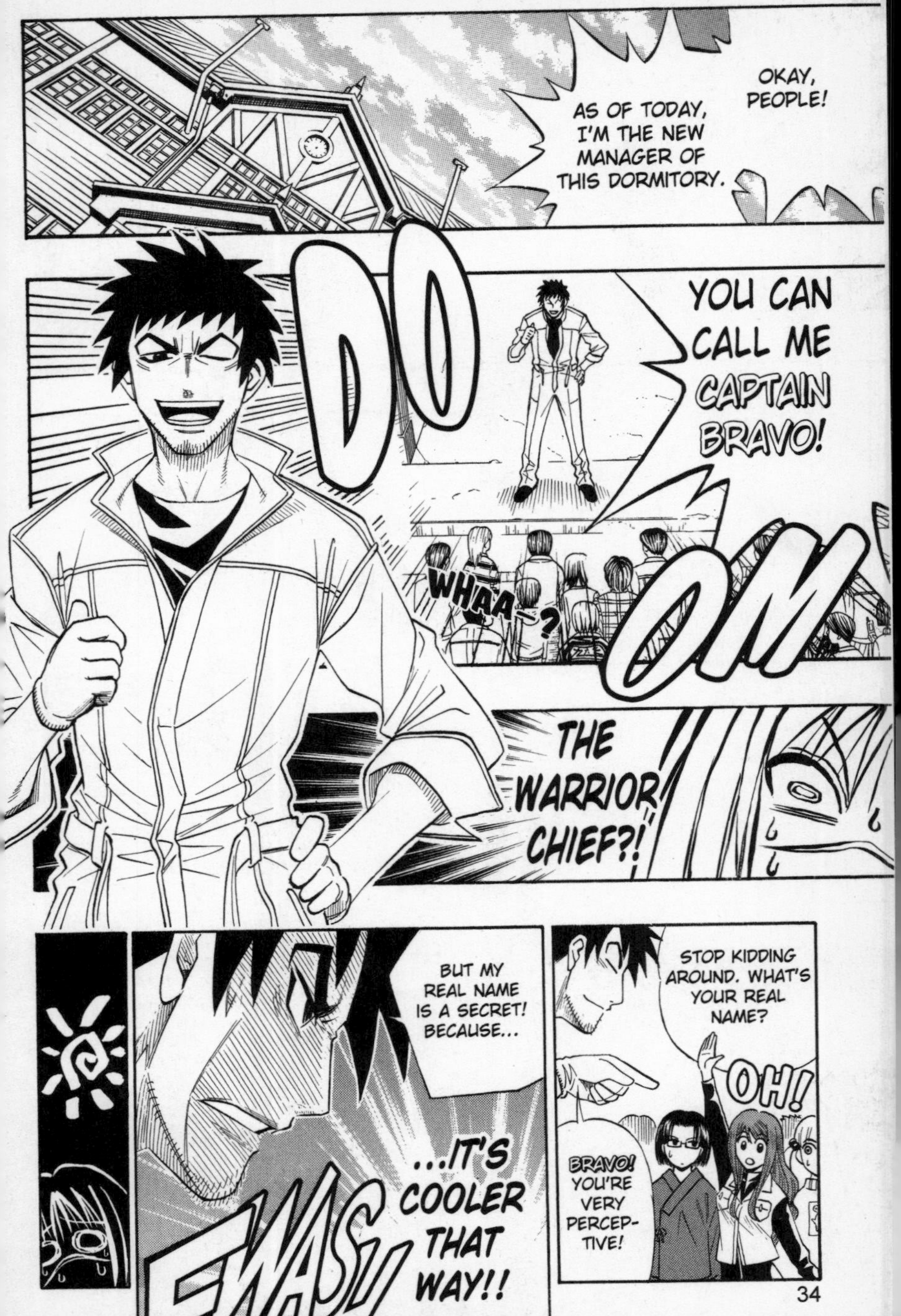
OKAY, PEOPLE!
AS OF TODAY, I'M THE NEW MANAGER OF THIS DORMITORY.
YOU CAN CALL ME CAPTAIN BRAVO!
DOOM
WHAA-?
THE WARRIOR CHIEF?!
STOP KIDDING AROUND. WHAT'S YOUR REAL NAME?
OH!
BRAVO! YOU'RE VERY PERCEP-TIVE!
BUT MY REAL NAME IS A SECRET! BECAUSE...
...IT'S COOLER THAT WAY!!

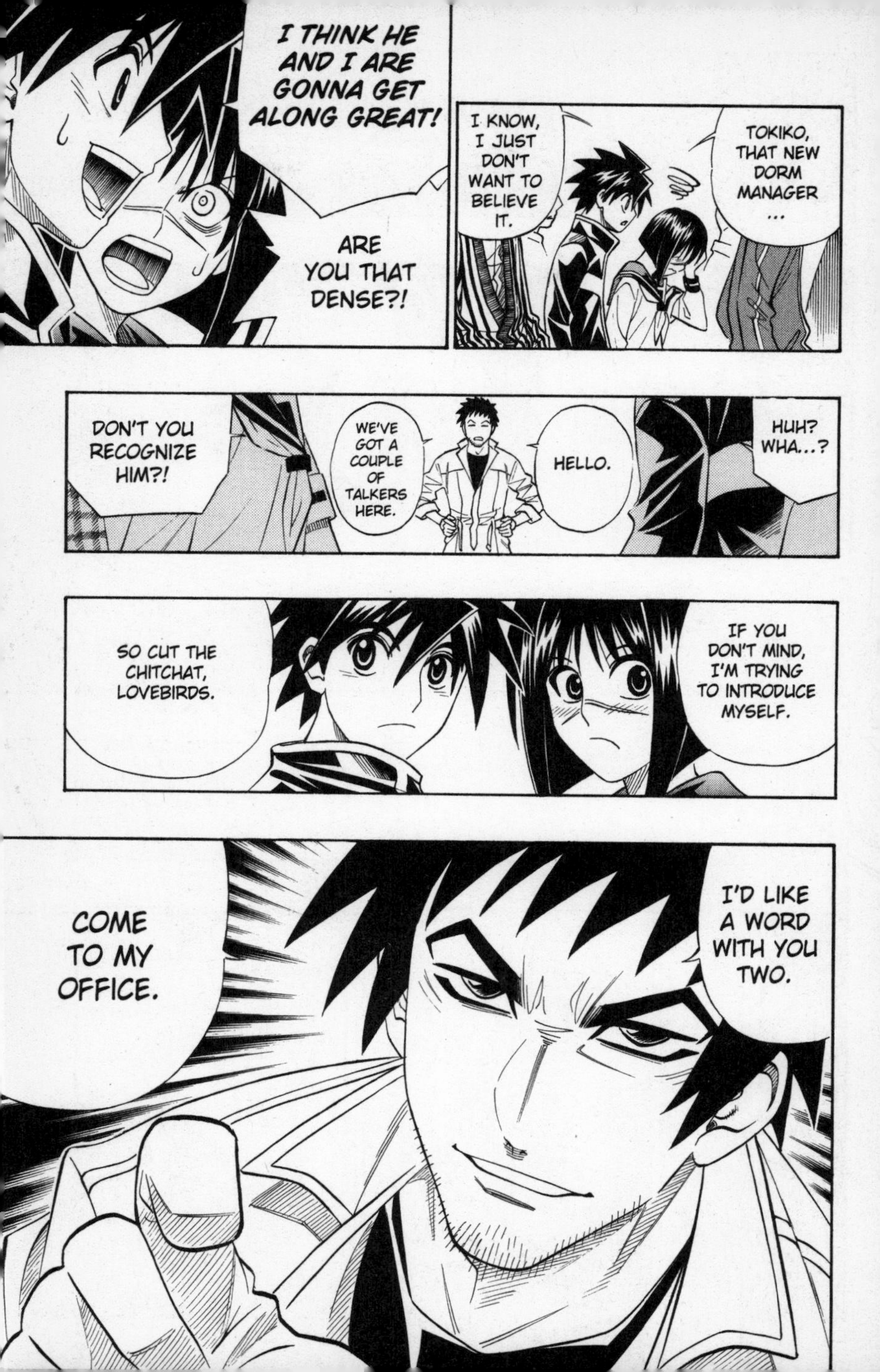
TOKIKO, THAT NEW DORM MANAGER ...
I KNOW, I JUST DON'T WANT TO BELIEVE IT.
I THINK HE AND I ARE GONNA GET ALONG GREAT!
ARE YOU THAT DENSE?!
HUH? WHA...?
HELLO.
WE'VE GOT A COUPLE OF TALKERS HERE.
DON'T YOU RECOGNIZE HIM?!
IF YOU DON'T MIND, I'M TRYING TO INTRODUCE MYSELF.
SO CUT THE CHITCHAT, LOVEBIRDS.
I'D LIKE A WORD WITH YOU TWO.
COME TO MY OFFICE.

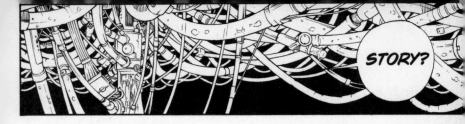

STORY?
WOOOOOO
YES.
IT'S ABOUT ME WHEN I WAS STILL HUMAN A CENTURY AGO.
IN THOSE DAYS NEW SCIENCES AND TECHNOLOGIES WERE FLOODING IN FROM ALL OVER THE WORLD.
ONE OF THEM WAS ALCHEMY, WHICH MOST PEOPLE HAD LONG SINCE DISMISSED AS CHARLATANRY.
BUT I SENSED THERE WAS MORE TO IT. SO I BEGAN TO DELVE INTO ITS MYSTERIES.
TO MY DISAPPOINTMENT, I FOUND THERE WERE LIMITS TO HOW FAR I COULD GO ON MY OWN.
MY STUDIES HAD CONSUMED A FORTUNE AND YEARS OF MY LIFE BY THE TIME I DISCOVERED THE HOMUNCULI AND THE KAKUGANE. AND I HAD COME TO A DEAD END.
KLINK
THEN ...
...I MET HIM.
HIM?

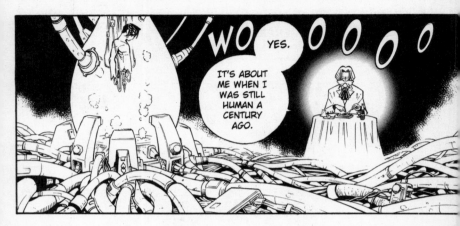

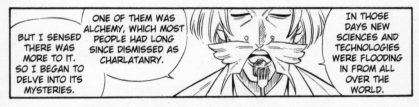

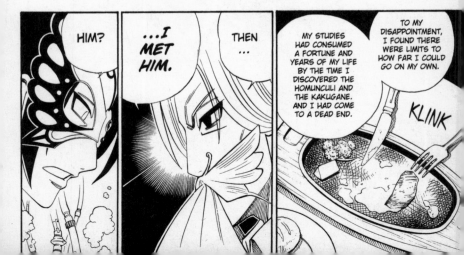

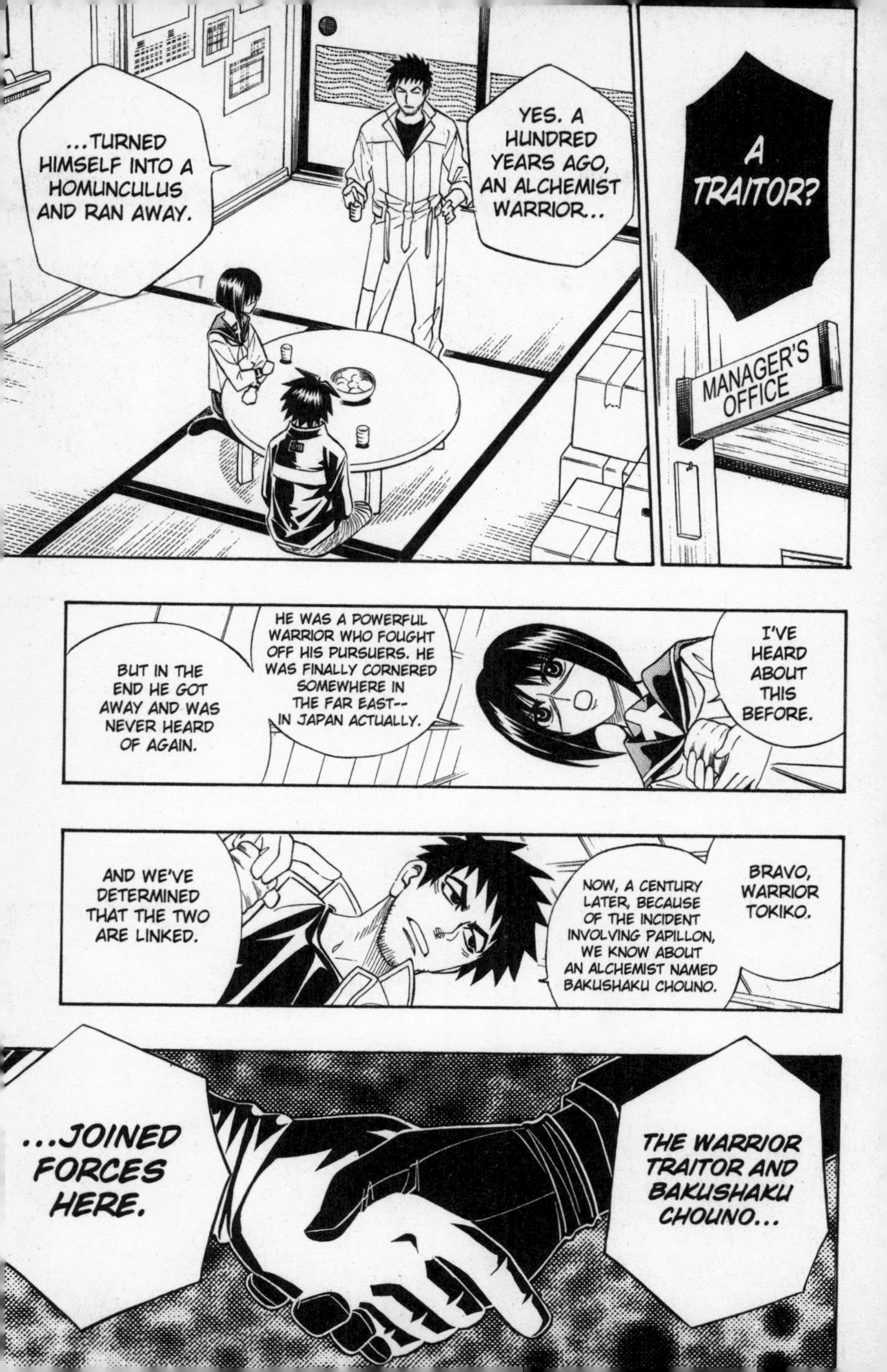
A TRAITOR?
MANAGER'S OFFICE
YES. A HUNDRED YEARS AGO, AN ALCHEMIST WARRIOR...
...TURNED HIMSELF INTO A HOMUNCULUS AND RAN AWAY.
I'VE HEARD ABOUT THIS BEFORE.
HE WAS A POWERFUL WARRIOR WHO FOUGHT OFF HIS PURSUERS. HE WAS FINALLY CORNERED SOMEWHERE IN THE FAR EAST-- IN JAPAN ACTUALLY.
BUT IN THE END HE GOT AWAY AND WAS NEVER HEARD OF AGAIN.
BRAVO, WARRIOR TOKIKO.
NOW, A CENTURY LATER, BECAUSE OF THE INCIDENT INVOLVING PAPILLON, WE KNOW ABOUT AN ALCHEMIST NAMED BAKUSHAKU CHOUNO.
AND WE'VE DETERMINED THAT THE TWO ARE LINKED.
THE WARRIOR TRAITOR AND BAKUSHAKU CHOUNO...
...JOINED FORCES HERE.

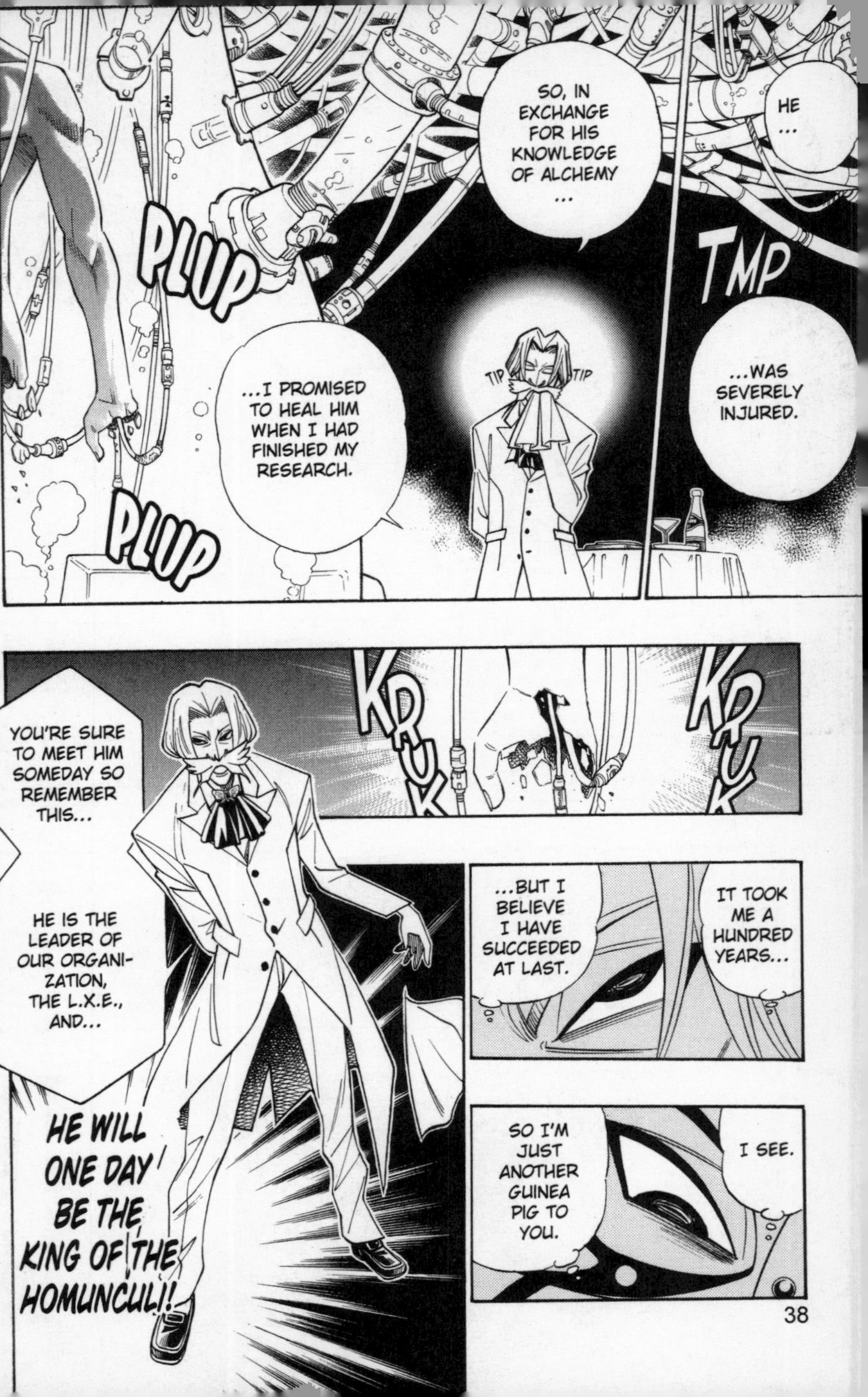
HE ...
TMP
...WAS SEVERELY INJURED.
SO, IN EXCHANGE FOR HIS KNOWLEDGE OF ALCHEMY ...
PLUP
...I PROMISED TO HEAL HIM WHEN I HAD FINISHED MY RESEARCH.
PLUP
TIP TIP
KRUK
KRUK
IT TOOK ME A HUNDRED YEARS...
...BUT I BELIEVE I HAVE SUCCEEDED AT LAST.
I SEE.
SO I'M JUST ANOTHER GUINEA PIG TO YOU.
YOU'RE SURE TO MEET HIM SOMEDAY SO REMEMBER THIS...
HE IS THE LEADER OF OUR ORGANI-ZATION, THE L.X.E., AND...
HE WILL ONE DAY BE THE KING OF THE HOMUNCULI!

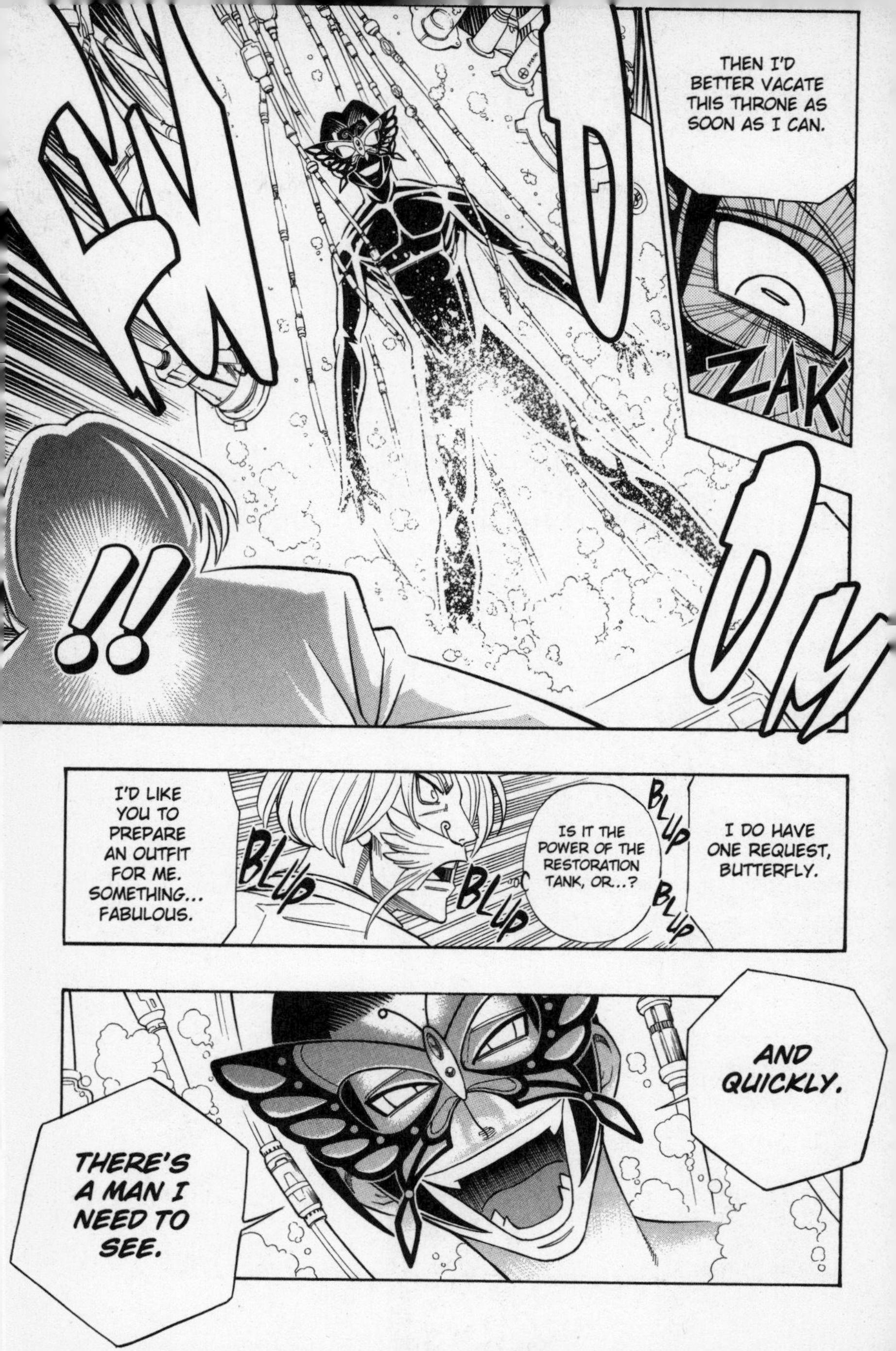
THEN I'D BETTER VACATE THIS THRONE AS SOON AS I CAN.
ZAK
!!
I DO HAVE ONE REQUEST, BUTTERFLY.
BLUP
BLUP
IS IT THE POWER OF THE RESTORATION TANK, OR...?
BLUP
BLUP
I'D LIKE YOU TO PREPARE AN OUTFIT FOR ME. SOMETHING... FABULOUS.
AND QUICKLY.
THERE'S A MAN I NEED TO SEE.

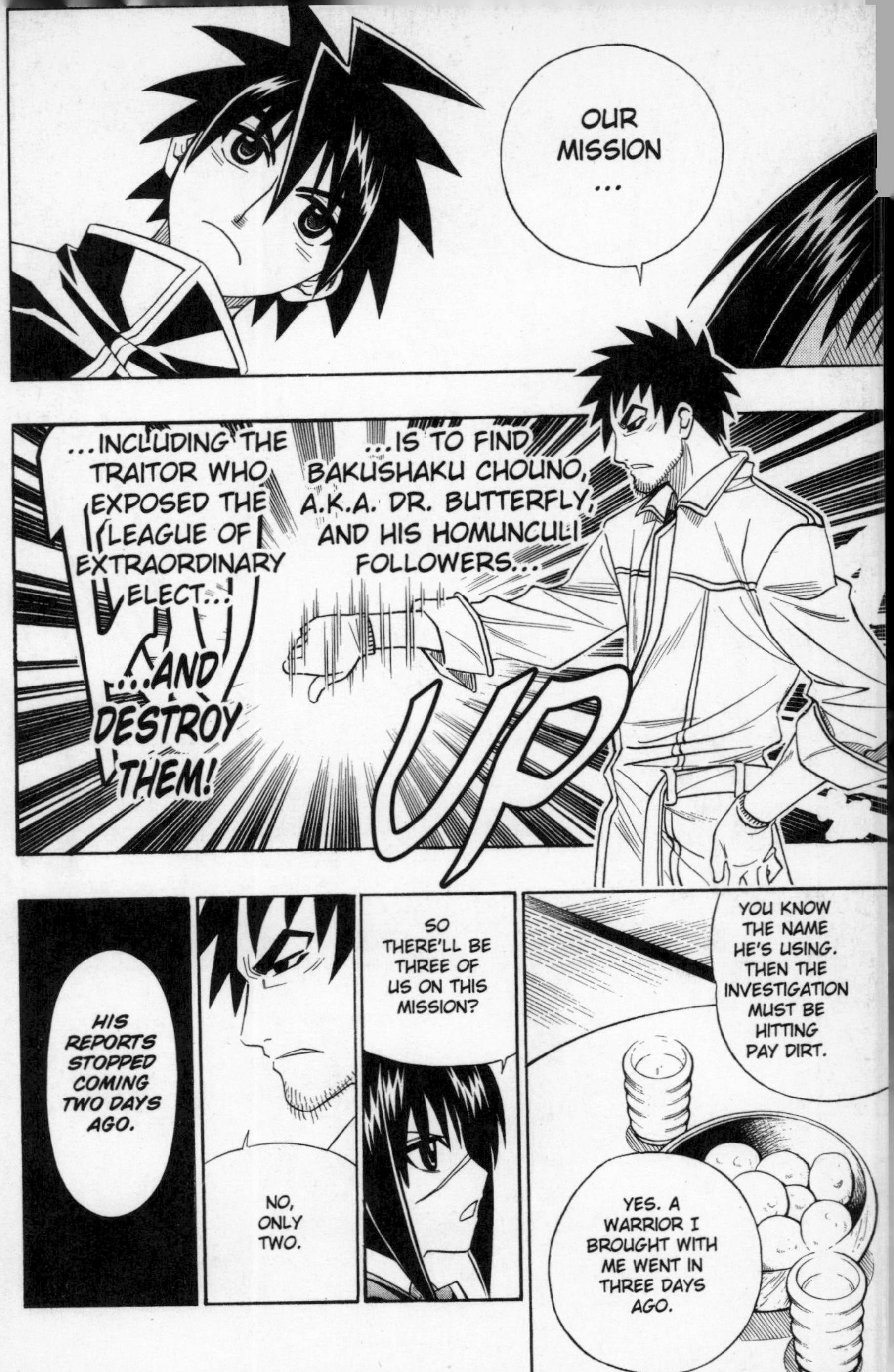
OUR MISSION ...
...IS TO FIND BAKUSHAKU CHOUNO, A.K.A. DR. BUTTERFLY, AND HIS HOMUNCULI FOLLOWERS...
...INCLUDING THE TRAITOR WHO EXPOSED THE LEAGUE OF EXTRAORDINARY ELECT...
...AND DESTROY THEM!
UP
YOU KNOW THE NAME HE'S USING. THEN THE INVESTIGATION MUST BE HITTING PAY DIRT.
YES. A WARRIOR I BROUGHT WITH ME WENT IN THREE DAYS AGO.
SO THERE'LL BE THREE OF US ON THIS MISSION?
NO, ONLY TWO.
HIS REPORTS STOPPED COMING TWO DAYS AGO.

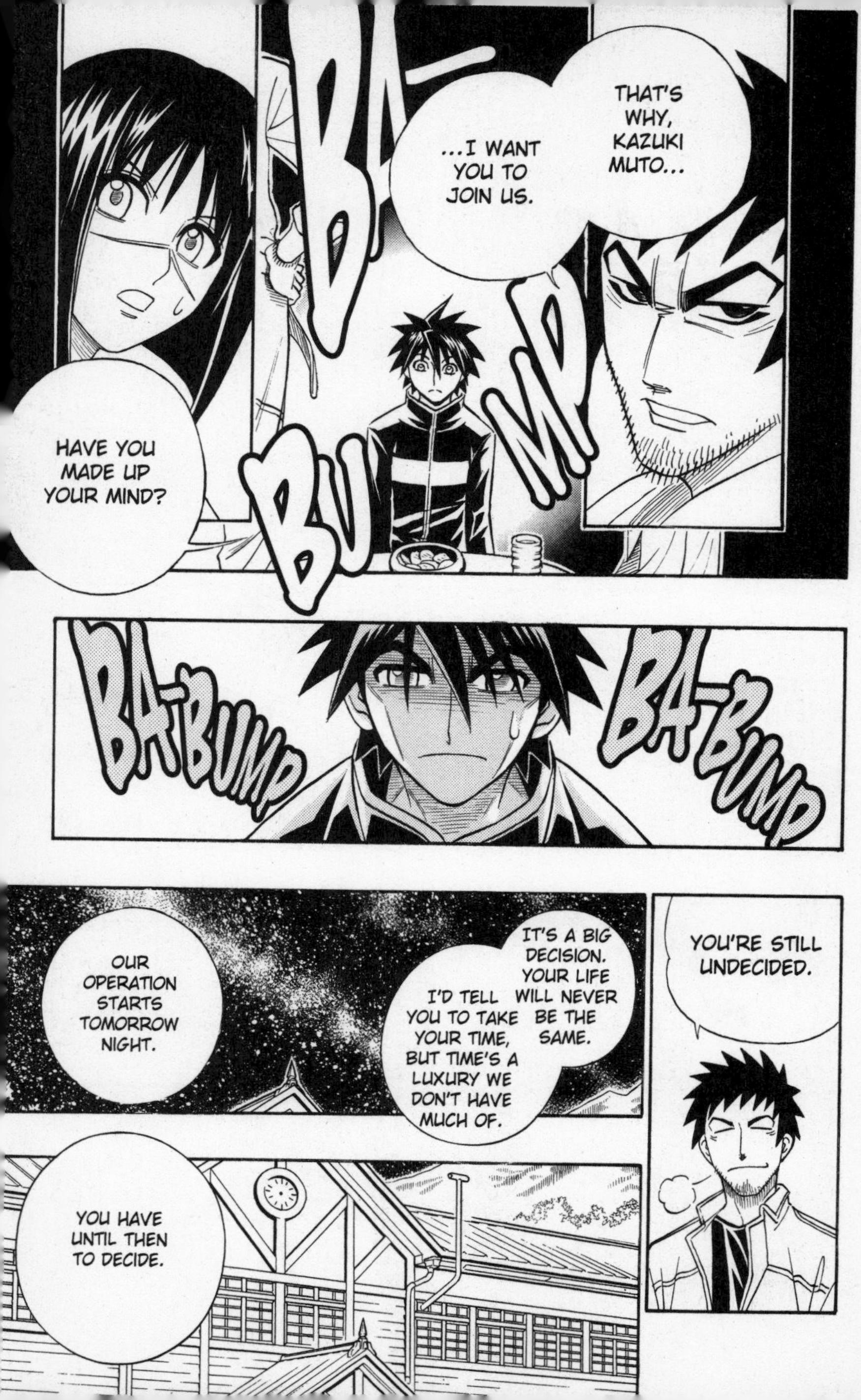
THAT'S WHY, KAZUKI MUTO...
...I WANT YOU TO JOIN US.
BA-BUMP
HAVE YOU MADE UP YOUR MIND?
BA-BUMP
BA-BUMP
YOU'RE STILL UNDECIDED.
IT'S A BIG DECISION. YOUR LIFE WILL NEVER BE THE SAME.
I'D TELL YOU TO TAKE YOUR TIME, BUT TIME'S A LUXURY WE DON'T HAVE MUCH OF.
OUR OPERATION STARTS TOMORROW NIGHT.
YOU HAVE UNTIL THEN TO DECIDE.

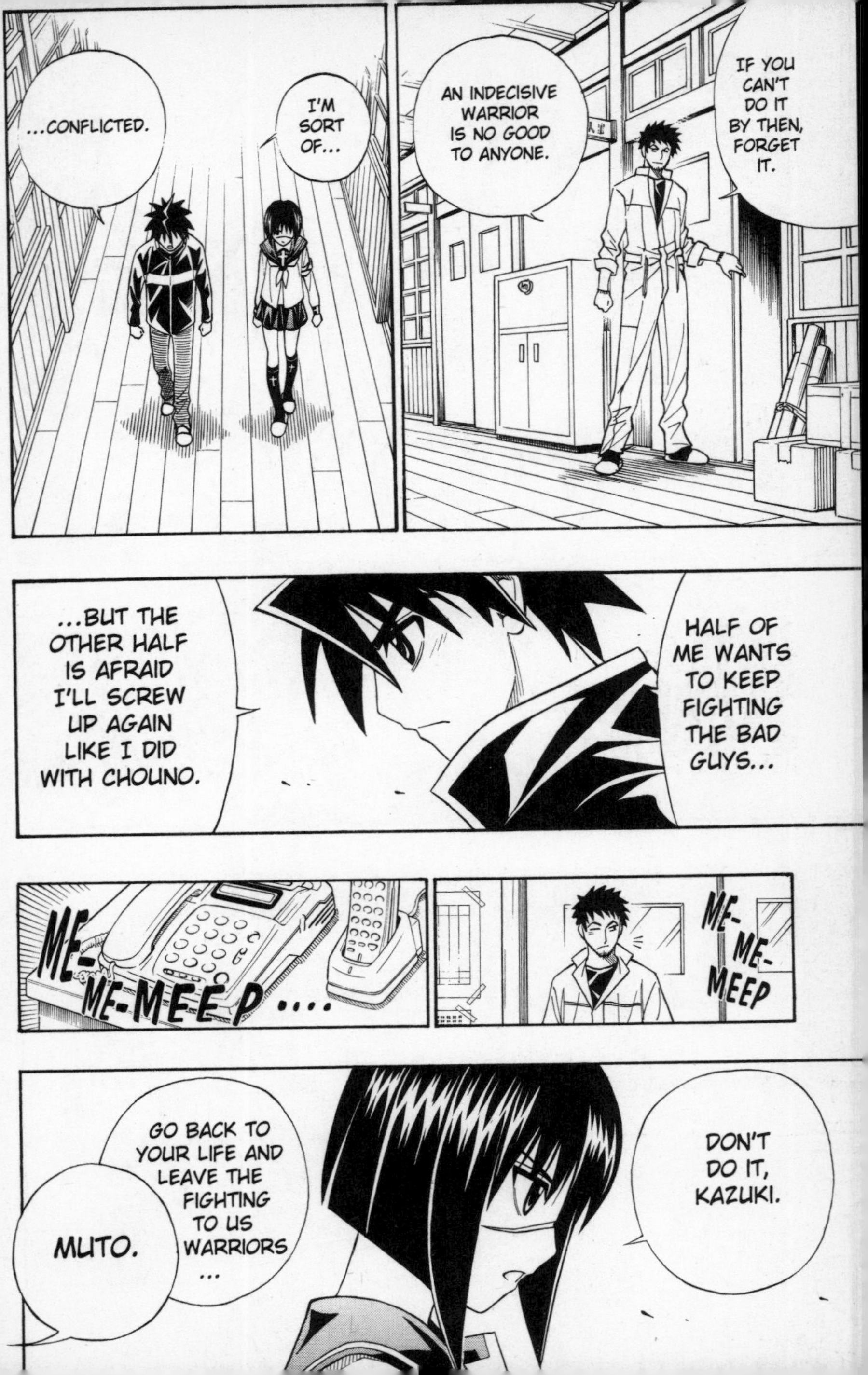
IF YOU CAN'T DO IT BY THEN, FORGET IT.
AN INDECISIVE WARRIOR IS NO GOOD TO ANYONE.
I'M SORT OF...
...CONFLICTED.
HALF OF ME WANTS TO KEEP FIGHTING THE BAD GUYS...
...BUT THE OTHER HALF IS AFRAID I'LL SCREW UP AGAIN LIKE I DID WITH CHOUNO.
ME-ME-MEEP
ME-ME-MEEP....
DON'T DO IT, KAZUKI.
GO BACK TO YOUR LIFE AND LEAVE THE FIGHTING TO US WARRIORS...
MUTO.

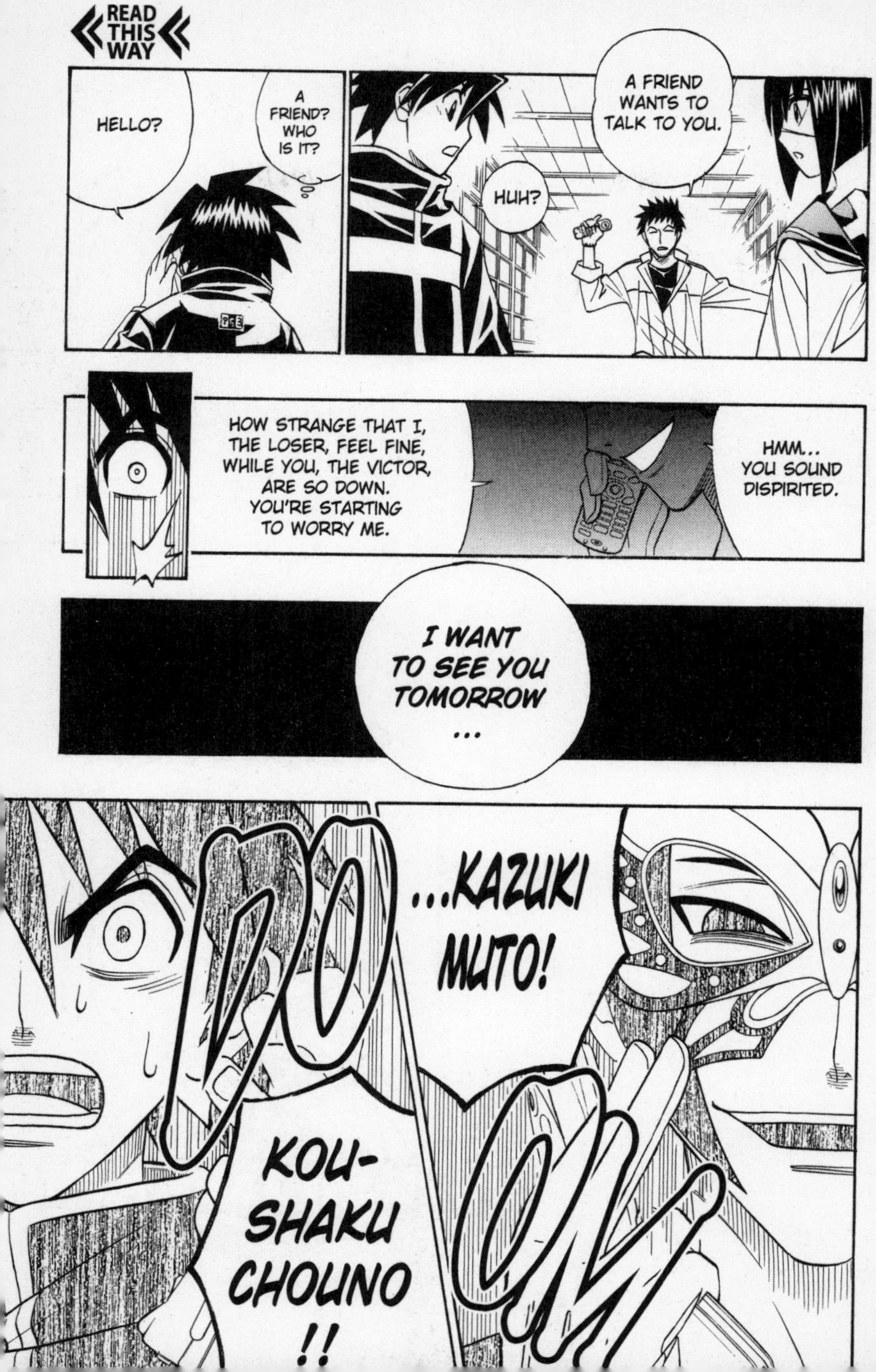
READ THIS WAY
A FRIEND WANTS TO TALK TO YOU.
HUH?
A FRIEND? WHO IS IT?
HELLO?
HMM... YOU SOUND DISPIRITED.
HOW STRANGE THAT I, THE LOSER, FEEL FINE, WHILE YOU, THE VICTOR, ARE SO DOWN. YOU'RE STARTING TO WORRY ME.
I WANT TO SEE YOU TOMORROW ...
...KAZUKI MUTO!
DOOM
KOU-SHAKU CHOUNO !!

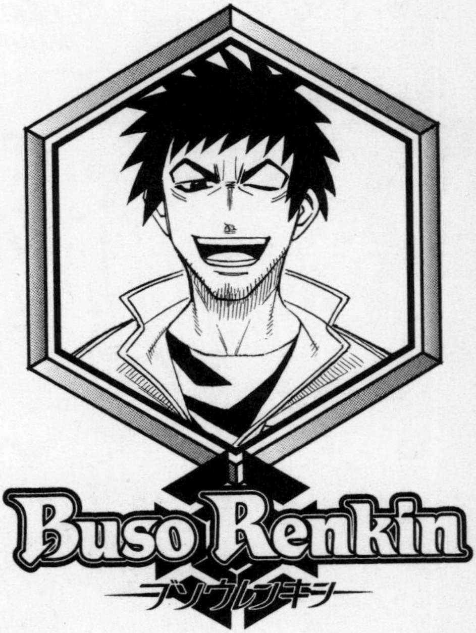
Buso Renkin
ブソウレンキン

CHAPTER 20: KAZUKI AND TOKIKO'S CHOICE, PART 2

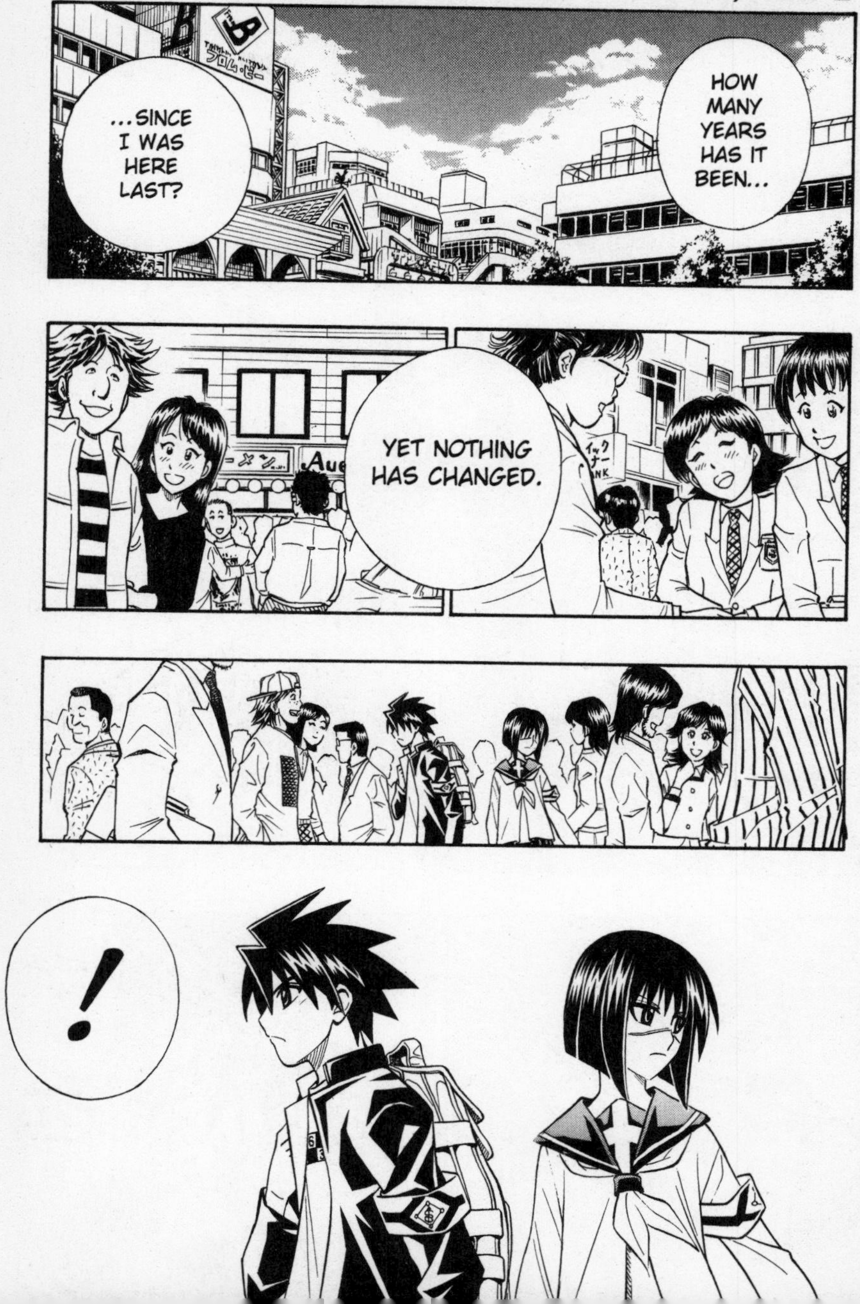
HOW MANY YEARS HAS IT BEEN...
...SINCE I WAS HERE LAST?
YET NOTHING HAS CHANGED.
!

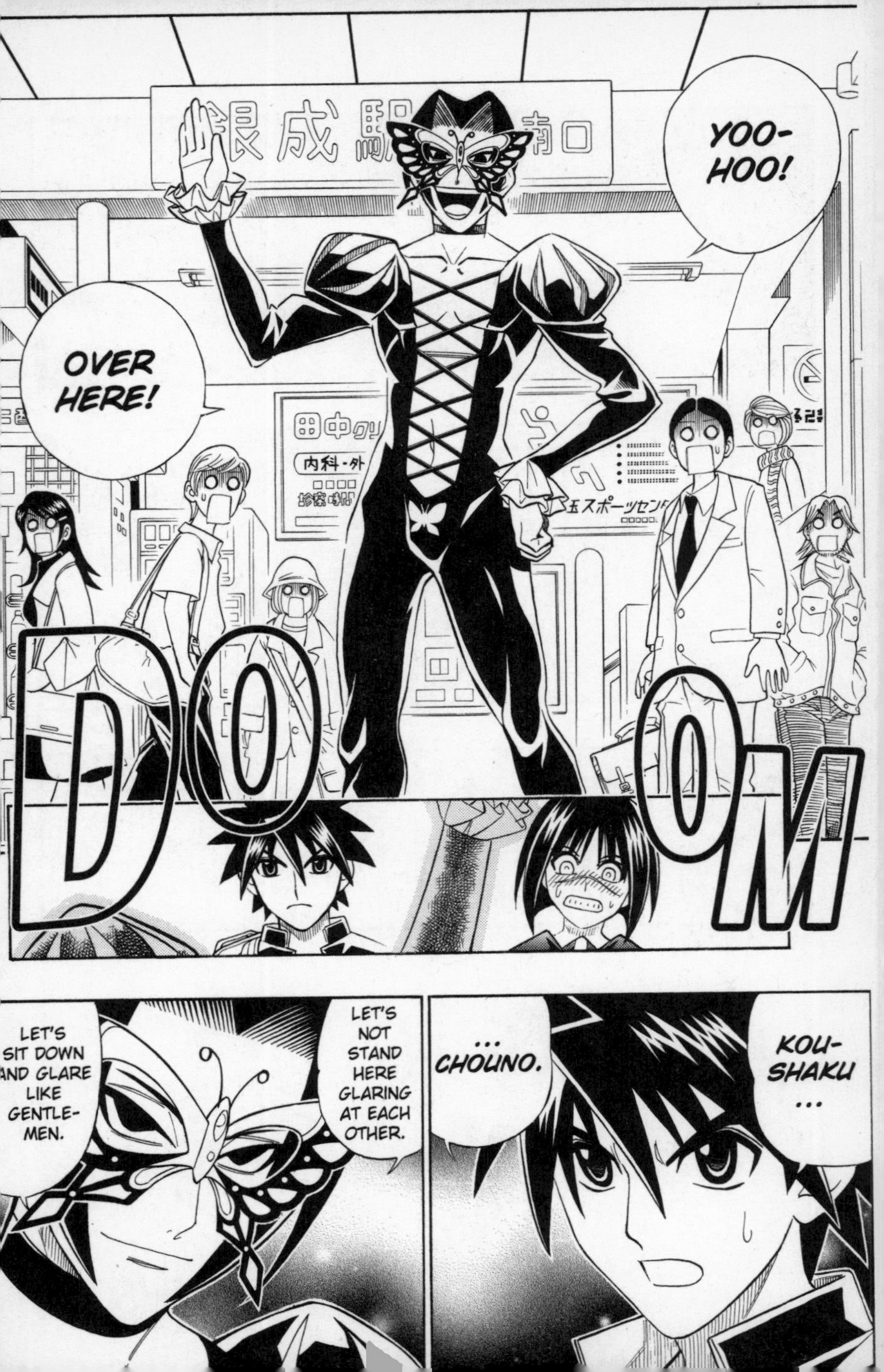
YOO-HOO!
OVER HERE!
DOOM
KOU-SHAKU...
...CHÔUNO.
LET'S NOT STAND HERE GLARING AT EACH OTHER.
LET'S SIT DOWN AND GLARE LIKE GENTLEMEN.

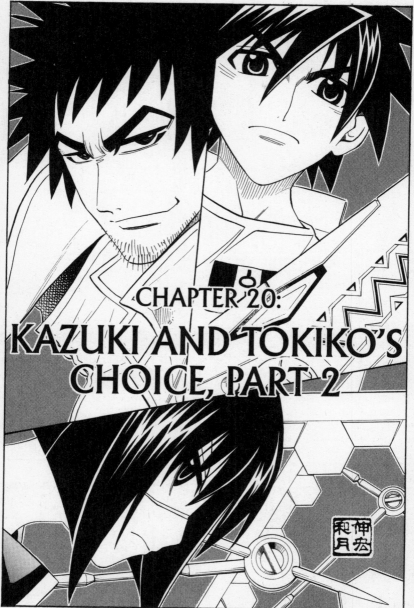

CHAPTER 20:
KAZUKI AND TOKIKO'S
CHOICE, PART 2

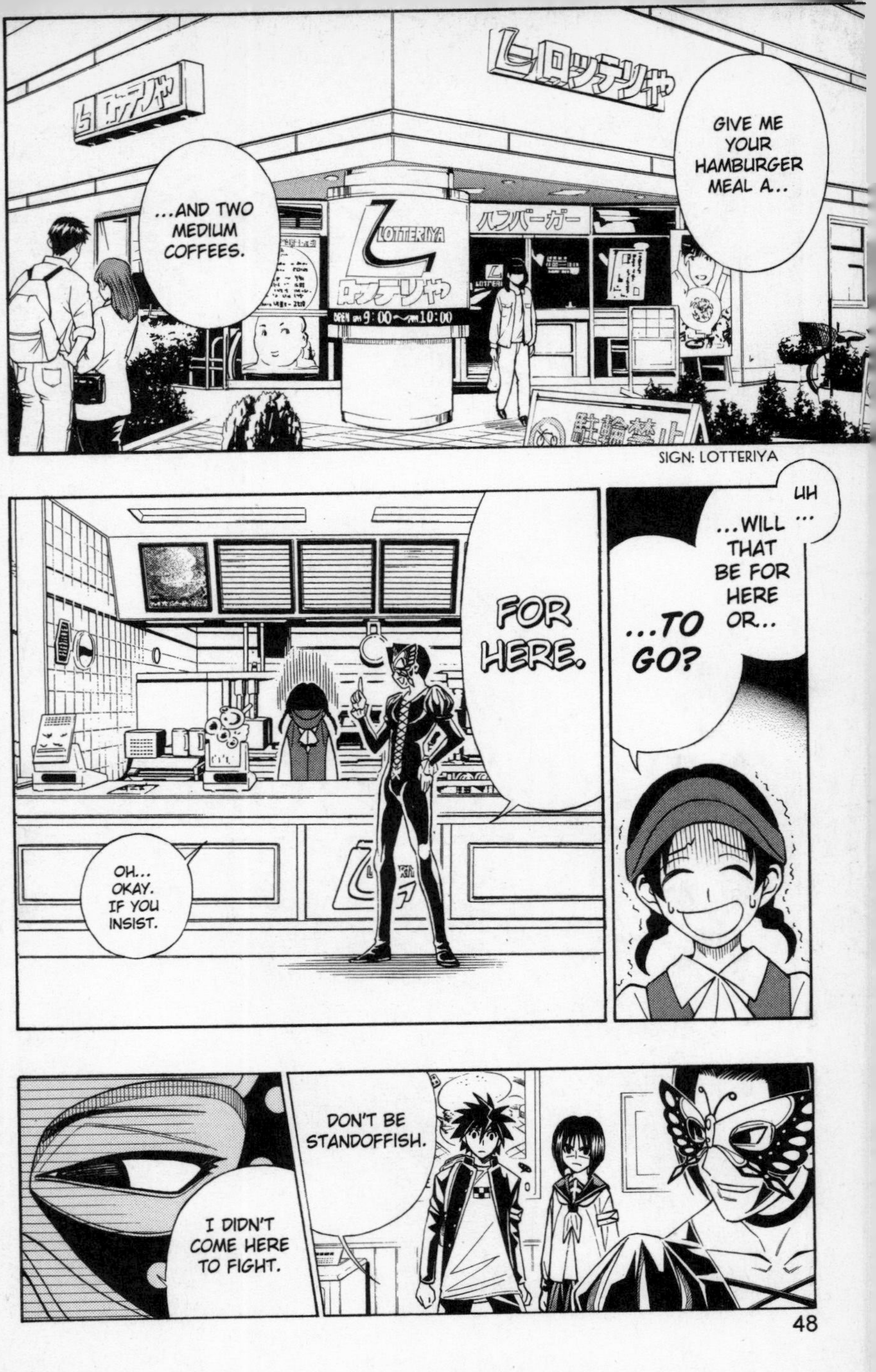
GIVE ME YOUR HAMBURGER MEAL A..
...AND TWO MEDIUM COFFEES.
UH ...
...WILL THAT BE FOR HERE OR...
...TO GO?
FOR HERE.
OH... OKAY. IF YOU INSIST.
DON'T BE STANDOFFISH.
I DIDN'T COME HERE TO FIGHT.

SIGN: LOTTERIYA

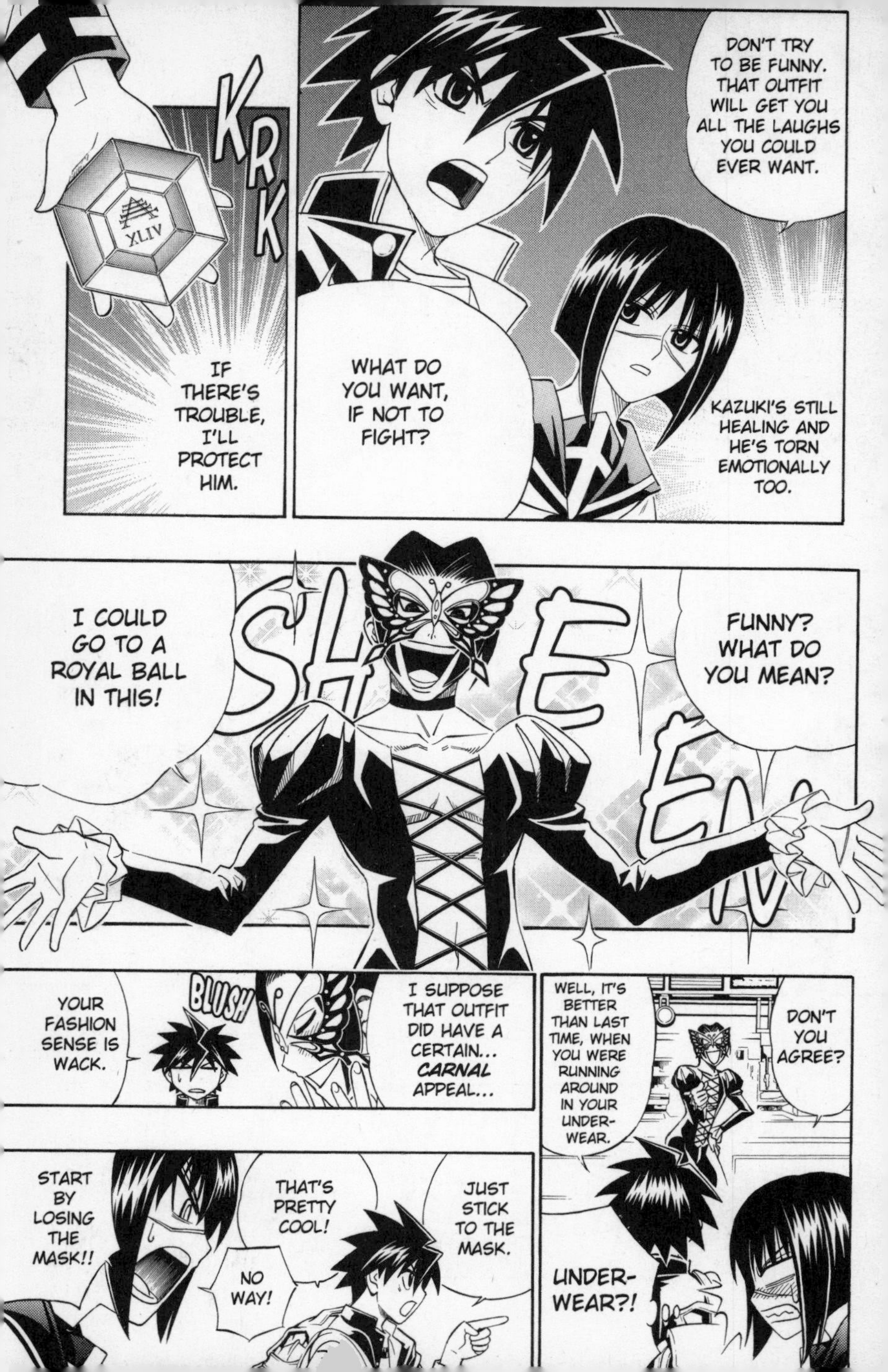
DON'T TRY TO BE FUNNY. THAT OUTFIT WILL GET YOU ALL THE LAUGHS YOU COULD EVER WANT.
WHAT DO YOU WANT, IF NOT TO FIGHT?
KAZUKI'S STILL HEALING AND HE'S TORN EMOTIONALLY TOO.
KRK
IF THERE'S TROUBLE, I'LL PROTECT HIM.
XLIV
FUNNY? WHAT DO YOU MEAN?
SHEEN
I COULD GO TO A ROYAL BALL IN THIS!
DON'T YOU AGREE?
WELL, IT'S BETTER THAN LAST TIME, WHEN YOU WERE RUNNING AROUND IN YOUR UNDER-WEAR.
UNDER-WEAR?!
I SUPPOSE THAT OUTFIT DID HAVE A CERTAIN... *CARNAL* APPEAL...
BLUSH
YOUR FASHION SENSE IS WACK.
JUST STICK TO THE MASK.
THAT'S PRETTY COOL!
NO WAY!
START BY LOSING THE MASK!!

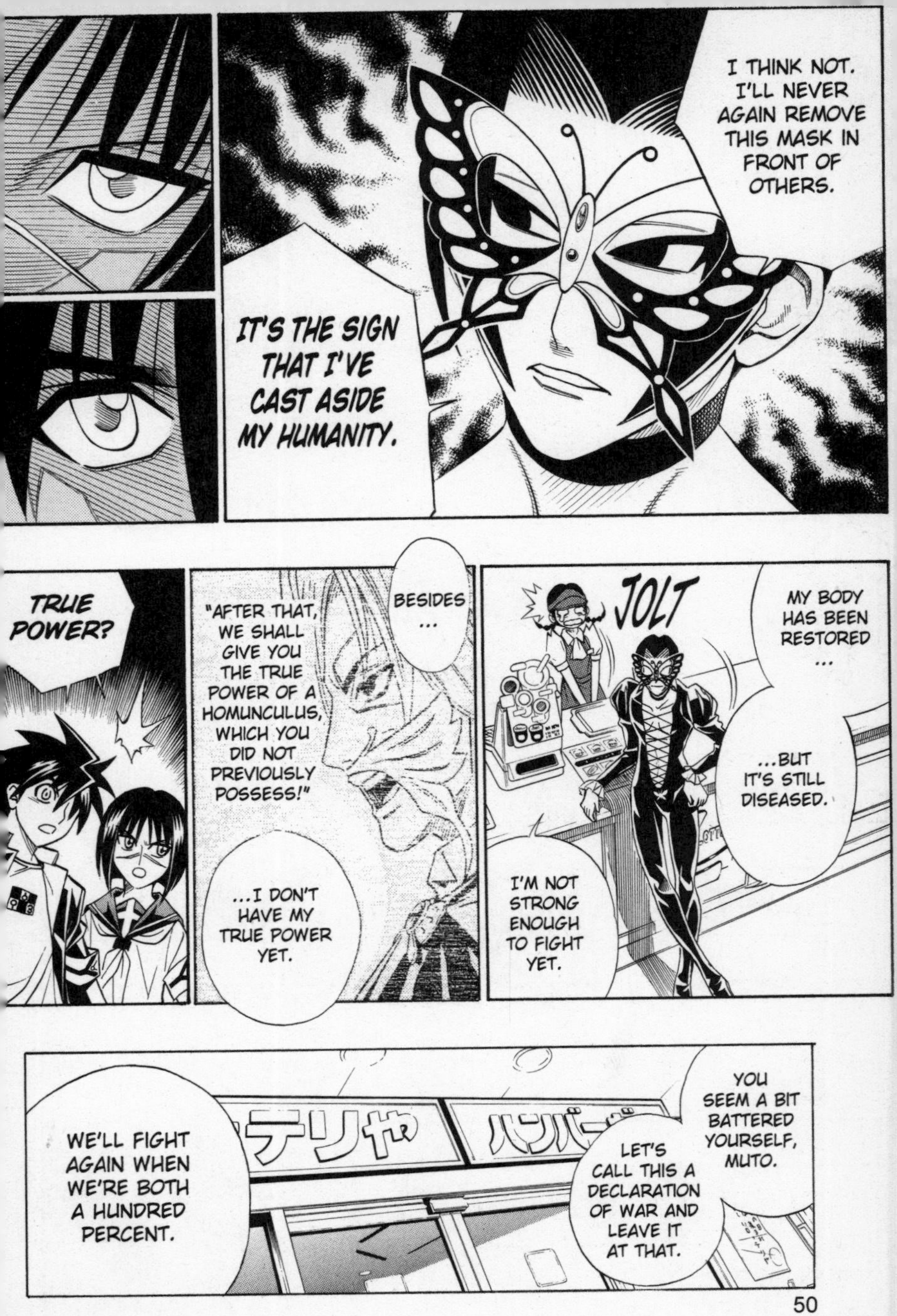
I THINK NOT. I'LL NEVER AGAIN REMOVE THIS MASK IN FRONT OF OTHERS.
IT'S THE SIGN THAT I'VE CAST ASIDE MY HUMANITY.
MY BODY HAS BEEN RESTORED ...
...BUT IT'S STILL DISEASED.
JOLT
I'M NOT STRONG ENOUGH TO FIGHT YET.
BESIDES ...
"AFTER THAT, WE SHALL GIVE YOU THE TRUE POWER OF A HOMUNCULUS, WHICH YOU DID NOT PREVIOUSLY POSSESS!"
...I DON'T HAVE MY TRUE POWER YET.
TRUE POWER?
YOU SEEM A BIT BATTERED YOURSELF, MUTO.
LET'S CALL THIS A DECLARATION OF WAR AND LEAVE IT AT THAT.
WE'LL FIGHT AGAIN WHEN WE'RE BOTH A HUNDRED PERCENT.

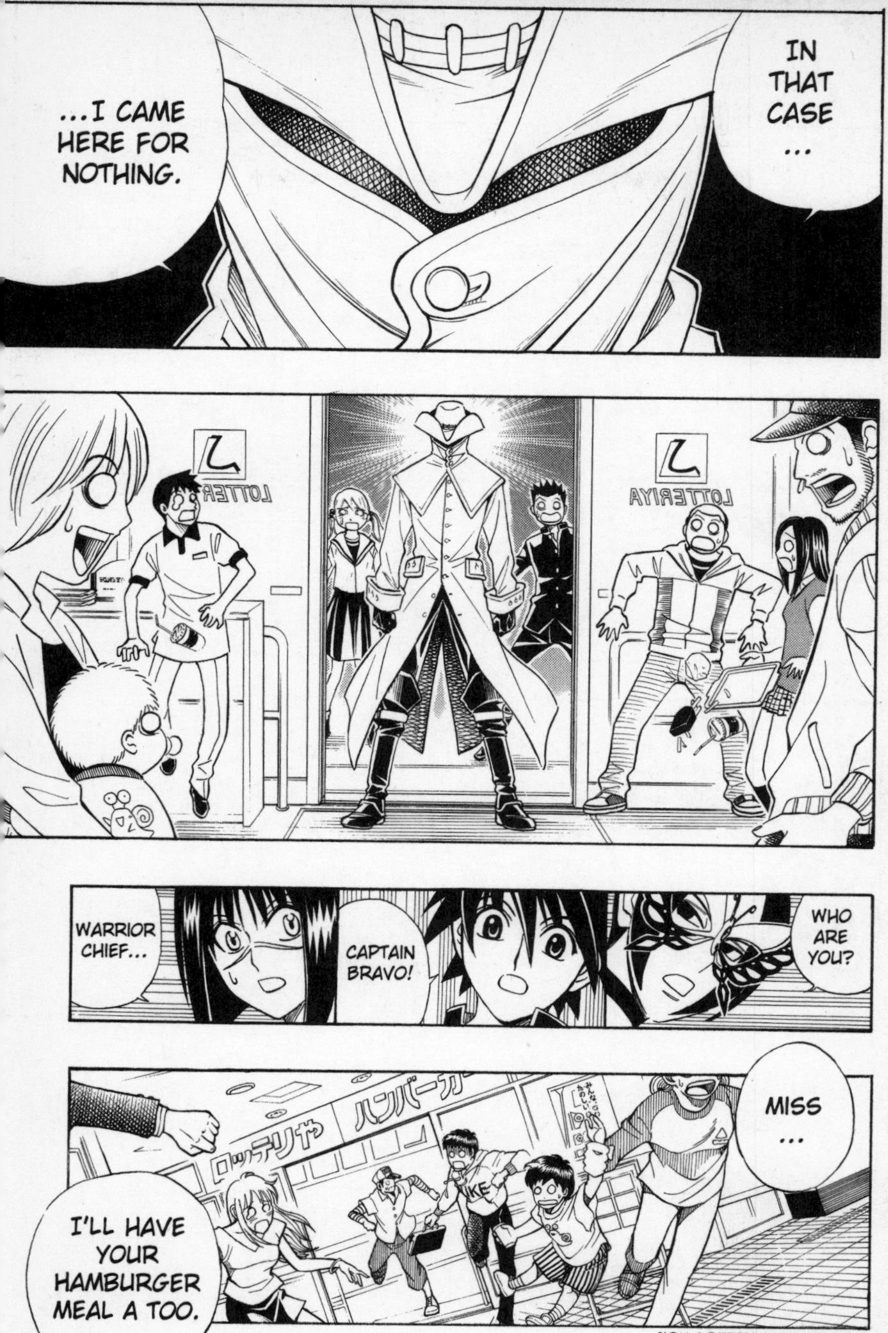
IN THAT CASE ...
...I CAME HERE FOR NOTHING.
LOTTERIYA
WHO ARE YOU?
CAPTAIN BRAVO!
WARRIOR CHIEF...
MISS ...
I'LL HAVE YOUR HAMBURGER MEAL A TOO.
ロッテリや
ハンバーガー

SIGN: LOTTERIYA HAMBURGER

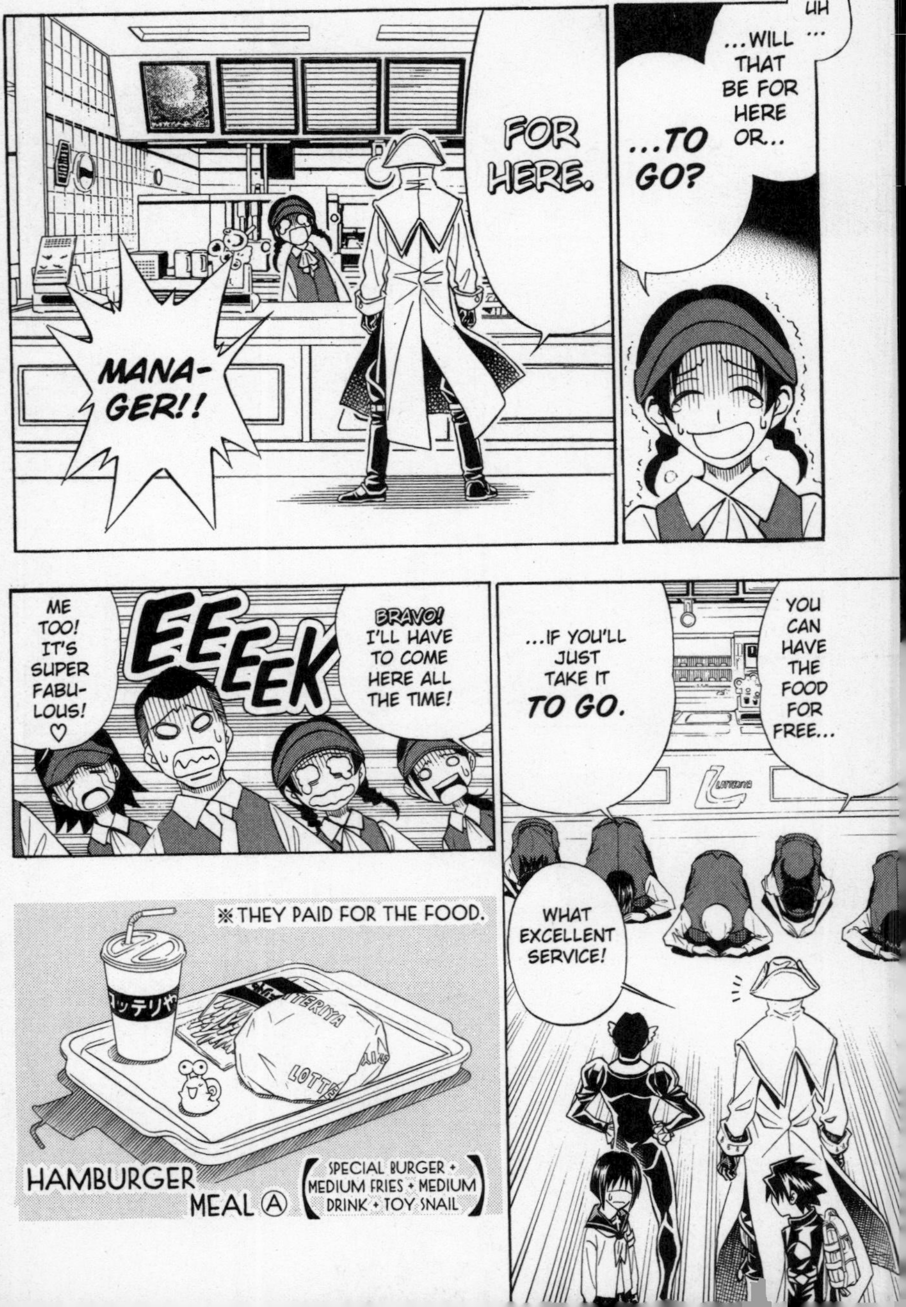
UH ...
...WILL THAT BE FOR HERE OR...
...TO GO?
FOR HERE.
MANA-GER!!
YOU CAN HAVE THE FOOD FOR FREE...
...IF YOU'LL JUST TAKE IT TO GO.
WHAT EXCELLENT SERVICE!
BRAVO! I'LL HAVE TO COME HERE ALL THE TIME!
EEEEK
ME TOO! IT'S SUPER FABU-LOUS! ♡
※THEY PAID FOR THE FOOD.
LOTTE
HAMBURGER MEAL Ⓐ
(SPECIAL BURGER + MEDIUM FRIES + MEDIUM DRINK + TOY SNAIL)

READ THIS WAY

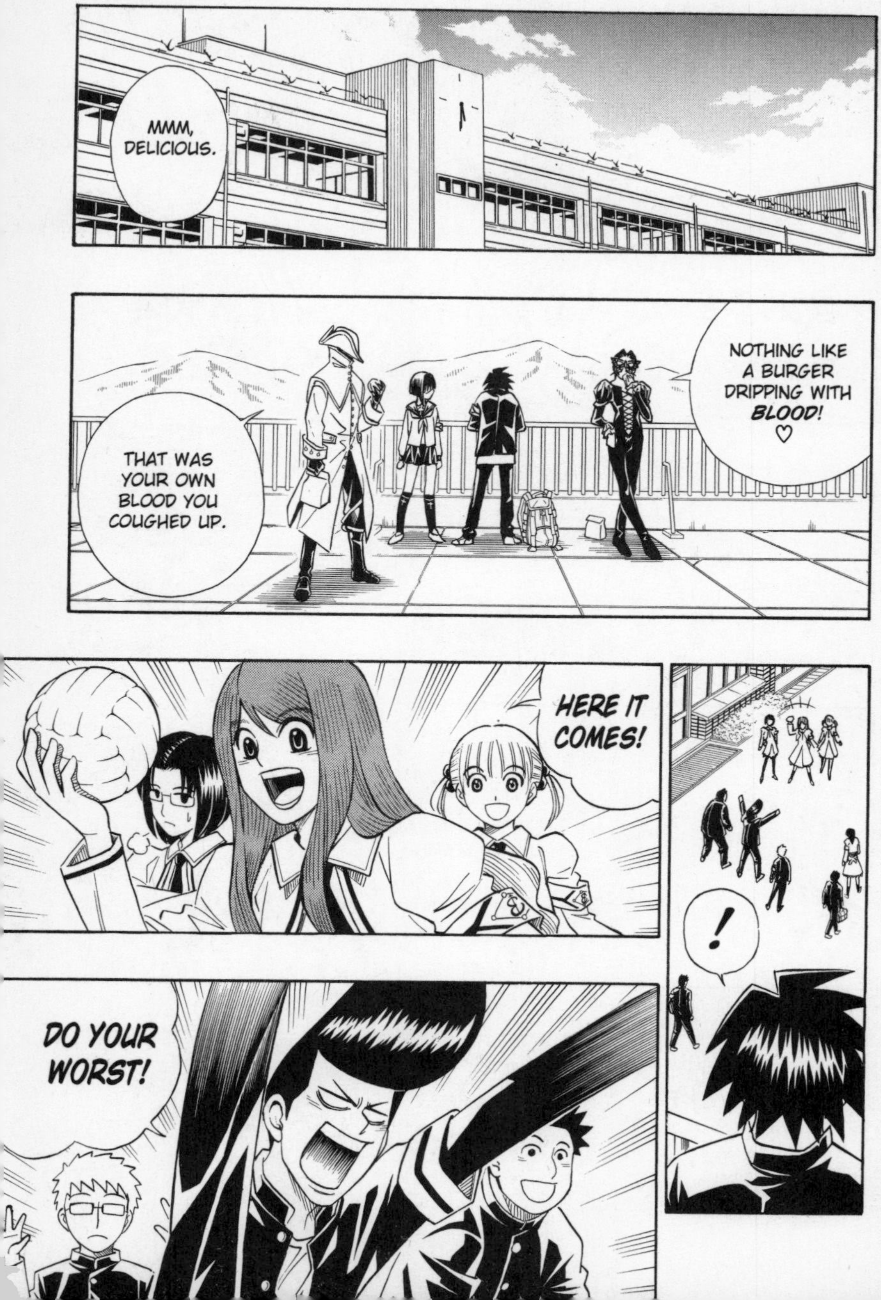
MMM, DELICIOUS.
NOTHING LIKE A BURGER DRIPPING WITH BLOOD! ♡
THAT WAS YOUR OWN BLOOD YOU COUGHED UP.
!
HERE IT COMES!
DO YOUR WORST!

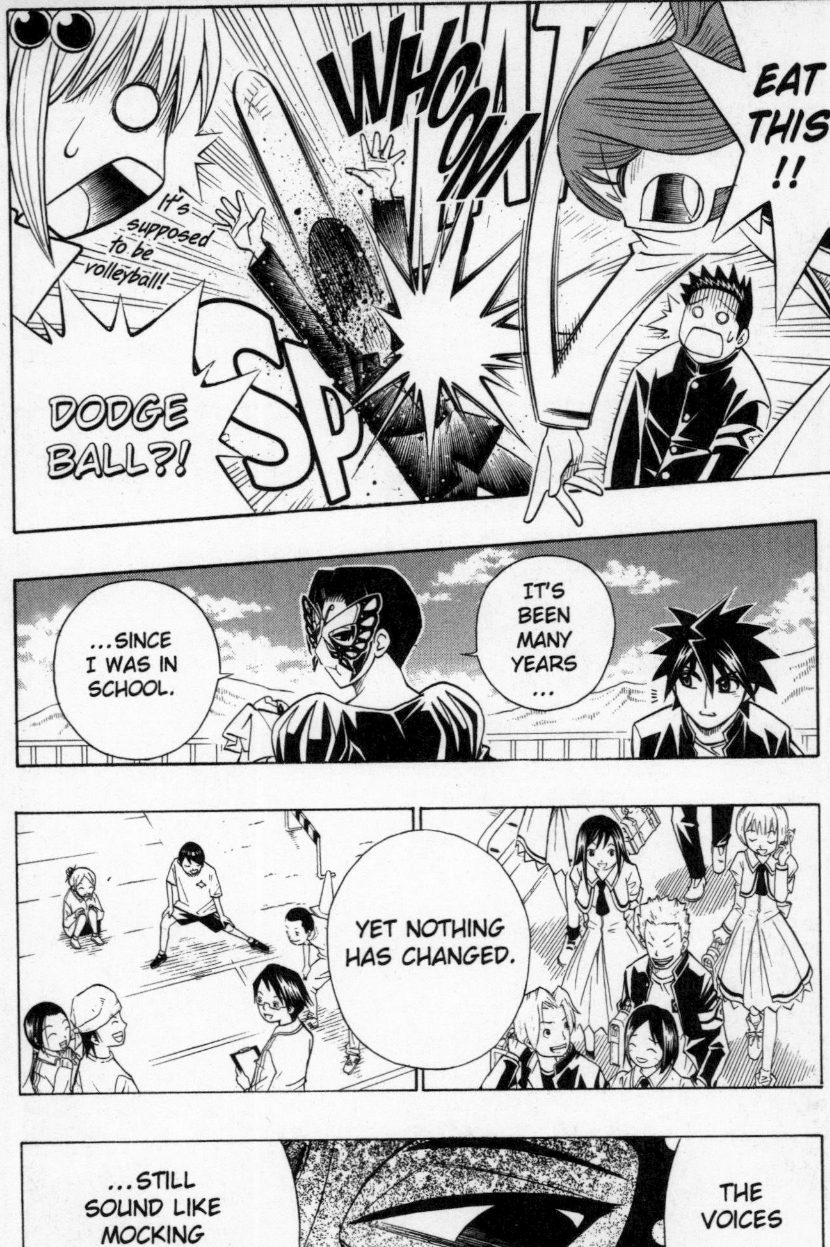
EAT THIS!!
WHOOM
It's supposed to be volleyball!
SP
DODGE BALL?!
IT'S BEEN MANY YEARS...
...SINCE I WAS IN SCHOOL.
YET NOTHING HAS CHANGED.
THE VOICES...
...STILL SOUND LIKE MOCKING JEERS TO ME.

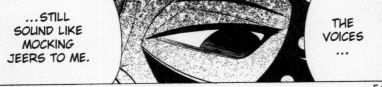

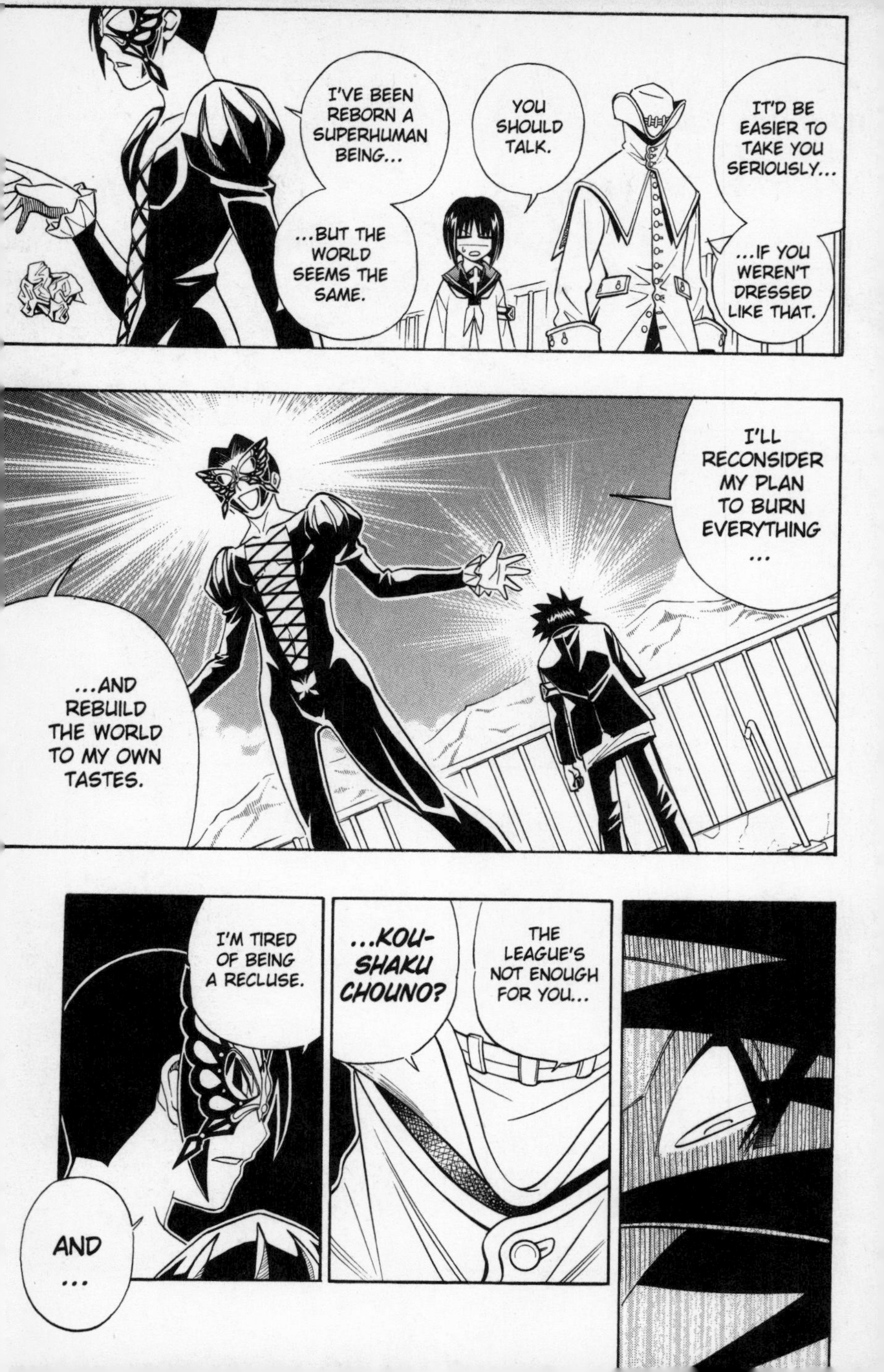
IT'D BE EASIER TO TAKE YOU SERIOUSLY...
...IF YOU WEREN'T DRESSED LIKE THAT.
YOU SHOULD TALK.
I'VE BEEN REBORN A SUPERHUMAN BEING...
...BUT THE WORLD SEEMS THE SAME.
I'LL RECONSIDER MY PLAN TO BURN EVERYTHING ...
...AND REBUILD THE WORLD TO MY OWN TASTES.
THE LEAGUE'S NOT ENOUGH FOR YOU...
...KOU-SHAKU CHOUNO?
I'M TIRED OF BEING A RECLUSE.
AND ...

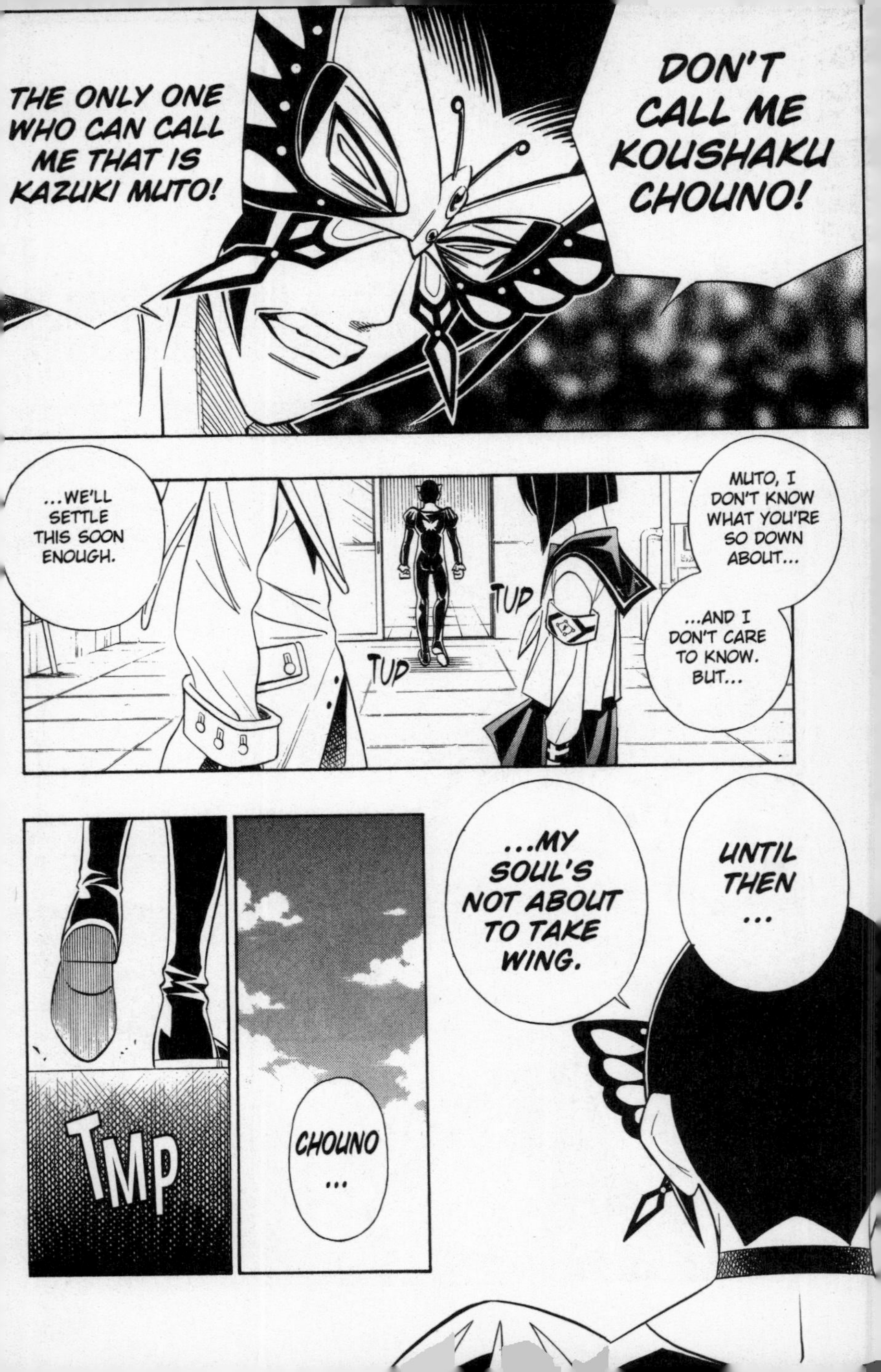
DON'T CALL ME KOUSHAKU CHOUNO!
THE ONLY ONE WHO CAN CALL ME THAT IS KAZUKI MUTO!
MUTO, I DON'T KNOW WHAT YOU'RE SO DOWN ABOUT...
...AND I DON'T CARE TO KNOW. BUT...
TUP
TUP
...WE'LL SETTLE THIS SOON ENOUGH.
UNTIL THEN ...
...MY SOUL'S NOT ABOUT TO TAKE WING.
CHOUNO ...
TMP

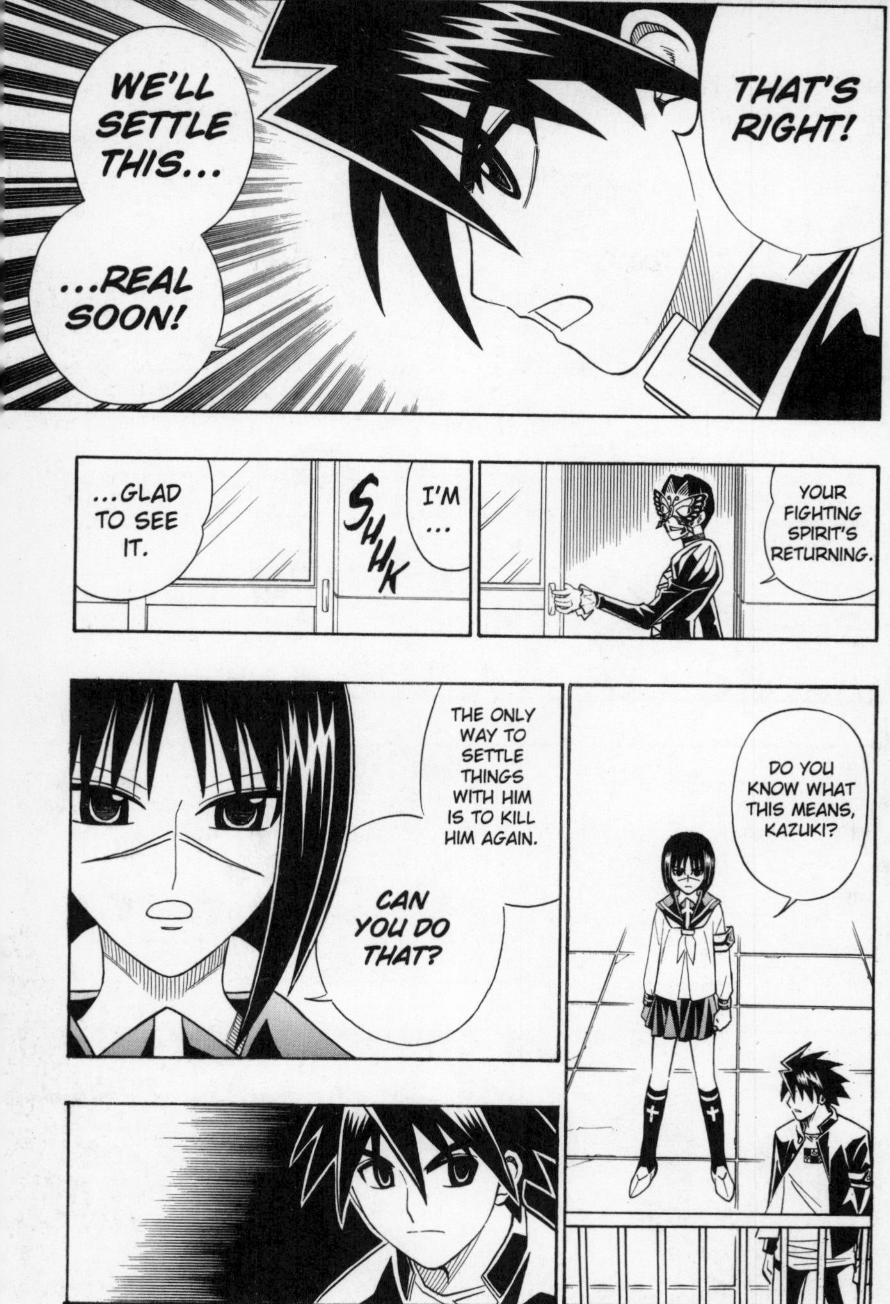
THAT'S RIGHT!
WE'LL SETTLE THIS...
...REAL SOON!
YOUR FIGHTING SPIRIT'S RETURNING.
I'M ...
SHUK
...GLAD TO SEE IT.
DO YOU KNOW WHAT THIS MEANS, KAZUKI?
THE ONLY WAY TO SETTLE THINGS WITH HIM IS TO KILL HIM AGAIN.
CAN YOU DO THAT?

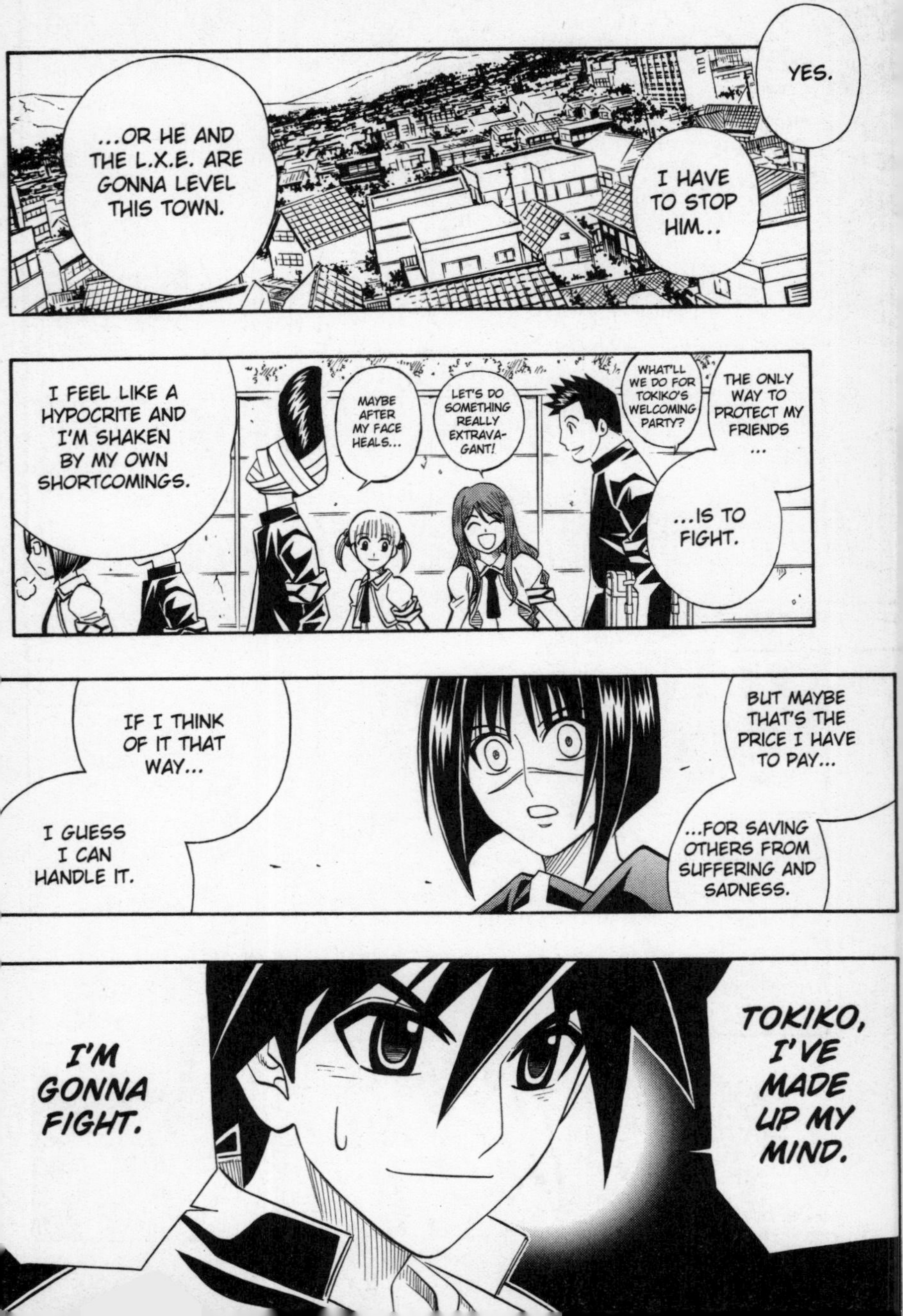
YES.
I HAVE TO STOP HIM...
...OR HE AND THE L.X.E. ARE GONNA LEVEL THIS TOWN.
THE ONLY WAY TO PROTECT MY FRIENDS ...
...IS TO FIGHT.
WHAT'LL WE DO FOR TOKIKO'S WELCOMING PARTY?
LET'S DO SOMETHING REALLY EXTRAVA-GANT!
MAYBE AFTER MY FACE HEALS...
I FEEL LIKE A HYPOCRITE AND I'M SHAKEN BY MY OWN SHORTCOMINGS.
BUT MAYBE THAT'S THE PRICE I HAVE TO PAY...
...FOR SAVING OTHERS FROM SUFFERING AND SADNESS.
IF I THINK OF IT THAT WAY...
I GUESS I CAN HANDLE IT.
TOKIKO, I'VE MADE UP MY MIND.
I'M GONNA FIGHT.

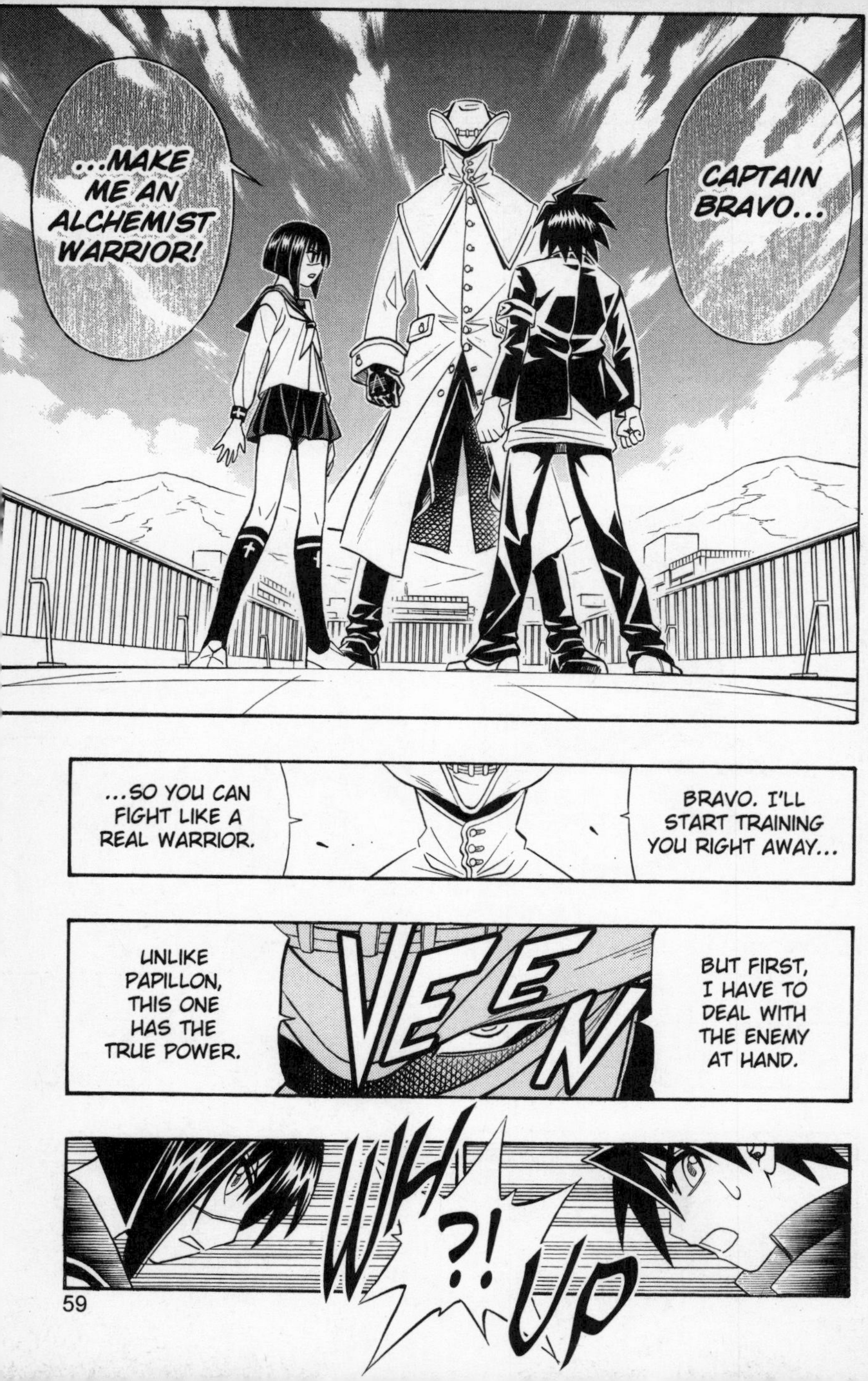
CAPTAIN BRAVO...
...MAKE ME AN ALCHEMIST WARRIOR!
BRAVO. I'LL START TRAINING YOU RIGHT AWAY...
...SO YOU CAN FIGHT LIKE A REAL WARRIOR.
BUT FIRST, I HAVE TO DEAL WITH THE ENEMY AT HAND.
VEEN
UNLIKE PAPILLON, THIS ONE HAS THE TRUE POWER.
WHUP
?!

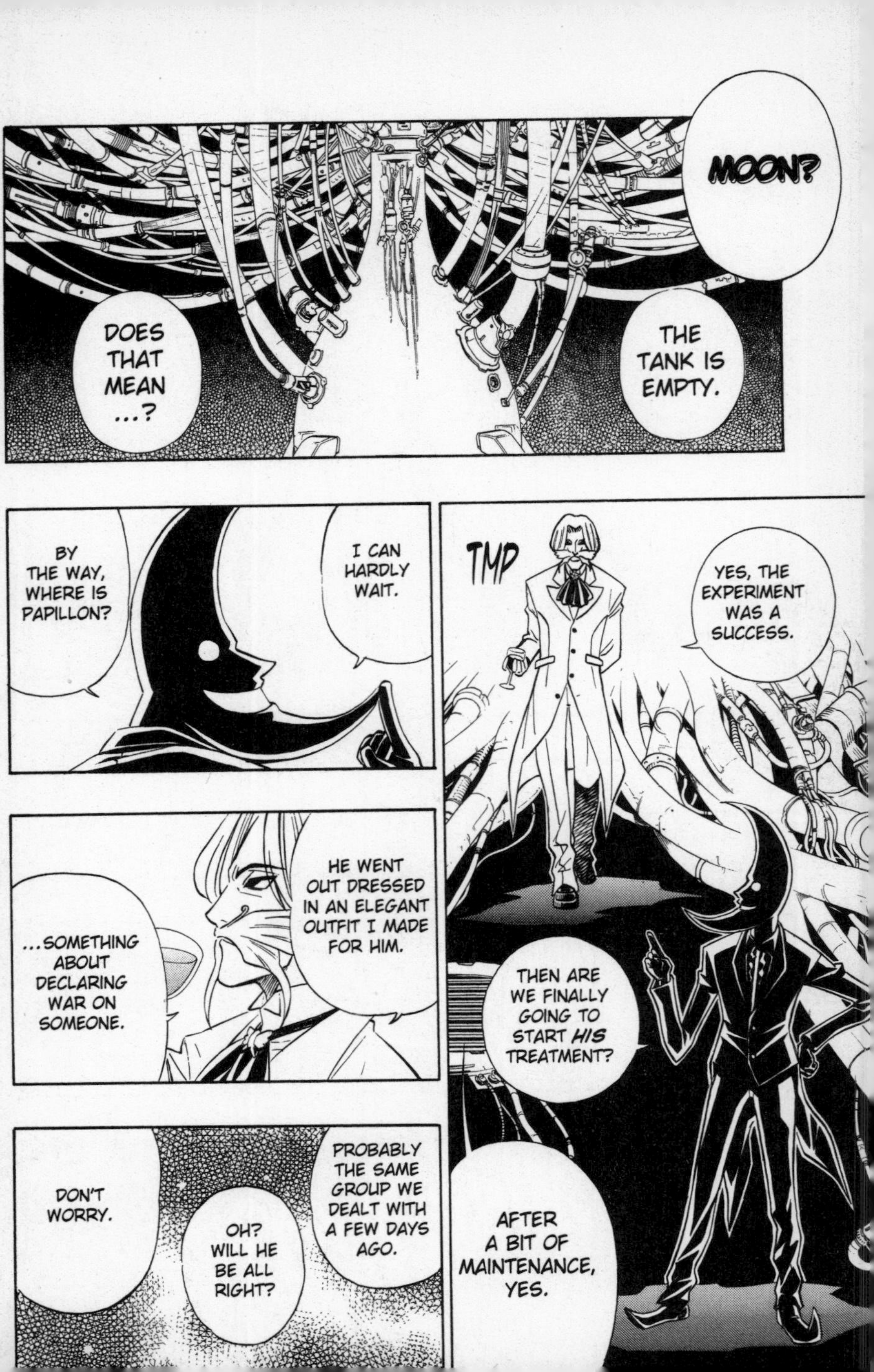
MOON?
THE TANK IS EMPTY.
DOES THAT MEAN ...?
TMP
YES, THE EXPERIMENT WAS A SUCCESS.
THEN ARE WE FINALLY GOING TO START *HIS* TREATMENT?
AFTER A BIT OF MAINTENANCE, YES.
I CAN HARDLY WAIT.
BY THE WAY, WHERE IS PAPILLON?
HE WENT OUT DRESSED IN AN ELEGANT OUTFIT I MADE FOR HIM.
...SOMETHING ABOUT DECLARING WAR ON SOMEONE.
PROBABLY THE SAME GROUP WE DEALT WITH A FEW DAYS AGO.
OH? WILL HE BE ALL RIGHT?
DON'T WORRY.

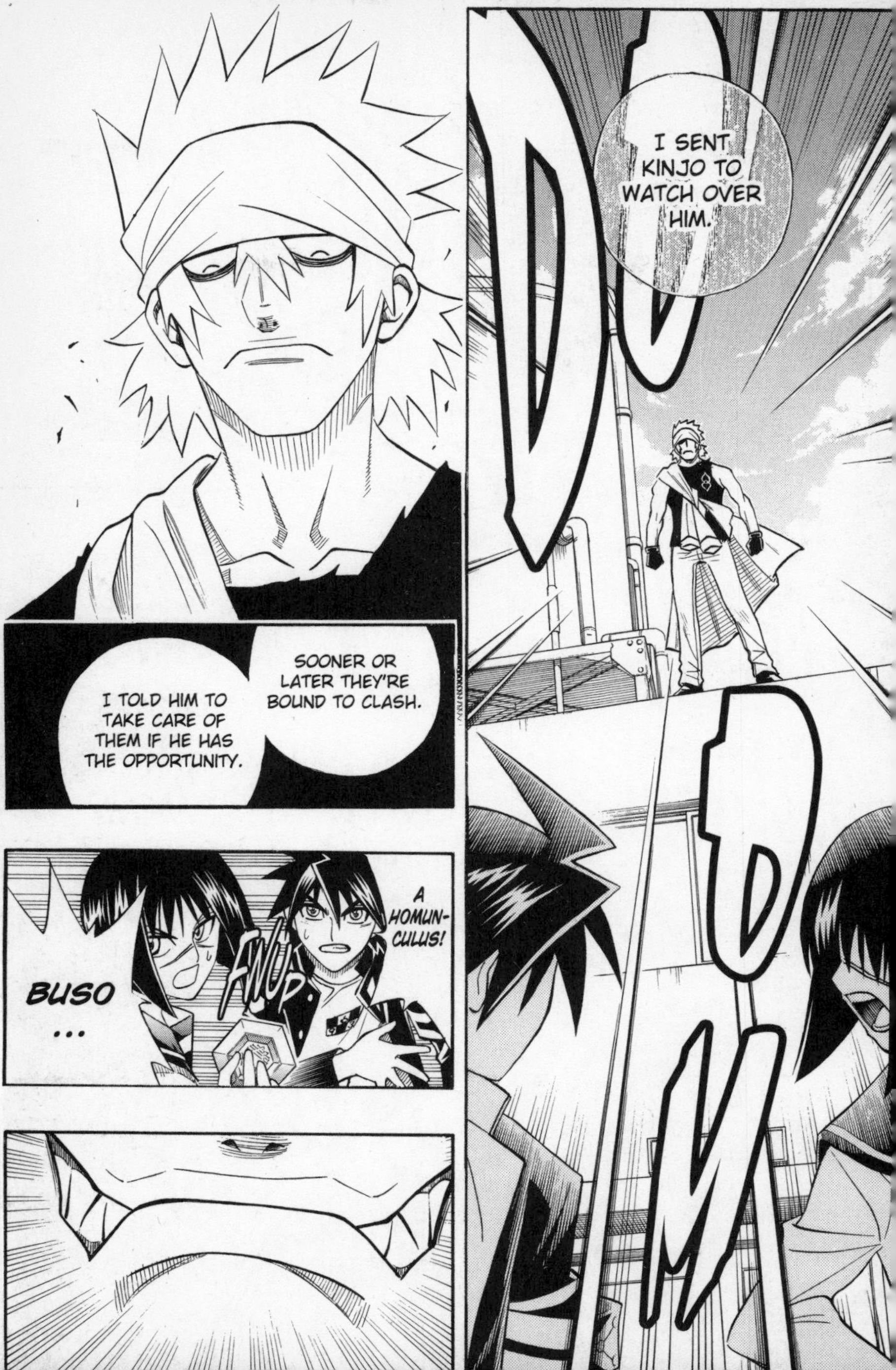
I SENT KINJO TO WATCH OVER HIM.
SOONER OR LATER THEY'RE BOUND TO CLASH.
I TOLD HIM TO TAKE CARE OF THEM IF HE HAS THE OPPORTUNITY.
A HOMUNCULUS!
FWUP
BUSO ...

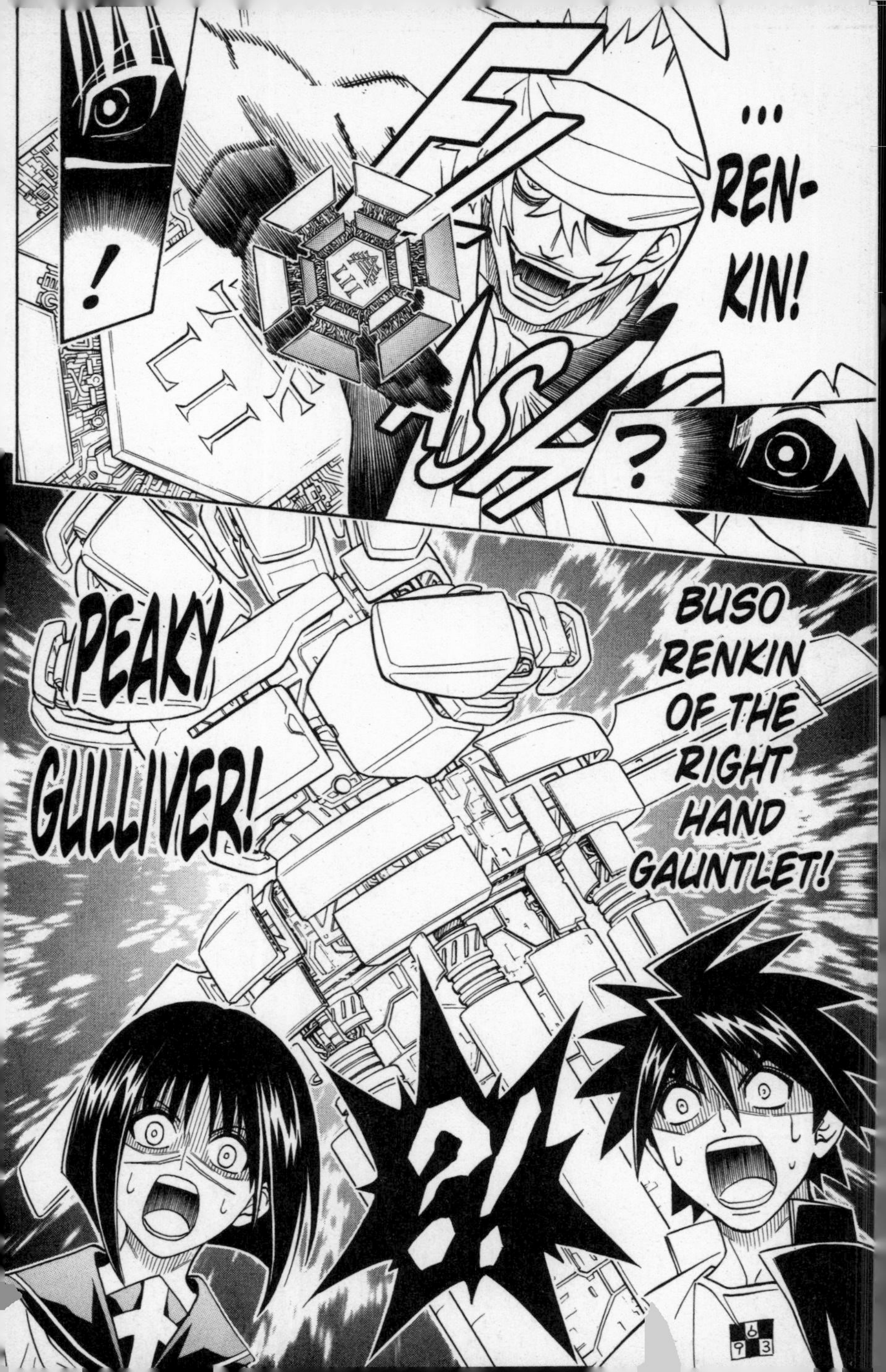
...
REN-KIN!
!
?
BUSO RENKIN OF THE RIGHT HAND GAUNTLET!
PEAKY GULLIVER!
?!

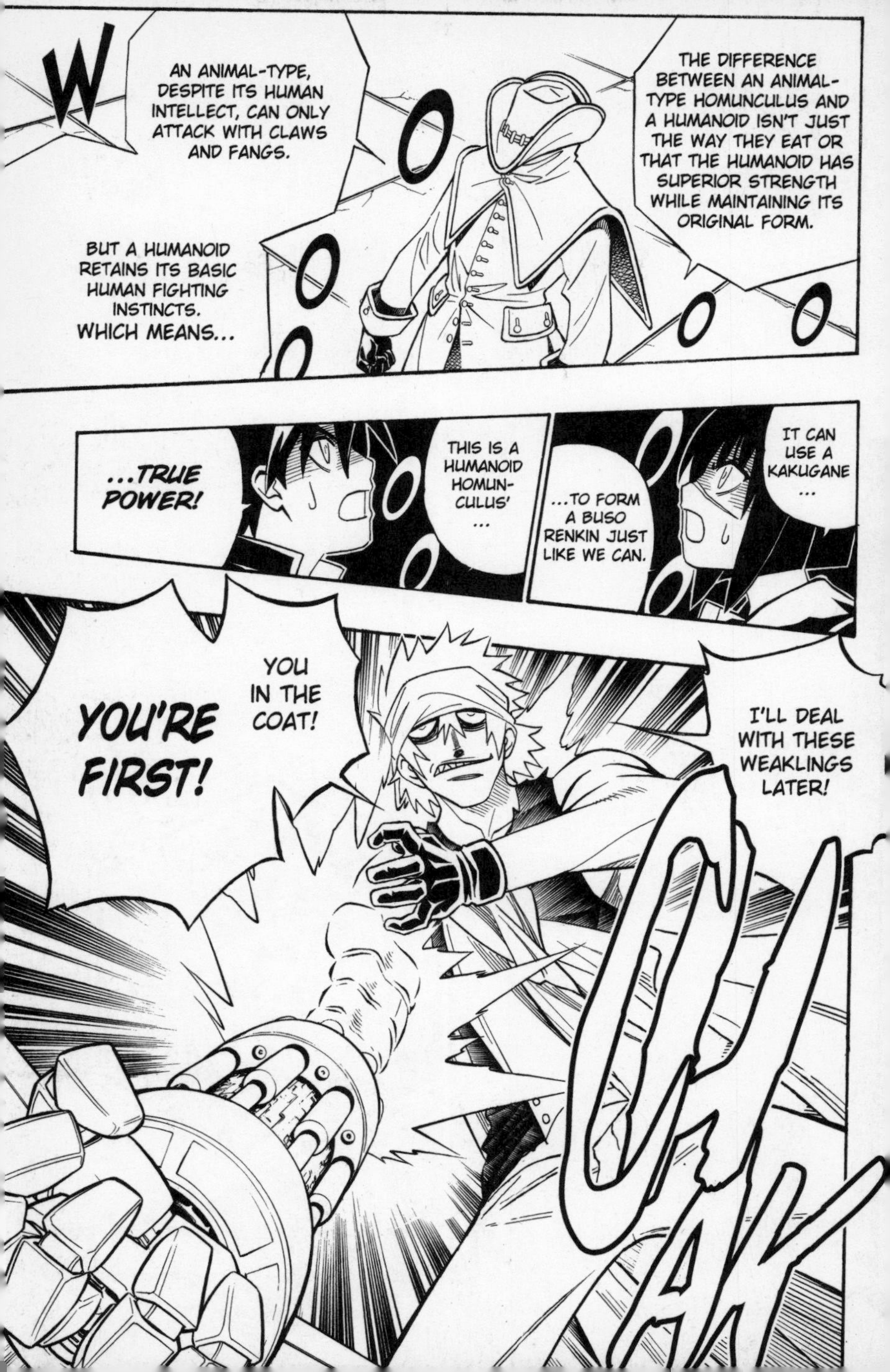
W
THE DIFFERENCE BETWEEN AN ANIMAL-TYPE HOMUNCULUS AND A HUMANOID ISN'T JUST THE WAY THEY EAT OR THAT THE HUMANOID HAS SUPERIOR STRENGTH WHILE MAINTAINING ITS ORIGINAL FORM.
AN ANIMAL-TYPE, DESPITE ITS HUMAN INTELLECT, CAN ONLY ATTACK WITH CLAWS AND FANGS.
BUT A HUMANOID RETAINS ITS BASIC HUMAN FIGHTING INSTINCTS. WHICH MEANS...
IT CAN USE A KAKUGANE ...
...TO FORM A BUSO RENKIN JUST LIKE WE CAN.
THIS IS A HUMANOID HOMUNCULUS' ...
...TRUE POWER!
I'LL DEAL WITH THESE WEAKLINGS LATER!
YOU IN THE COAT!
YOU'RE FIRST!
CHAK

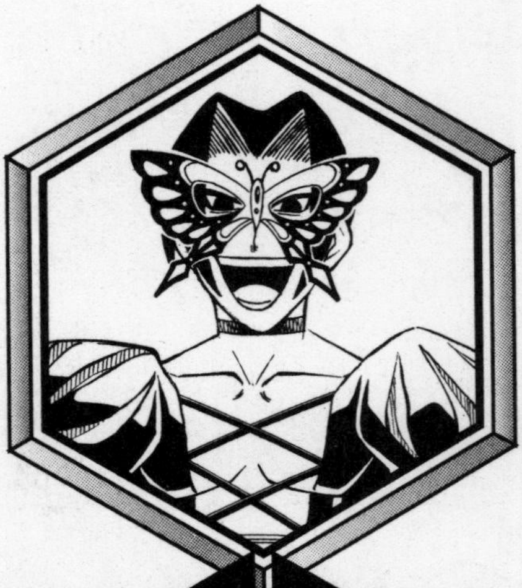

Buso Renkin
ブソウレンキン

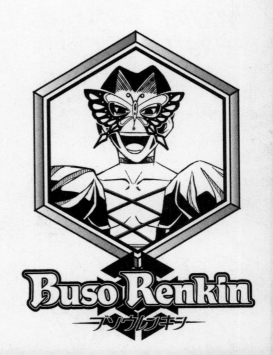

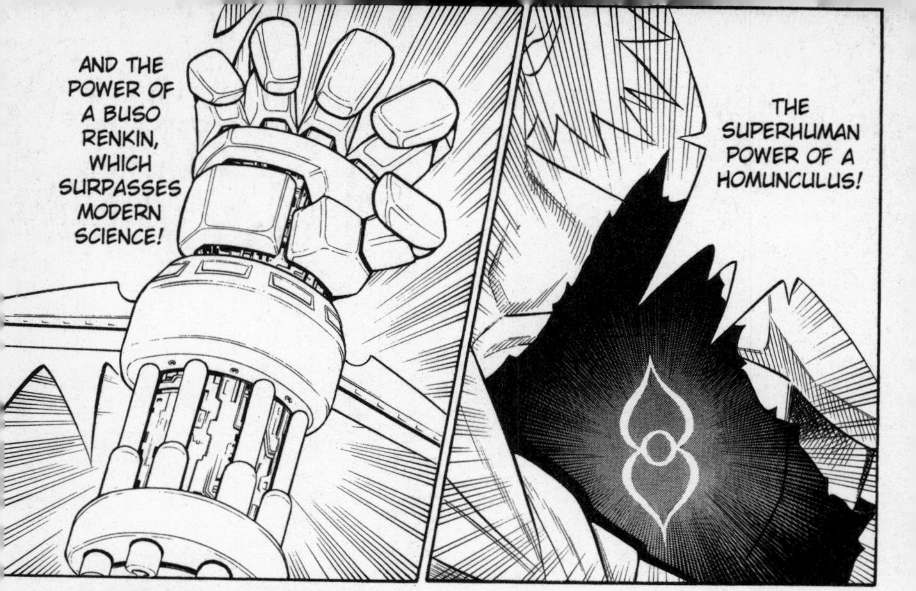
THE SUPERHUMAN POWER OF A HOMUNCULUS!
AND THE POWER OF A BUSO RENKIN, WHICH SURPASSES MODERN SCIENCE!

CHAPTER 21: KAZUKI AND TOKIKO'S CHOICE, PART 3

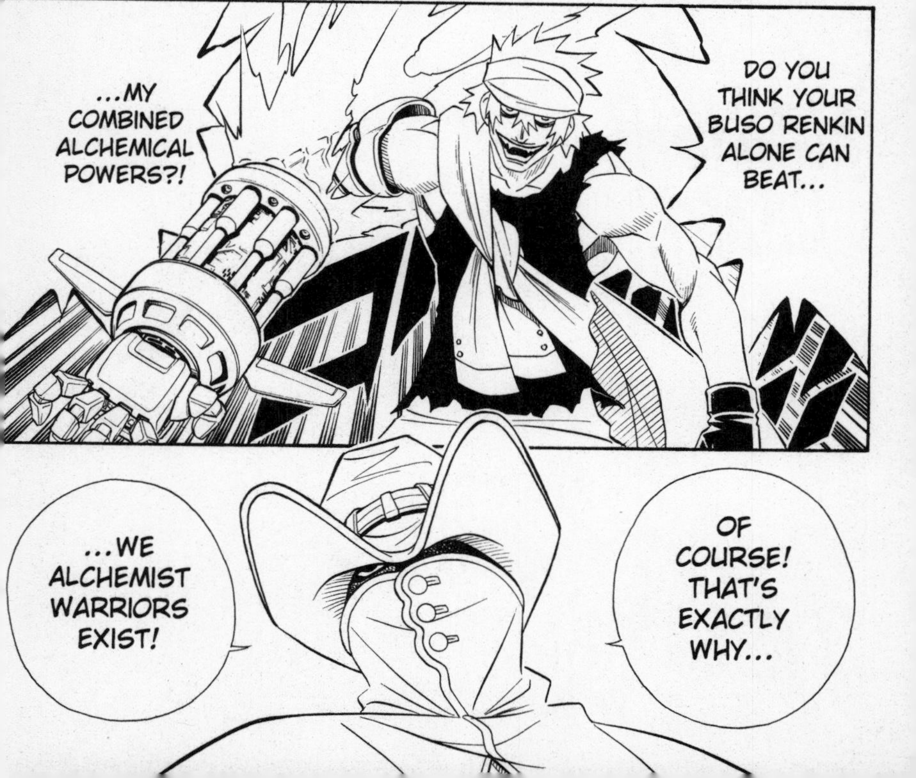
DO YOU THINK YOUR BUSO RENKIN ALONE CAN BEAT...
...MY COMBINED ALCHEMICAL POWERS?!
OF COURSE! THAT'S EXACTLY WHY...
...WE ALCHEMIST WARRIORS EXIST!

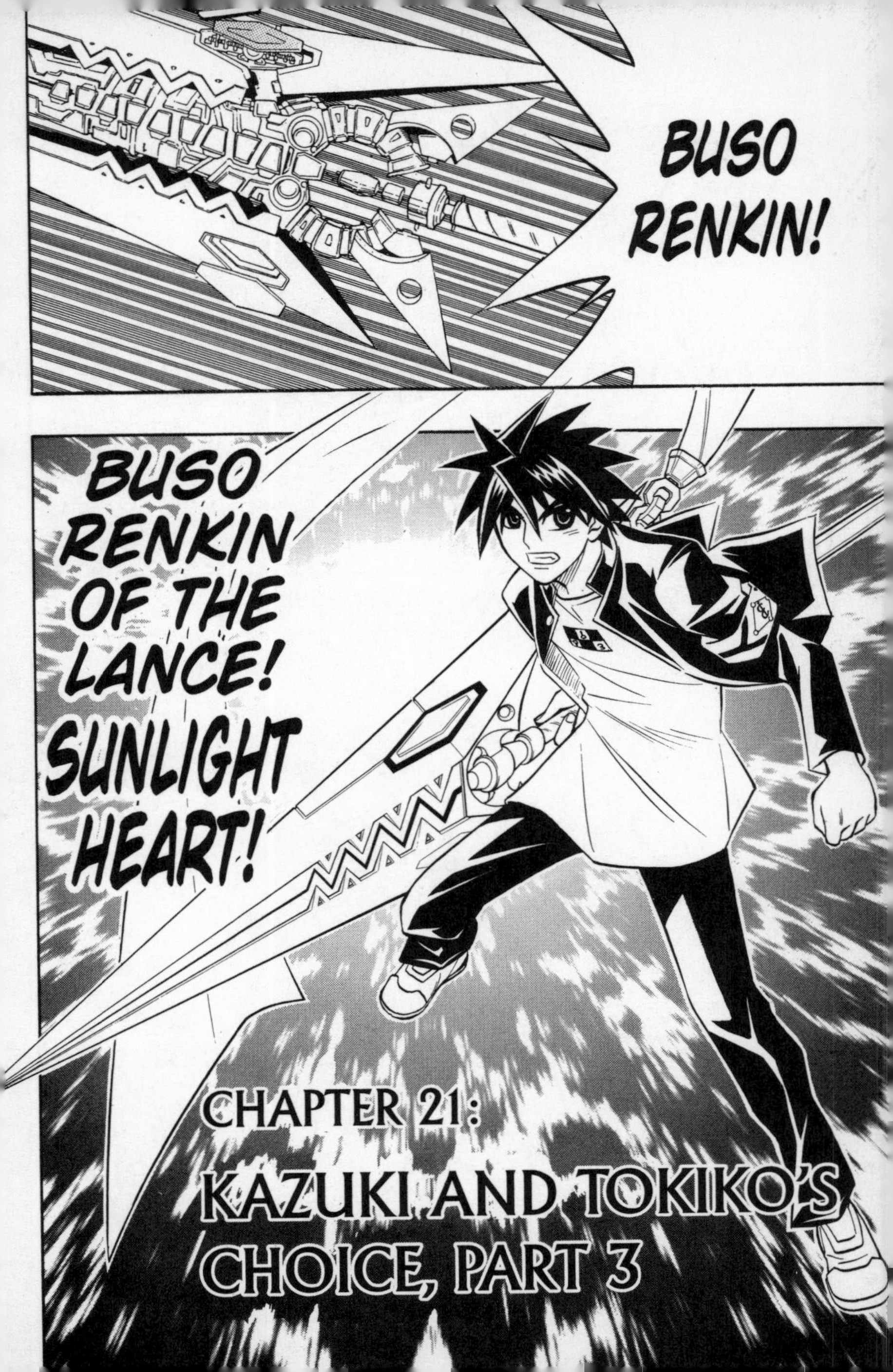
BUSO RENKIN!
BUSO RENKIN OF THE LANCE! SUNLIGHT HEART!
CHAPTER 21:
KAZUKI AND TOKIKO'S CHOICE, PART 3

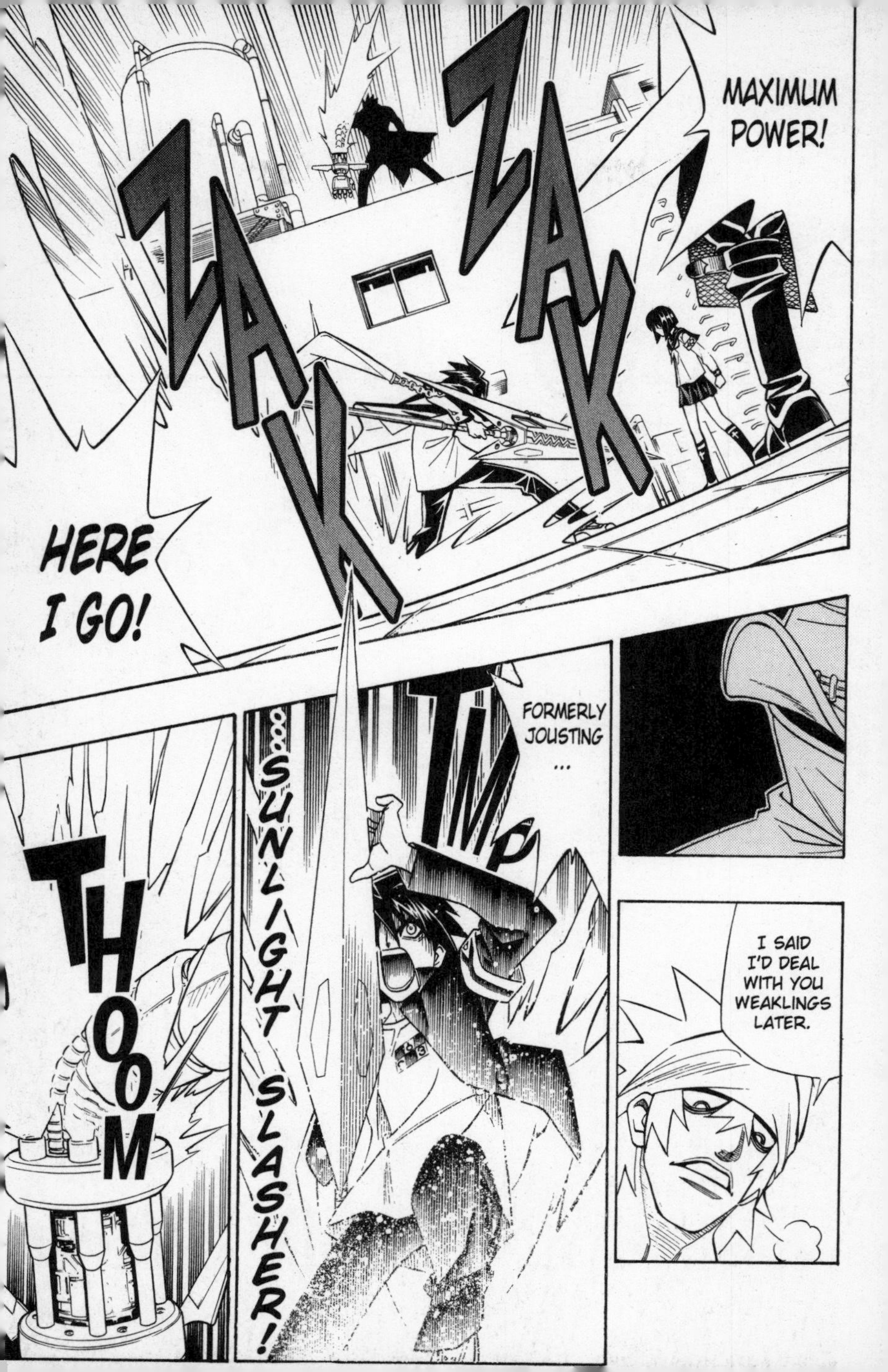
MAXIMUM POWER!
ZAK ZAK
HERE I GO!
I SAID I'D DEAL WITH YOU WEAKLINGS LATER.
FORMERLY JOUSTING ...
TMP
SUNLIGHT SLASHER!
THOOOM

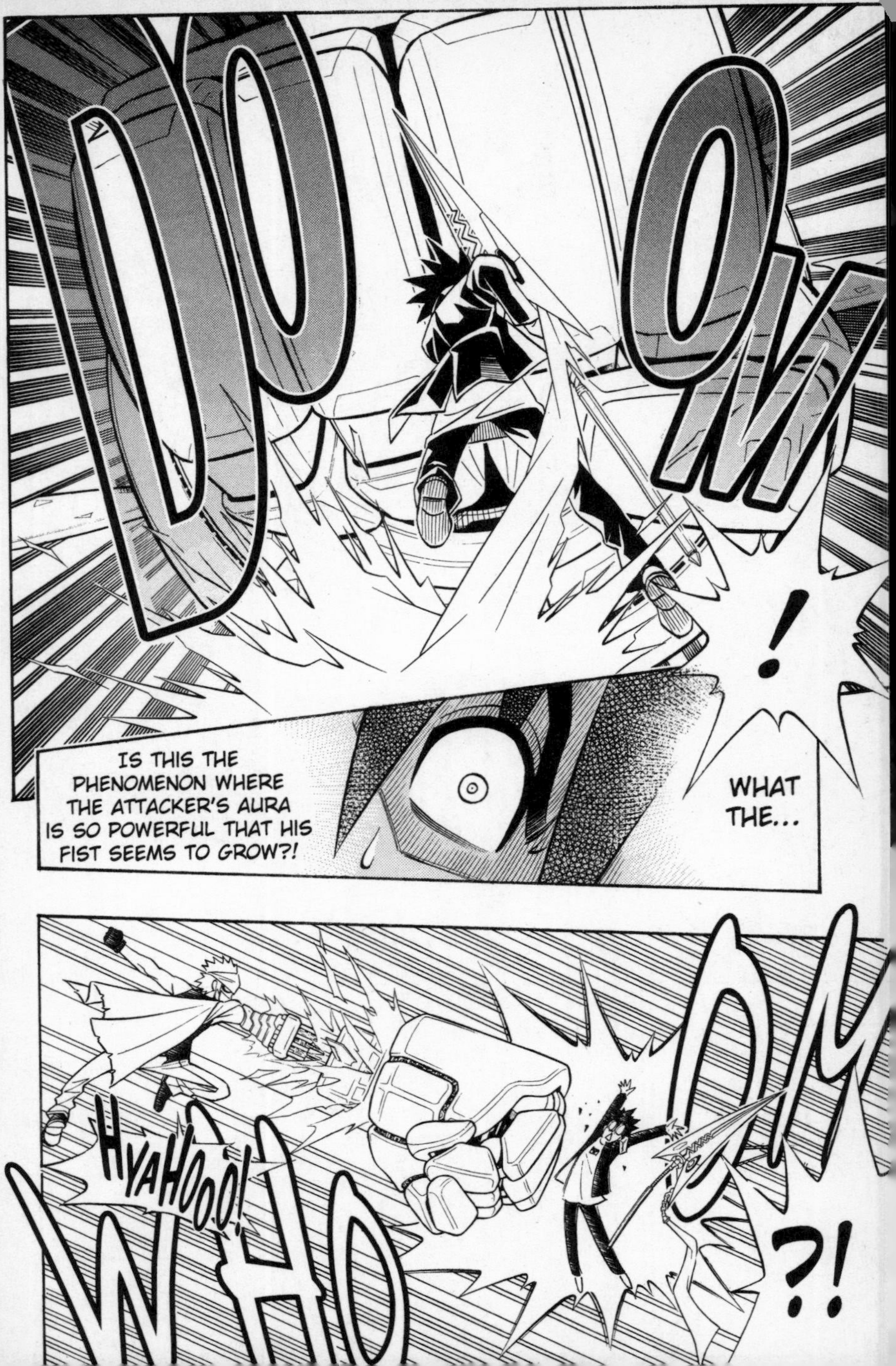
DOOM
!
WHAT THE...
IS THIS THE PHENOMENON WHERE THE ATTACKER'S AURA IS SO POWERFUL THAT HIS FIST SEEMS TO GROW?!
?!
HYAHOOO!
WHOOM

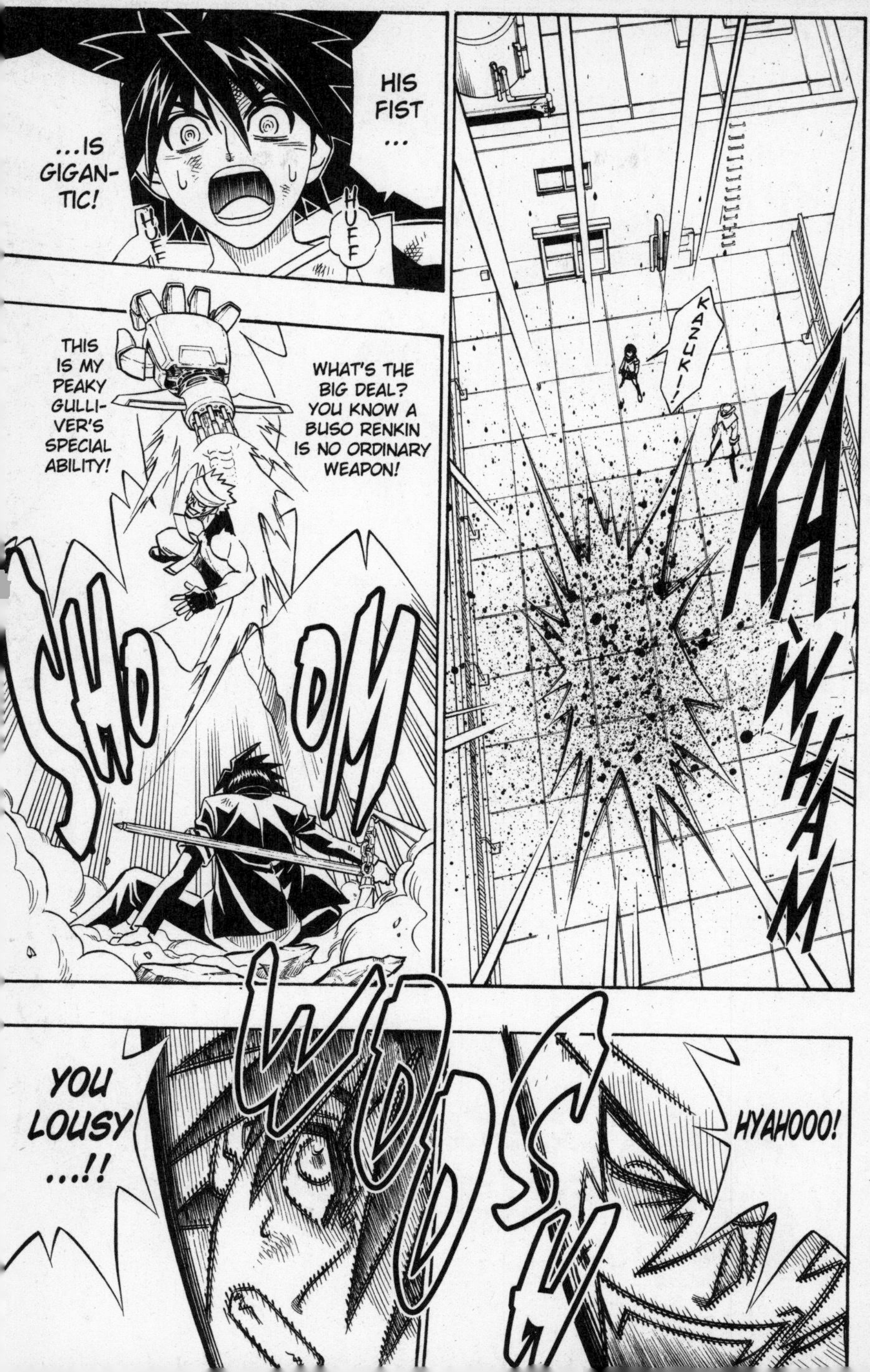
KAZUKI!
KA-WHAM
HIS FIST...
...IS GIGANTIC!
HUFF
HUFF
WHAT'S THE BIG DEAL? YOU KNOW A BUSO RENKIN IS NO ORDINARY WEAPON!
THIS IS MY PEAKY GULLIVER'S SPECIAL ABILITY!
SHOOM
HYAHOOO!
WOOSH
YOU LOUSY ...!!

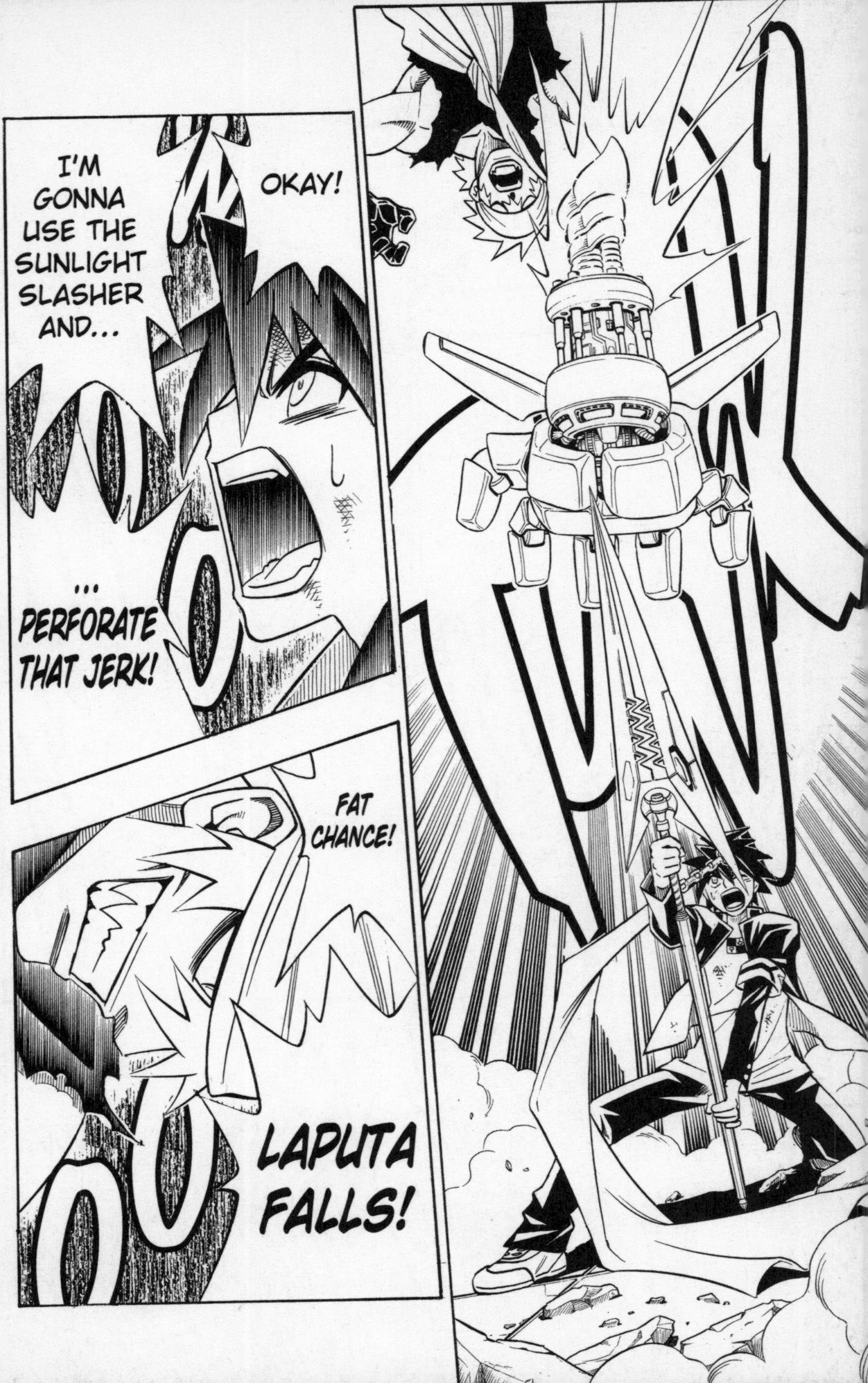
I'M GONNA USE THE SUNLIGHT SLASHER AND...
OKAY!
... PERFORATE THAT JERK!
FAT CHANCE!
LAPUTA FALLS!

HYAHOOO!

!!

KA-ZUKI!!

GAH!

KOFF!

ZANG

KREEEK

DID YOU THINK A MERE HUMAN COULD DEFEAT A HOMUNCULUS IN A CONTEST OF STRENGTH?!

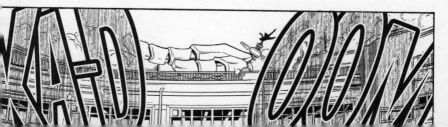

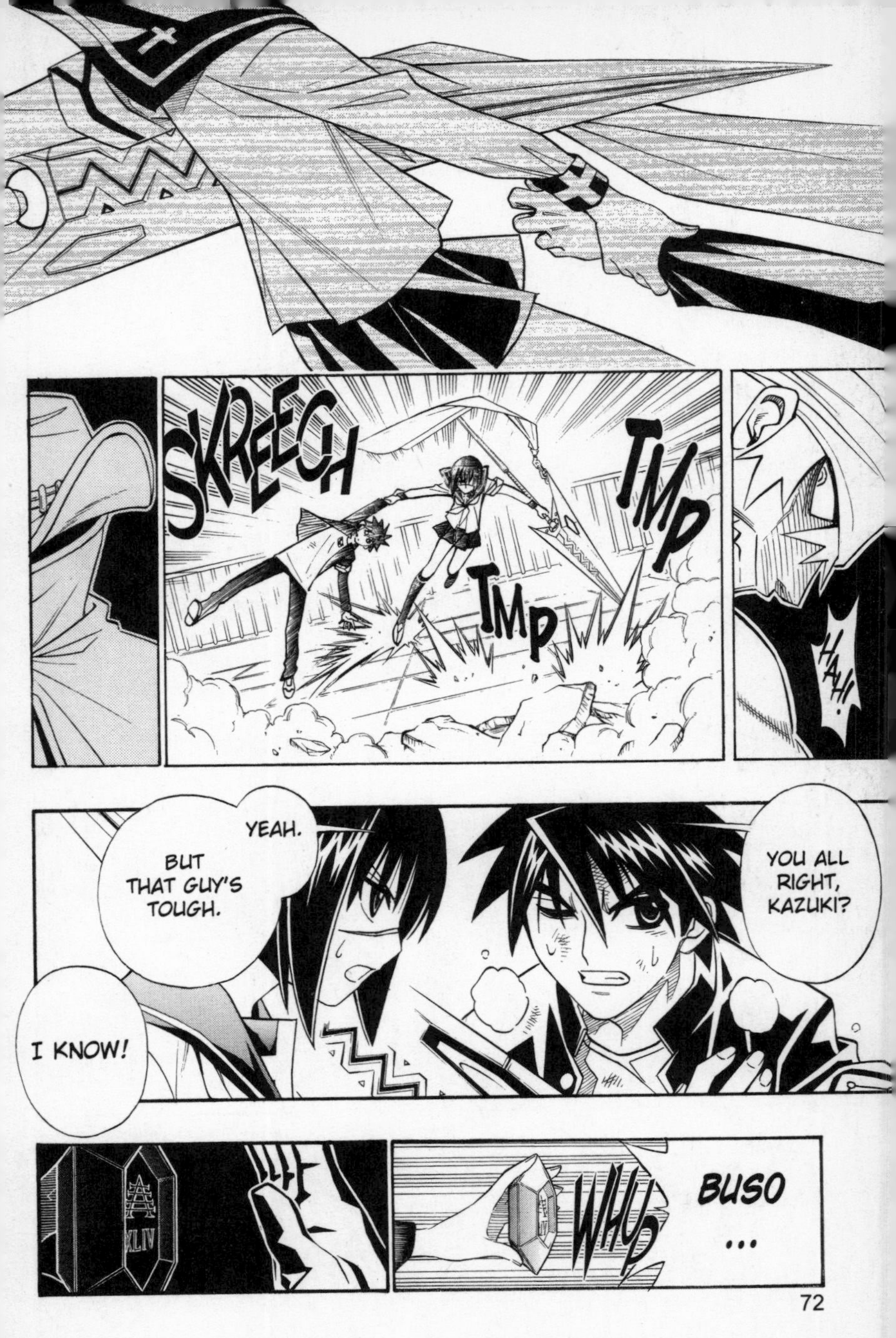
HAH!
SKREECH
TMP
TMP
YOU ALL RIGHT, KAZUKI?
YEAH.
BUT THAT GUY'S TOUGH.
I KNOW!
WHUD
BUSO ...

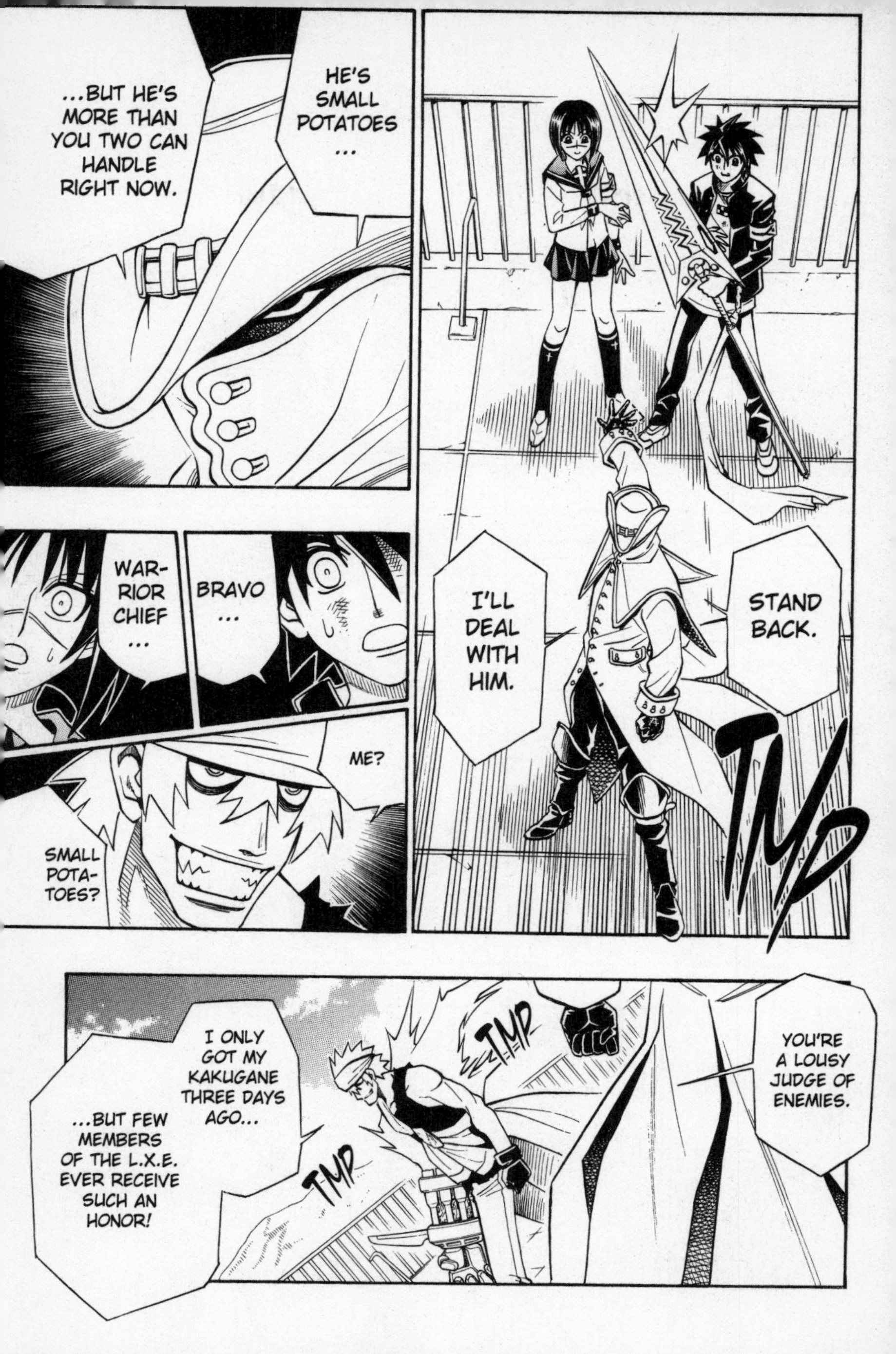
STAND BACK.
I'LL DEAL WITH HIM.
TMP
HE'S SMALL POTATOES...
...BUT HE'S MORE THAN YOU TWO CAN HANDLE RIGHT NOW.
BRAVO...
WARRIOR CHIEF...
ME?
SMALL POTATOES?
YOU'RE A LOUSY JUDGE OF ENEMIES.
TMP
TMP
I ONLY GOT MY KAKUGANE THREE DAYS AGO...
...BUT FEW MEMBERS OF THE L.X.E. EVER RECEIVE SUCH AN HONOR!

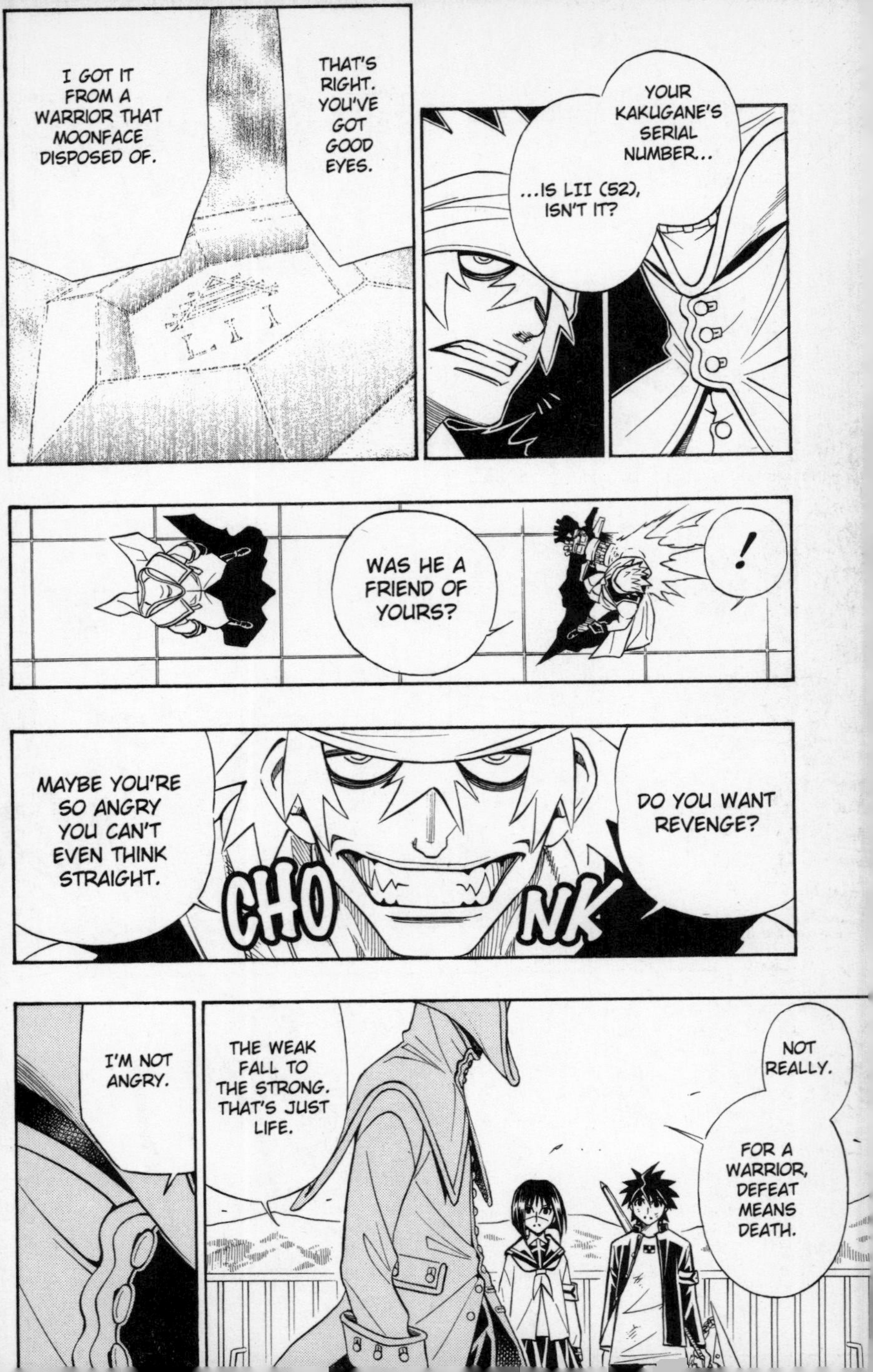
YOUR KAKUGANE'S SERIAL NUMBER...
...IS LII (52), ISN'T IT?
THAT'S RIGHT. YOU'VE GOT GOOD EYES.
I GOT IT FROM A WARRIOR THAT MOONFACE DISPOSED OF.
!
WAS HE A FRIEND OF YOURS?
DO YOU WANT REVENGE?
CHONK
MAYBE YOU'RE SO ANGRY YOU CAN'T EVEN THINK STRAIGHT.
NOT REALLY.
FOR A WARRIOR, DEFEAT MEANS DEATH.
THE WEAK FALL TO THE STRONG. THAT'S JUST LIFE.
I'M NOT ANGRY.

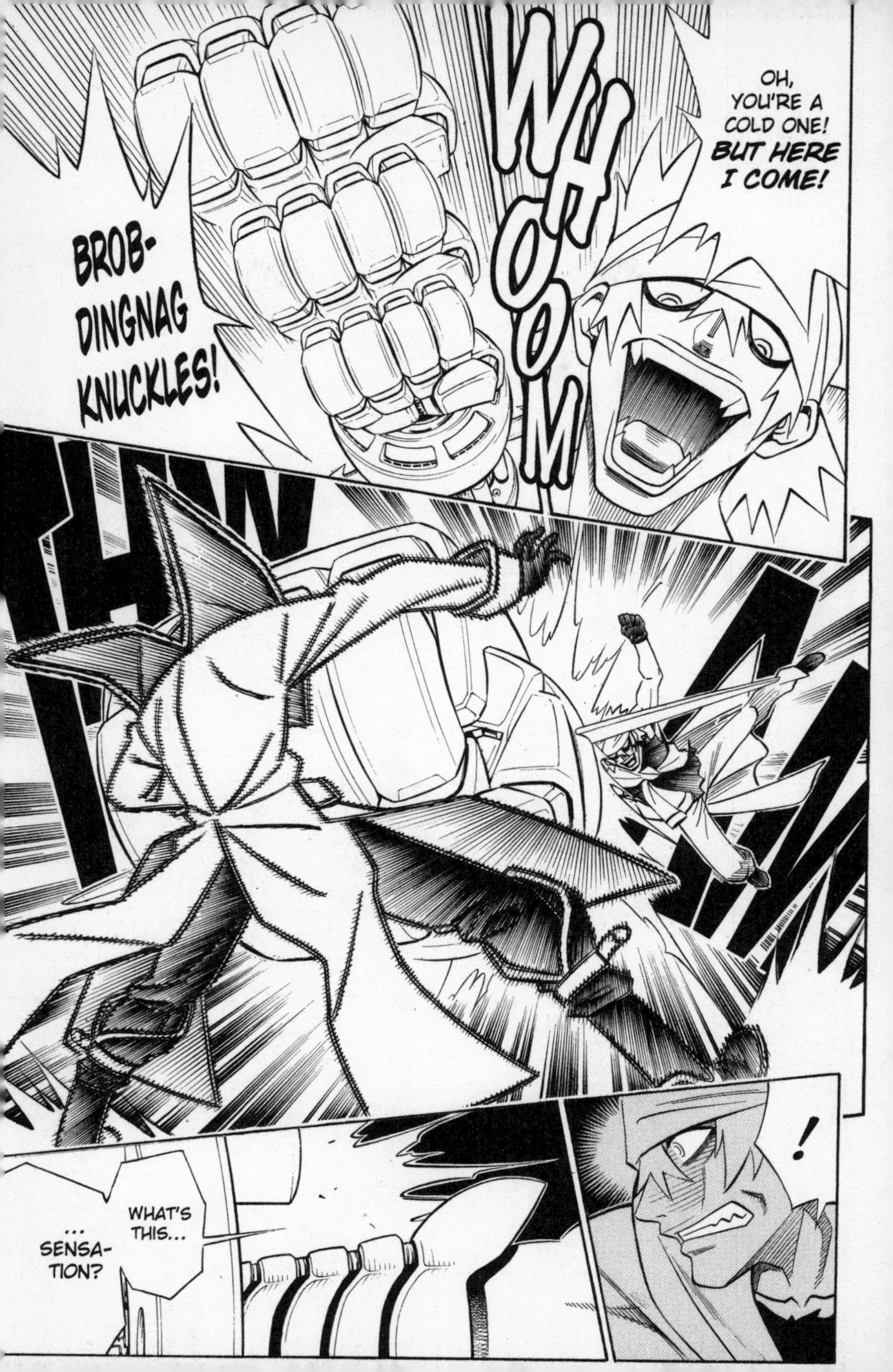

OH, YOU'RE A COLD ONE! BUT HERE I COME!
WHOOOM
BROB-DINGNAG KNUCKLES!
!
WHAT'S THIS...
...SENSA-TION?

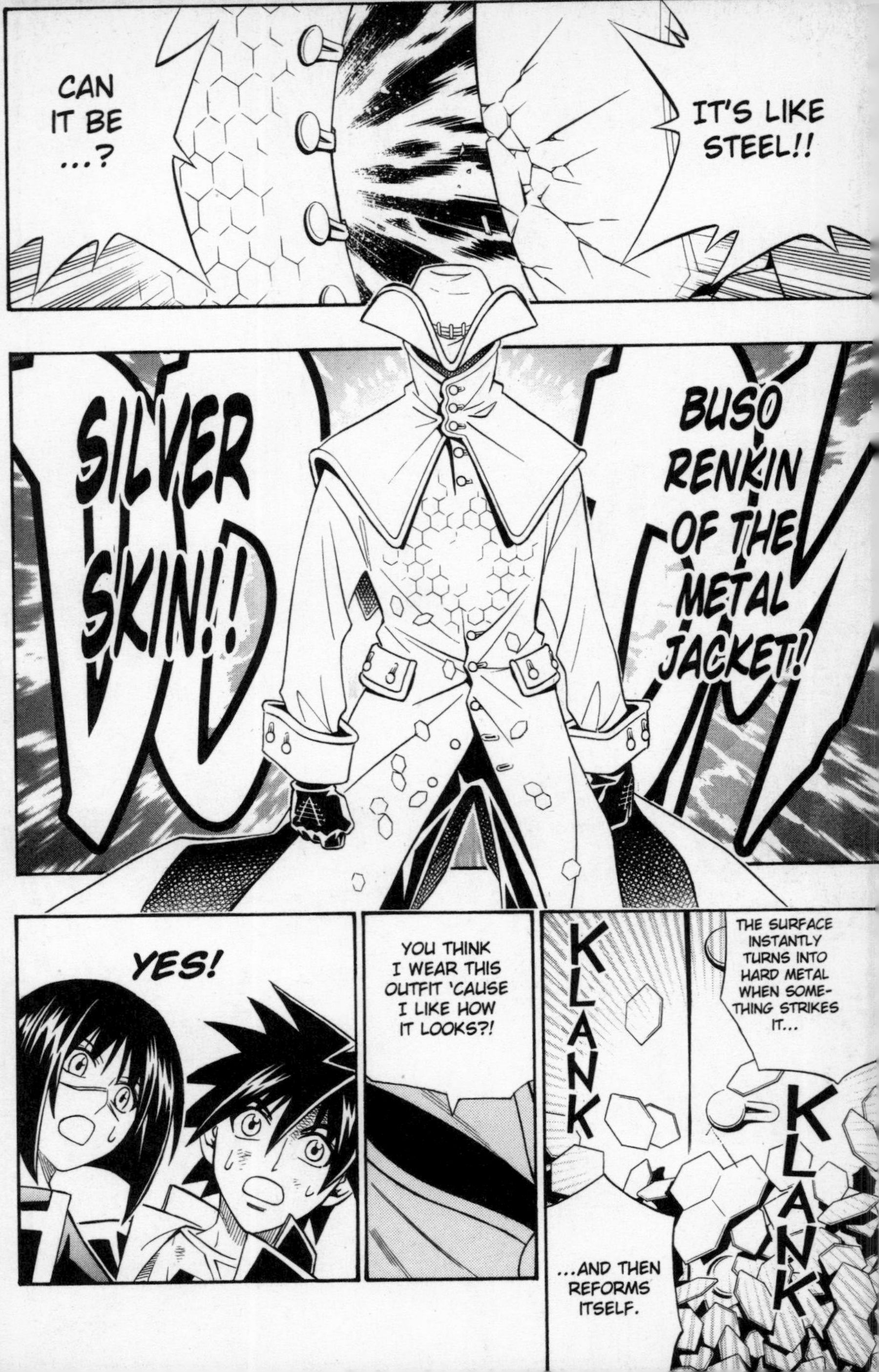
IT'S LIKE STEEL!!
CAN IT BE ...?
BUSO RENKIN OF THE METAL JACKET!
SILVER SKIN!!
THE SURFACE INSTANTLY TURNS INTO HARD METAL WHEN SOME-THING STRIKES IT...
KLANK
KLANK
...AND THEN REFORMS ITSELF.
YOU THINK I WEAR THIS OUTFIT 'CAUSE I LIKE HOW IT LOOKS?!
YES!

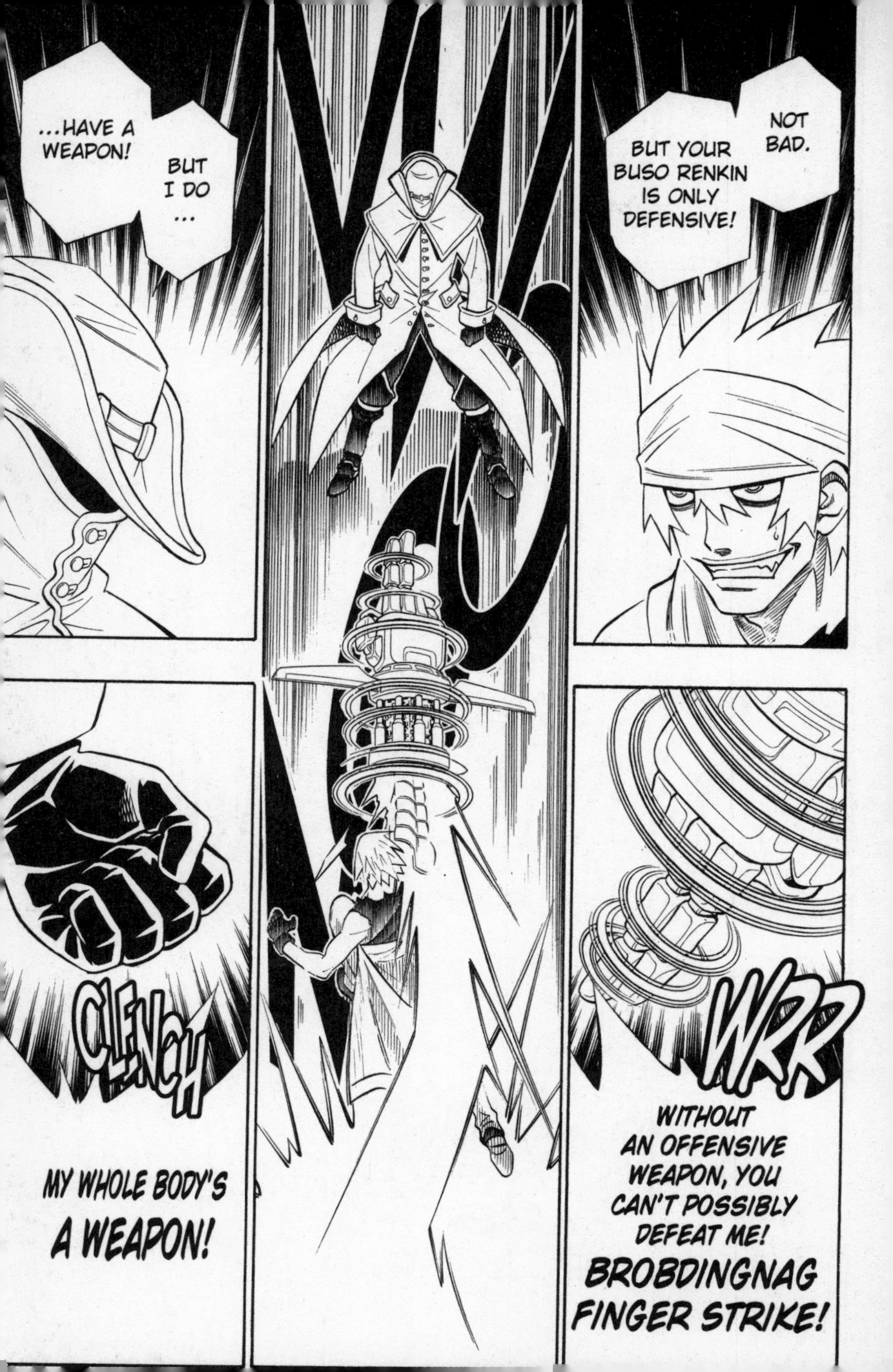
NOT BAD.
BUT YOUR BUSO RENKIN IS ONLY DEFENSIVE!
WRR
WITHOUT AN OFFENSIVE WEAPON, YOU CAN'T POSSIBLY DEFEAT ME!
BROBDINGNAG FINGER STRIKE!
...HAVE A WEAPON!
BUT I DO...
CLENCH
MY WHOLE BODY'S A WEAPON!

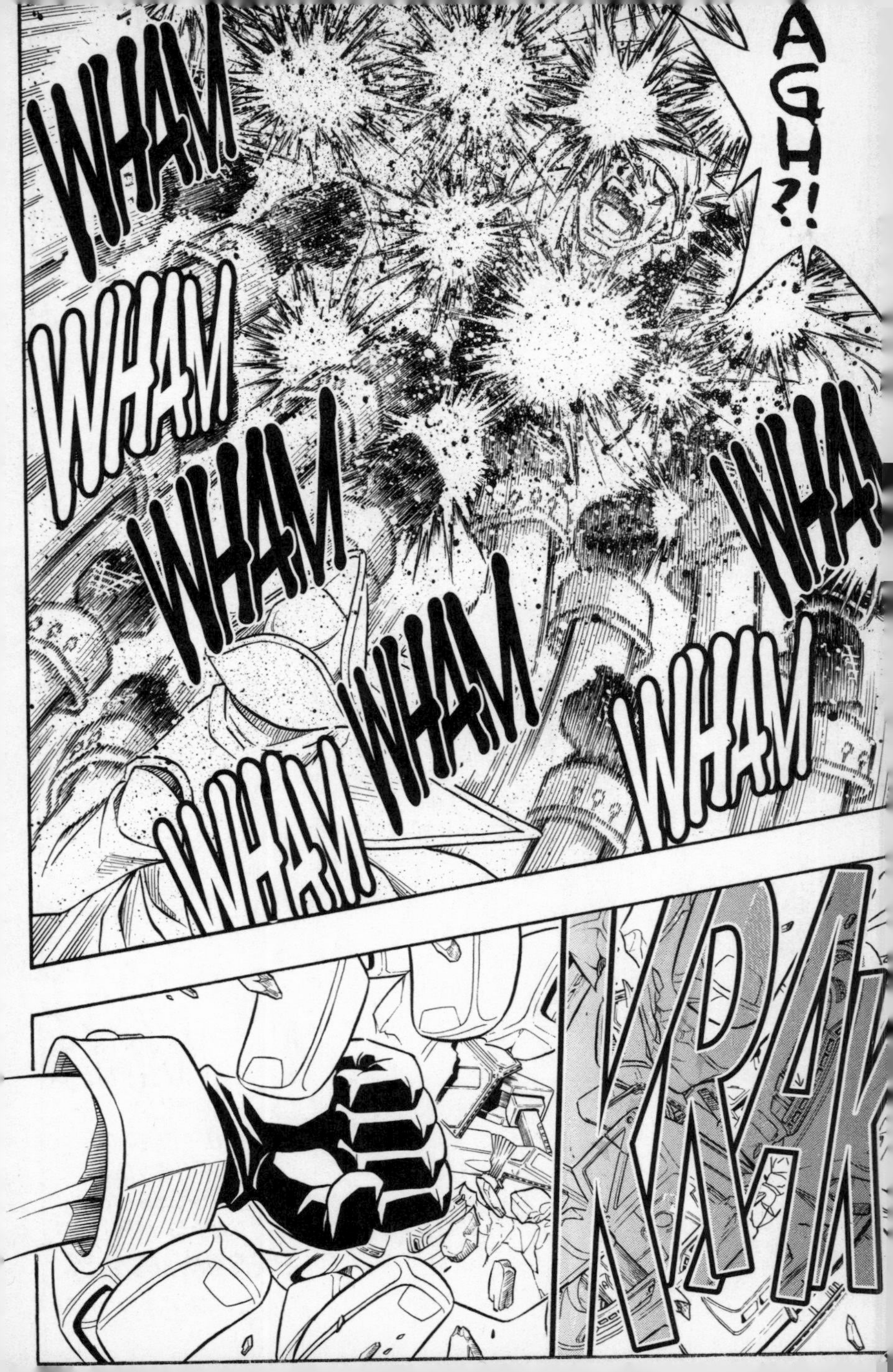
AGH?!
WHA
WHAM
WHAM
WHAM
WHAM
WHAM
WHAM
KRAK

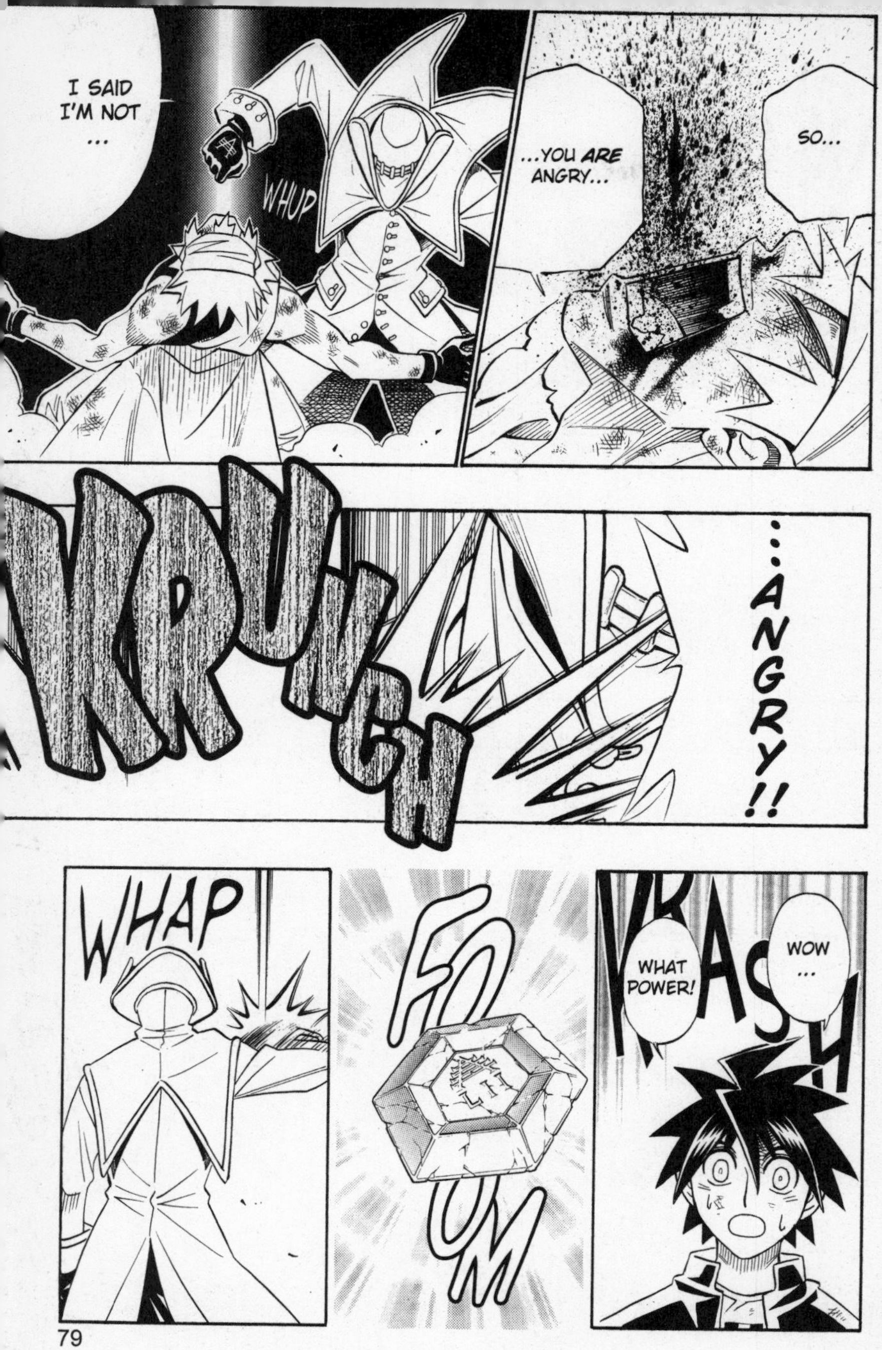
SO...
...YOU ARE ANGRY...
I SAID I'M NOT ...
WHUP
...ANGRY!!
KRUNCH
KRASH
WOW ...
WHAT POWER!
FOOM
WHAP

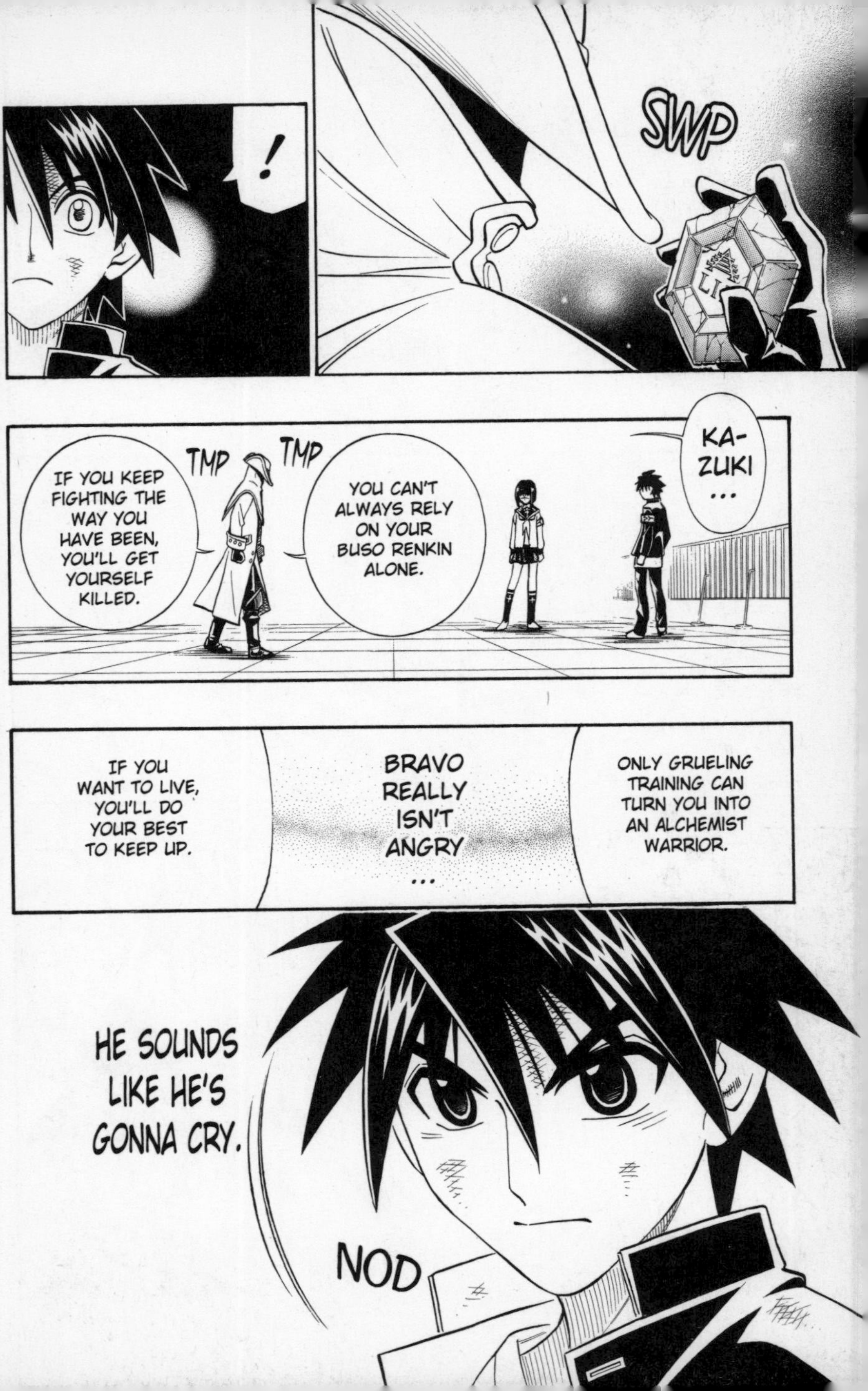
SWP
!
KA-ZUKI...
TMP
YOU CAN'T ALWAYS RELY ON YOUR BUSO RENKIN ALONE.
TMP
IF YOU KEEP FIGHTING THE WAY YOU HAVE BEEN, YOU'LL GET YOURSELF KILLED.
ONLY GRUELING TRAINING CAN TURN YOU INTO AN ALCHEMIST WARRIOR.
BRAVO REALLY ISN'T ANGRY...
IF YOU WANT TO LIVE, YOU'LL DO YOUR BEST TO KEEP UP.
HE SOUNDS LIKE HE'S GONNA CRY.
NOD

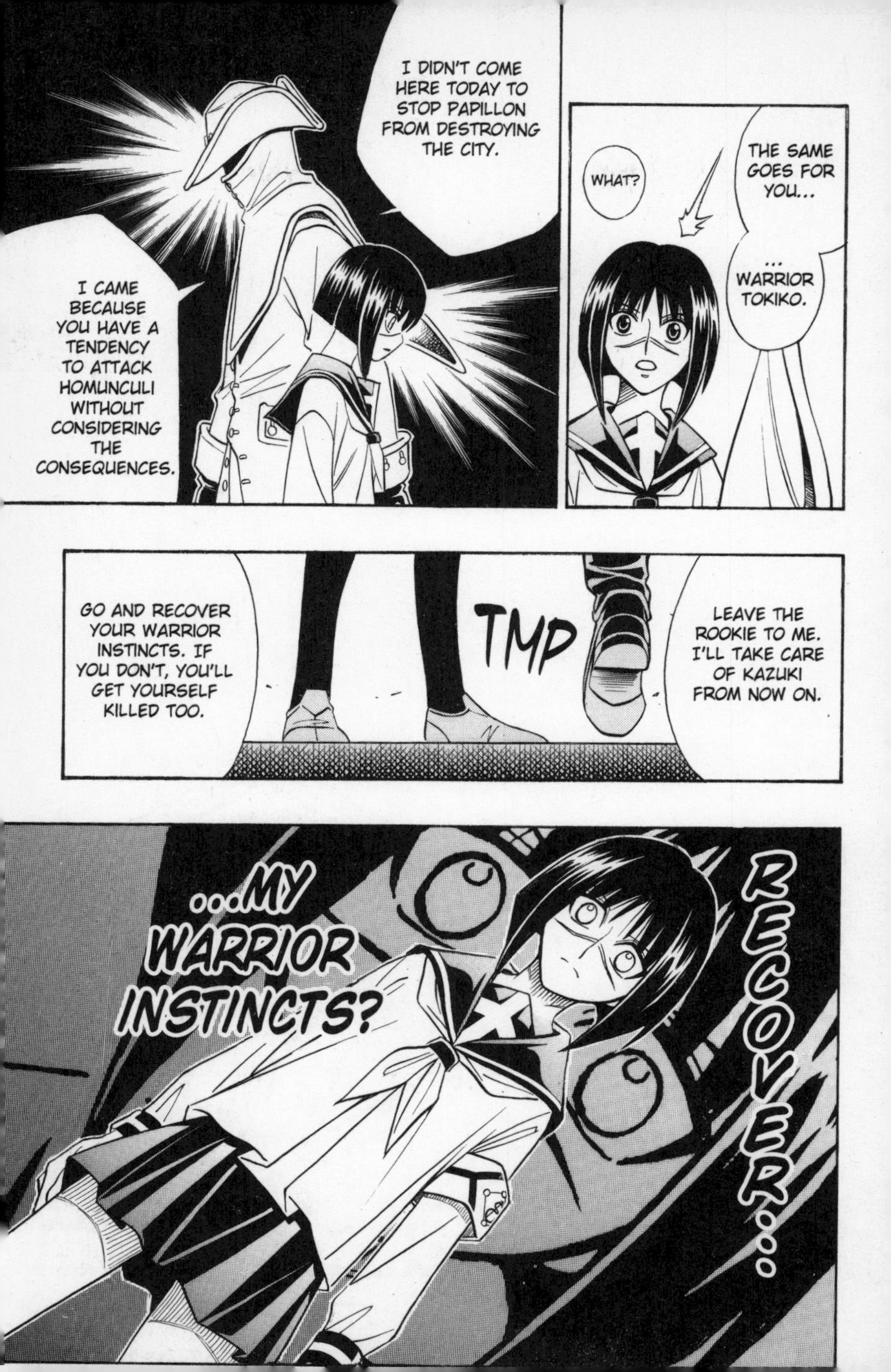
THE SAME GOES FOR YOU...
WHAT?
... WARRIOR TOKIKO.
I DIDN'T COME HERE TODAY TO STOP PAPILLON FROM DESTROYING THE CITY.
I CAME BECAUSE YOU HAVE A TENDENCY TO ATTACK HOMUNCULI WITHOUT CONSIDERING THE CONSEQUENCES.
LEAVE THE ROOKIE TO ME. I'LL TAKE CARE OF KAZUKI FROM NOW ON.
TMP
GO AND RECOVER YOUR WARRIOR INSTINCTS. IF YOU DON'T, YOU'LL GET YOURSELF KILLED TOO.
RECOVER...
...MY WARRIOR INSTINCTS?

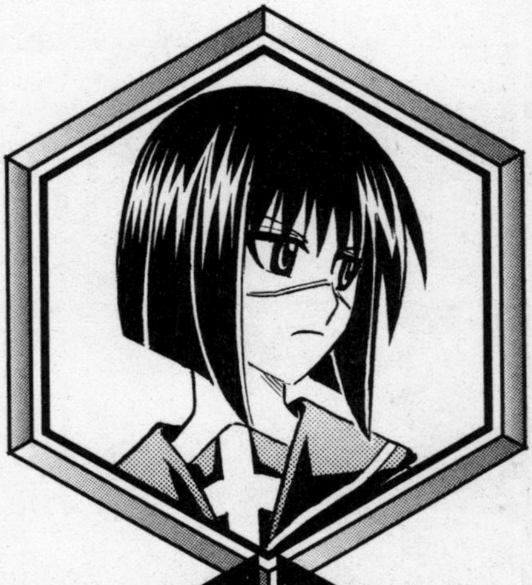

Buso Renkin
ブソウレンキン

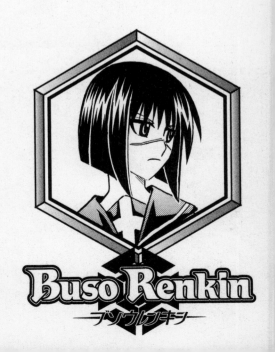

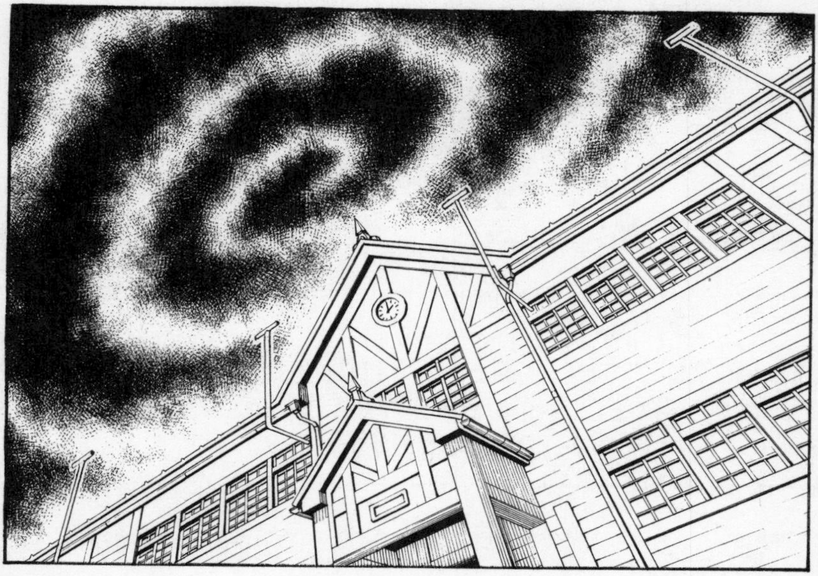

CHAPTER 22:

NIGHT IN THE DORMITORY

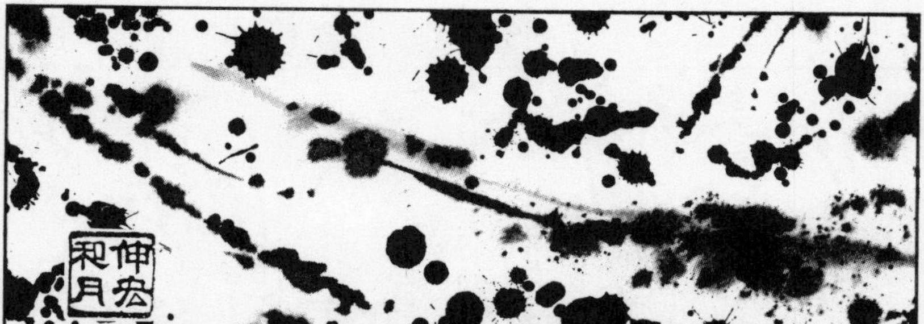
伸宏
和月

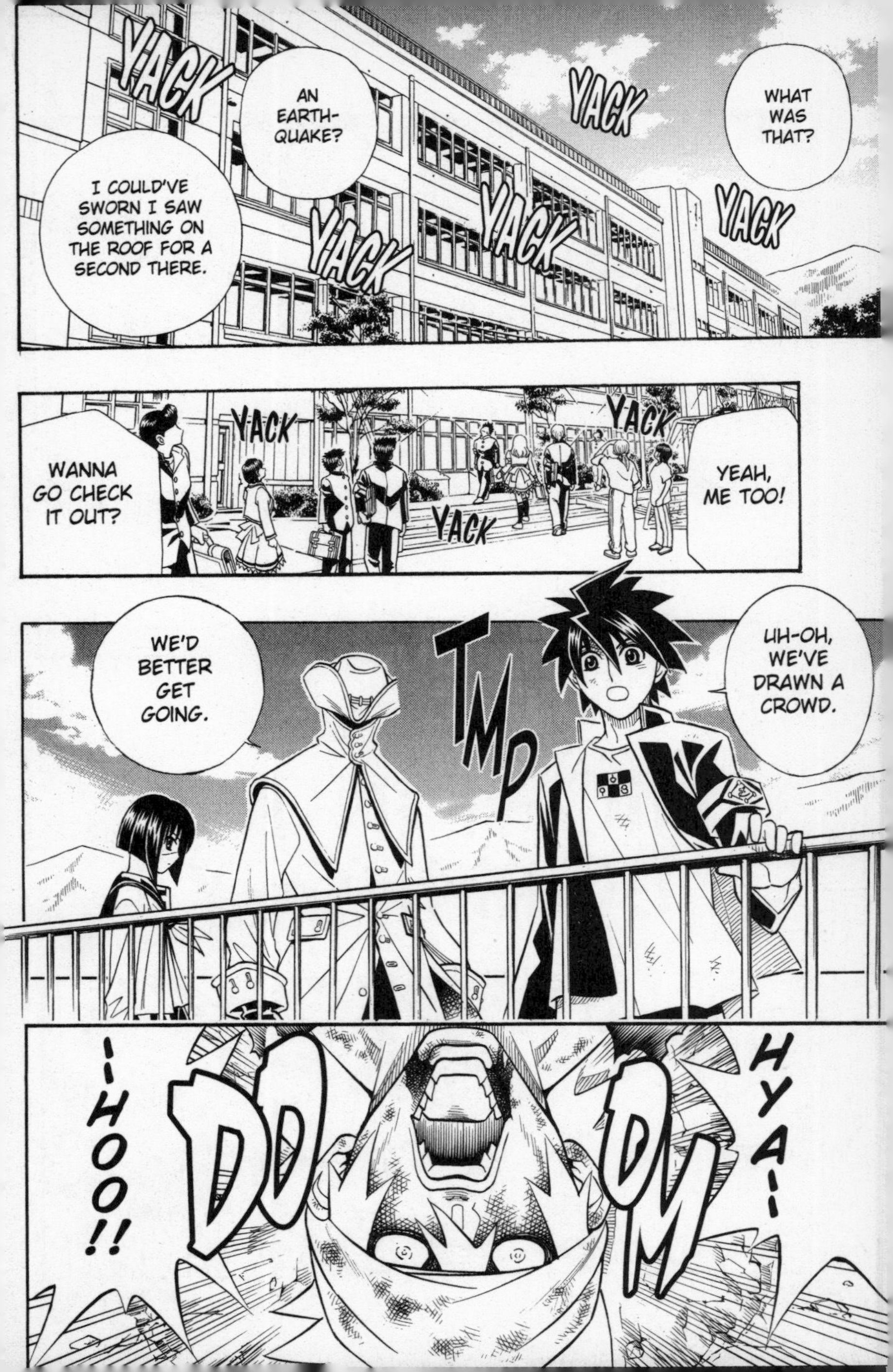
WHAT WAS THAT?
YACK
YACK
YACK
AN EARTH-QUAKE?
YACK
YACK
I COULD'VE SWORN I SAW SOMETHING ON THE ROOF FOR A SECOND THERE.
YEAH, ME TOO!
YACK
YACK
YACK
WANNA GO CHECK IT OUT?
UH-OH, WE'VE DRAWN A CROWD.
TMP
WE'D BETTER GET GOING.
HYA!
DOOM
HOO!!

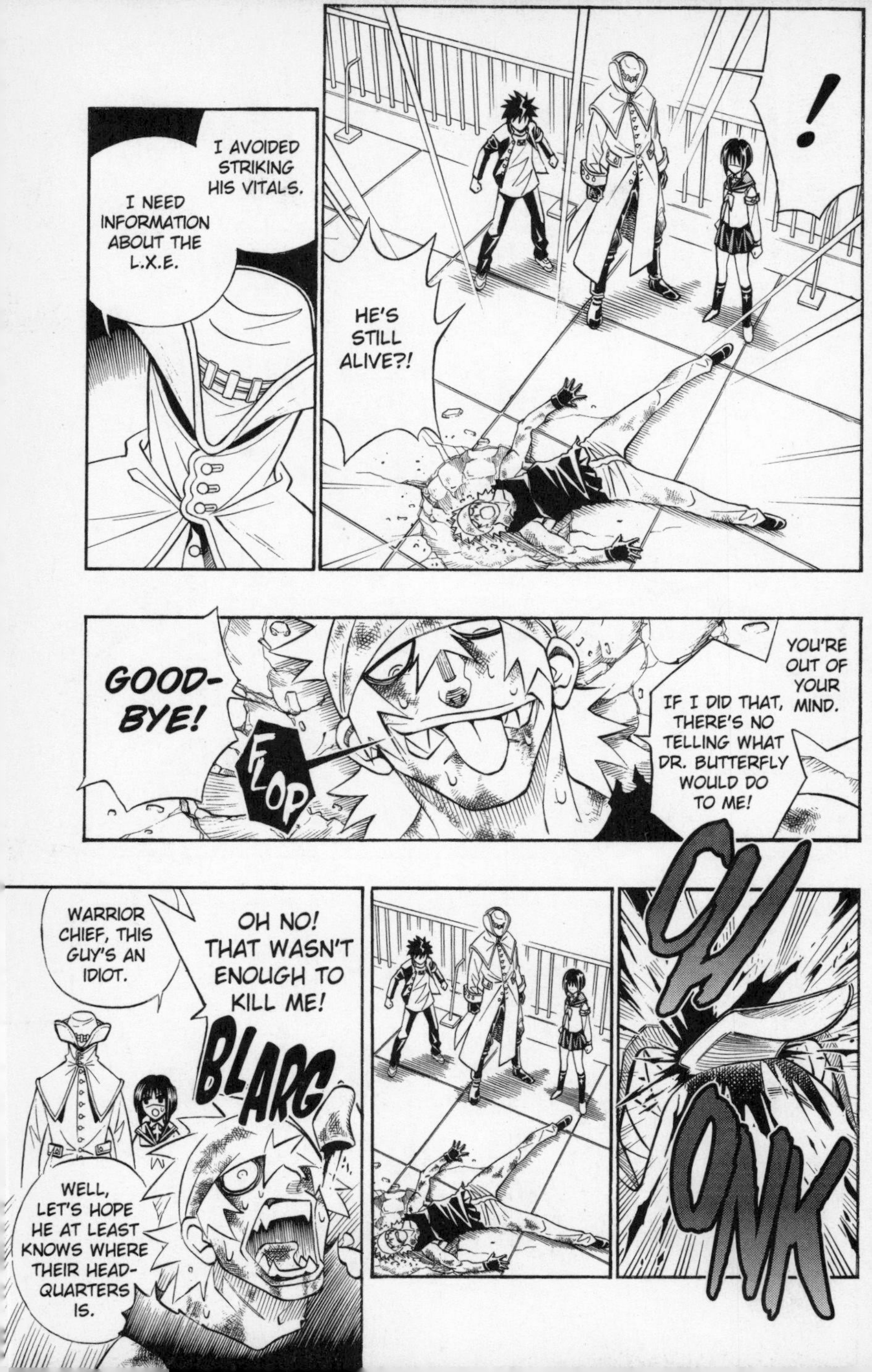
!
HE'S STILL ALIVE?!
I AVOIDED STRIKING HIS VITALS.
I NEED INFORMATION ABOUT THE L.X.E.
YOU'RE OUT OF YOUR MIND.
IF I DID THAT, THERE'S NO TELLING WHAT DR. BUTTERFLY WOULD DO TO ME!
FLOP
GOOD-BYE!
CHONK
OH NO! THAT WASN'T ENOUGH TO KILL ME!
WARRIOR CHIEF, THIS GUY'S AN IDIOT.
BLARG
WELL, LET'S HOPE HE AT LEAST KNOWS WHERE THEIR HEAD-QUARTERS IS.

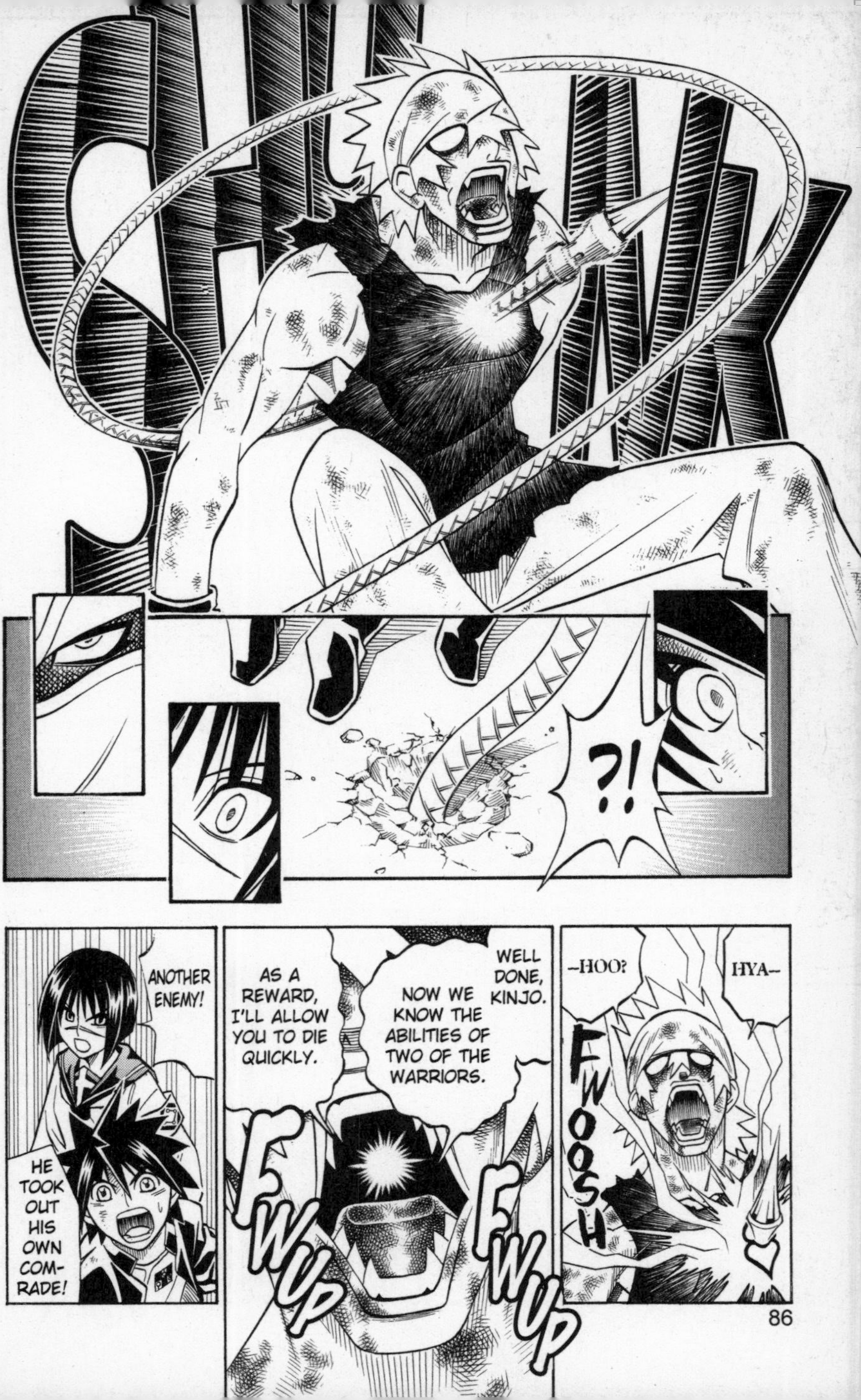
SHUNK
?!
HYA–
–HOO?
FWOOSH
WELL DONE, KINJO.
NOW WE KNOW THE ABILITIES OF TWO OF THE WARRIORS.
AS A REWARD, I'LL ALLOW YOU TO DIE QUICKLY.
FWUP
FWUP
ANOTHER ENEMY!
HE TOOK OUT HIS OWN COM-RADE!

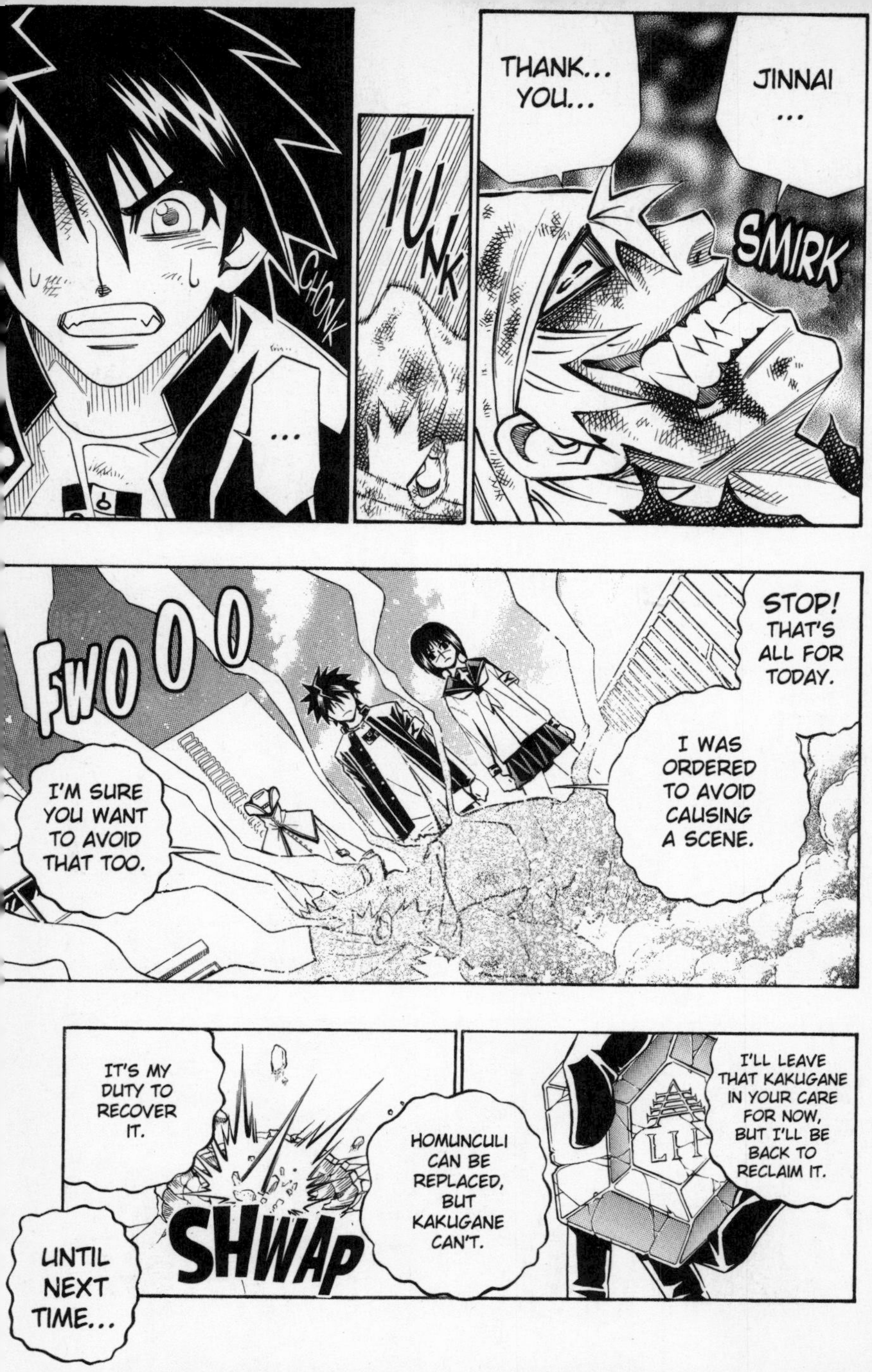
THANK... YOU...
JINNAI ...
SMIRK
TUNK
CHONK
...
STOP! THAT'S ALL FOR TODAY.
I WAS ORDERED TO AVOID CAUSING A SCENE.
I'M SURE YOU WANT TO AVOID THAT TOO.
FWOOO
I'LL LEAVE THAT KAKUGANE IN YOUR CARE FOR NOW, BUT I'LL BE BACK TO RECLAIM IT.
LH
HOMUNCULI CAN BE REPLACED, BUT KAKUGANE CAN'T.
IT'S MY DUTY TO RECOVER IT.
SHWAP
UNTIL NEXT TIME...

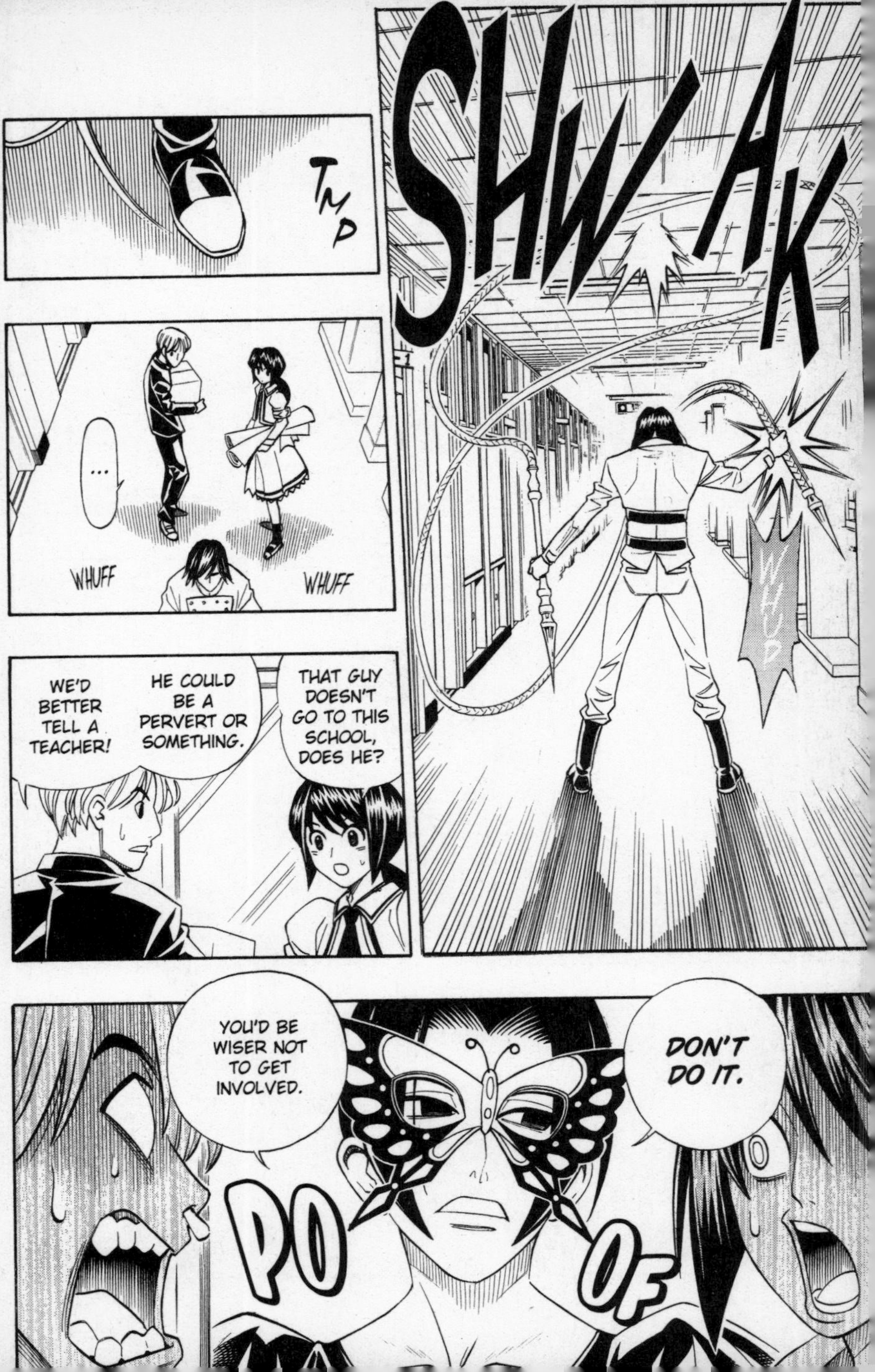
SHWAK
WHUD
TMP
...
WHUFF
WHUFF
THAT GUY DOESN'T GO TO THIS SCHOOL, DOES HE?
HE COULD BE A PERVERT OR SOMETHING.
WE'D BETTER TELL A TEACHER!
DON'T DO IT.
YOU'D BE WISER NOT TO GET INVOLVED.
POOF

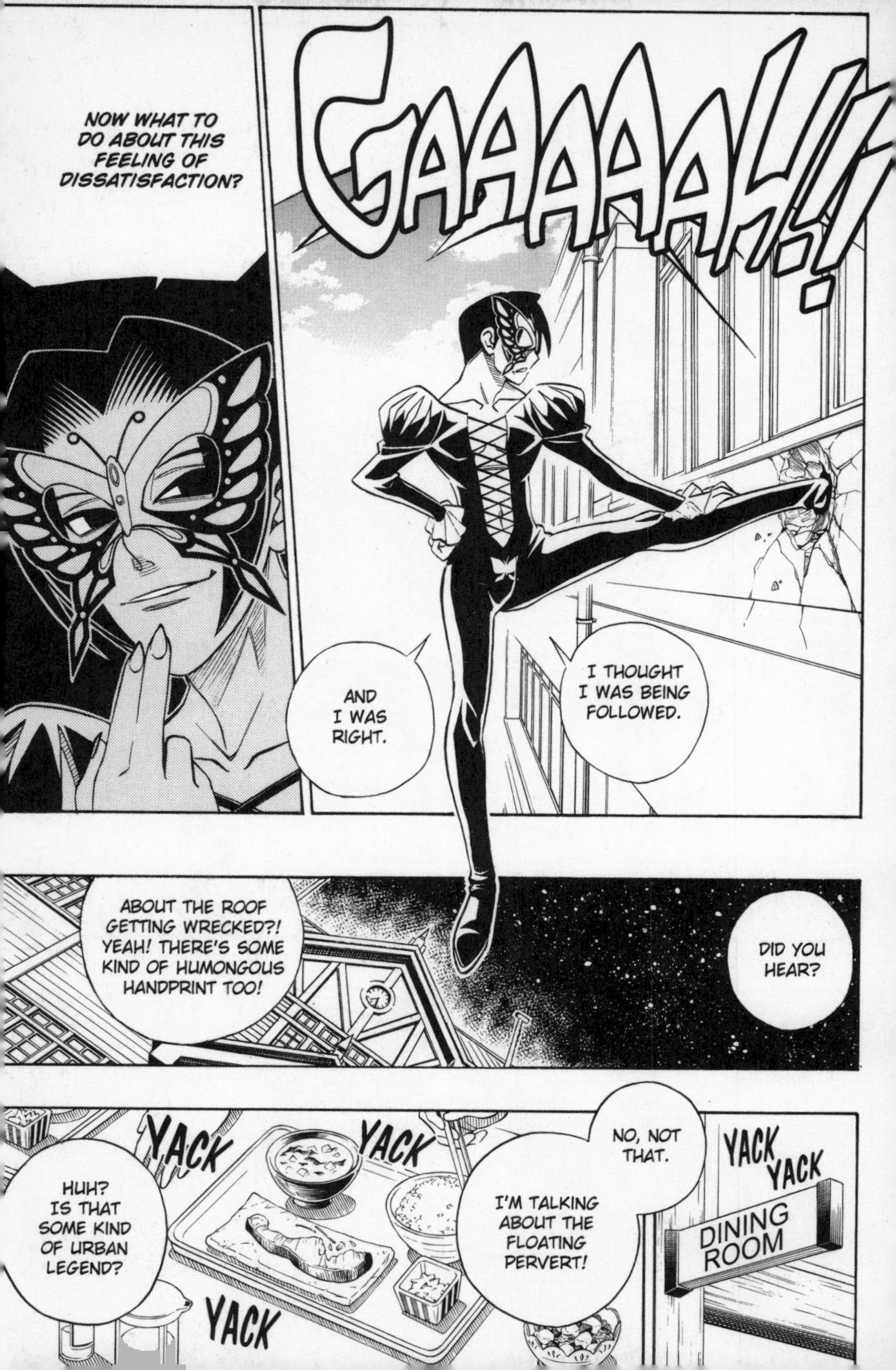
GAAAAH!!
I THOUGHT I WAS BEING FOLLOWED.
AND I WAS RIGHT.
NOW WHAT TO DO ABOUT THIS FEELING OF DISSATISFACTION?
DID YOU HEAR?
ABOUT THE ROOF GETTING WRECKED?! YEAH! THERE'S SOME KIND OF HUMONGOUS HANDPRINT TOO!
YACK YACK
DINING ROOM
NO, NOT THAT.
I'M TALKING ABOUT THE FLOATING PERVERT!
YACK
YACK
HUH? IS THAT SOME KIND OF URBAN LEGEND?
YACK

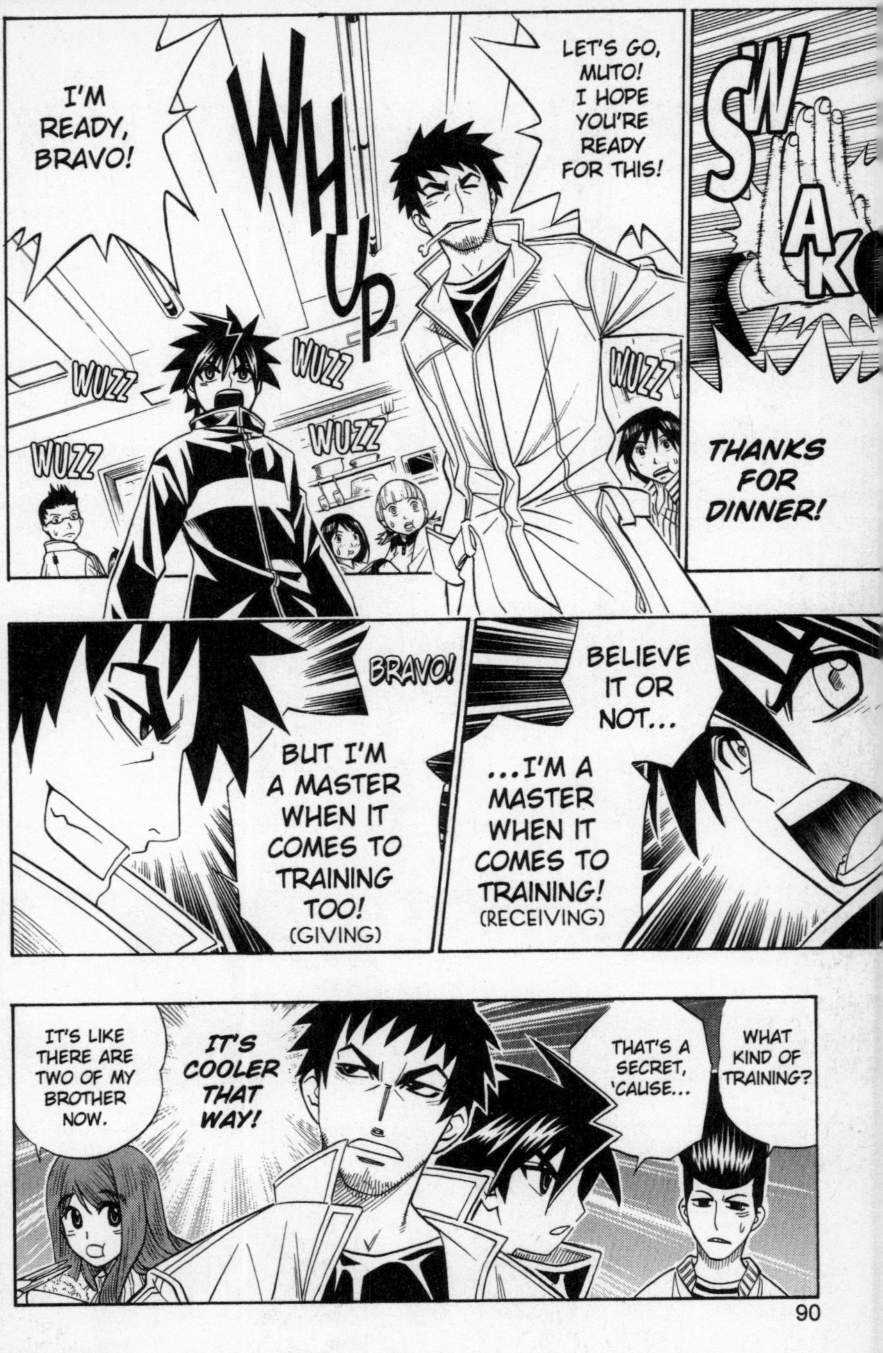
SWAK
THANKS FOR DINNER!
LET'S GO, MUTO! I HOPE YOU'RE READY FOR THIS!
WHUP
I'M READY, BRAVO!
WUZZ
WUZZ
WUZZ
WUZZ
WUZZ
BELIEVE IT OR NOT...
...I'M A MASTER WHEN IT COMES TO TRAINING!
(RECEIVING)
BRAVO!
BUT I'M A MASTER WHEN IT COMES TO TRAINING TOO!
(GIVING)
WHAT KIND OF TRAINING?
THAT'S A SECRET, 'CAUSE...
IT'S COOLER THAT WAY!
IT'S LIKE THERE ARE TWO OF MY BROTHER NOW.

READ THIS WAY

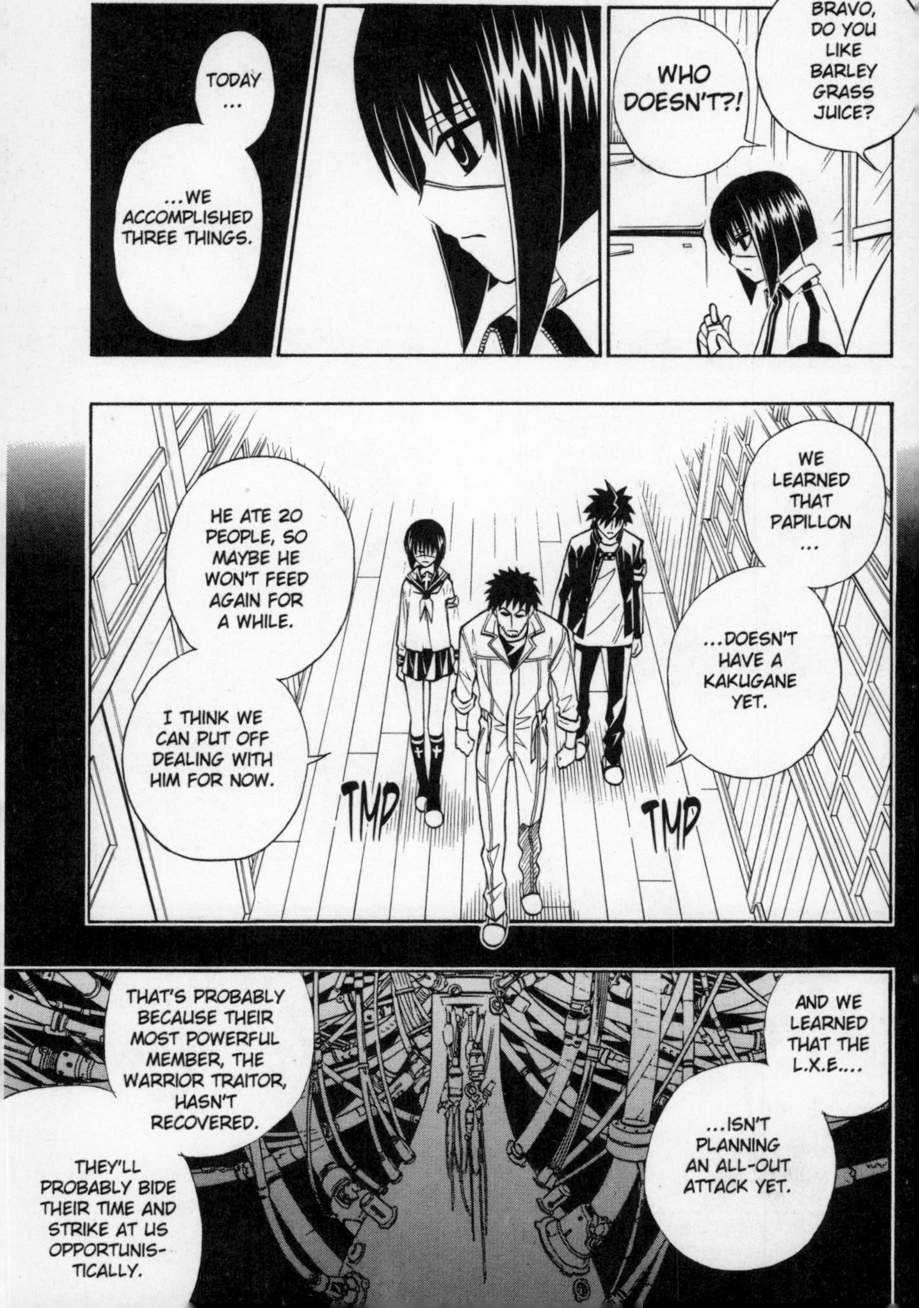
BRAVO, DO YOU LIKE BARLEY GRASS JUICE?
WHO DOESN'T?!
TODAY ...
...WE ACCOMPLISHED THREE THINGS.
WE LEARNED THAT PAPILLON ...
...DOESN'T HAVE A KAKUGANE YET.
HE ATE 20 PEOPLE, SO MAYBE HE WON'T FEED AGAIN FOR A WHILE.
I THINK WE CAN PUT OFF DEALING WITH HIM FOR NOW.
TMP
TMP
AND WE LEARNED THAT THE L.X.E....
...ISN'T PLANNING AN ALL-OUT ATTACK YET.
THAT'S PROBABLY BECAUSE THEIR MOST POWERFUL MEMBER, THE WARRIOR TRAITOR, HASN'T RECOVERED.
THEY'LL PROBABLY BIDE THEIR TIME AND STRIKE AT US OPPORTUNIS-TICALLY.

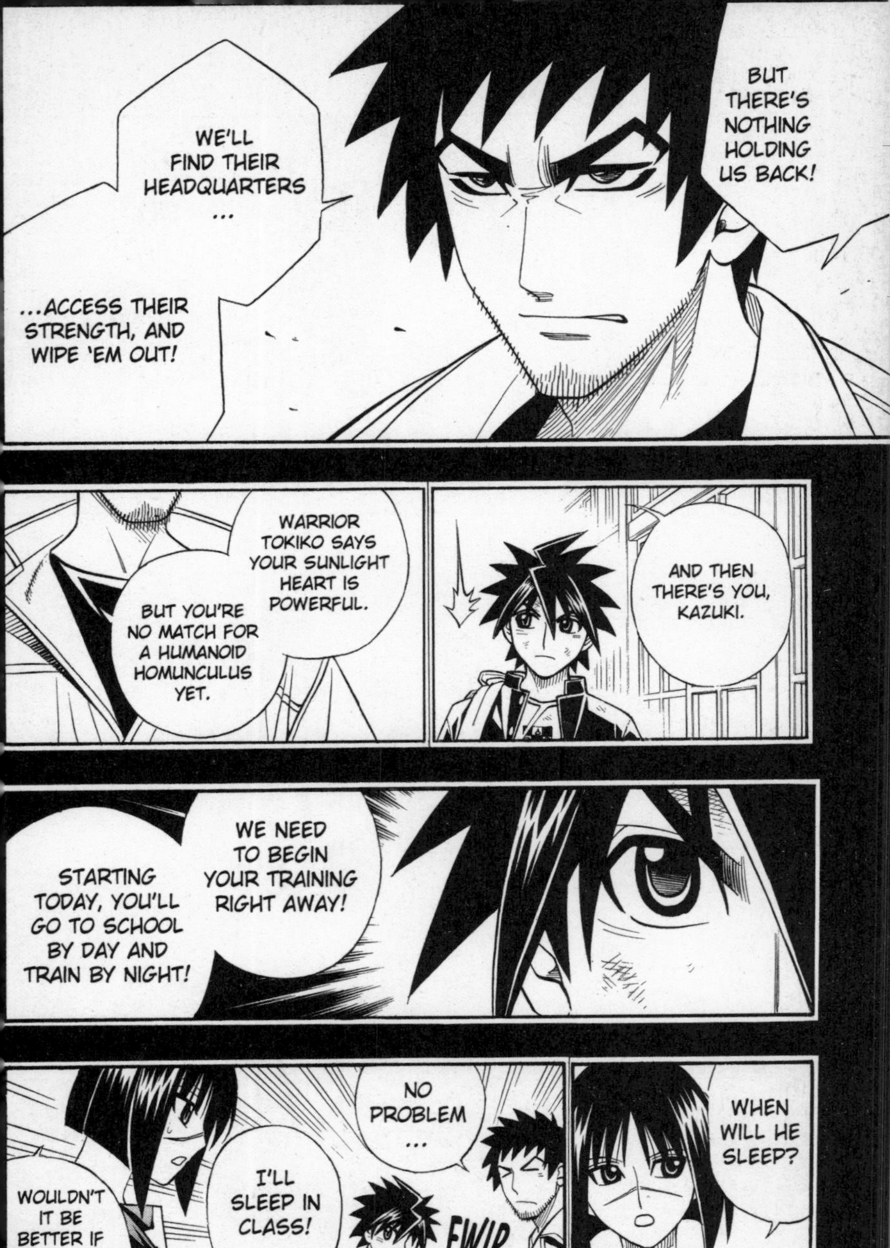
BUT THERE'S NOTHING HOLDING US BACK!
WE'LL FIND THEIR HEADQUARTERS ...
...ACCESS THEIR STRENGTH, AND WIPE 'EM OUT!
AND THEN THERE'S YOU, KAZUKI.
WARRIOR TOKIKO SAYS YOUR SUNLIGHT HEART IS POWERFUL.
BUT YOU'RE NO MATCH FOR A HUMANOID HOMUNCULUS YET.
WE NEED TO BEGIN YOUR TRAINING RIGHT AWAY!
STARTING TODAY, YOU'LL GO TO SCHOOL BY DAY AND TRAIN BY NIGHT!
WHEN WILL HE SLEEP?
NO PROBLEM ...
I'LL SLEEP IN CLASS!
FWIP
WOULDN'T IT BE BETTER IF HE JUST TOOK SOME TIME OFF?

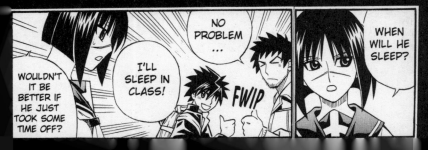

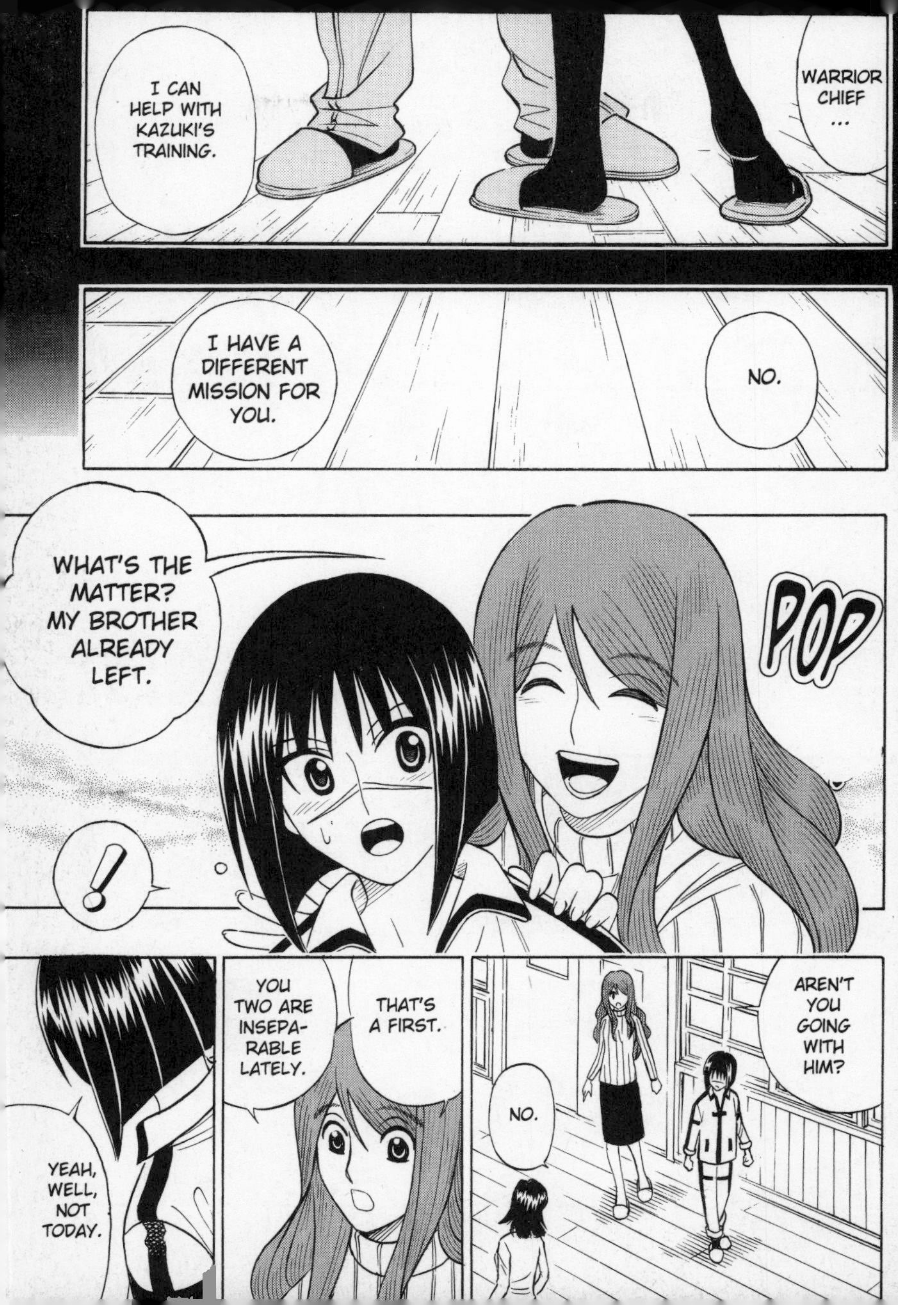
WARRIOR CHIEF ...
I CAN HELP WITH KAZUKI'S TRAINING.
NO.
I HAVE A DIFFERENT MISSION FOR YOU.
POP
WHAT'S THE MATTER? MY BROTHER ALREADY LEFT.
!
AREN'T YOU GOING WITH HIM?
NO.
THAT'S A FIRST.
YOU TWO ARE INSEPA-RABLE LATELY.
YEAH, WELL, NOT TODAY.

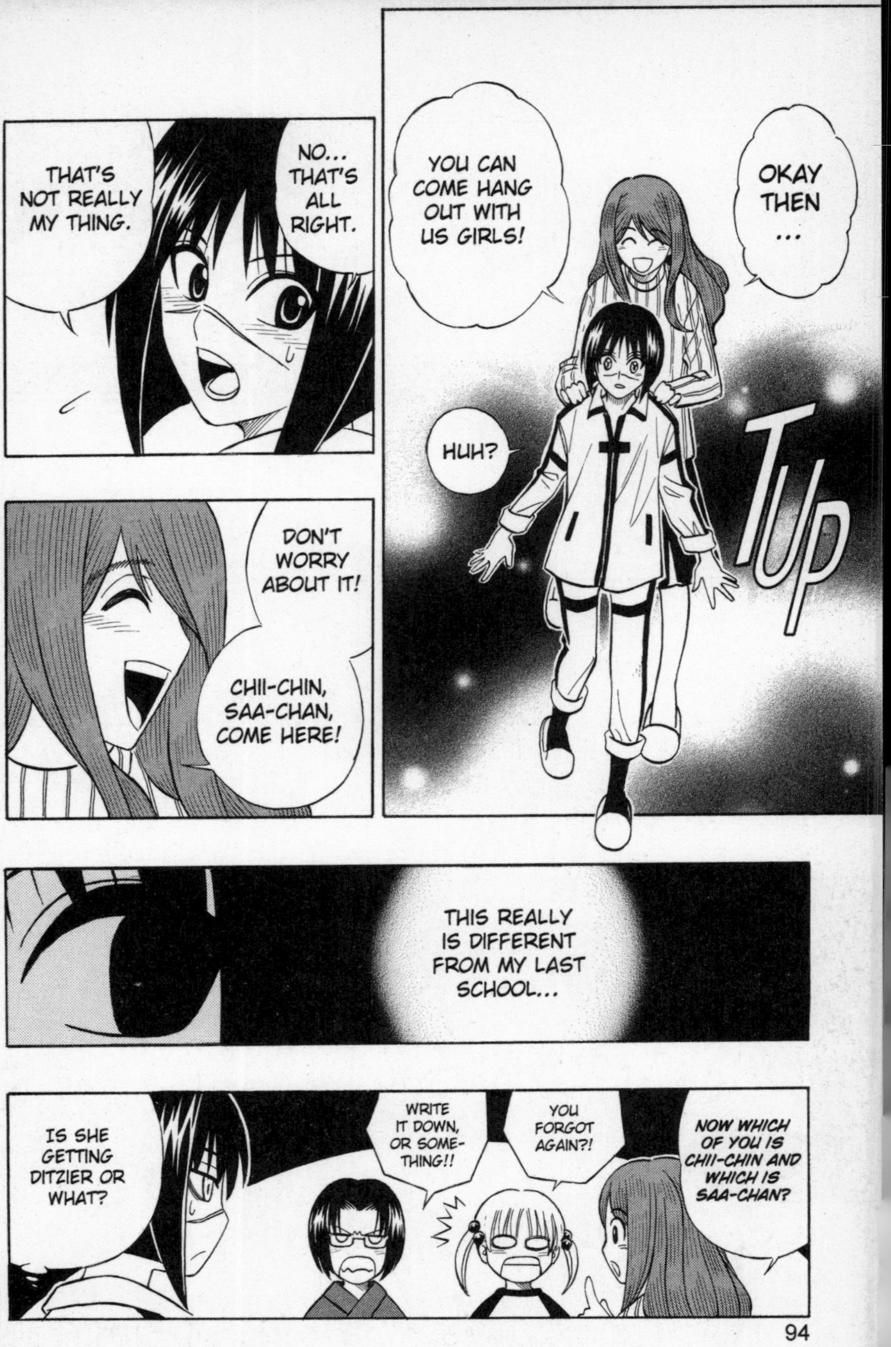
OKAY THEN ...
YOU CAN COME HANG OUT WITH US GIRLS!
HUH?
TUP
NO... THAT'S ALL RIGHT.
THAT'S NOT REALLY MY THING.
DON'T WORRY ABOUT IT!
CHII-CHIN, SAA-CHAN, COME HERE!
THIS REALLY IS DIFFERENT FROM MY LAST SCHOOL...
NOW WHICH OF YOU IS CHII-CHIN AND WHICH IS SAA-CHAN?
YOU FORGOT AGAIN?!
WRITE IT DOWN, OR SOME-THING!!
IS SHE GETTING DITZIER OR WHAT?

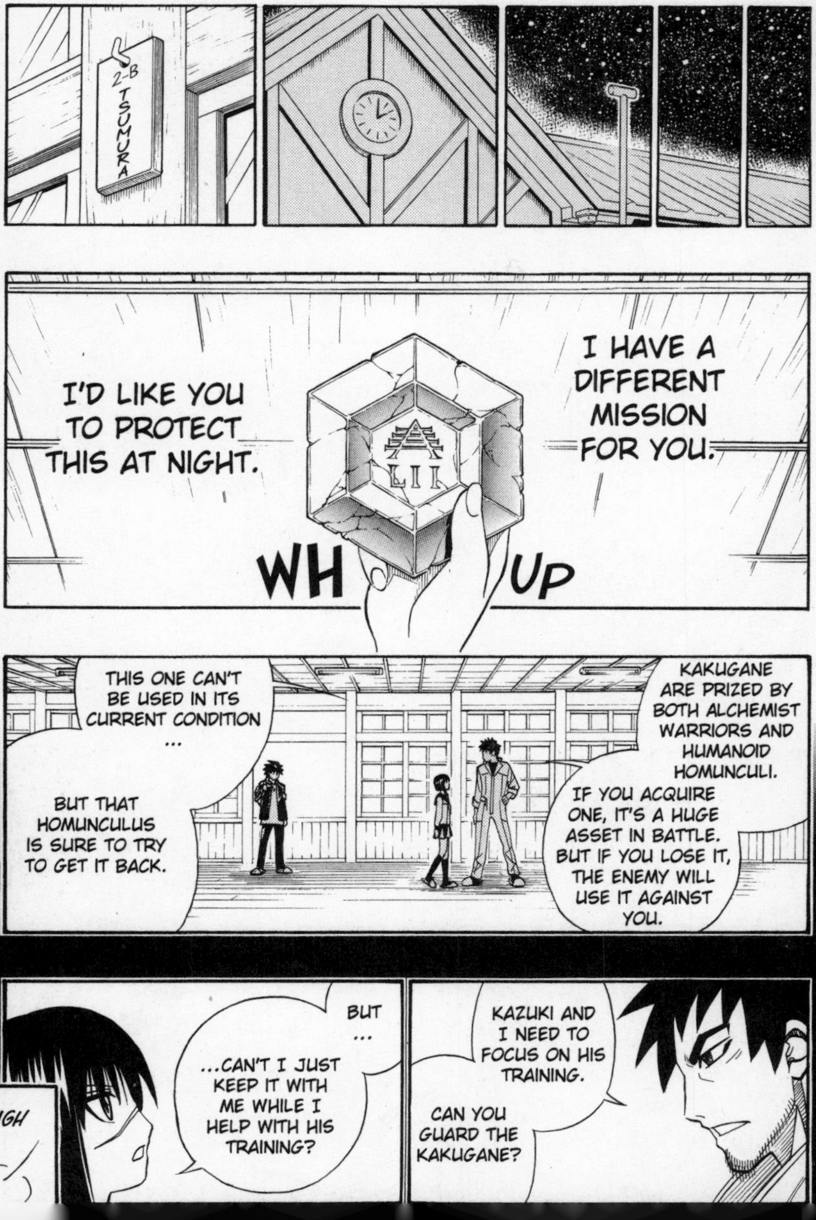
2-B TSUMURA
I HAVE A DIFFERENT MISSION FOR YOU.
I'D LIKE YOU TO PROTECT THIS AT NIGHT.
WH UP
KAKUGANE ARE PRIZED BY BOTH ALCHEMIST WARRIORS AND HUMANOID HOMUNCULI.
IF YOU ACQUIRE ONE, IT'S A HUGE ASSET IN BATTLE. BUT IF YOU LOSE IT, THE ENEMY WILL USE IT AGAINST YOU.
THIS ONE CAN'T BE USED IN ITS CURRENT CONDITION ...
BUT THAT HOMUNCULUS IS SURE TO TRY TO GET IT BACK.
KAZUKI AND I NEED TO FOCUS ON HIS TRAINING.
CAN YOU GUARD THE KAKUGANE?
BUT ...
...CAN'T I JUST KEEP IT WITH ME WHILE I HELP WITH HIS TRAINING?
SIGH

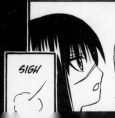

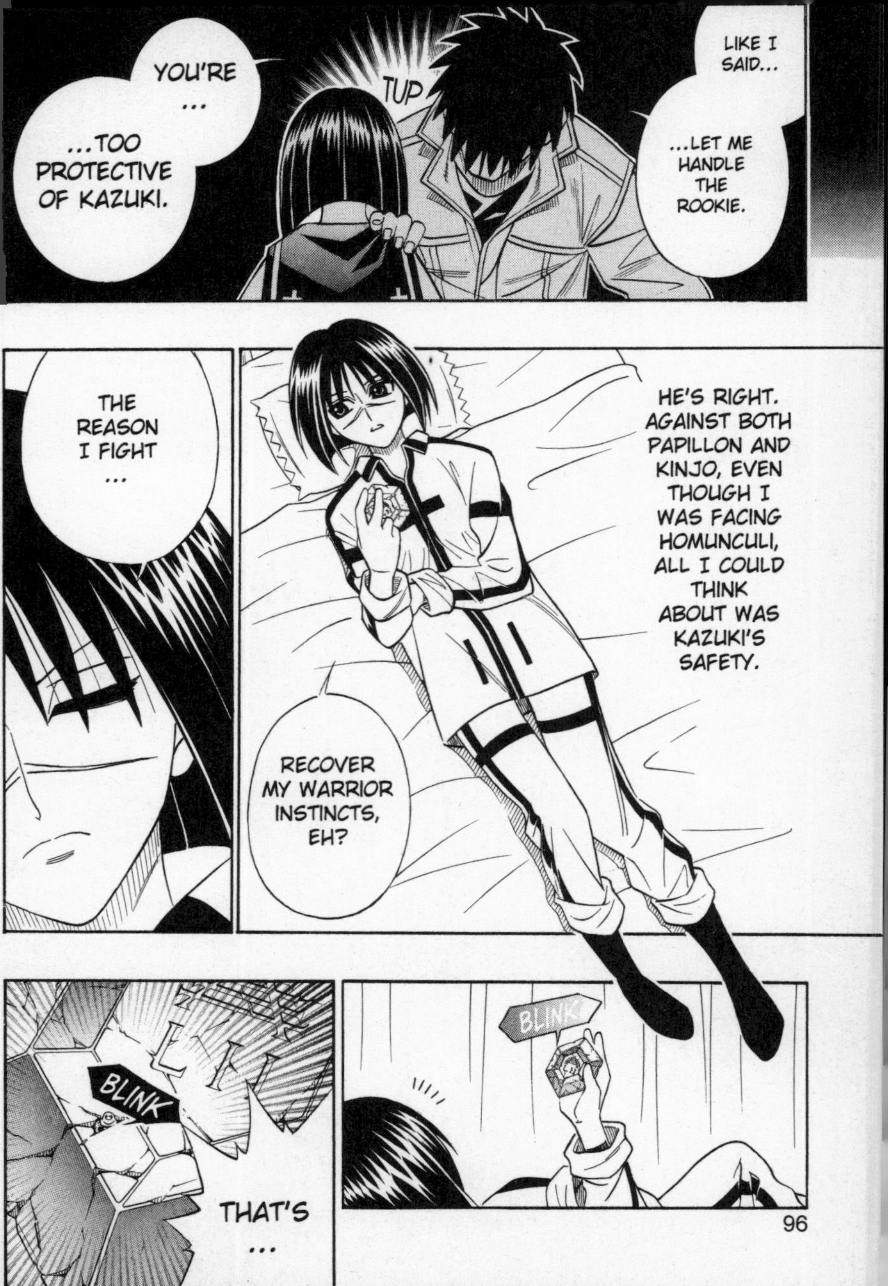

LIKE I SAID...
...LET ME HANDLE THE ROOKIE.
TUP
YOU'RE ...
...TOO PROTECTIVE OF KAZUKI.
HE'S RIGHT. AGAINST BOTH PAPILLON AND KINJO, EVEN THOUGH I WAS FACING HOMUNCULI, ALL I COULD THINK ABOUT WAS KAZUKI'S SAFETY.
RECOVER MY WARRIOR INSTINCTS, EH?
THE REASON I FIGHT ...
BLINK
BLINK
THAT'S ...

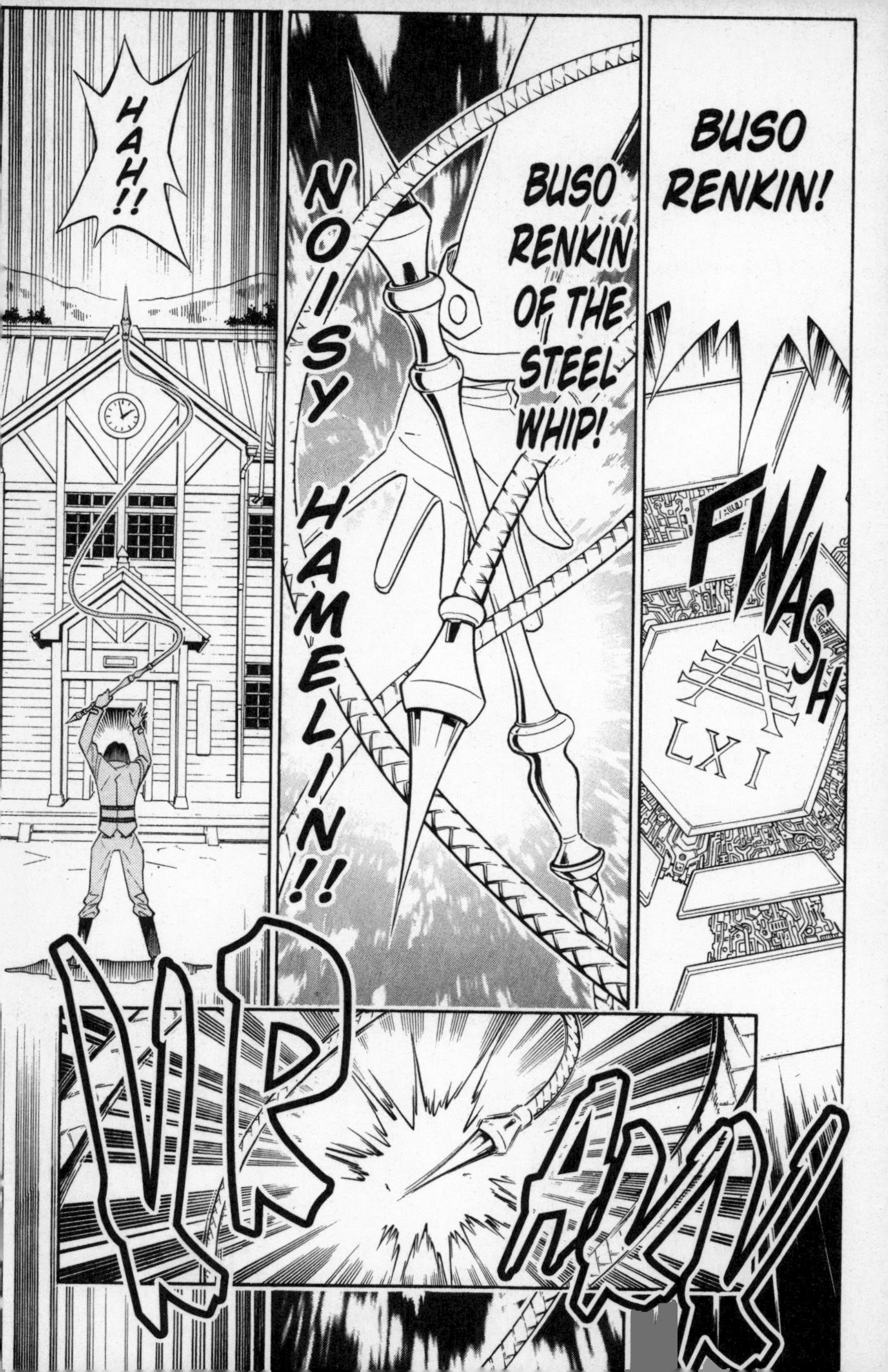
BUSO RENKIN!
FWASH
LXI
BUSO RENKIN OF THE STEEL WHIP!
NOISY HAMELIN!!
HAH!!

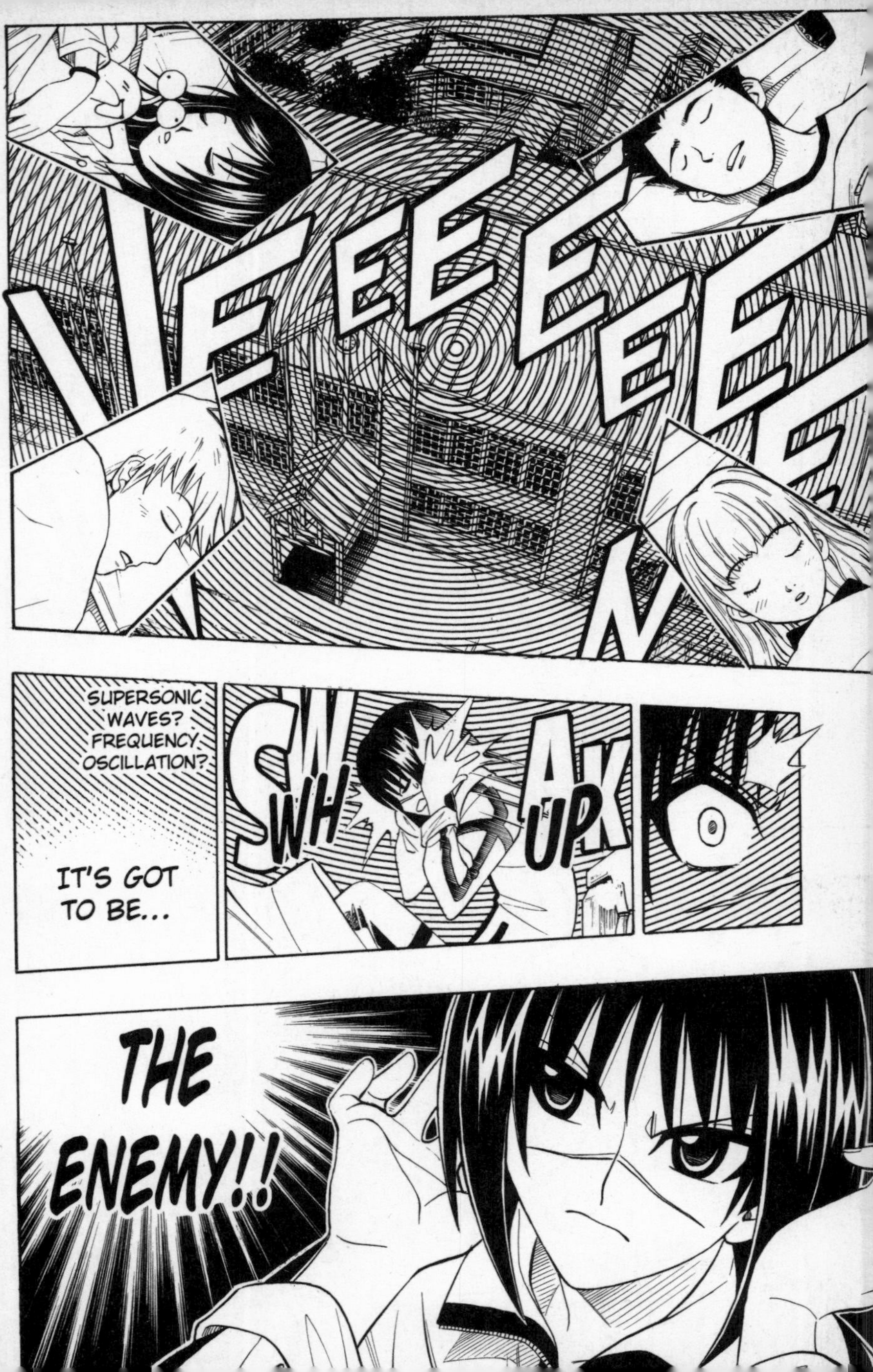
VEEEEEEEEN
SWAK
WHUP
SUPERSONIC WAVES? FREQUENCY OSCILLATION?
IT'S GOT TO BE...
THE ENEMY!!

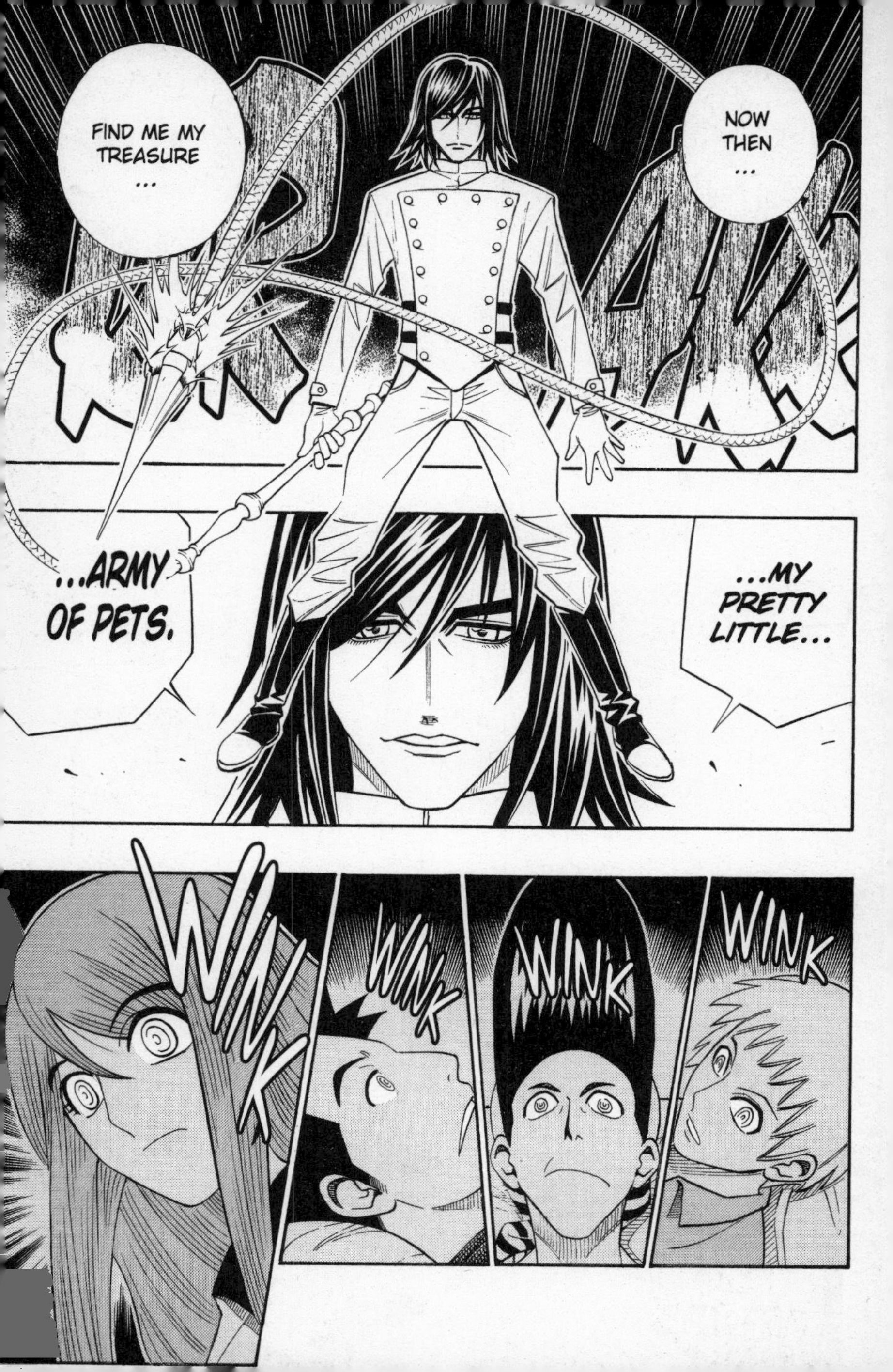
NOW THEN ...
FIND ME MY TREASURE ...
...MY PRETTY LITTLE...
...ARMY OF PETS.
WINK
WINK
WINK
WINK

- Height: 177cm; Weight: 85kg
- Born: April 21; Aries; Blood Type: B; Age 21
- Likes: Things that are very "Hyahoo," street fights
- Dislikes: Cats, detail-oriented people
- Hobby: Watching professional wrestling
- Special Ability: Able to talk without moving his tongue
- Affiliation: L.X.E.

Character File No. 15

Homunculus Kinjo

Author's Notes

- Because he was my first Kakugane-armed Homunculus, I put a lot of work into him, but he ended up just being a character that said "Hyahoo" a lot. Still, I really like his weirdness. Too bad I couldn't draw him a while longer. It's sad.
- He's a reworking of Banshin Inui from my previous series, *Rurouni Kenshin*.
- I regret that he became a throwaway character, but I'm happy with the way he turned out overall. I'll keep trying to create interesting characters like him.

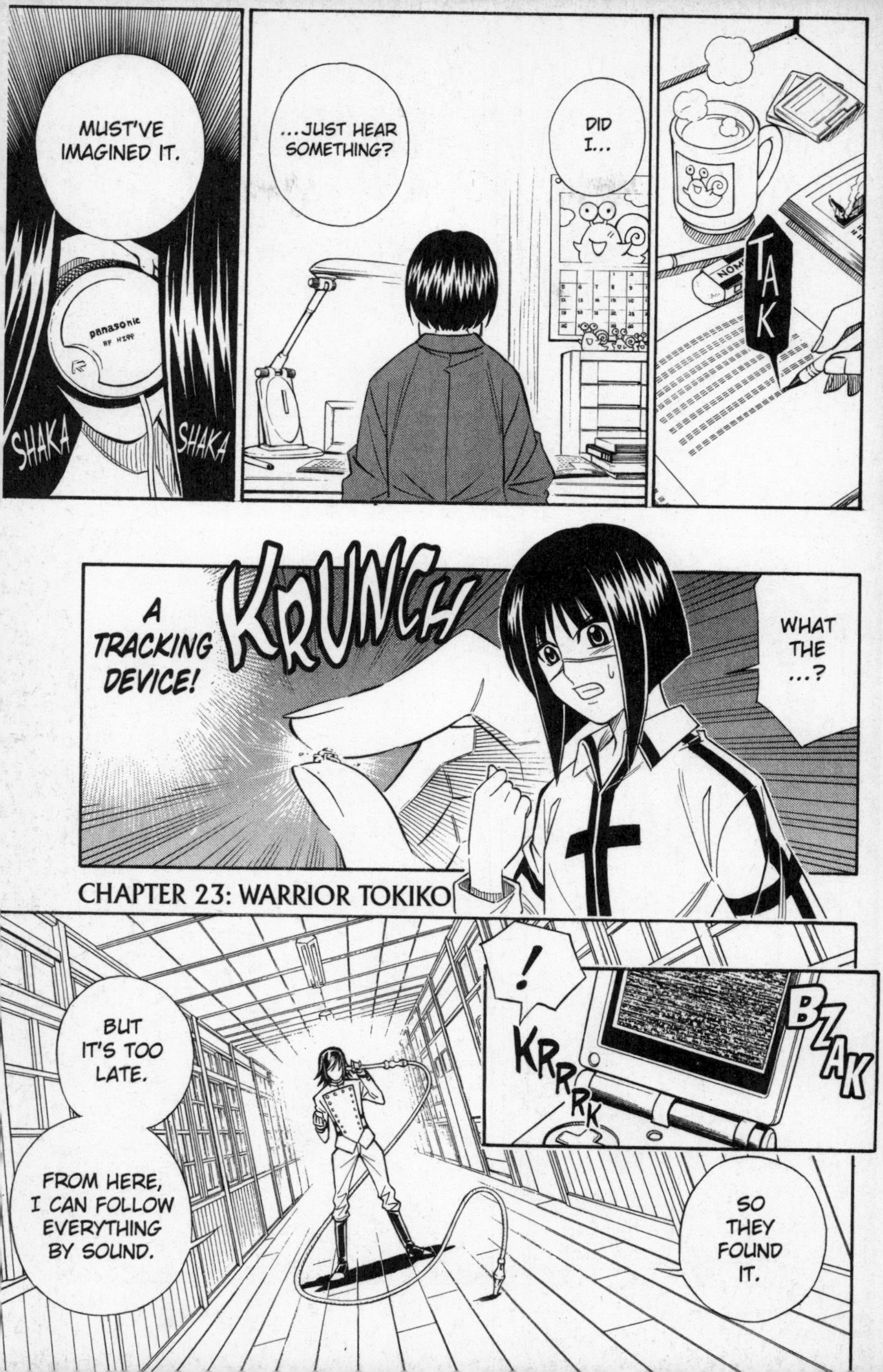
TAK
DID I...
...JUST HEAR SOMETHING?
MUST'VE IMAGINED IT.
panasonic
SHAKA
SHAKA
WHAT THE ...?
KRUNCH
A TRACKING DEVICE!
CHAPTER 23: WARRIOR TOKIKO
!
KRRRRK
BZAK
SO THEY FOUND IT.
BUT IT'S TOO LATE.
FROM HERE, I CAN FOLLOW EVERYTHING BY SOUND.

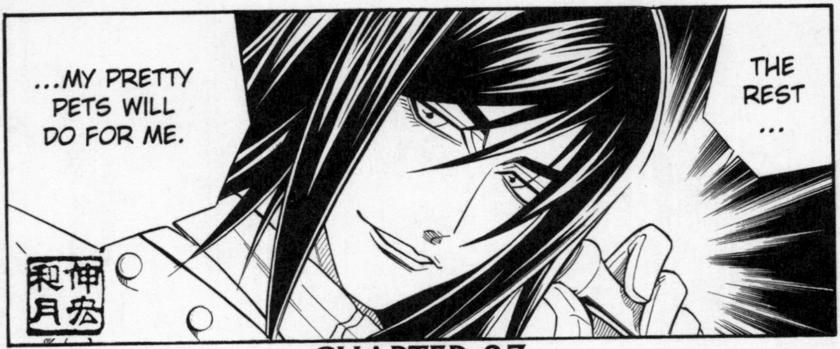
THE REST...
...MY PRETTY PETS WILL DO FOR ME.

CHAPTER 23:

WARRIOR TOKIKO

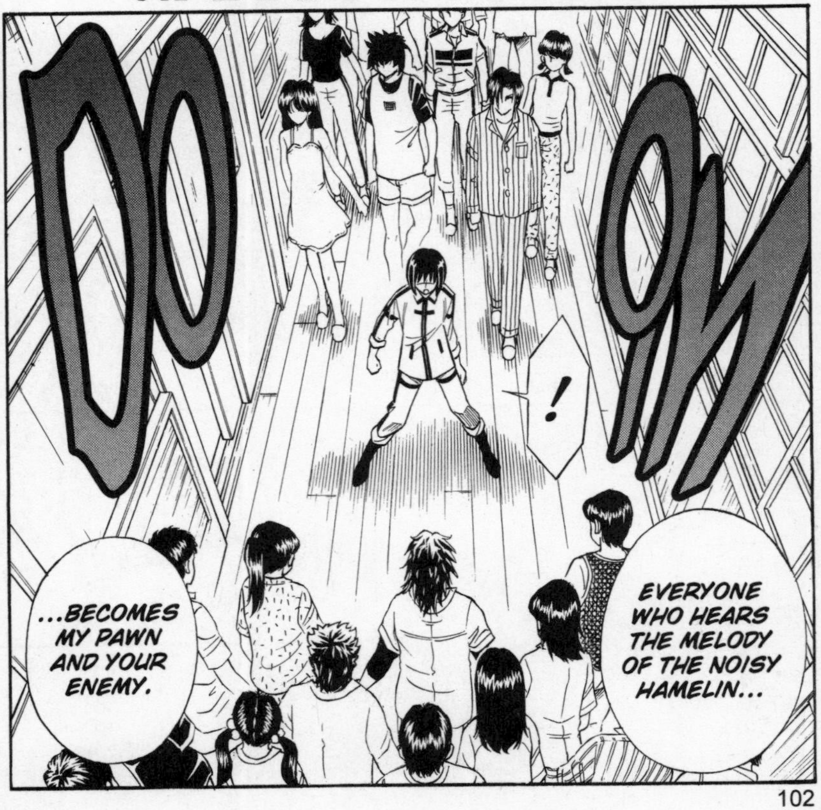
DOOM
!
EVERYONE WHO HEARS THE MELODY OF THE NOISY HAMELIN...
...BECOMES MY PAWN AND YOUR ENEMY.

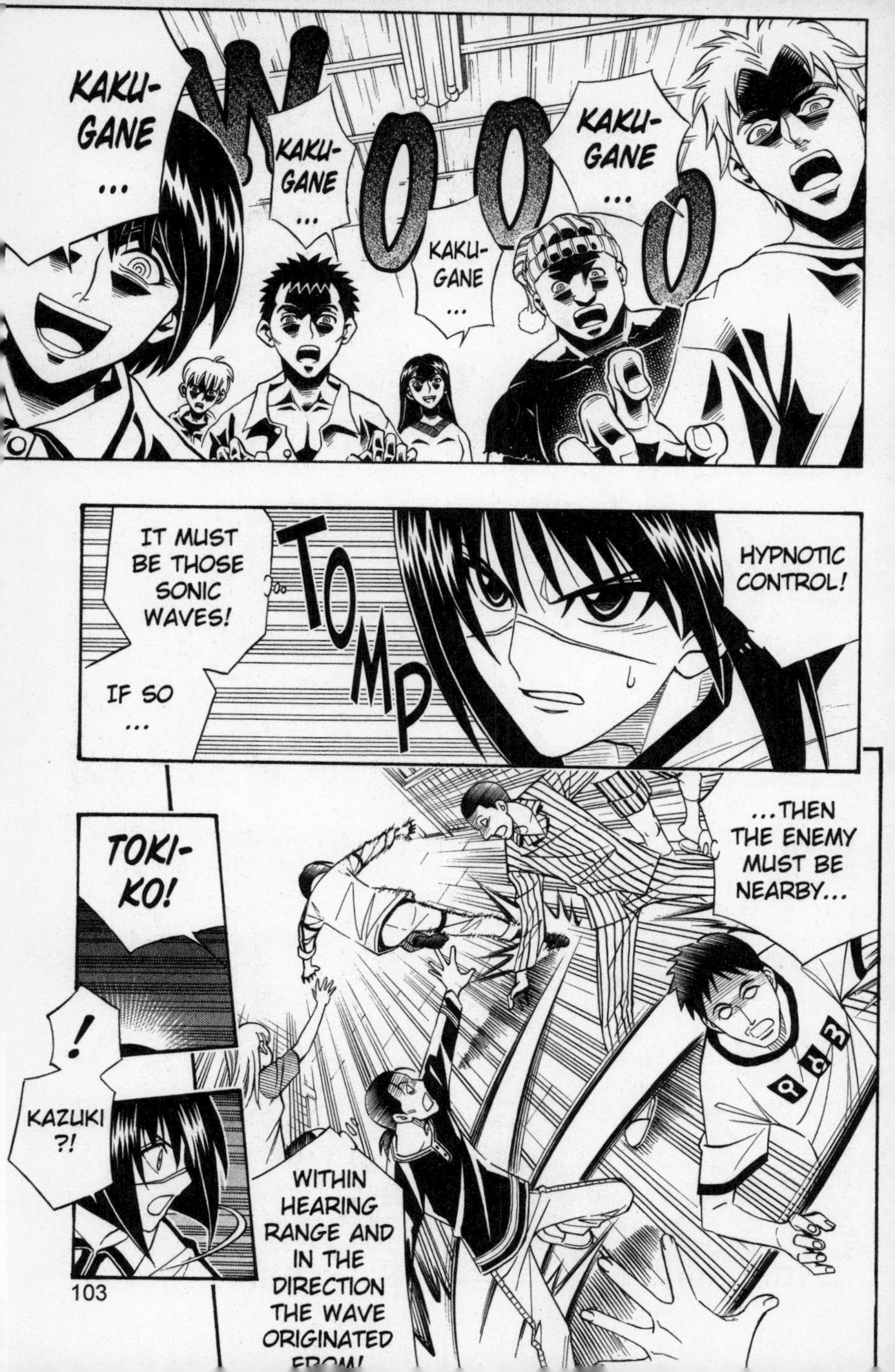
WOOOO
KAKU-GANE ...
KAKU-GANE ...
KAKU-GANE ...
KAKU-GANE ...
HYPNOTIC CONTROL!
TOMP
IT MUST BE THOSE SONIC WAVES!
IF SO ...
...THEN THE ENEMY MUST BE NEARBY...
WITHIN HEARING RANGE AND IN THE DIRECTION THE WAVE ORIGINATED FROM!
TOKI-KO!
!
KAZUKI ?!

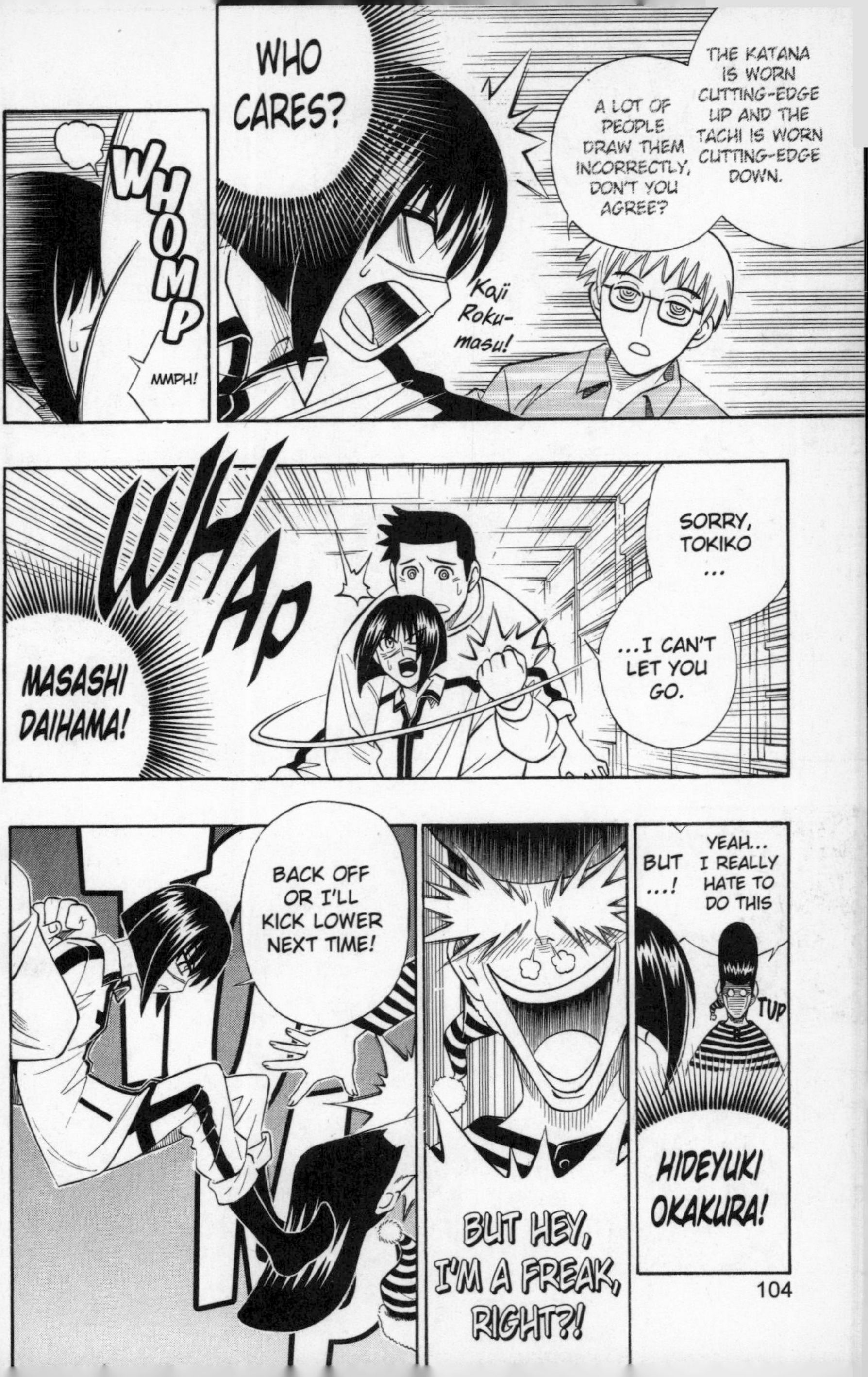

THE KATANA IS WORN CUTTING-EDGE UP AND THE TACHI IS WORN CUTTING-EDGE DOWN.
A LOT OF PEOPLE DRAW THEM INCORRECTLY, DON'T YOU AGREE?
Kaji Rokumasu!
WHO CARES?
WHOMP
MMPH!
SORRY, TOKIKO ...
...I CAN'T LET YOU GO.
WHAP
MASASHI DAIHAMA!
YEAH... I REALLY HATE TO DO THIS
BUT ...!
TUP
HIDEYUKI OKAKURA!
BUT HEY, I'M A FREAK, RIGHT?!
BACK OFF OR I'LL KICK LOWER NEXT TIME!

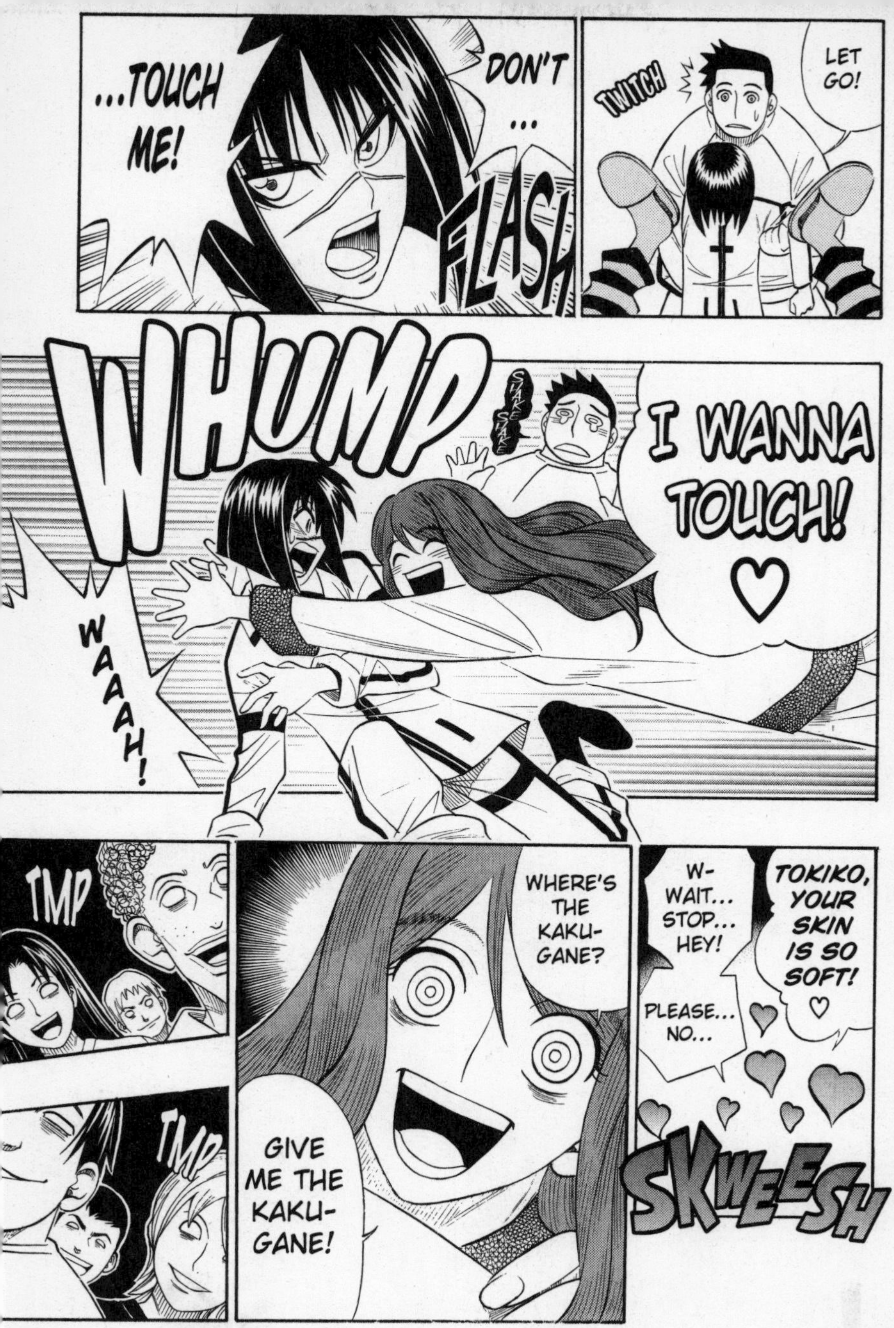
LET GO!
TWITCH
DON'T ...
...TOUCH ME!
FLASH
I WANNA TOUCH! ♥
SHAKE SHAKE
WHUMP
WAAAAH!
TOKIKO, YOUR SKIN IS SO SOFT! ♥
W-WAIT... STOP... HEY!
PLEASE... NO...
SKWEESH
WHERE'S THE KAKU-GANE?
GIVE ME THE KAKU-GANE!
TMP
TMP

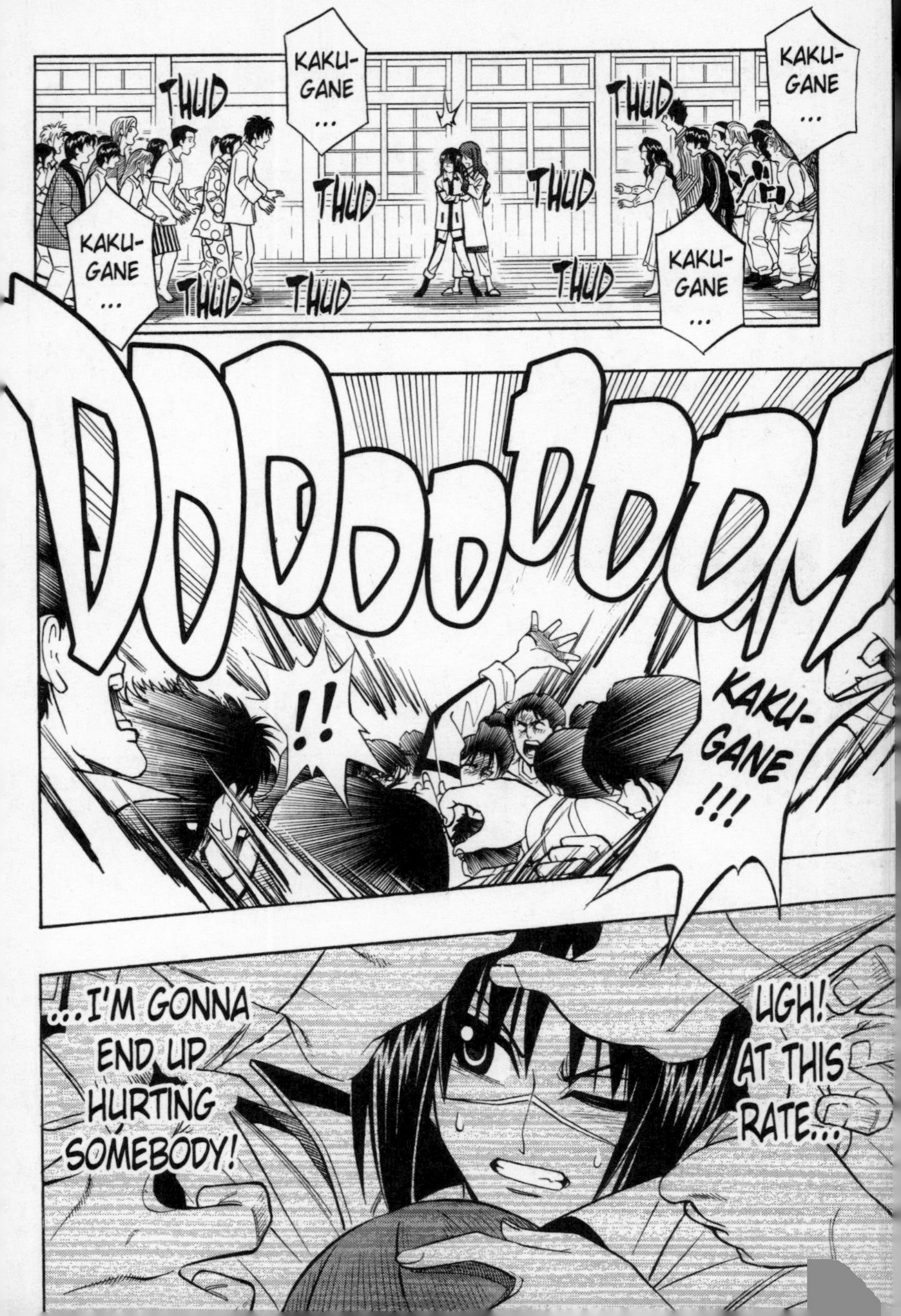
KAKU-GANE ...
THUD
KAKU-GANE ...
THUD
THUD
THUD
KAKU-GANE ...
THUD
THUD
THUD
KAKU-GANE ...
KAKU-GANE !!!
!!
UGH! AT THIS RATE...
...I'M GONNA END UP HURTING SOMEBODY!

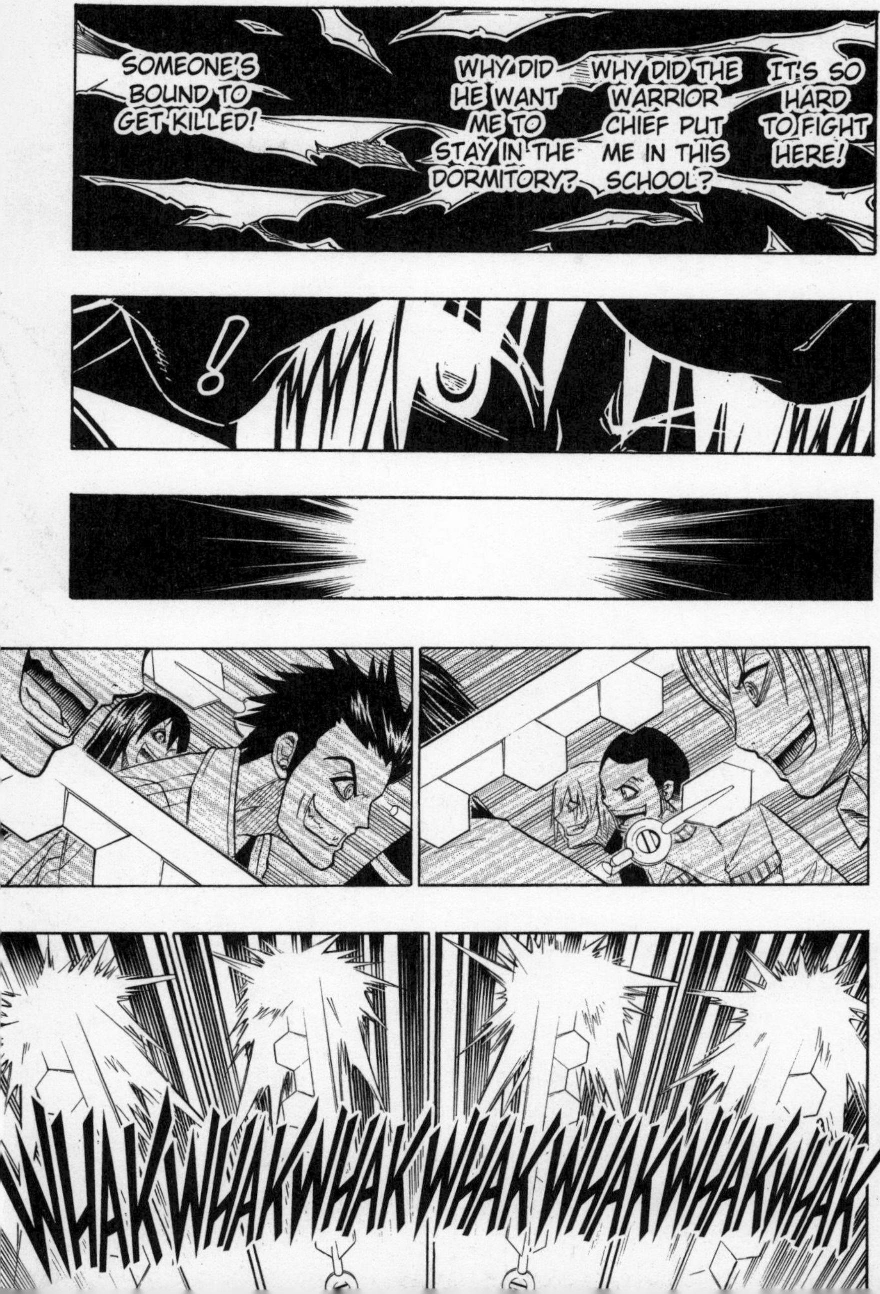
IT'S SO HARD TO FIGHT HERE!
WHY DID THE WARRIOR CHIEF PUT ME IN THIS SCHOOL?
WHY DID HE WANT ME TO STAY IN THE DORMITORY?
SOMEONE'S BOUND TO GET KILLED!
!
WHAK WHAK WHAK WHAK WHAK WHAK WHAK

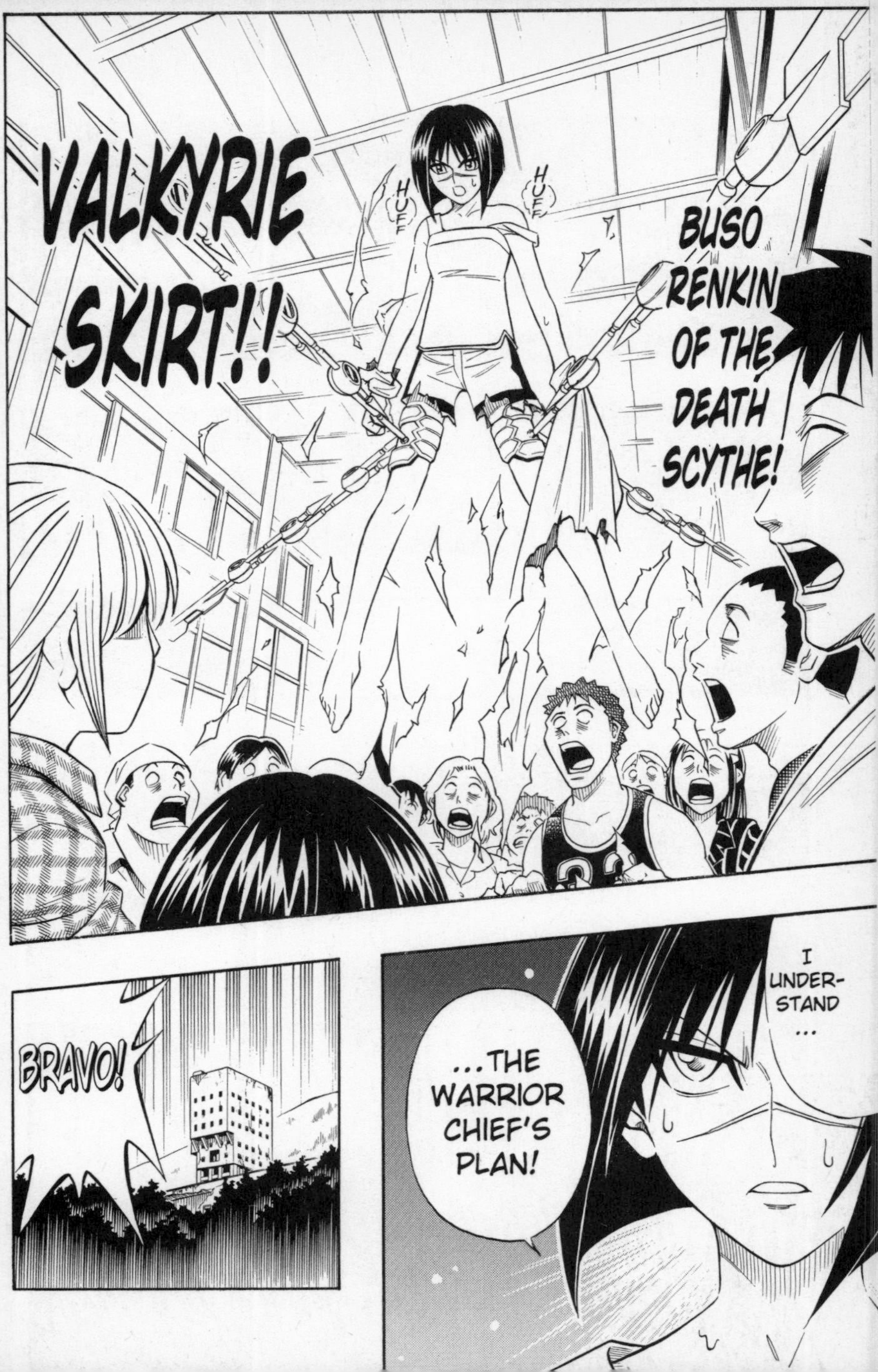
BUSO RENKIN OF THE DEATH SCYTHE!
HUFF HUFF
HUFF
VALKYRIE SKIRT!!
I UNDER-STAND ...
...THE WARRIOR CHIEF'S PLAN!
BRAVO!

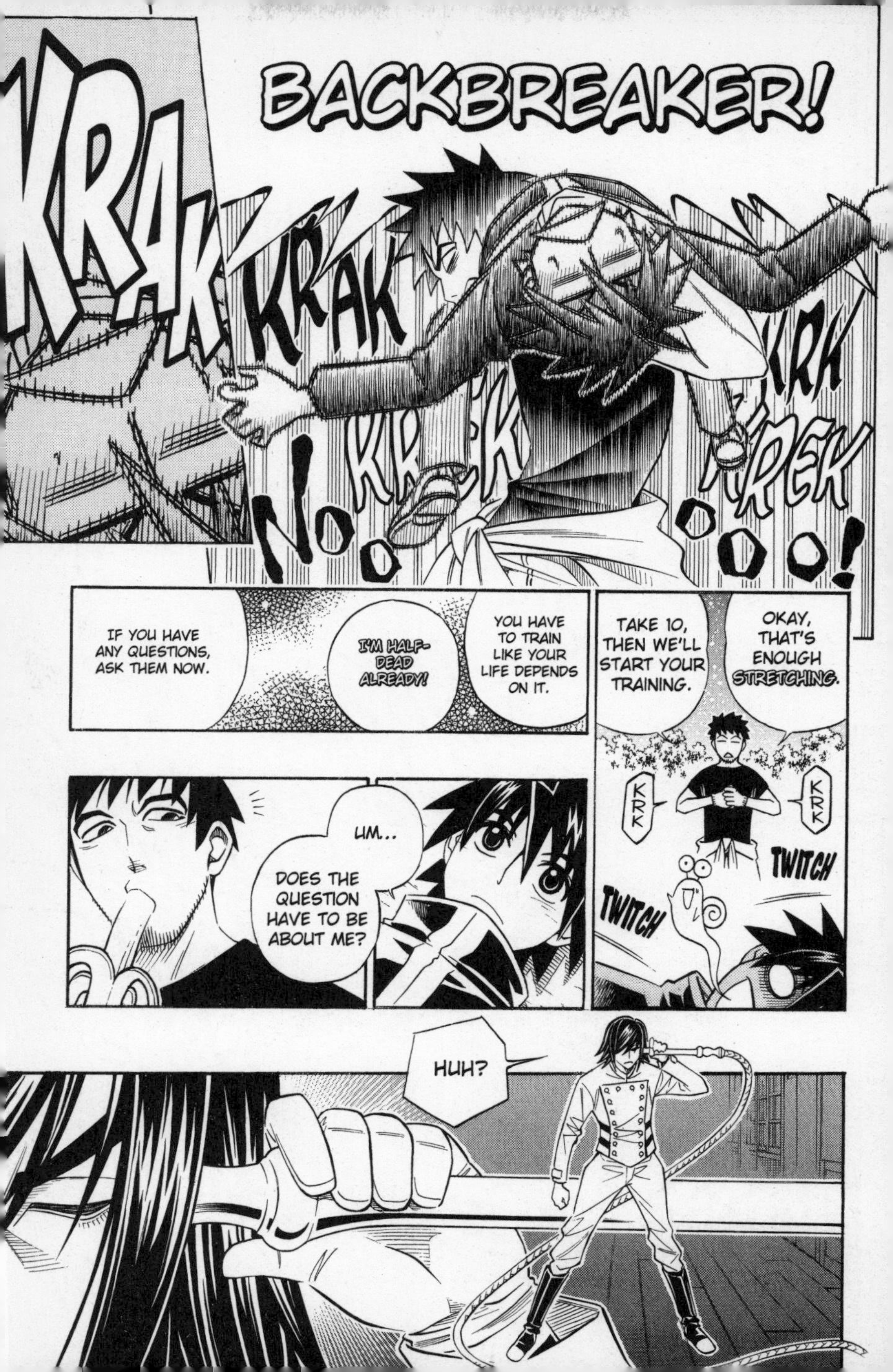
BACKBREAKER!
KRAK
KRAK
KRAK
KREK
KREK
NOOOOO!
OKAY, THAT'S ENOUGH STRETCHING.
TAKE 10, THEN WE'LL START YOUR TRAINING.
KRK
KRK
TWITCH
TWITCH
YOU HAVE TO TRAIN LIKE YOUR LIFE DEPENDS ON IT.
I'M HALF-DEAD ALREADY!
IF YOU HAVE ANY QUESTIONS, ASK THEM NOW.
UM...
DOES THE QUESTION HAVE TO BE ABOUT ME?
HUH?

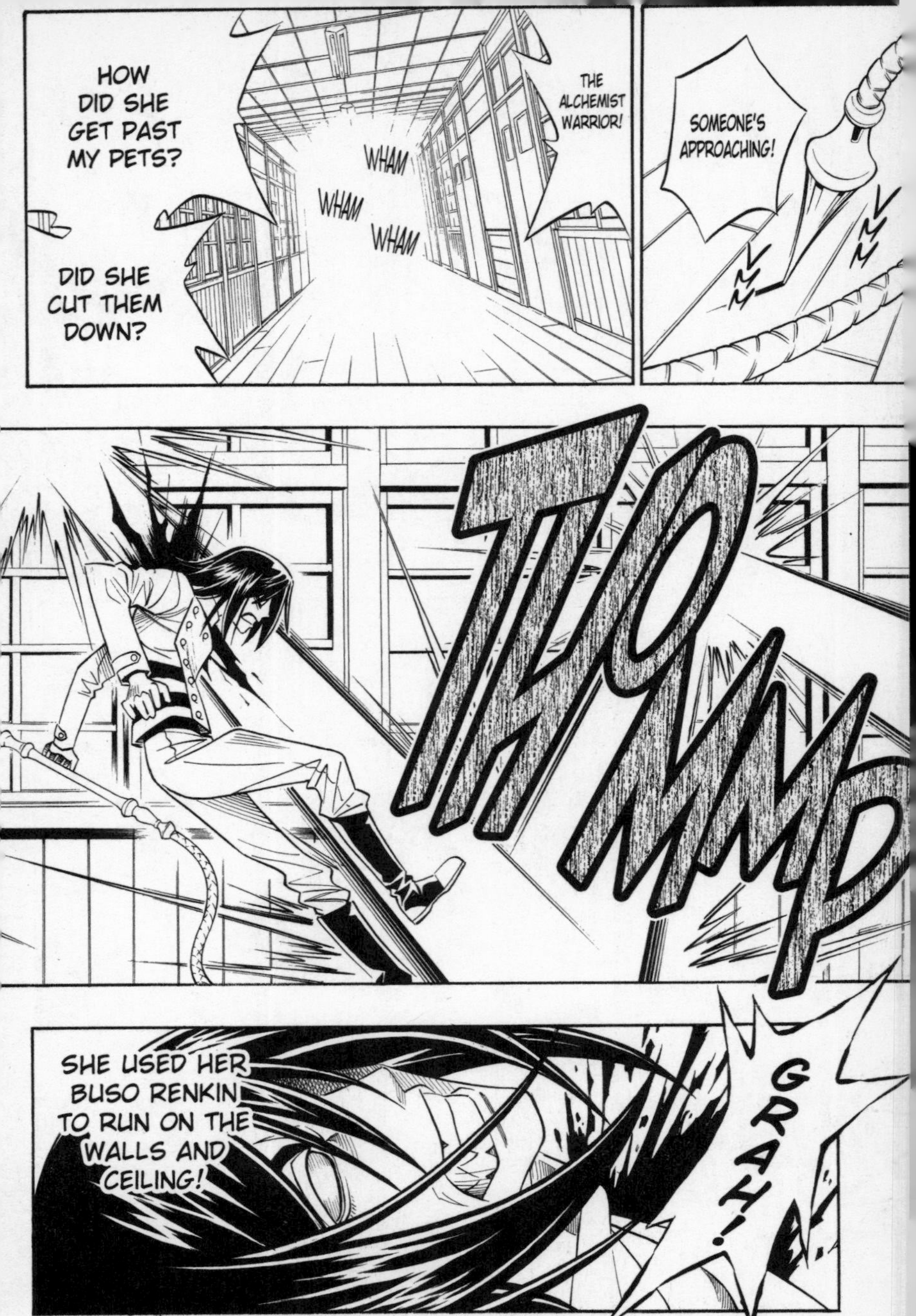
SOMEONE'S APPROACHING!
VMM
VMM
THE ALCHEMIST WARRIOR!
HOW DID SHE GET PAST MY PETS?
WHAM
WHAM
WHAM
DID SHE CUT THEM DOWN?
THOMP
GRAH!
SHE USED HER BUSO RENKIN TO RUN ON THE WALLS AND CEILING!

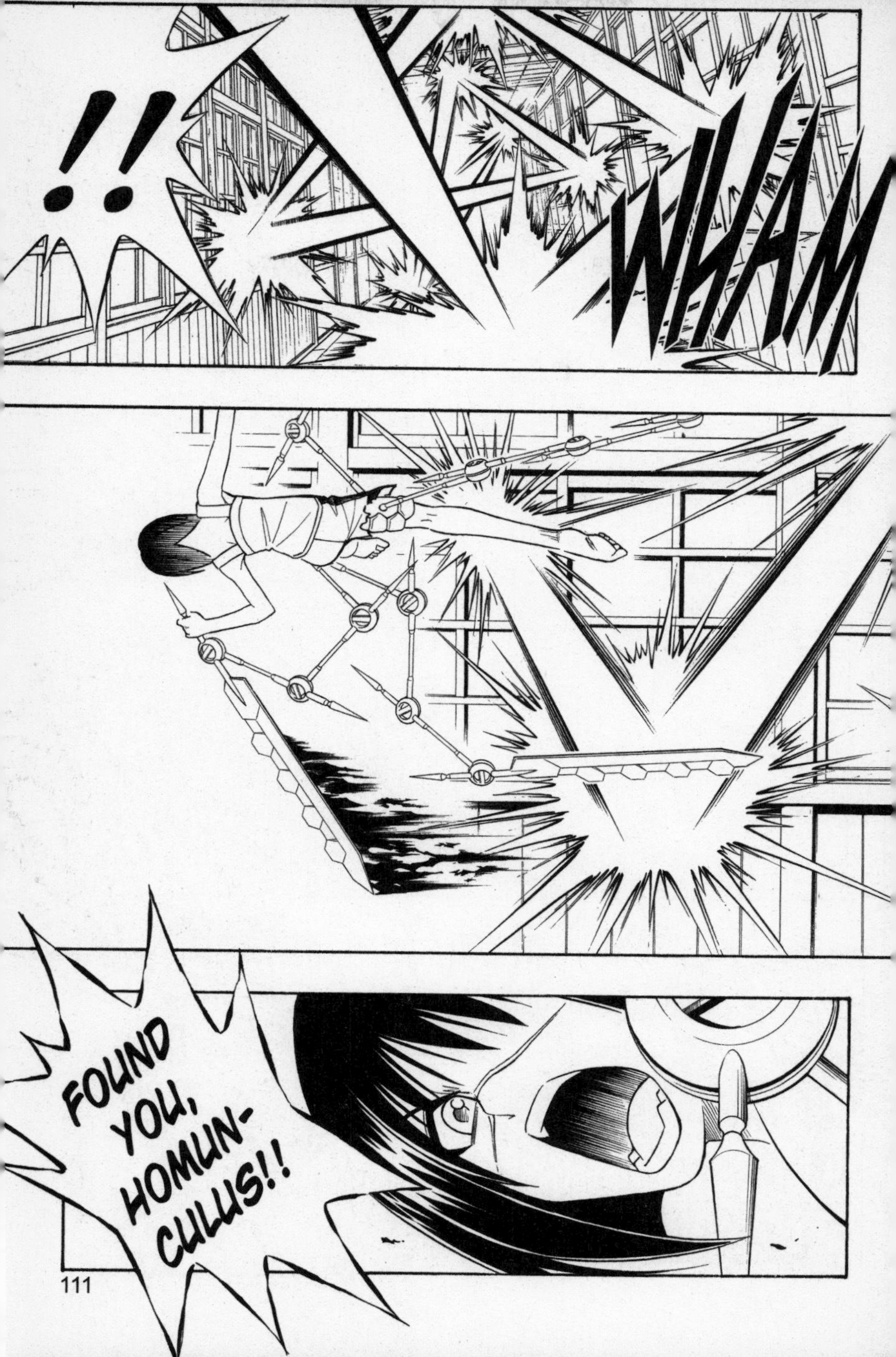
WHAM
!!
FOUND YOU, HOMUN-CULUS!!

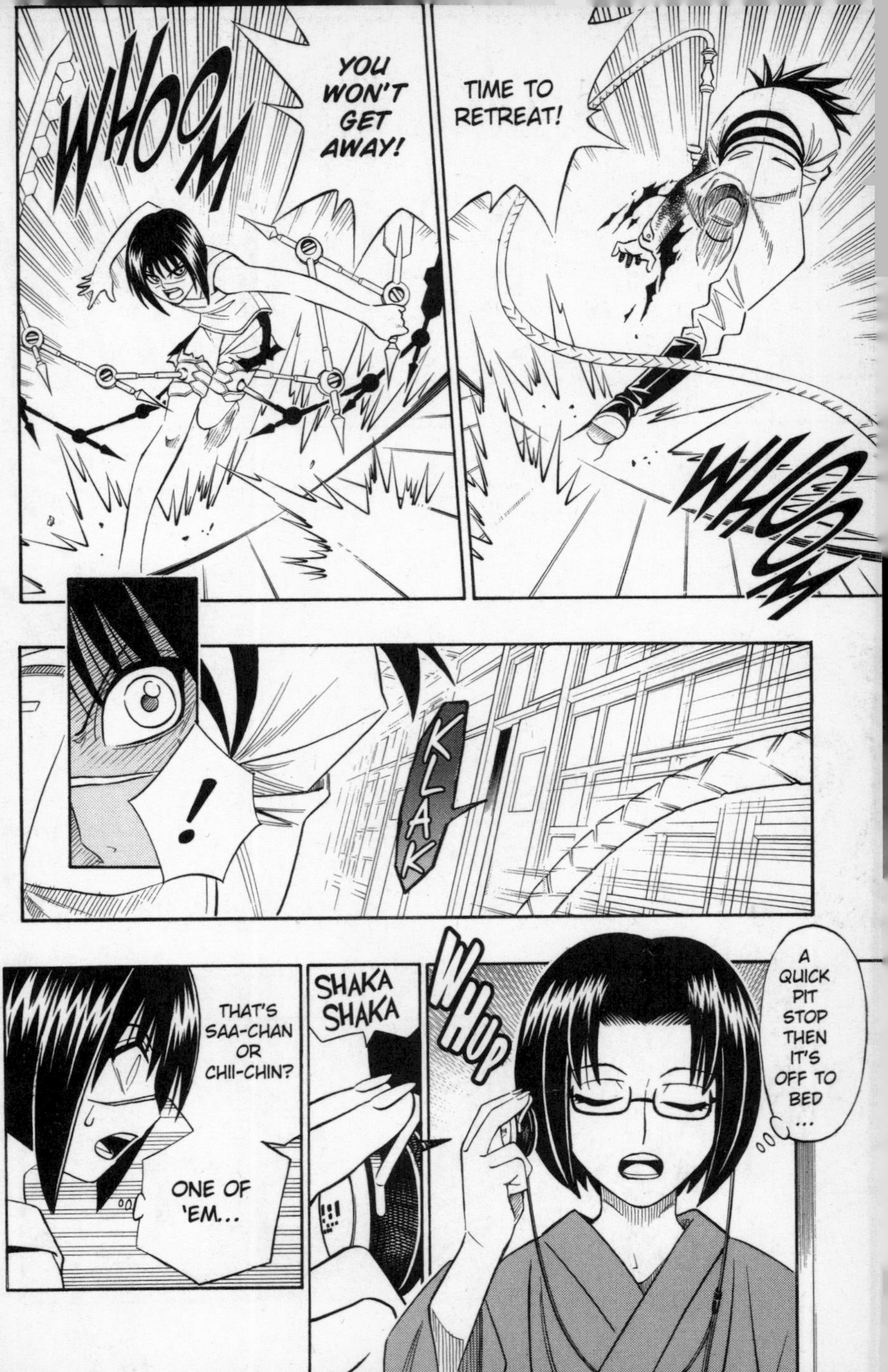
TIME TO RETREAT!
WHOOM
YOU WON'T GET AWAY!
WHOOM
KLAK
!
A QUICK PIT STOP THEN IT'S OFF TO BED...
WHUP
SHAKA SHAKA
THAT'S SAA-CHAN OR CHII-CHIN?
ONE OF 'EM...

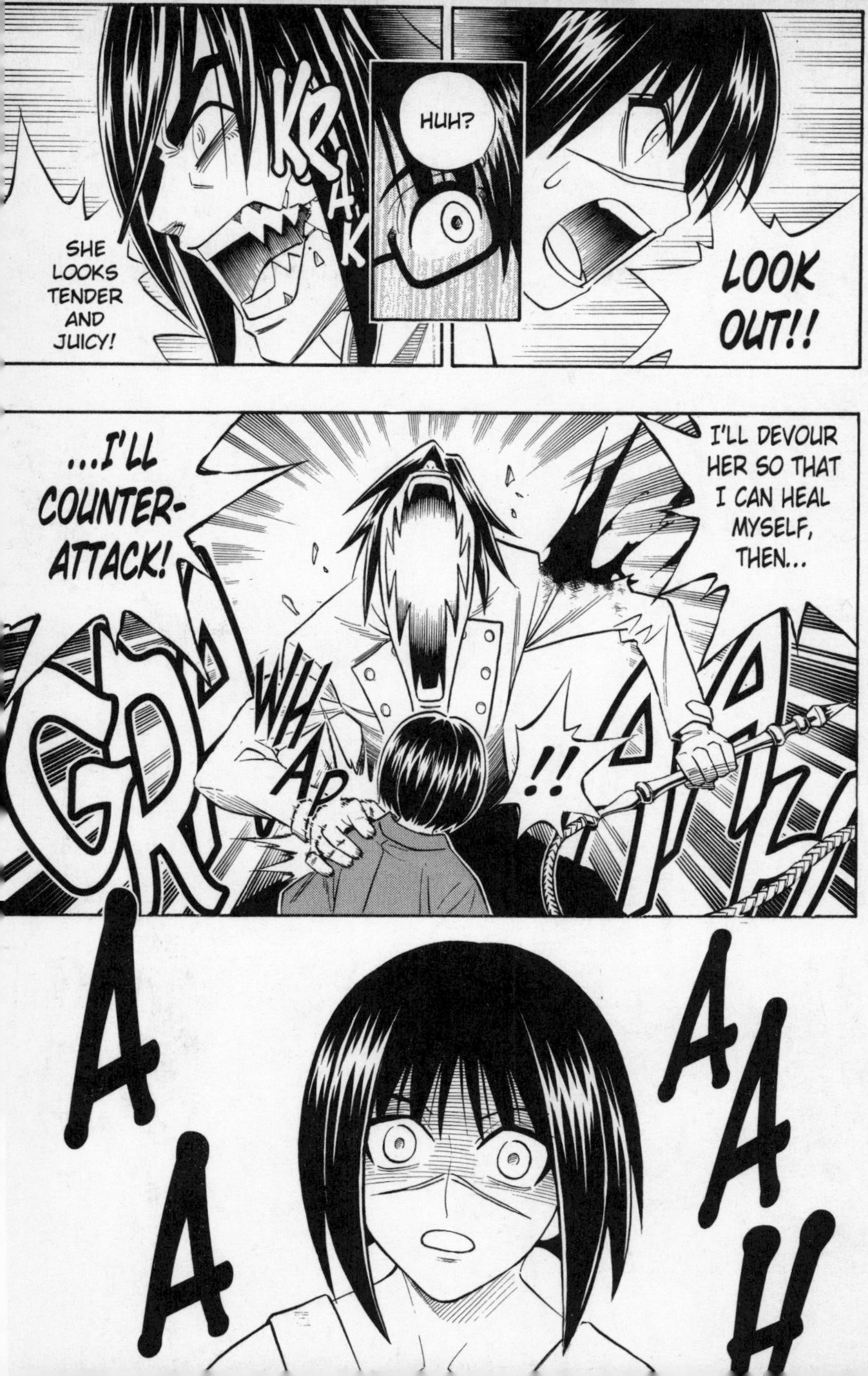
LOOK OUT!!
HUH?
KRAK
SHE LOOKS TENDER AND JUICY!
I'LL DEVOUR HER SO THAT I CAN HEAL MYSELF, THEN...
...I'LL COUNTER-ATTACK!
WHAP
!!
AAAAAAH

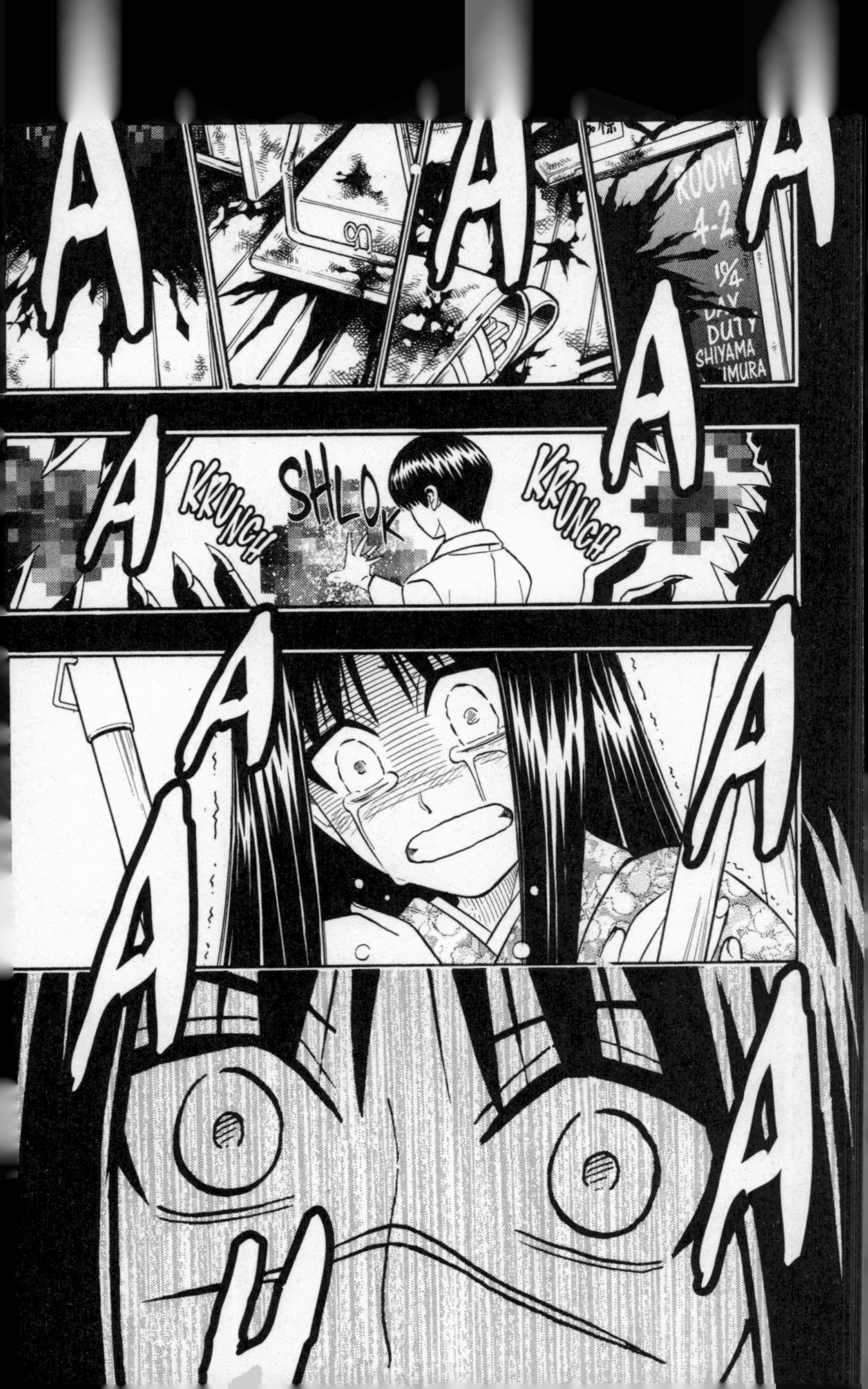
ROOM
4-2
DUTY
SHIYAMA
IMURA
A A A A A A A A A A A A A
KRUNCH
SHLOK
KRUNCH

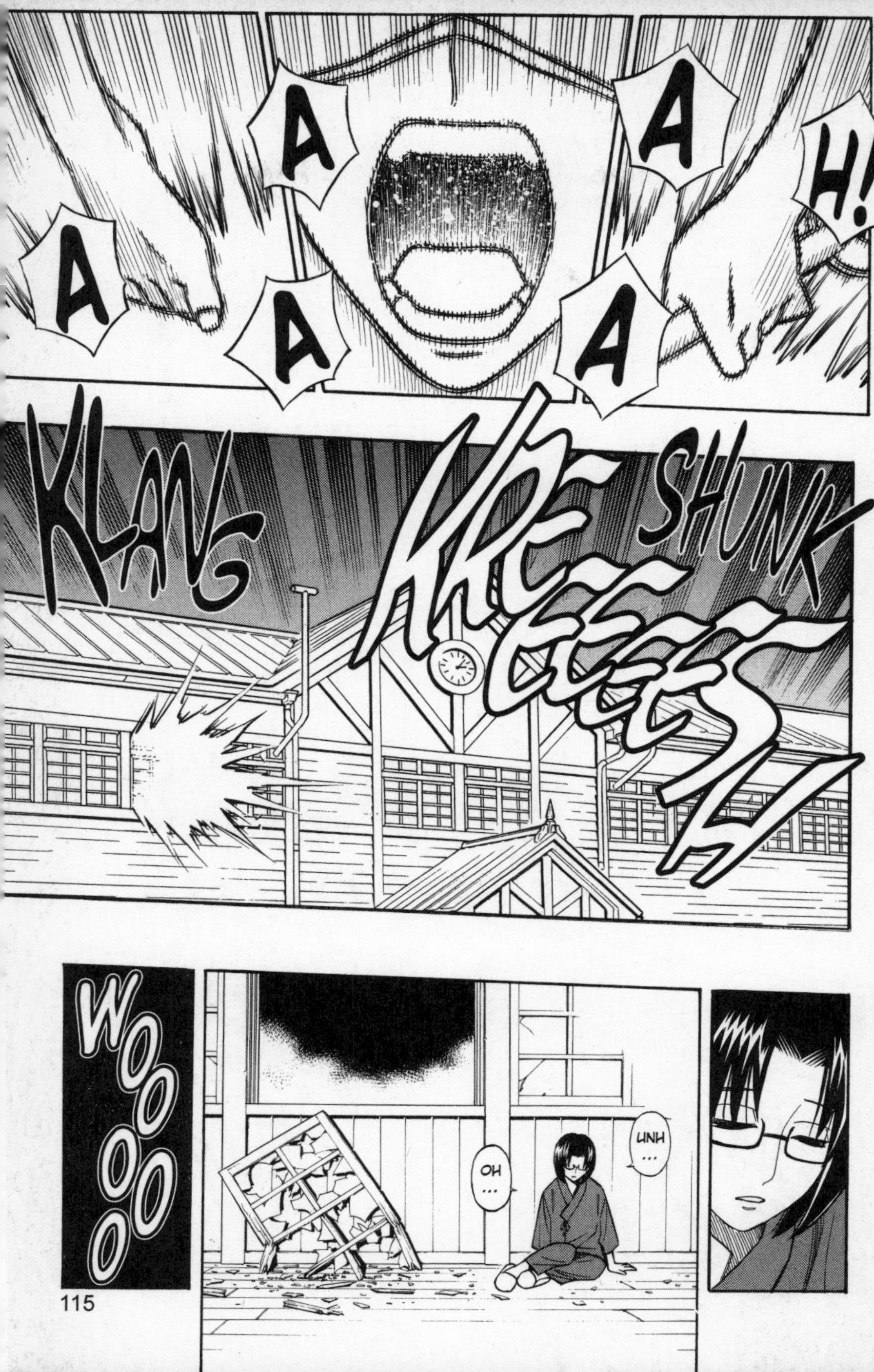
AAAAAAH!
SHUNK
KREEEEESH
KLANG
UNH ...
OH ...
WOOOOOO

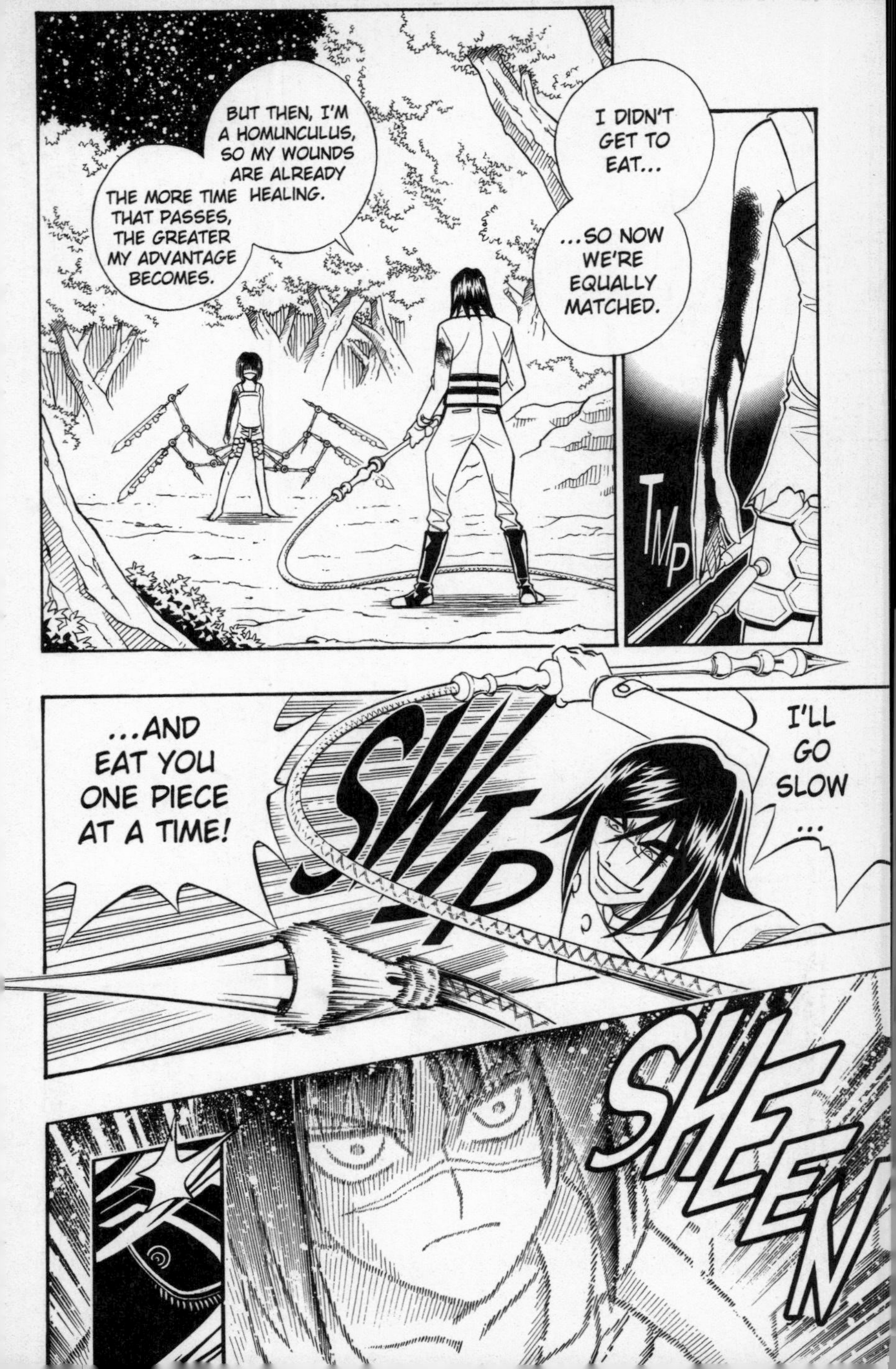
I DIDN'T GET TO EAT...
...SO NOW WE'RE EQUALLY MATCHED.
TMP
BUT THEN, I'M A HOMUNCULUS, SO MY WOUNDS ARE ALREADY HEALING.
THE MORE TIME THAT PASSES, THE GREATER MY ADVANTAGE BECOMES.
I'LL GO SLOW...
SWIP
...AND EAT YOU ONE PIECE AT A TIME!
SHEEN

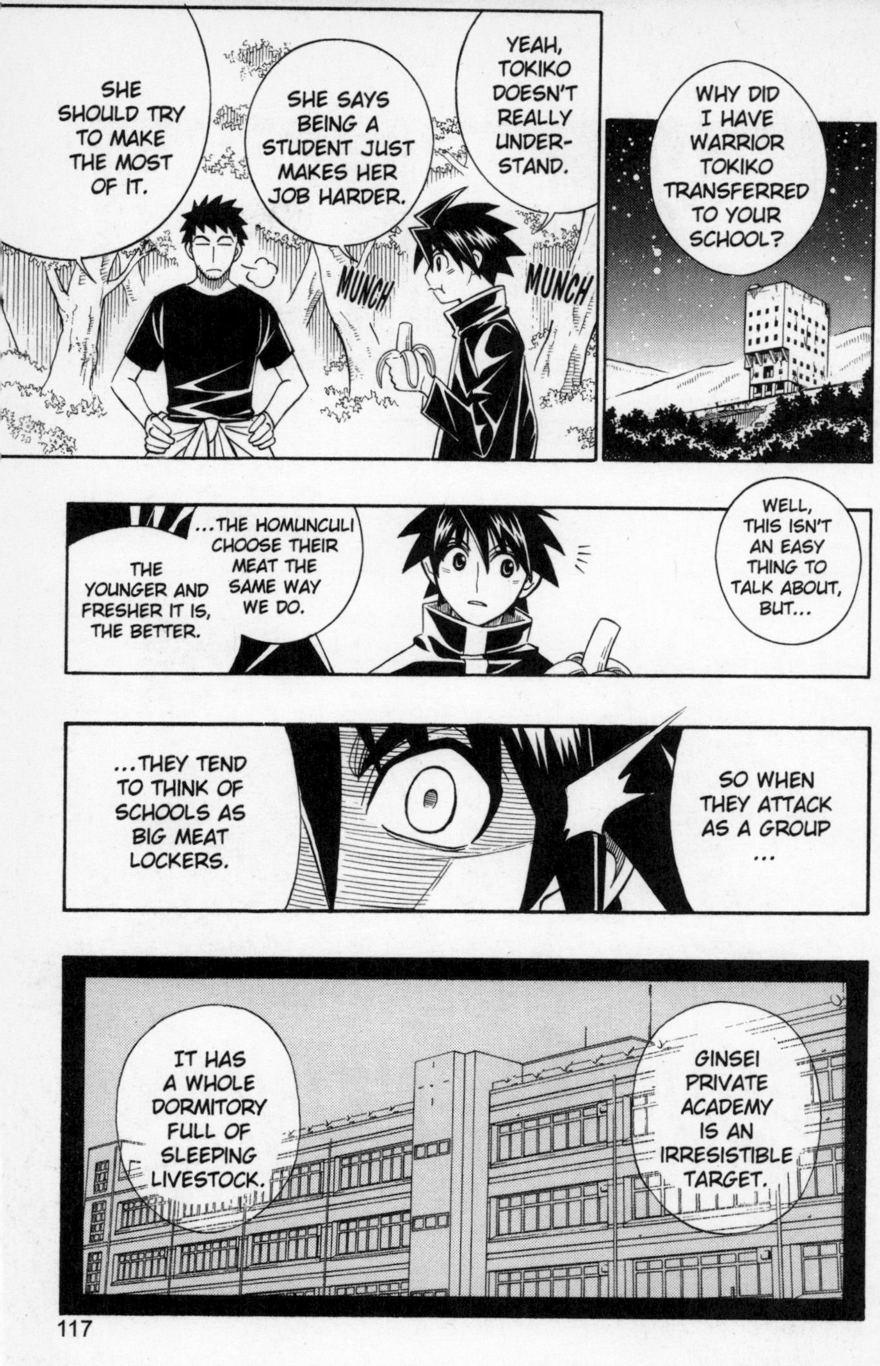
WHY DID I HAVE WARRIOR TOKIKO TRANSFERRED TO YOUR SCHOOL?
YEAH, TOKIKO DOESN'T REALLY UNDER-STAND.
MUNCH
SHE SAYS BEING A STUDENT JUST MAKES HER JOB HARDER.
MUNCH
SHE SHOULD TRY TO MAKE THE MOST OF IT.
WELL, THIS ISN'T AN EASY THING TO TALK ABOUT, BUT...
...THE HOMUNCULI CHOOSE THEIR MEAT THE SAME WAY WE DO.
THE YOUNGER AND FRESHER IT IS, THE BETTER.
SO WHEN THEY ATTACK AS A GROUP ...
...THEY TEND TO THINK OF SCHOOLS AS BIG MEAT LOCKERS.
GINSEI PRIVATE ACADEMY IS AN IRRESISTIBLE TARGET.
IT HAS A WHOLE DORMITORY FULL OF SLEEPING LIVESTOCK.

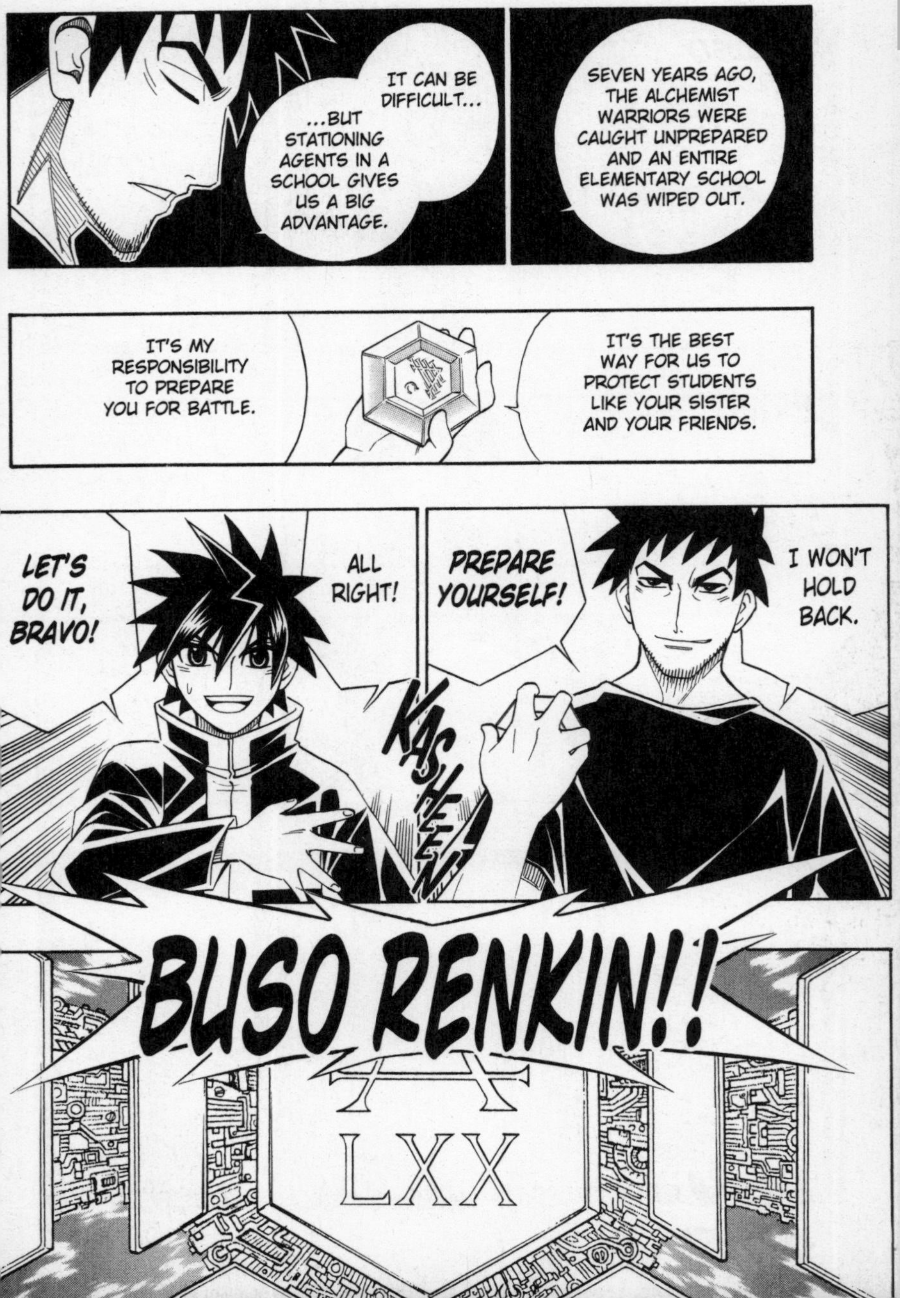
SEVEN YEARS AGO, THE ALCHEMIST WARRIORS WERE CAUGHT UNPREPARED AND AN ENTIRE ELEMENTARY SCHOOL WAS WIPED OUT.
IT CAN BE DIFFICULT...
...BUT STATIONING AGENTS IN A SCHOOL GIVES US A BIG ADVANTAGE.
IT'S THE BEST WAY FOR US TO PROTECT STUDENTS LIKE YOUR SISTER AND YOUR FRIENDS.
IT'S MY RESPONSIBILITY TO PREPARE YOU FOR BATTLE.
I WON'T HOLD BACK.
PREPARE YOURSELF!
ALL RIGHT!
LET'S DO IT, BRAVO!
KASHEEN
BUSO RENKIN!!
LXX

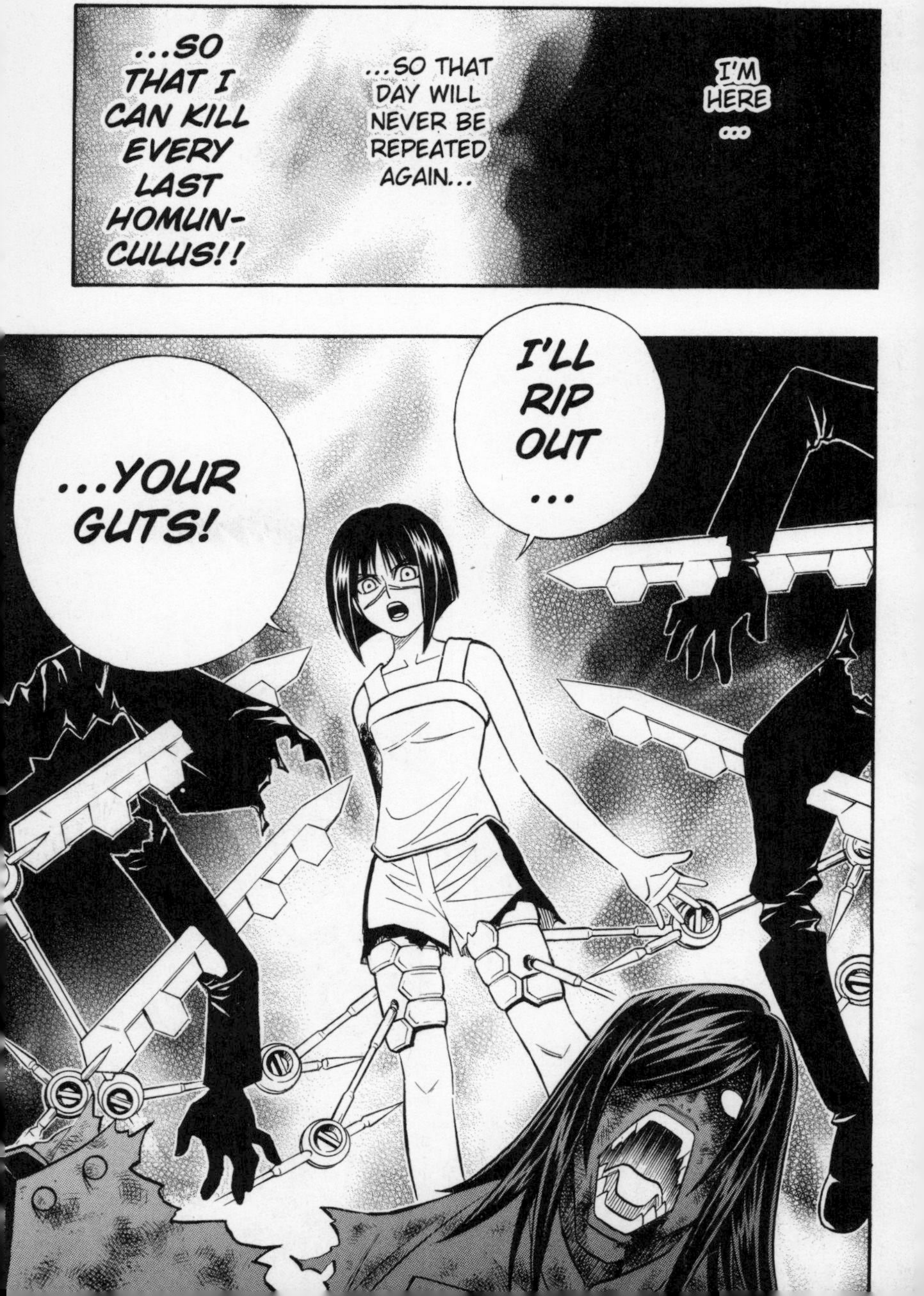
I'M HERE ...
...SO THAT DAY WILL NEVER BE REPEATED AGAIN...
...SO THAT I CAN KILL EVERY LAST HOMUN-CULUS!!
I'LL RIP OUT ...
...YOUR GUTS!

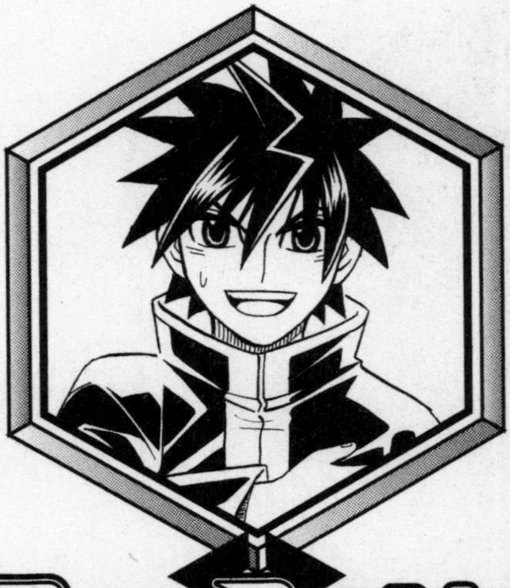

Buso Renkin

ブソウレンキン

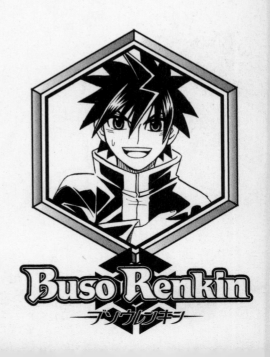

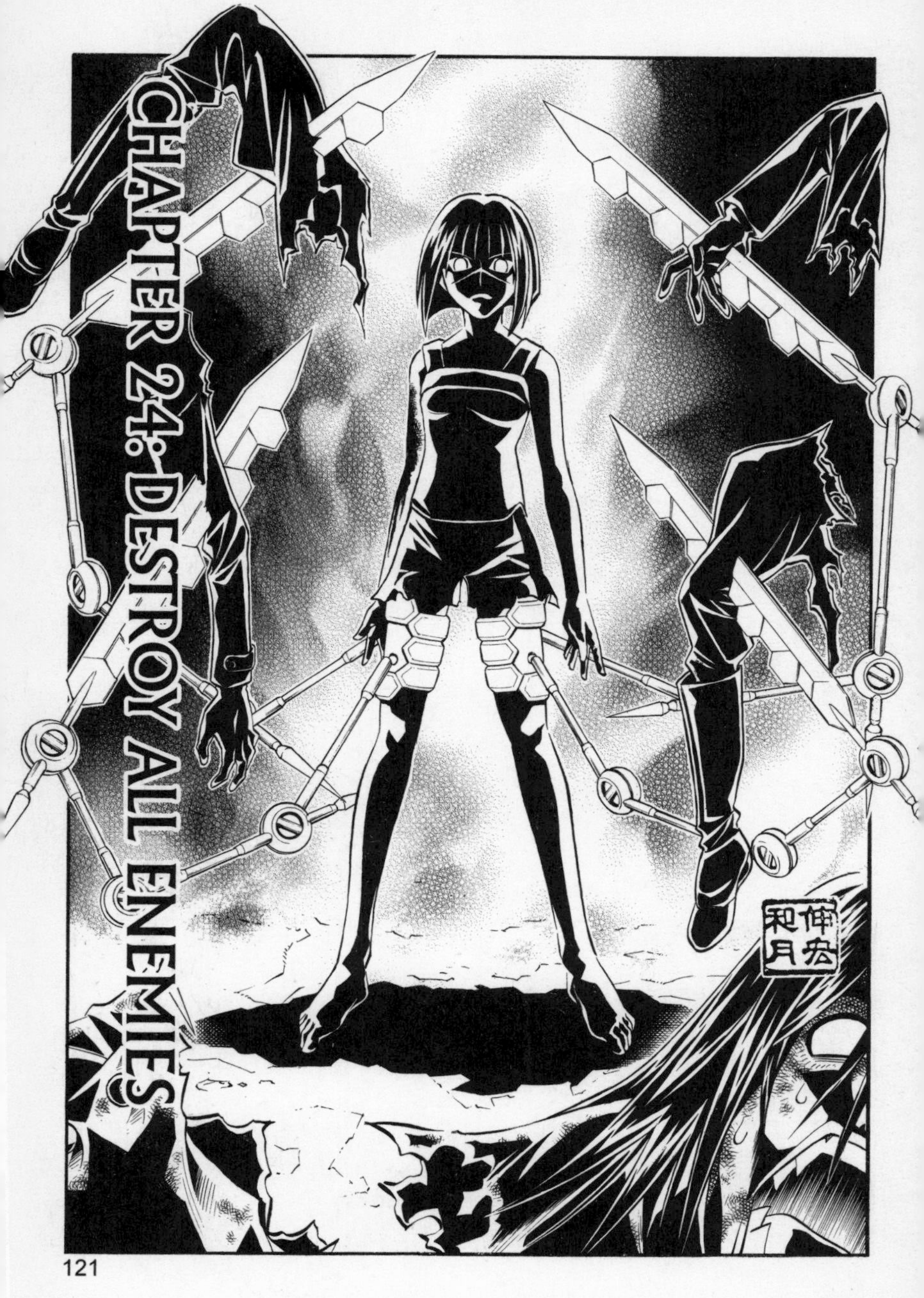
CHAPTER 24: DESTROY ALL ENEMIES
伸宏
和月

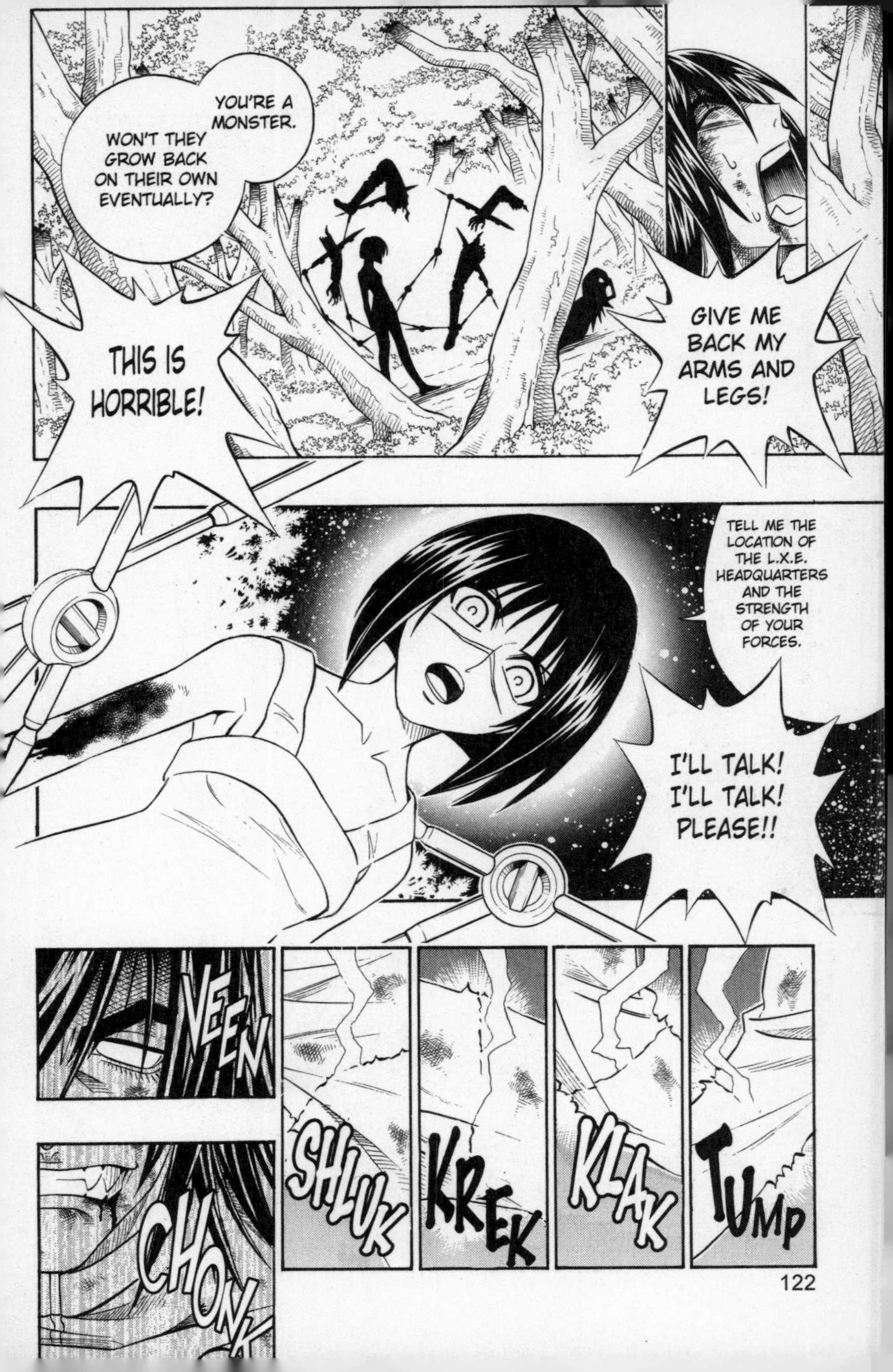
GIVE ME BACK MY ARMS AND LEGS!
YOU'RE A MONSTER.
WON'T THEY GROW BACK ON THEIR OWN EVENTUALLY?
THIS IS HORRIBLE!
TELL ME THE LOCATION OF THE L.X.E. HEADQUARTERS AND THE STRENGTH OF YOUR FORCES.
I'LL TALK! I'LL TALK! PLEASE!!
TUMP
KLAK
KREK
SHLUK
VEEN
CHONK

READ THIS WAY

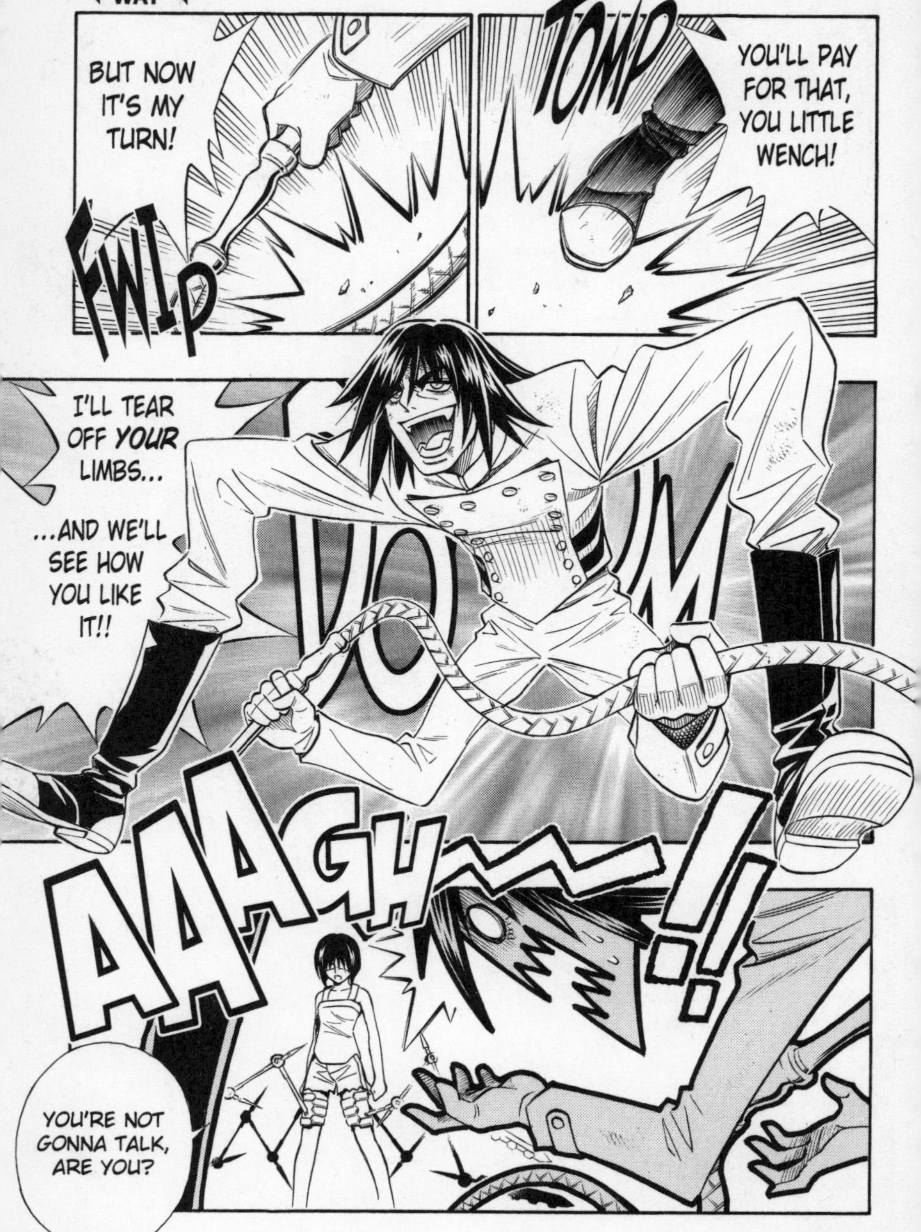
TOMP
YOU'LL PAY FOR THAT, YOU LITTLE WENCH!
BUT NOW IT'S MY TURN!
FWIP
I'LL TEAR OFF *YOUR* LIMBS...
...AND WE'LL SEE HOW YOU LIKE IT!!
VOOM
AAAGH!!
YOU'RE NOT GONNA TALK, ARE YOU?

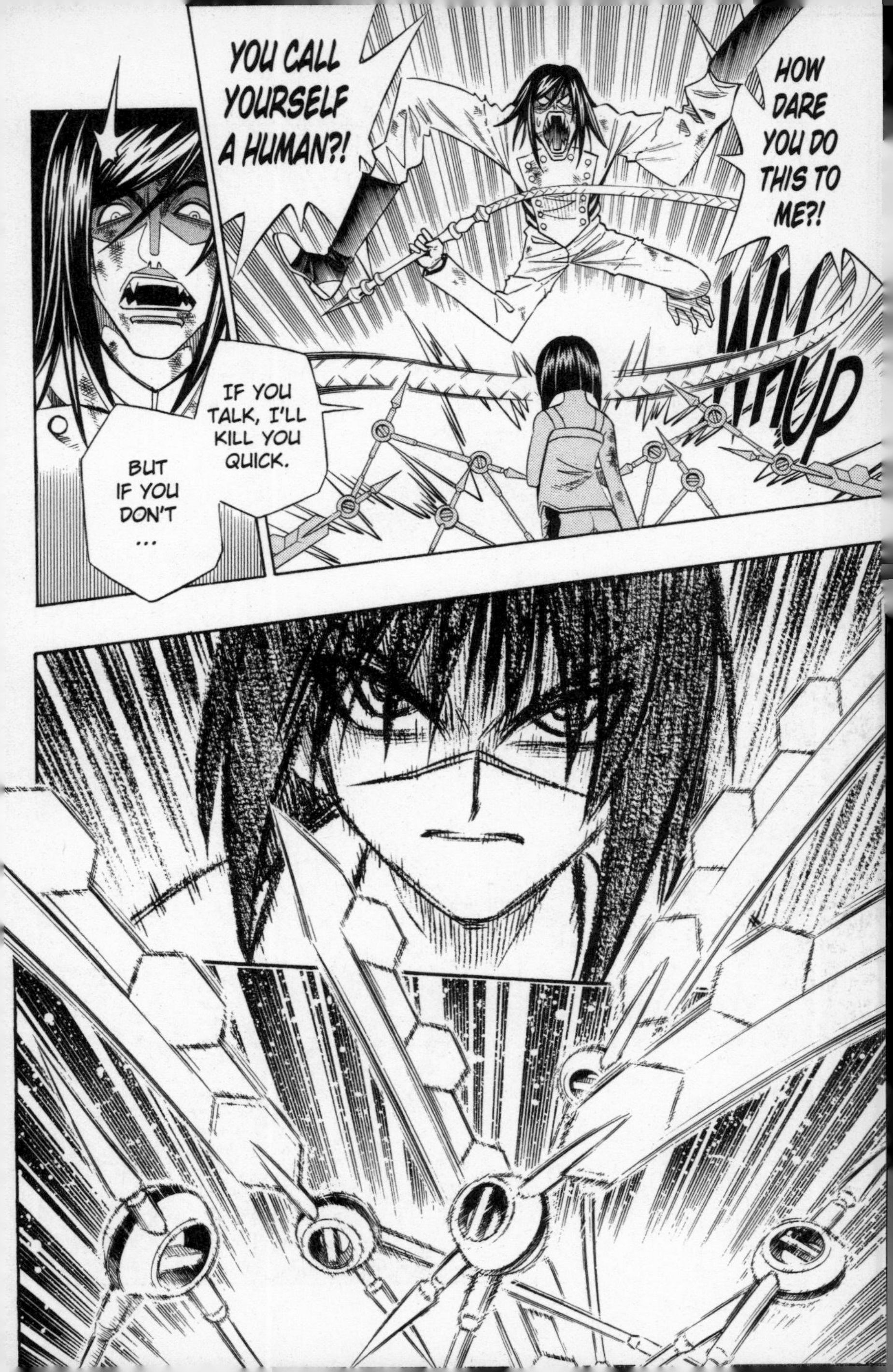
HOW DARE YOU DO THIS TO ME?!
YOU CALL YOURSELF A HUMAN?!
WHUP
IF YOU TALK, I'LL KILL YOU QUICK.
BUT IF YOU DON'T ...

HUFF...

HUFF...

IT HURTS ...

IT HURTS ...

AGH ...

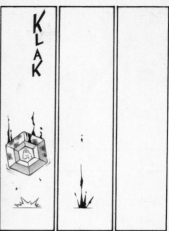

KLAK

ZZZAK

"IF YOU DON'T, YOU'LL SUFFER THE TORMENTS OF HELL BEFORE YOU DIE."

TWITCH

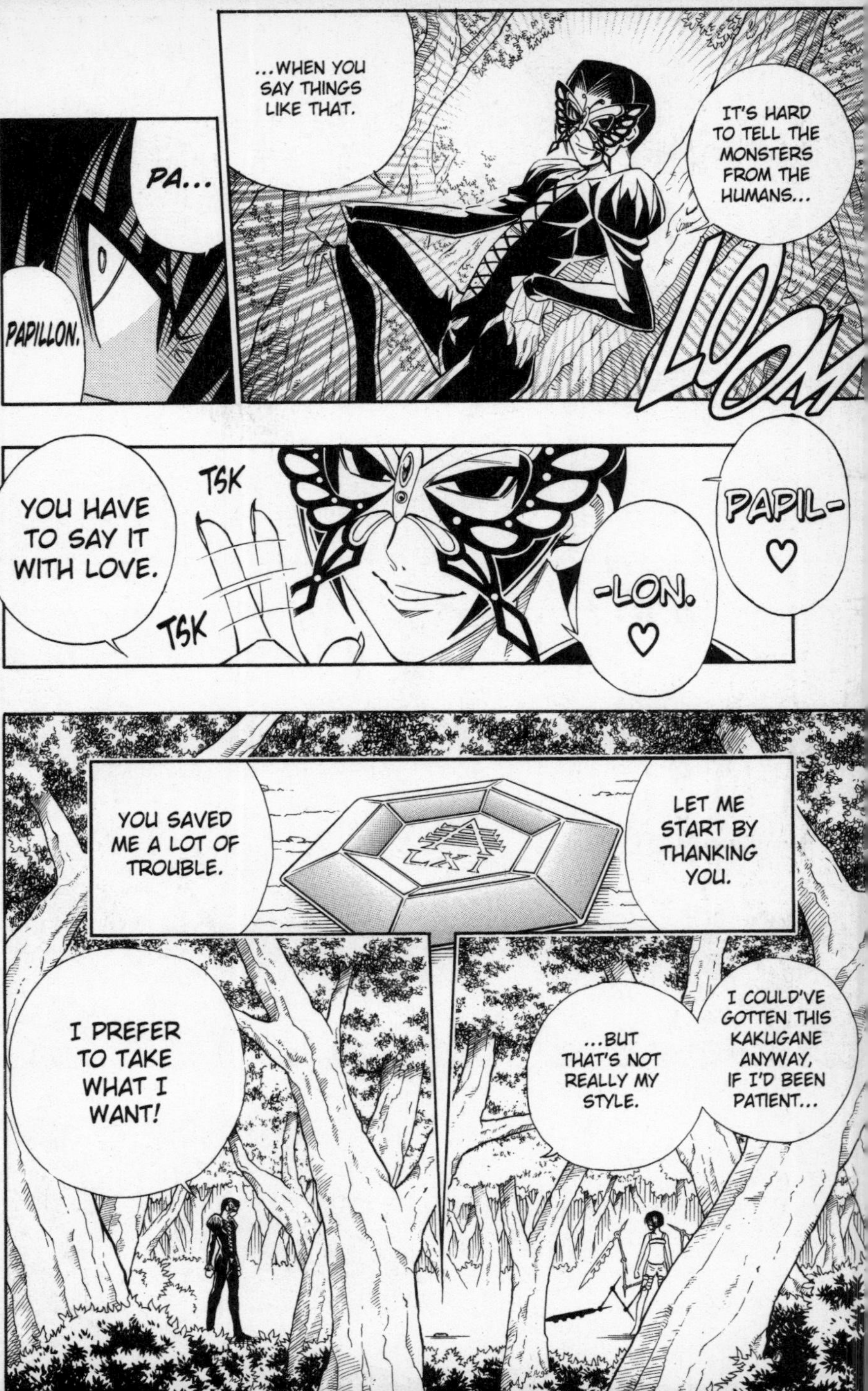
IT'S HARD TO TELL THE MONSTERS FROM THE HUMANS...
...WHEN YOU SAY THINGS LIKE THAT.
LOOM
PA...
PAPILLON.
PAPIL- ♡
-LON. ♡
TSK
TSK
YOU HAVE TO SAY IT WITH LOVE.
LET ME START BY THANKING YOU.
YOU SAVED ME A LOT OF TROUBLE.
LXI
I COULD'VE GOTTEN THIS KAKUGANE ANYWAY, IF I'D BEEN PATIENT...
...BUT THAT'S NOT REALLY MY STYLE.
I PREFER TO TAKE WHAT I WANT!

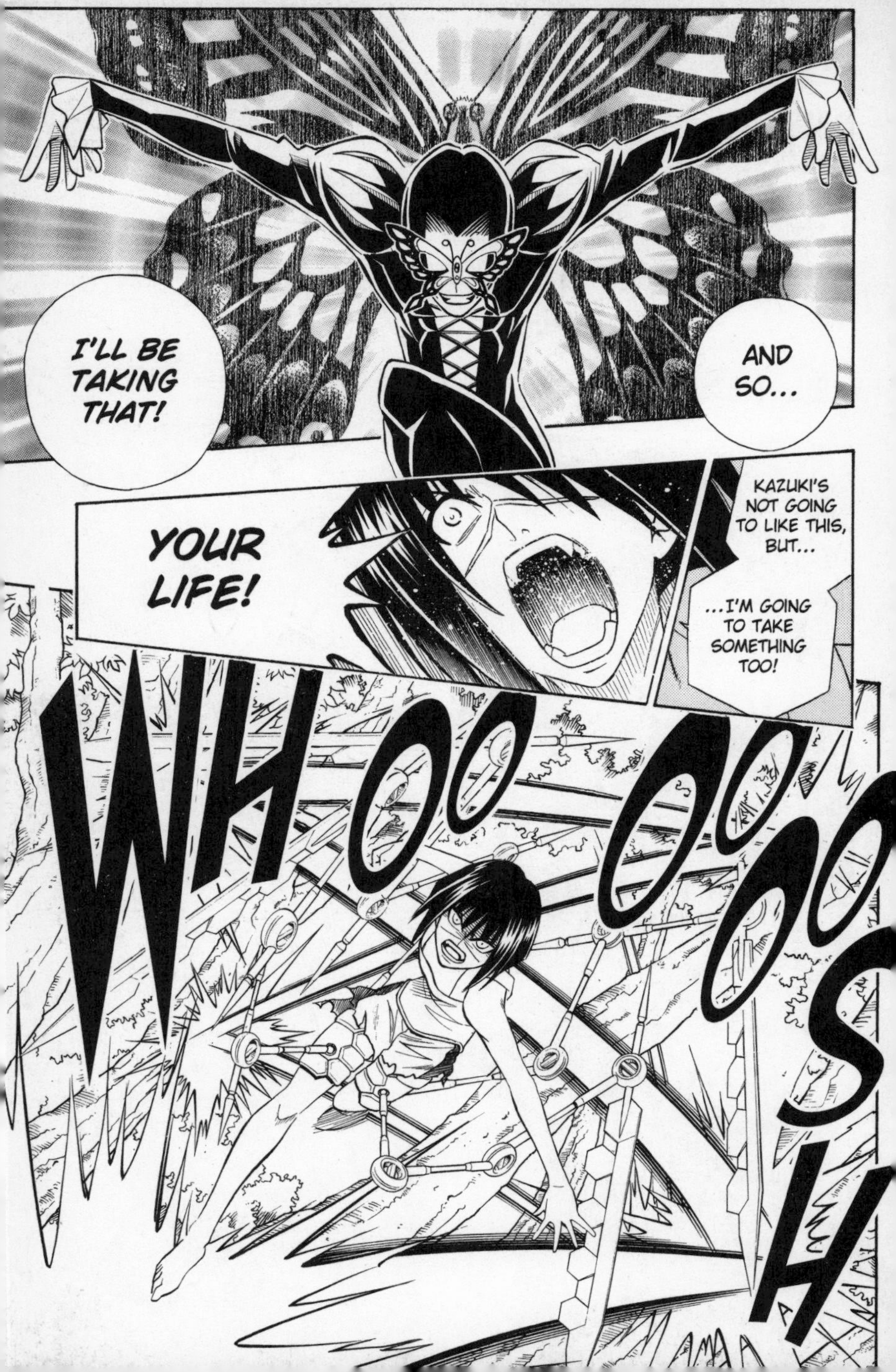
AND SO...
I'LL BE TAKING THAT!
KAZUKI'S NOT GOING TO LIKE THIS, BUT...
...I'M GOING TO TAKE SOMETHING TOO!
YOUR LIFE!
WHOOOOOOOOSH

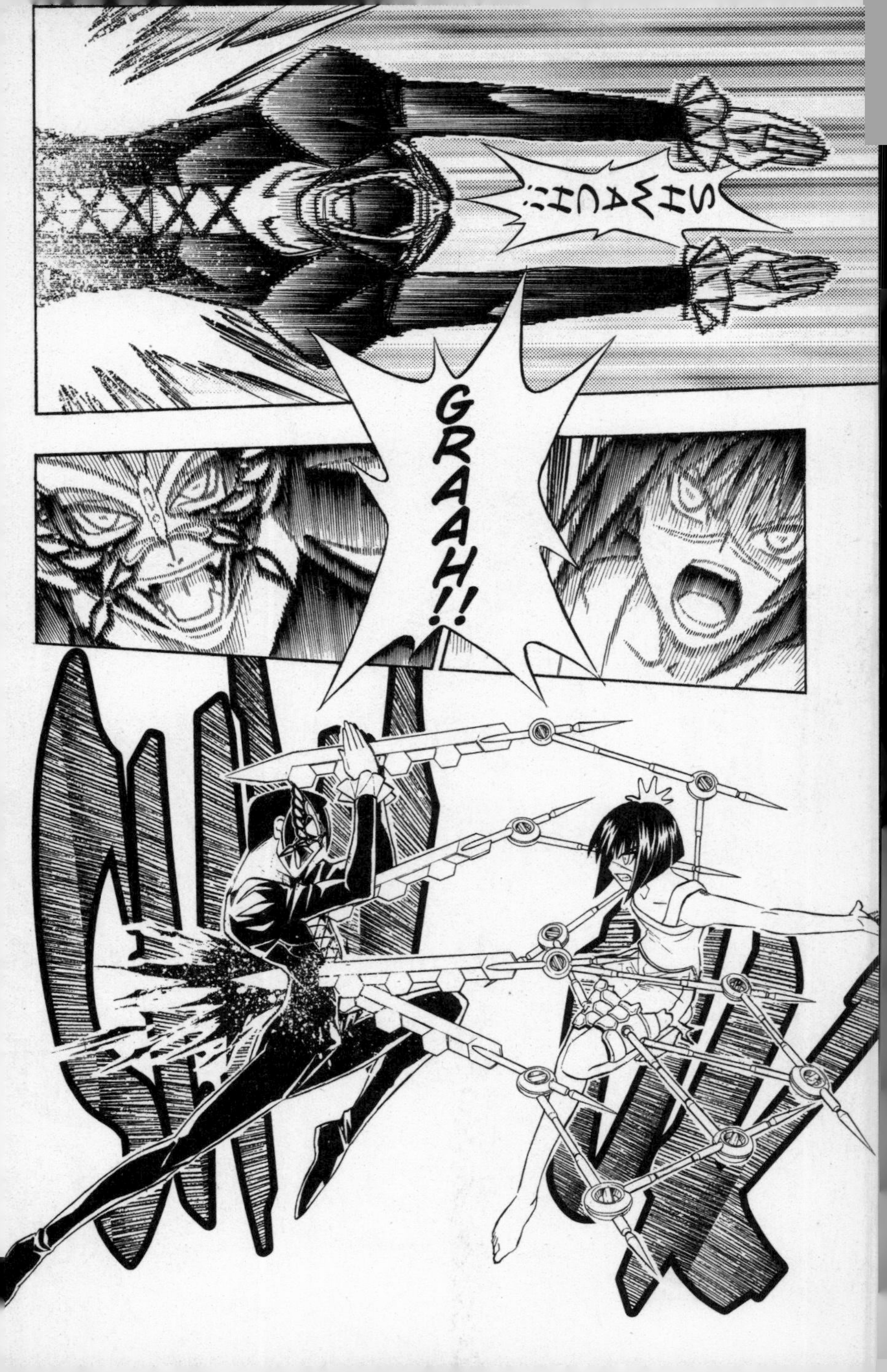
SHWACH!!
GRAAAH!!

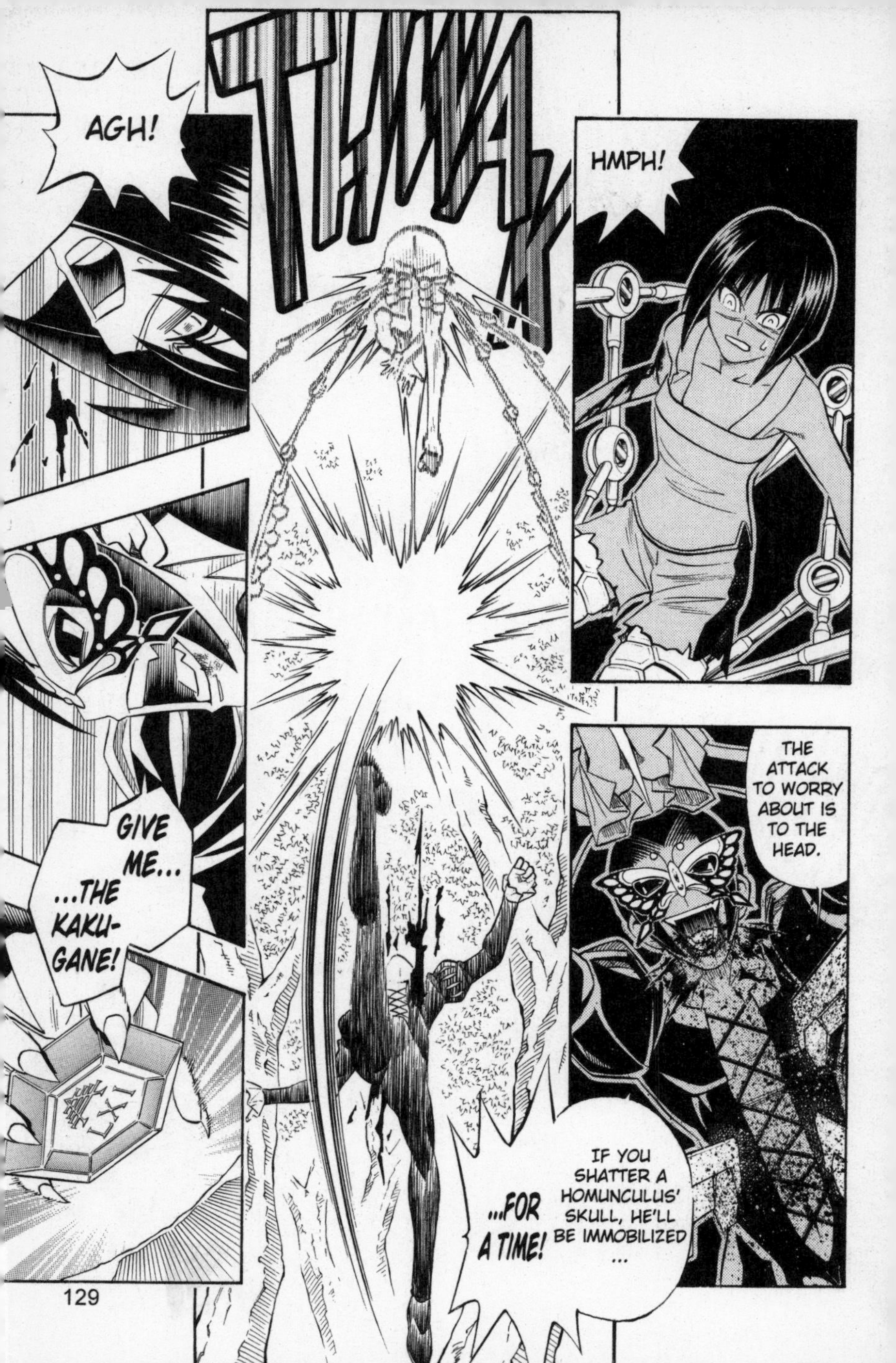
HMPH!
THE ATTACK TO WORRY ABOUT IS TO THE HEAD.
IF YOU SHATTER A HOMUNCULUS' SKULL, HE'LL BE IMMOBILIZED...
...FOR A TIME!
THWAK
AGH!
GIVE ME... ...THE KAKU-GANE!

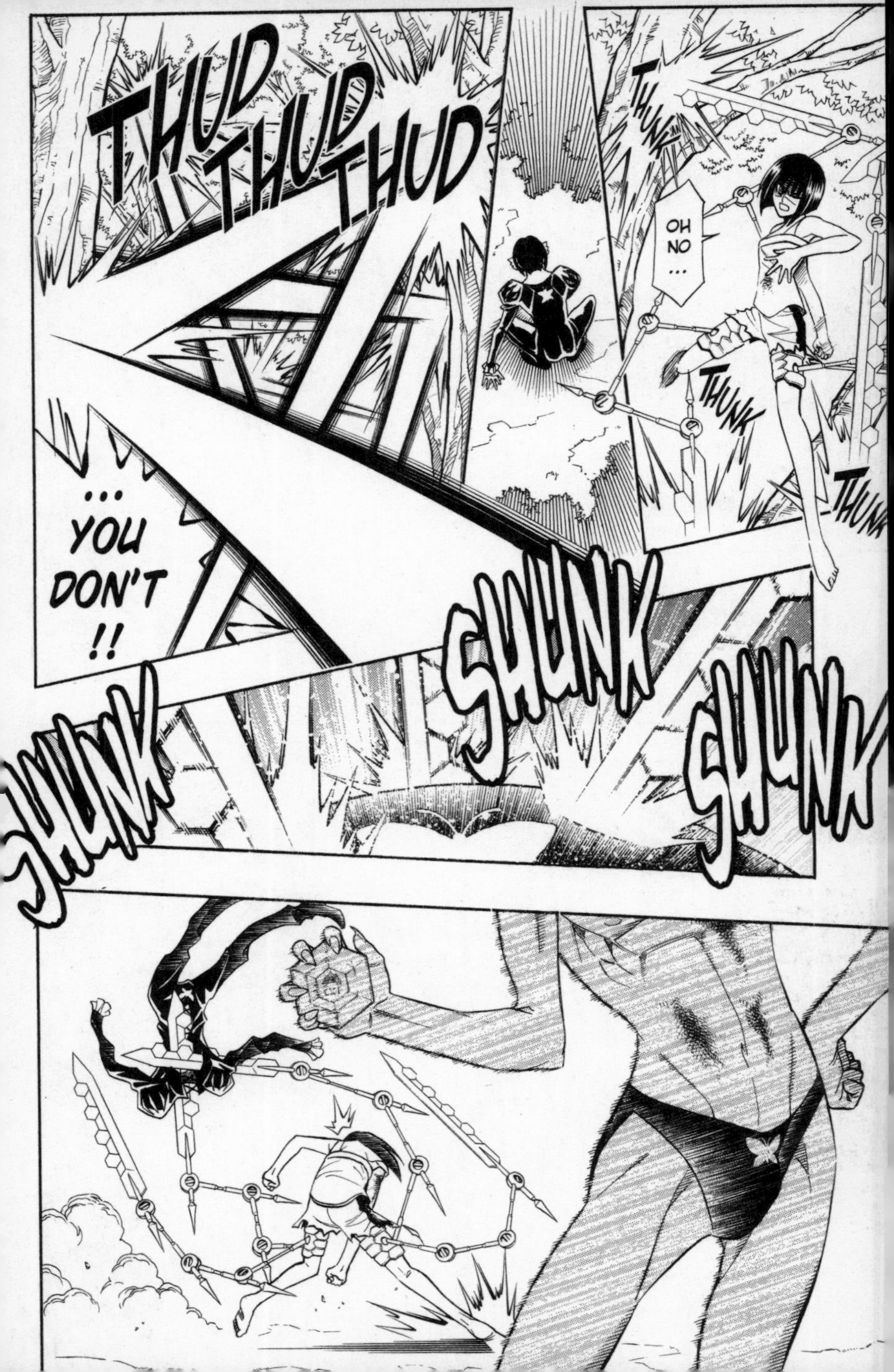
THUNK
OH NO ...
THUNK
THUNK
THUD THUD THUD
... YOU DON'T !!
SHUNK
SHUNK
SHUNK

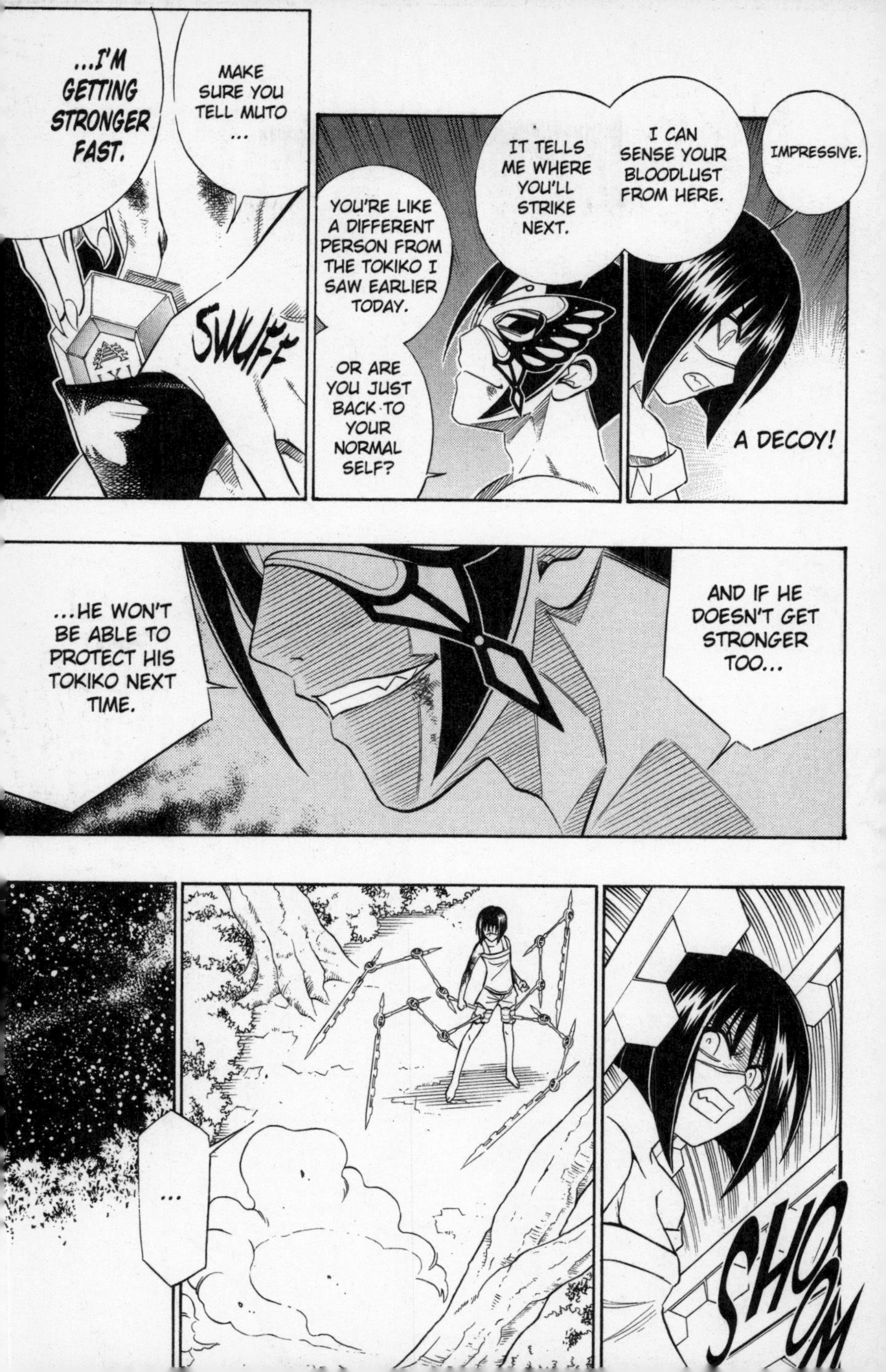
IMPRESSIVE.
A DECOY!
I CAN SENSE YOUR BLOODLUST FROM HERE.
IT TELLS ME WHERE YOU'LL STRIKE NEXT.
YOU'RE LIKE A DIFFERENT PERSON FROM THE TOKIKO I SAW EARLIER TODAY.
OR ARE YOU JUST BACK TO YOUR NORMAL SELF?
MAKE SURE YOU TELL MUTO ...
...I'M GETTING STRONGER FAST.
SWUFF
AND IF HE DOESN'T GET STRONGER TOO...
...HE WON'T BE ABLE TO PROTECT HIS TOKIKO NEXT TIME.
SHOM
...

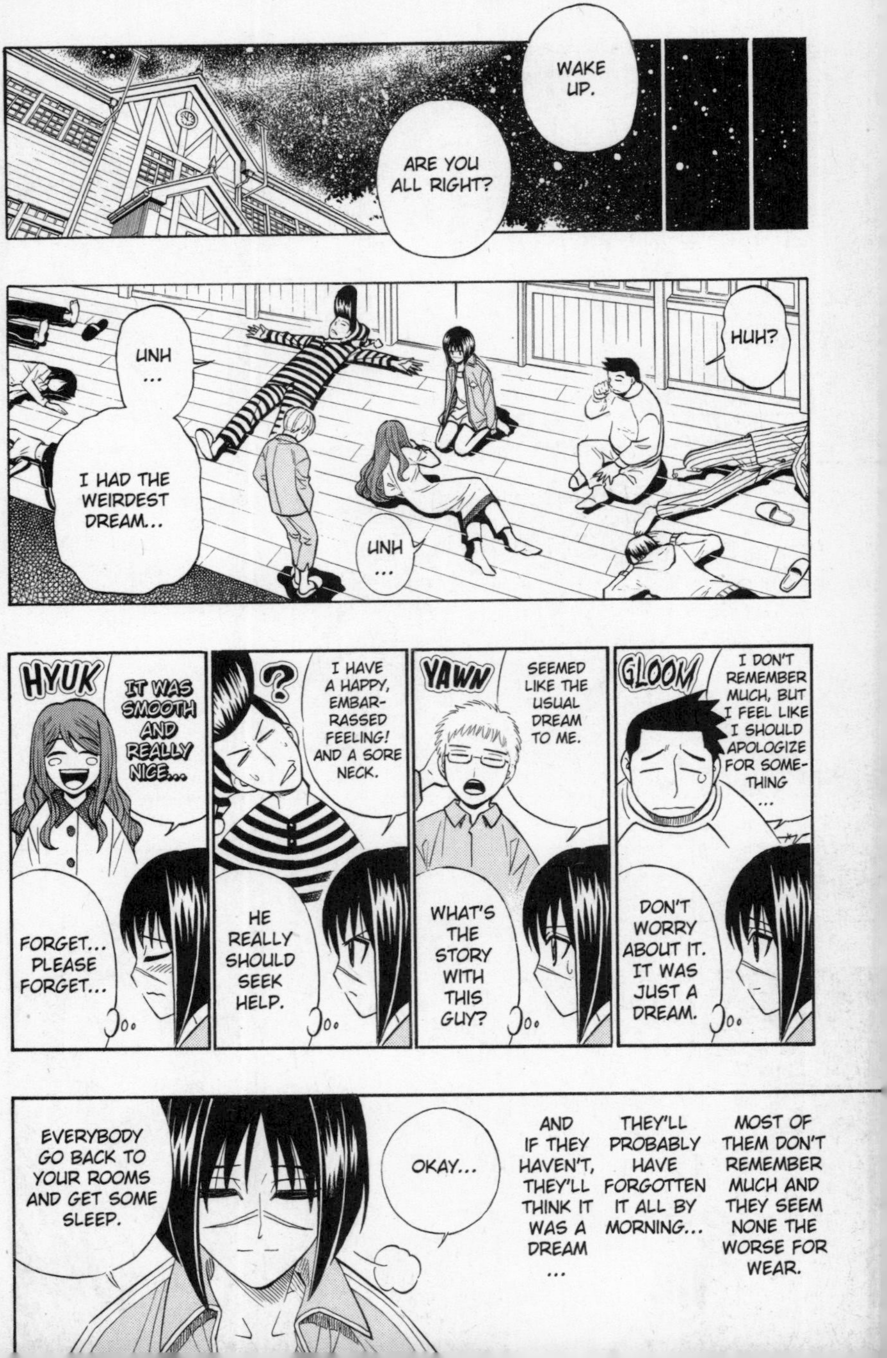
WAKE UP.
ARE YOU ALL RIGHT?
HUH?
UNH ...
I HAD THE WEIRDEST DREAM...
UNH ...
GLOOM
I DON'T REMEMBER MUCH, BUT I FEEL LIKE I SHOULD APOLOGIZE FOR SOMETHING ...
DON'T WORRY ABOUT IT. IT WAS JUST A DREAM.
YAWN
SEEMED LIKE THE USUAL DREAM TO ME.
WHAT'S THE STORY WITH THIS GUY?
?
I HAVE A HAPPY, EMBARRASSED FEELING! AND A SORE NECK.
HE REALLY SHOULD SEEK HELP.
HYUK
IT WAS SMOOTH AND REALLY NICE...
FORGET... PLEASE FORGET...
MOST OF THEM DON'T REMEMBER MUCH AND THEY SEEM NONE THE WORSE FOR WEAR.
THEY'LL PROBABLY HAVE FORGOTTEN IT ALL BY MORNING...
AND IF THEY HAVEN'T, THEY'LL THINK IT WAS A DREAM ...
OKAY...
EVERYBODY GO BACK TO YOUR ROOMS AND GET SOME SLEEP.

READ THIS WAY

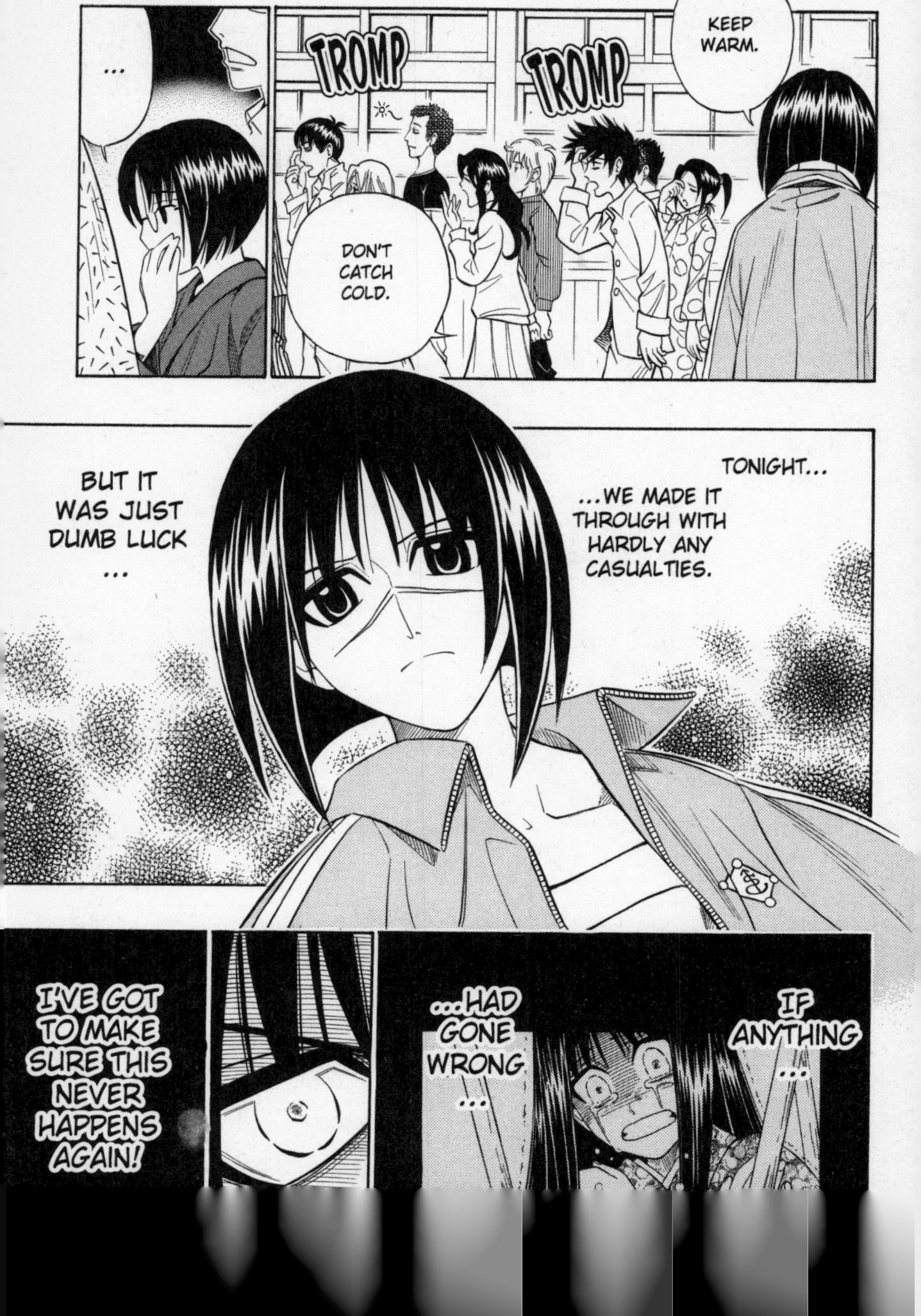
KEEP WARM.
TROMP
TROMP
DON'T CATCH COLD.
...
TONIGHT...
...WE MADE IT THROUGH WITH HARDLY ANY CASUALTIES.
BUT IT WAS JUST DUMB LUCK...
IF ANYTHING...
...HAD GONE WRONG...
I'VE GOT TO MAKE SURE THIS NEVER HAPPENS AGAIN!

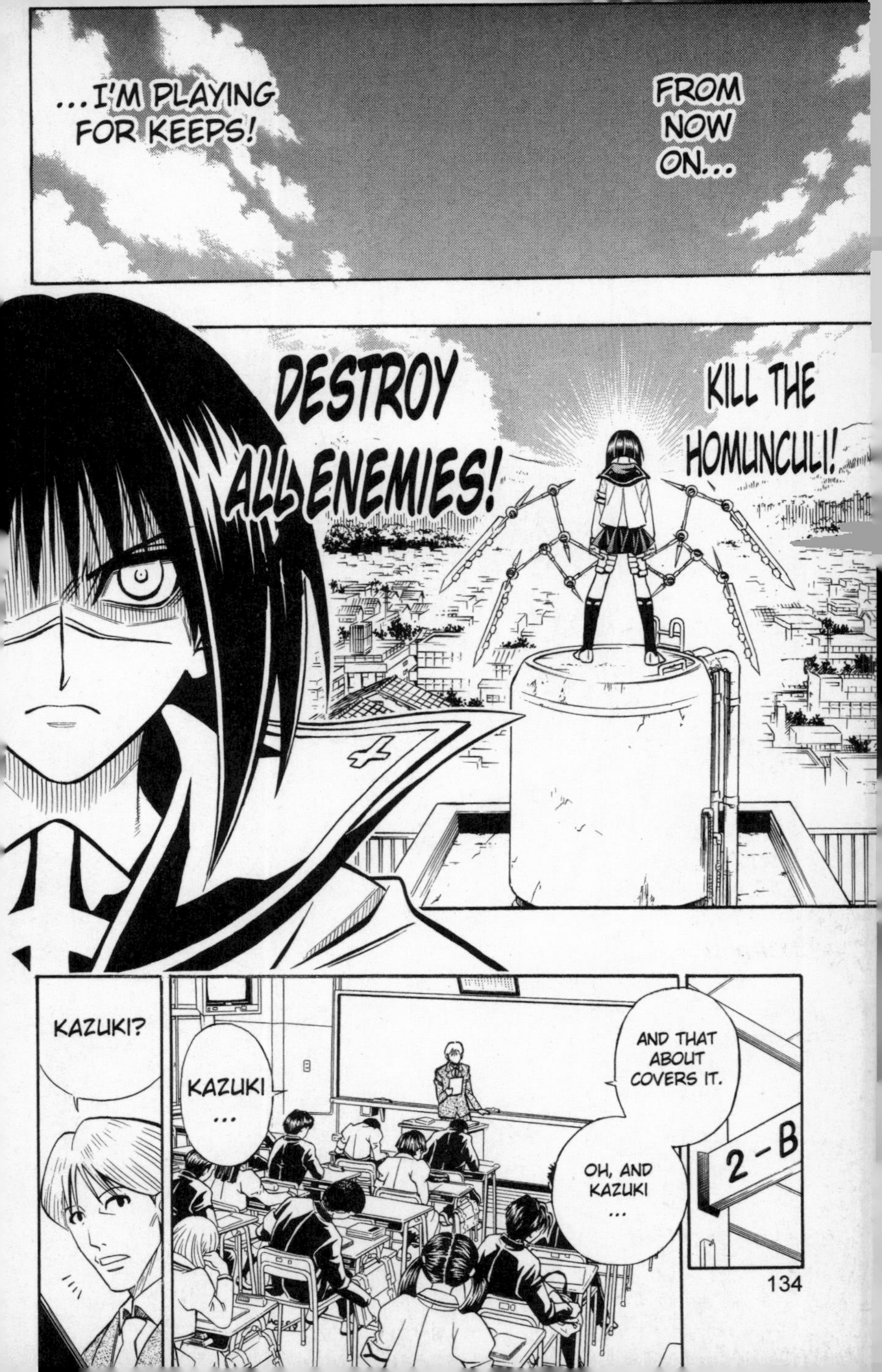
FROM NOW ON...
...I'M PLAYING FOR KEEPS!
KILL THE HOMUNCULI!
DESTROY ALL ENEMIES!
2-B
AND THAT ABOUT COVERS IT.
OH, AND KAZUKI ...
KAZUKI ...
KAZUKI?

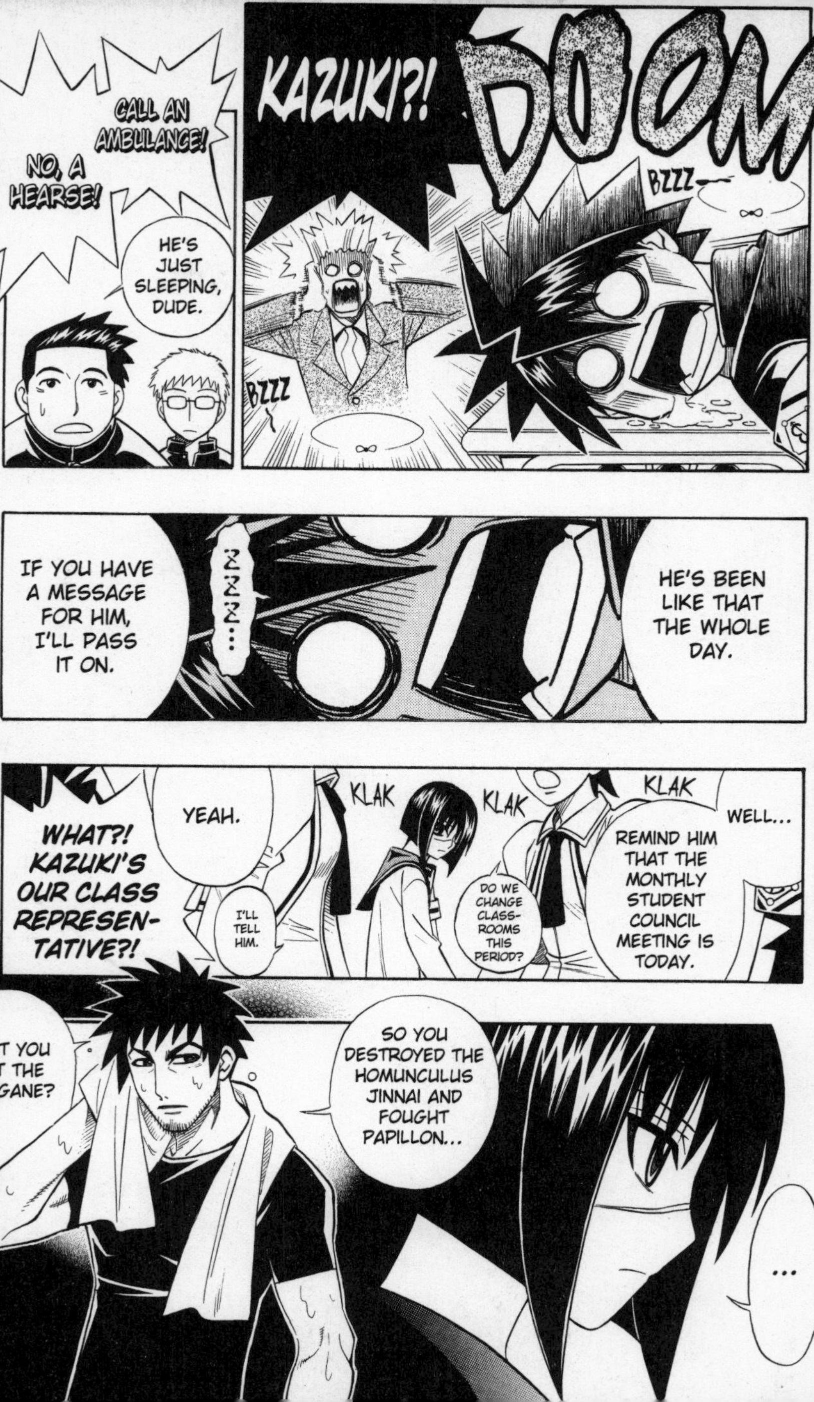
DOOM
BZZZ
KAZUKI?!
BZZZ
CALL AN AMBULANCE!
NO, A HEARSE!
HE'S JUST SLEEPING, DUDE.
HE'S BEEN LIKE THAT THE WHOLE DAY.
ZZZZ...
IF YOU HAVE A MESSAGE FOR HIM, I'LL PASS IT ON.
WELL...
REMIND HIM THAT THE MONTHLY STUDENT COUNCIL MEETING IS TODAY.
KLAK
DO WE CHANGE CLASS-ROOMS THIS PERIOD?
KLAK
KLAK
YEAH.
I'LL TELL HIM.
WHAT?! KAZUKI'S OUR CLASS REPRESEN-TATIVE?!
...
SO YOU DESTROYED THE HOMUNCULUS JINNAI AND FOUGHT PAPILLON...
...BUT YOU LOST THE KAKUGANE?

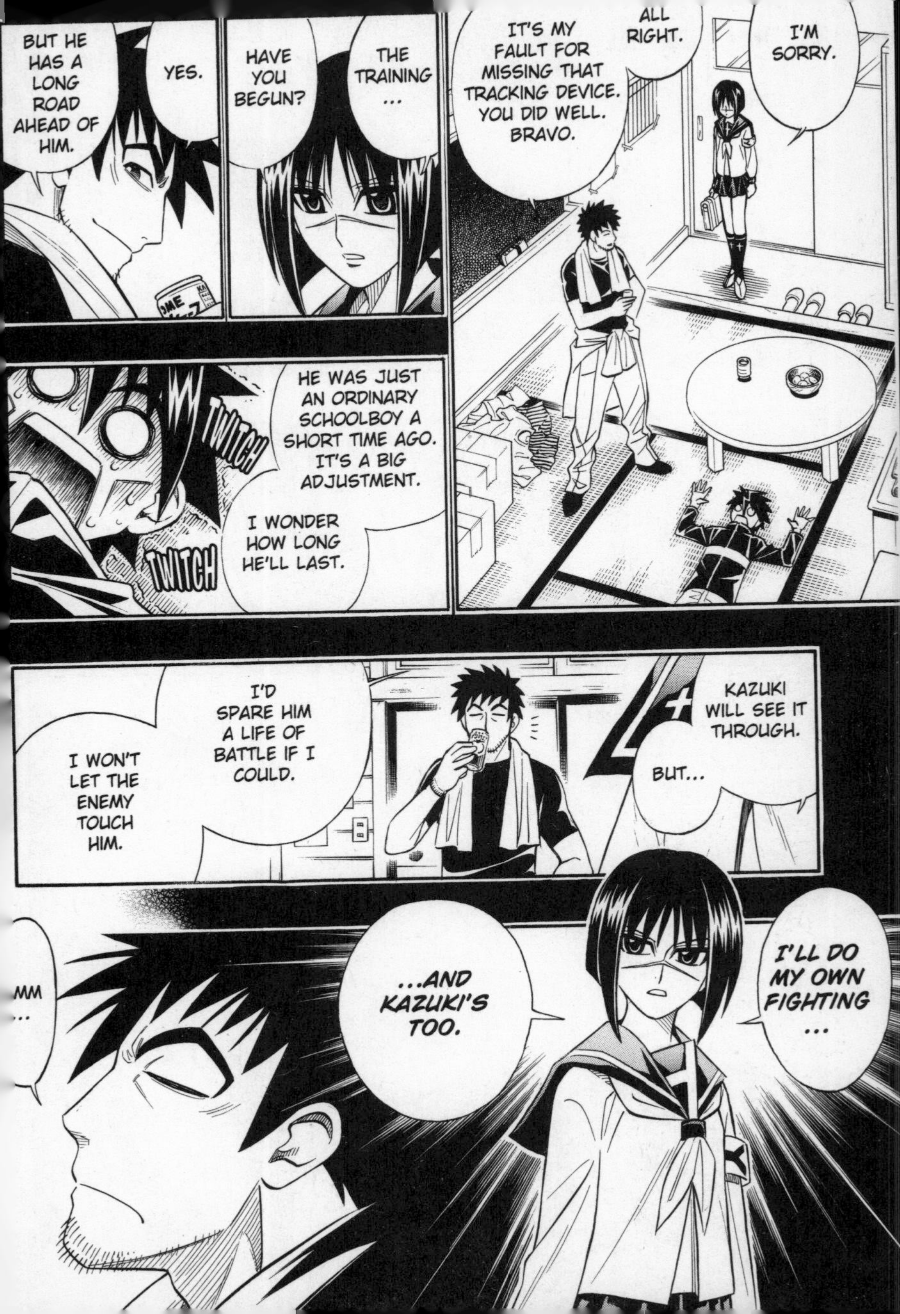
I'M SORRY.
ALL RIGHT.
IT'S MY FAULT FOR MISSING THAT TRACKING DEVICE. YOU DID WELL. BRAVO.
THE TRAINING ...
HAVE YOU BEGUN?
YES.
BUT HE HAS A LONG ROAD AHEAD OF HIM.
HE WAS JUST AN ORDINARY SCHOOLBOY A SHORT TIME AGO. IT'S A BIG ADJUSTMENT.
I WONDER HOW LONG HE'LL LAST.
TWITCH
TWITCH
KAZUKI WILL SEE IT THROUGH.
BUT...
I'D SPARE HIM A LIFE OF BATTLE IF I COULD.
I WON'T LET THE ENEMY TOUCH HIM.
I'LL DO MY OWN FIGHTING ...
...AND KAZUKI'S TOO.
MM ...

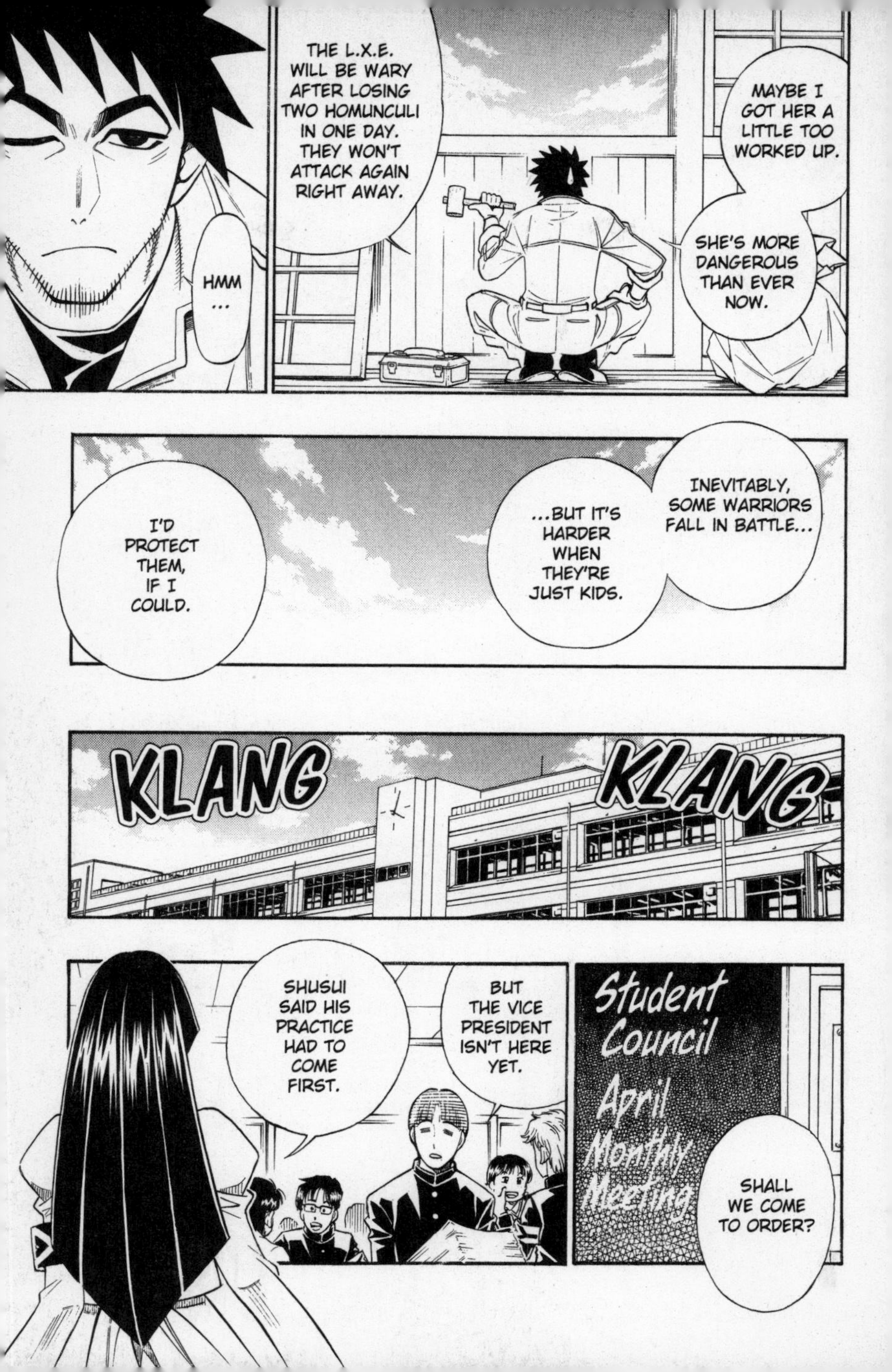
MAYBE I GOT HER A LITTLE TOO WORKED UP.
SHE'S MORE DANGEROUS THAN EVER NOW.
THE L.X.E. WILL BE WARY AFTER LOSING TWO HOMUNCULI IN ONE DAY. THEY WON'T ATTACK AGAIN RIGHT AWAY.
HMM ...
INEVITABLY, SOME WARRIORS FALL IN BATTLE...
...BUT IT'S HARDER WHEN THEY'RE JUST KIDS.
I'D PROTECT THEM, IF I COULD.
KLANG
KLANG
Student Council
April Monthly Meeting
SHALL WE COME TO ORDER?
BUT THE VICE PRESIDENT ISN'T HERE YET.
SHUSUI SAID HIS PRACTICE HAD TO COME FIRST.

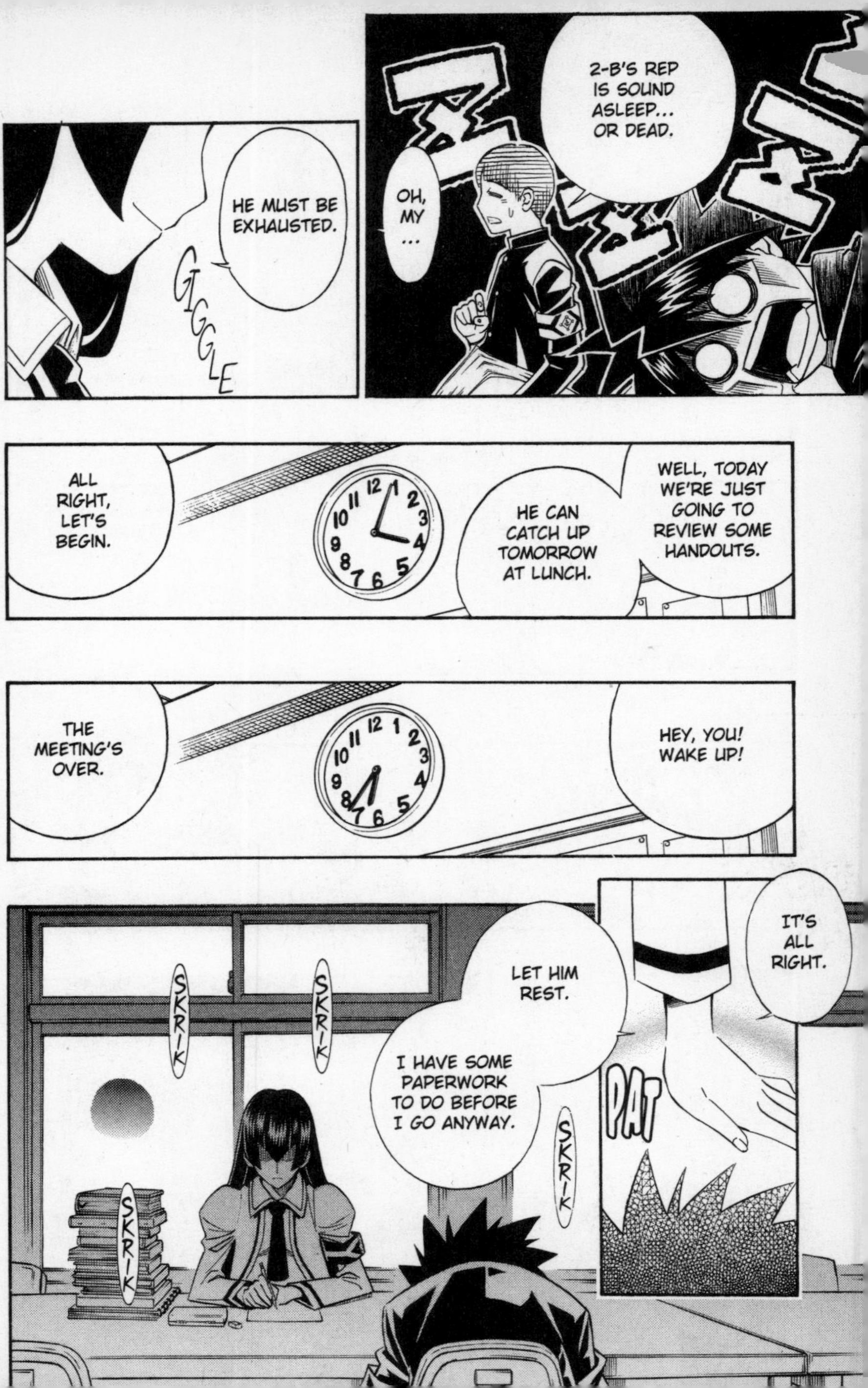

2-B'S REP IS SOUND ASLEEP... OR DEAD.
OH, MY ...
HE MUST BE EXHAUSTED.
GIGGLE
WELL, TODAY WE'RE JUST GOING TO REVIEW SOME HANDOUTS.
HE CAN CATCH UP TOMORROW AT LUNCH.
ALL RIGHT, LET'S BEGIN.
HEY, YOU! WAKE UP!
THE MEETING'S OVER.
IT'S ALL RIGHT.
PAT
LET HIM REST.
I HAVE SOME PAPERWORK TO DO BEFORE I GO ANYWAY.
SKRIK
SKRIK
SKRIK
SKRIK

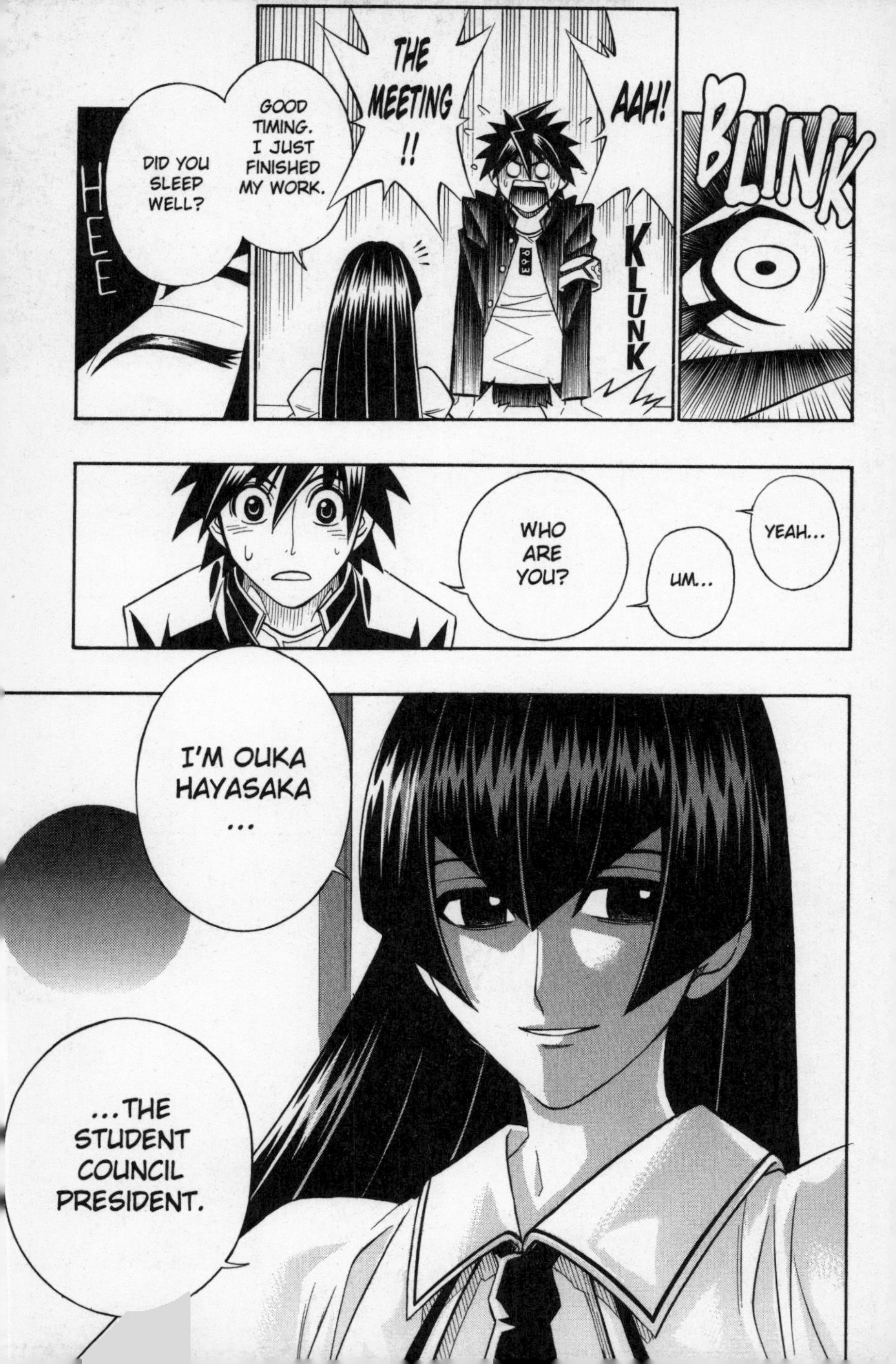
BLINK
KLUNK
AAH!
THE MEETING!!
GOOD TIMING. I JUST FINISHED MY WORK.
DID YOU SLEEP WELL?
HEE
YEAH...
UM...
WHO ARE YOU?
I'M OUKA HAYASAKA...
...THE STUDENT COUNCIL PRESIDENT.

- Height: 177cm; Weight: 65kg
- Born: March 21; Aries; Blood Type B; Age 21
- Likes: 1/f Yuragi (sonic pattern of fluctuation)
- Dislikes: Dogs, flamboyant people
- Hobby: Listening to music
- Special Ability: Breeding pets
- Affiliation: L.X.E.

Character File No. 16
Homunculus Jinnai

Author's Notes

- I created this character after my original idea to have the Homunculus Hanabuki fight in the dormitory got canned.
- He was inspired by Hyoko Otowa from Rurouni Kenshin. He's the opposite of Kinjo. His outfit is based on the one worn by the American comic book character, the Rocketeer. Or rather, it's evocative of that era's flight attire. The more I research 19th and early 20th century fashions, the more I'm attracted to them.
- When I came up with this character, I didn't want him to just be good-looking. So Jinnai's sort of handsome, but sort of creepy too. I like how he turned out.
- I've always wanted to switch the arms and legs around on an immortal character. Those of you who collect action figures know where I'm coming from.

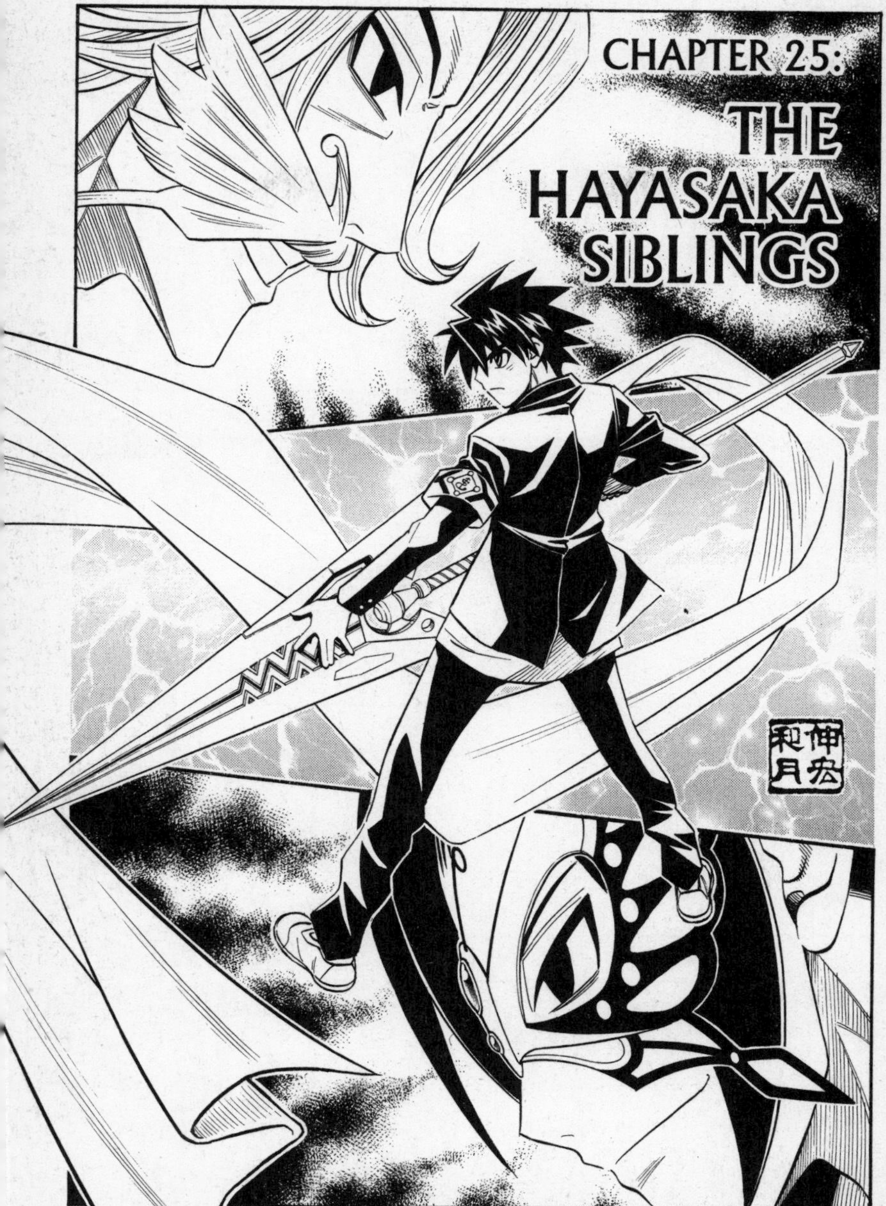
CHAPTER 25:
THE HAYASAKA SIBLINGS

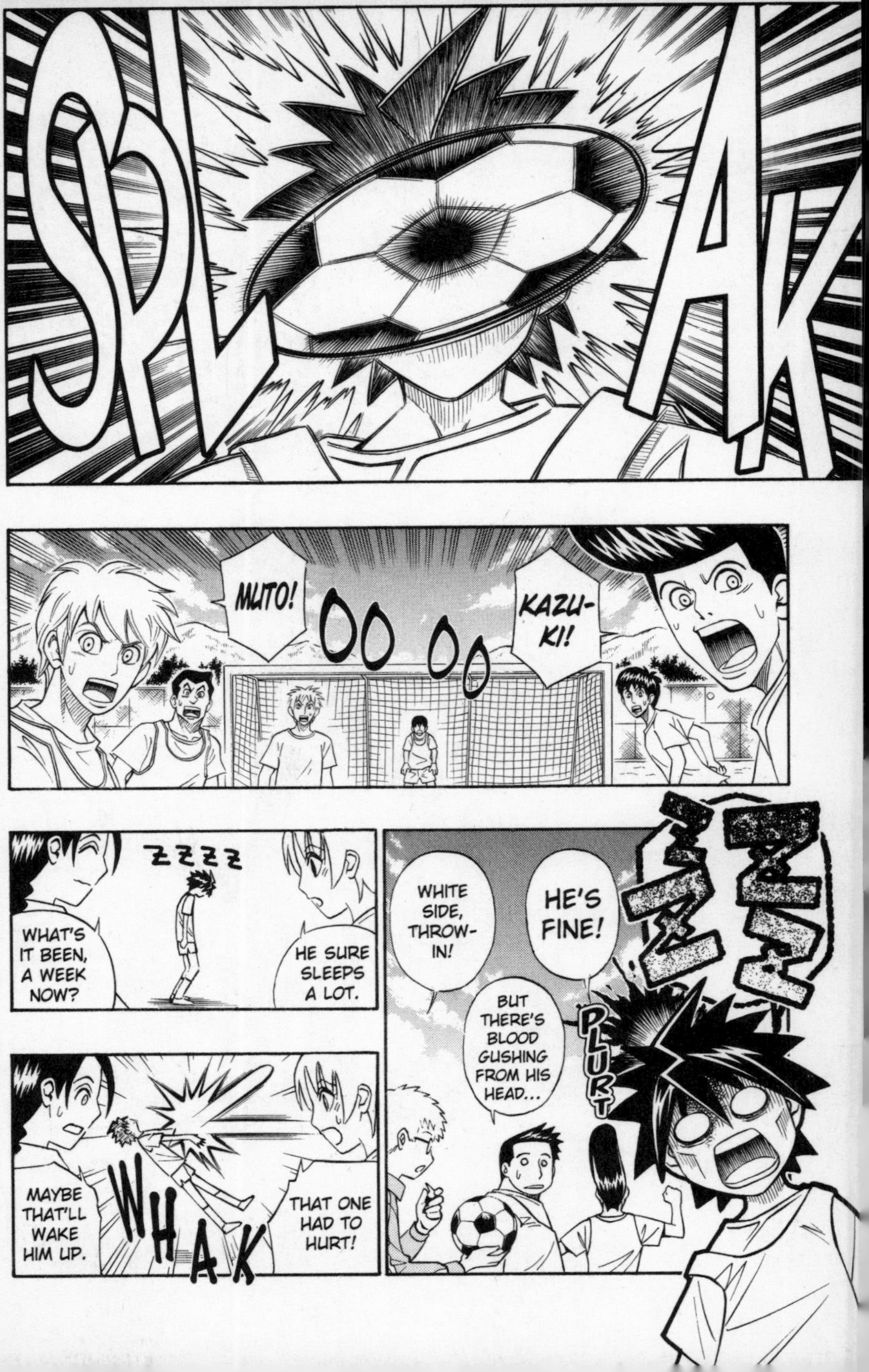
SPLAK
KAZU-KI!
MUTO!
HE'S FINE!
WHITE SIDE, THROW-IN!
BUT THERE'S BLOOD GUSHING FROM HIS HEAD...
PLURT
HE SURE SLEEPS A LOT.
ZZZZ
WHAT'S IT BEEN, A WEEK NOW?
THAT ONE HAD TO HURT!
WHAK
MAYBE THAT'LL WAKE HIM UP.

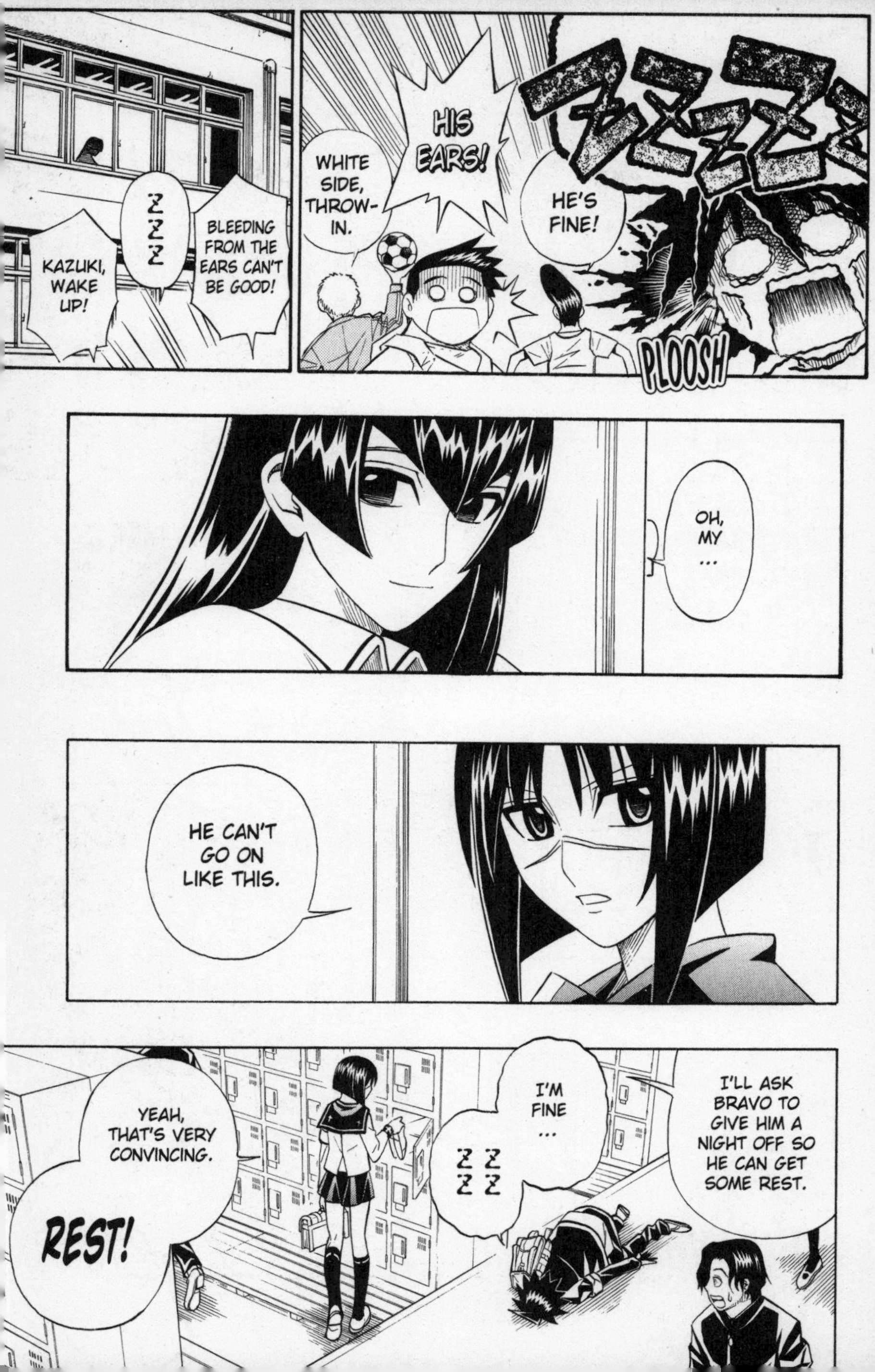
HE'S FINE!
HIS EARS!
WHITE SIDE, THROW-IN.
PLOOSH
BLEEDING FROM THE EARS CAN'T BE GOOD!
Z Z Z
KAZUKI, WAKE UP!
OH, MY ...
HE CAN'T GO ON LIKE THIS.
I'LL ASK BRAVO TO GIVE HIM A NIGHT OFF SO HE CAN GET SOME REST.
I'M FINE ...
Z Z Z Z
YEAH, THAT'S VERY CONVINCING.
REST!

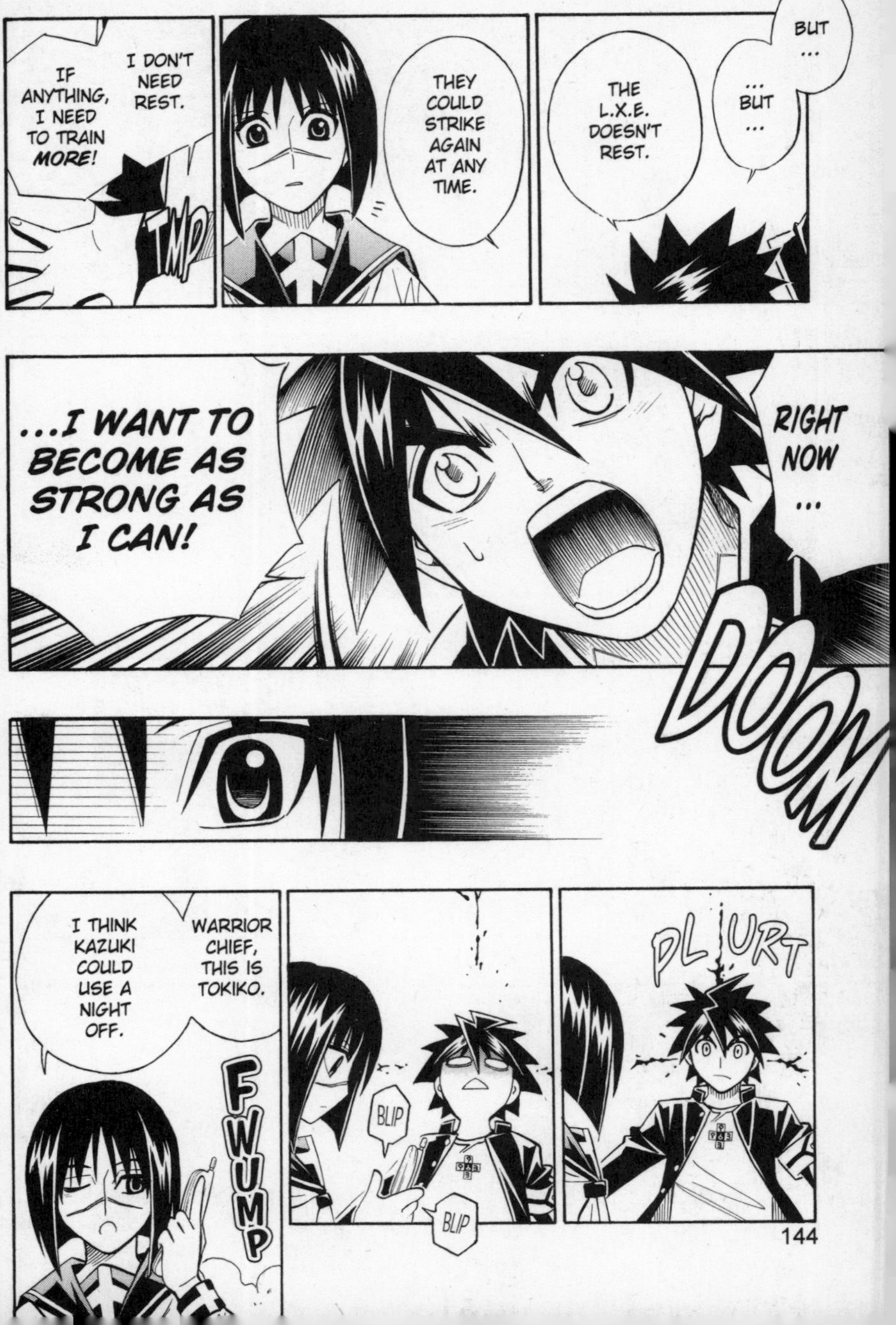
BUT ...
... BUT ...
THE L.X.E. DOESN'T REST.
THEY COULD STRIKE AGAIN AT ANY TIME.
I DON'T NEED REST.
IF ANYTHING, I NEED TO TRAIN *MORE!*
TMP
RIGHT NOW ...
...I WANT TO BECOME AS STRONG AS I CAN!
DOOM
PLURT
BLIP
BLIP
WARRIOR CHIEF, THIS IS TOKIKO.
I THINK KAZUKI COULD USE A NIGHT OFF.
FWUMP

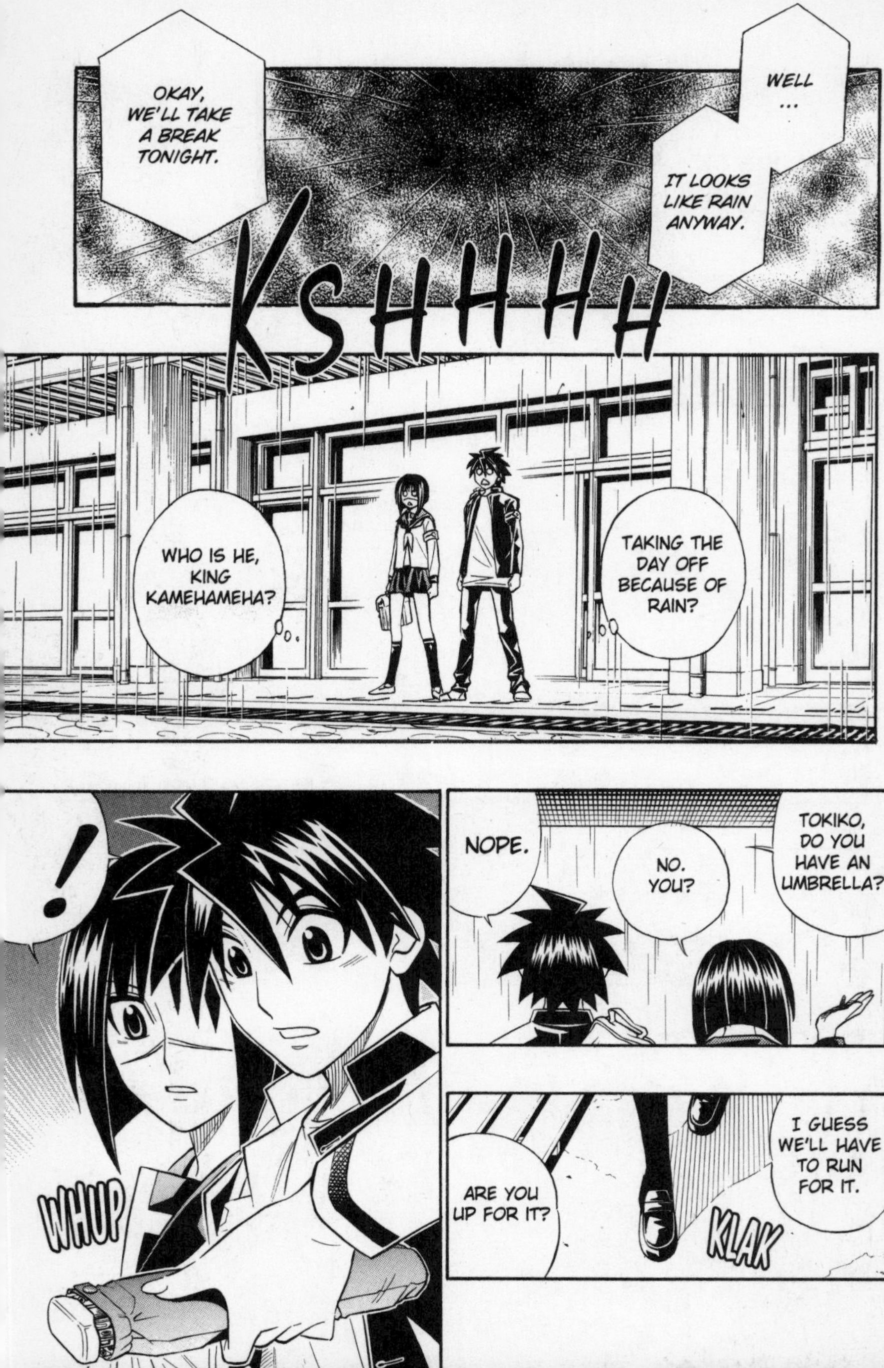
WELL ...
IT LOOKS LIKE RAIN ANYWAY.
OKAY, WE'LL TAKE A BREAK TONIGHT.
KSHHHHH
TAKING THE DAY OFF BECAUSE OF RAIN?
WHO IS HE, KING KAMEHAMEHA?
TOKIKO, DO YOU HAVE AN UMBRELLA?
NO. YOU?
NOPE.
I GUESS WE'LL HAVE TO RUN FOR IT.
ARE YOU UP FOR IT?
KLAK
!
WHUP

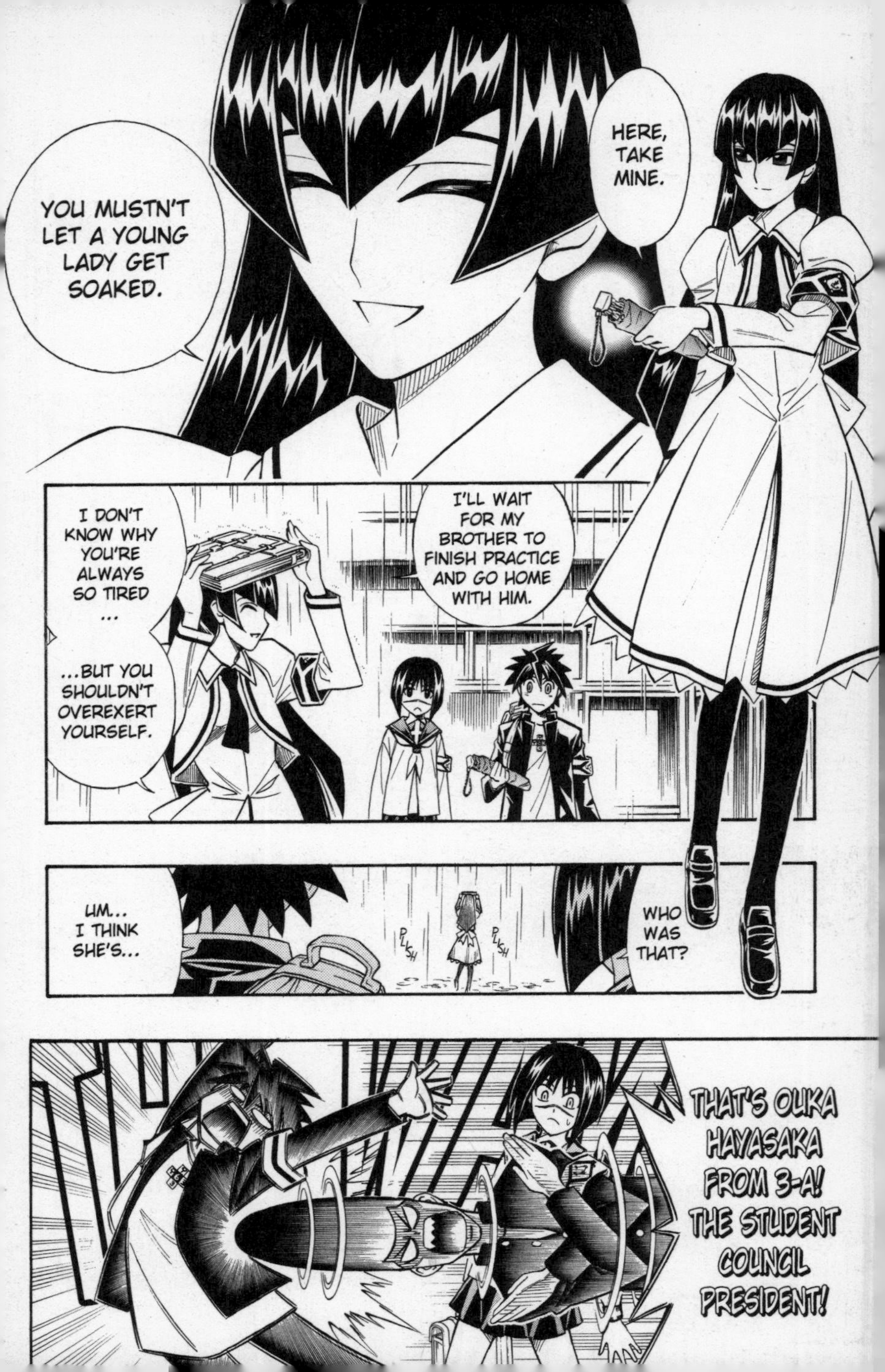
HERE, TAKE MINE.
YOU MUSTN'T LET A YOUNG LADY GET SOAKED.
I'LL WAIT FOR MY BROTHER TO FINISH PRACTICE AND GO HOME WITH HIM.
I DON'T KNOW WHY YOU'RE ALWAYS SO TIRED ...
...BUT YOU SHOULDN'T OVEREXERT YOURSELF.
WHO WAS THAT?
PLISH
PLISH
UM... I THINK SHE'S...
THAT'S OUKA HAYASAKA FROM 3-A! THE STUDENT COUNCIL PRESIDENT!

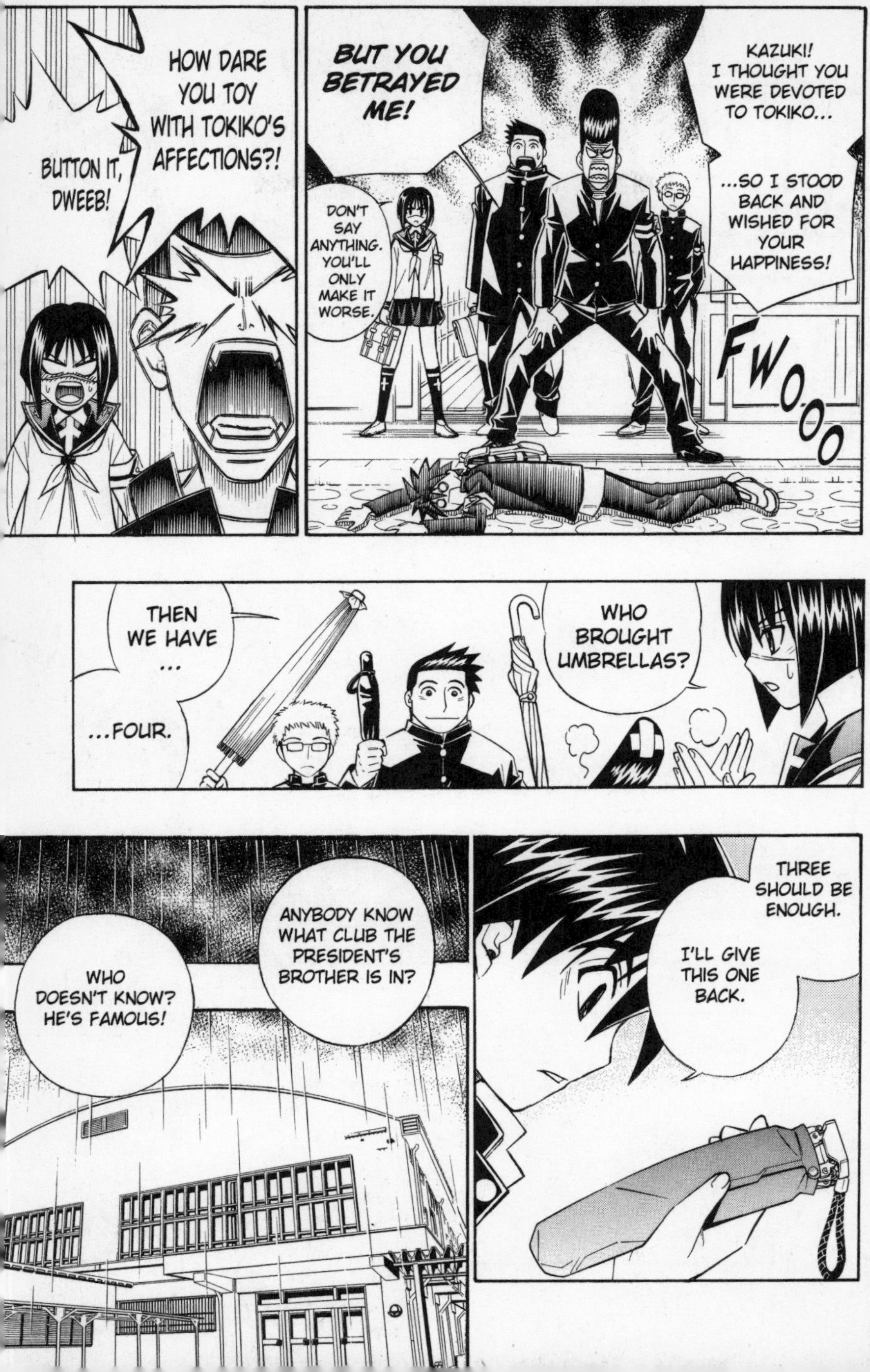
KAZUKI! I THOUGHT YOU WERE DEVOTED TO TOKIKO...
...SO I STOOD BACK AND WISHED FOR YOUR HAPPINESS!
FWOOO
BUT YOU BETRAYED ME!
DON'T SAY ANYTHING. YOU'LL ONLY MAKE IT WORSE.
HOW DARE YOU TOY WITH TOKIKO'S AFFECTIONS?!
BUTTON IT, DWEEB!
WHO BROUGHT UMBRELLAS?
THEN WE HAVE ...
...FOUR.
THREE SHOULD BE ENOUGH.
I'LL GIVE THIS ONE BACK.
ANYBODY KNOW WHAT CLUB THE PRESIDENT'S BROTHER IS IN?
WHO DOESN'T KNOW? HE'S FAMOUS!

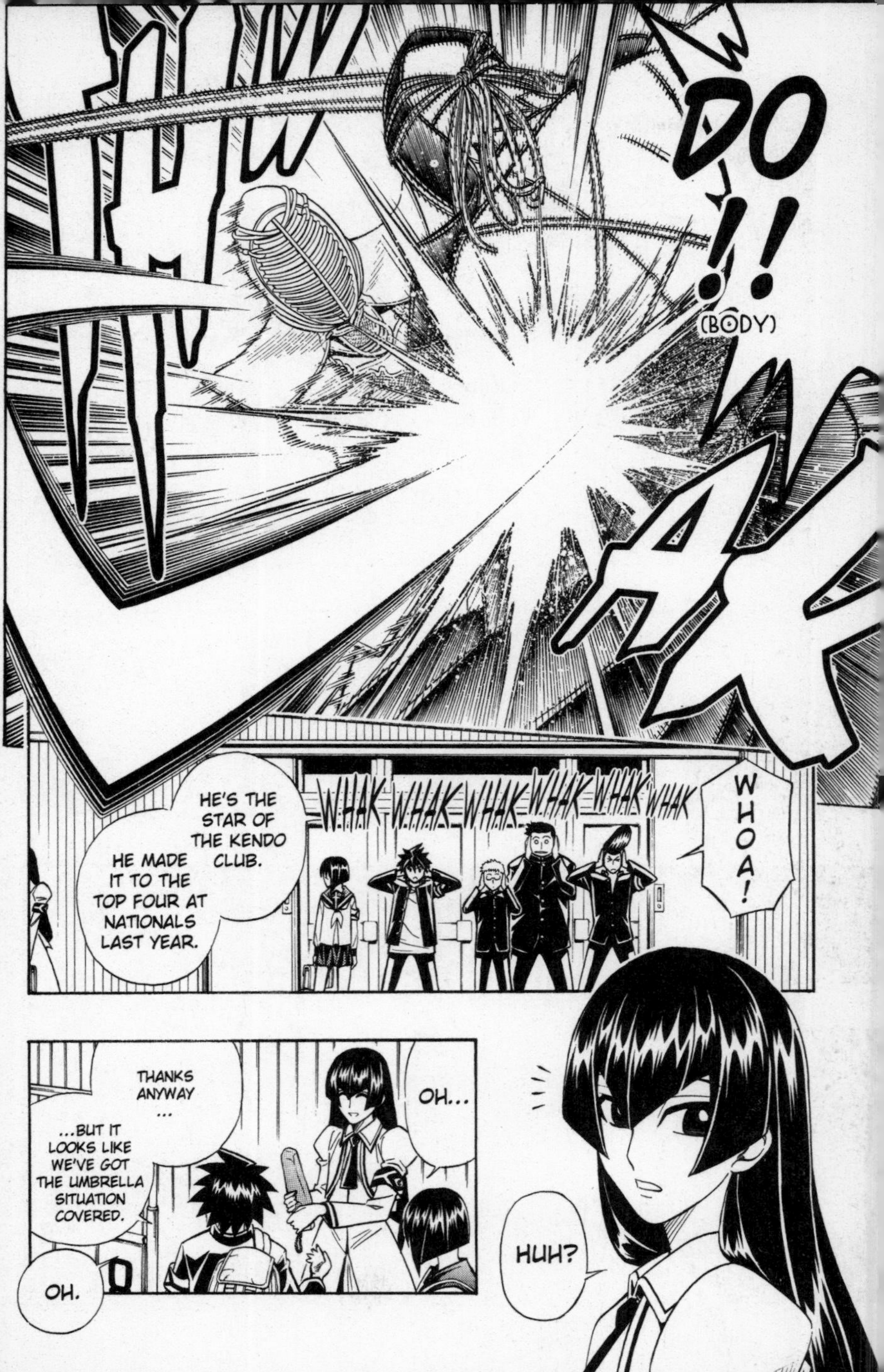
DO!!
(BODY)
WHOA!
WHAK WHAK WHAK WHAK WHAK WHAK
HE'S THE STAR OF THE KENDO CLUB.
HE MADE IT TO THE TOP FOUR AT NATIONALS LAST YEAR.
HUH?
OH...
THANKS ANYWAY ...
...BUT IT LOOKS LIKE WE'VE GOT THE UMBRELLA SITUATION COVERED.
OH.

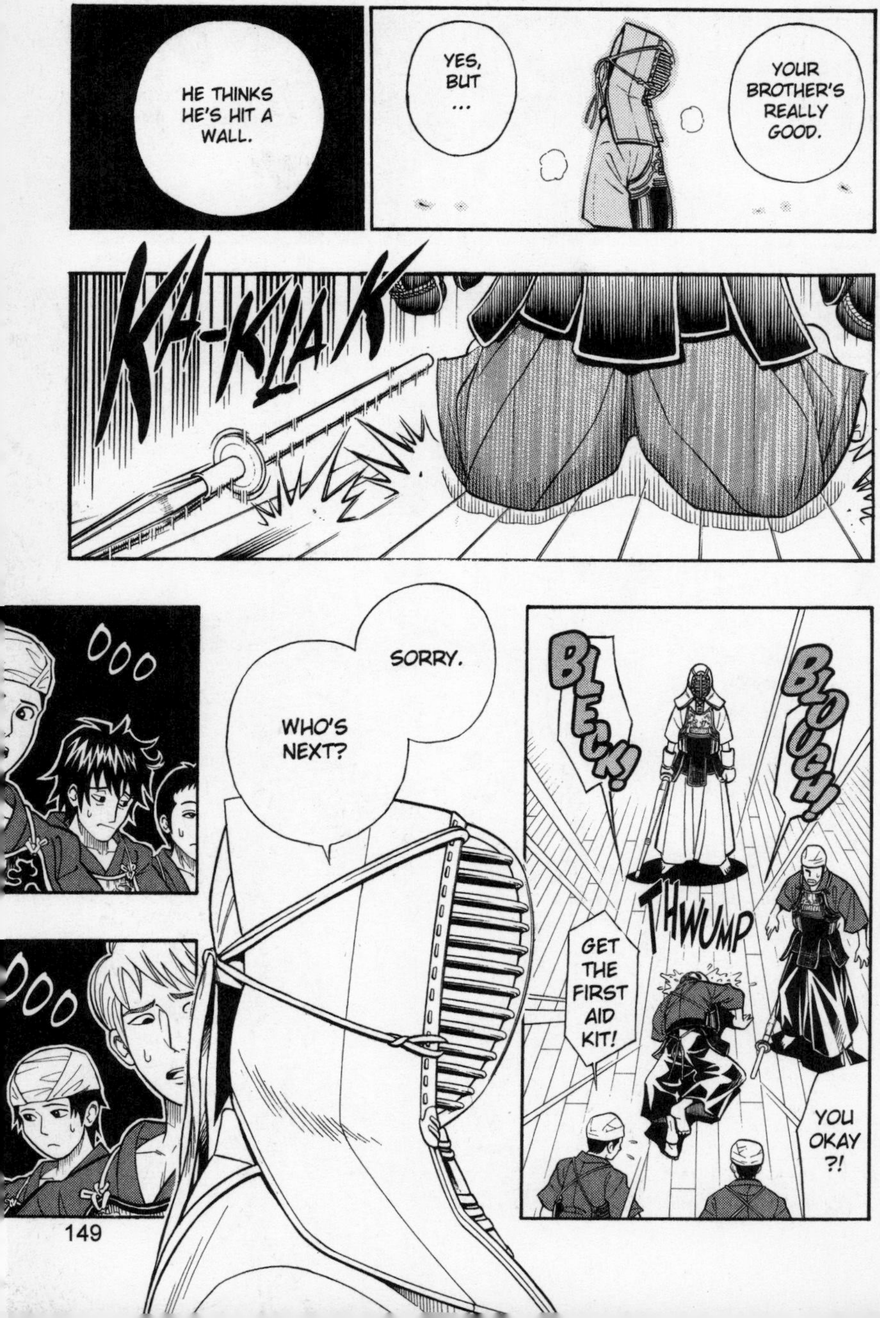
YOUR BROTHER'S REALLY GOOD.
YES, BUT ...
HE THINKS HE'S HIT A WALL.
KA-KLAK
BLOUGH!
BLECK!
THWUMP
GET THE FIRST AID KIT!
YOU OKAY ?!
SORRY.
WHO'S NEXT?
OOO
OOO

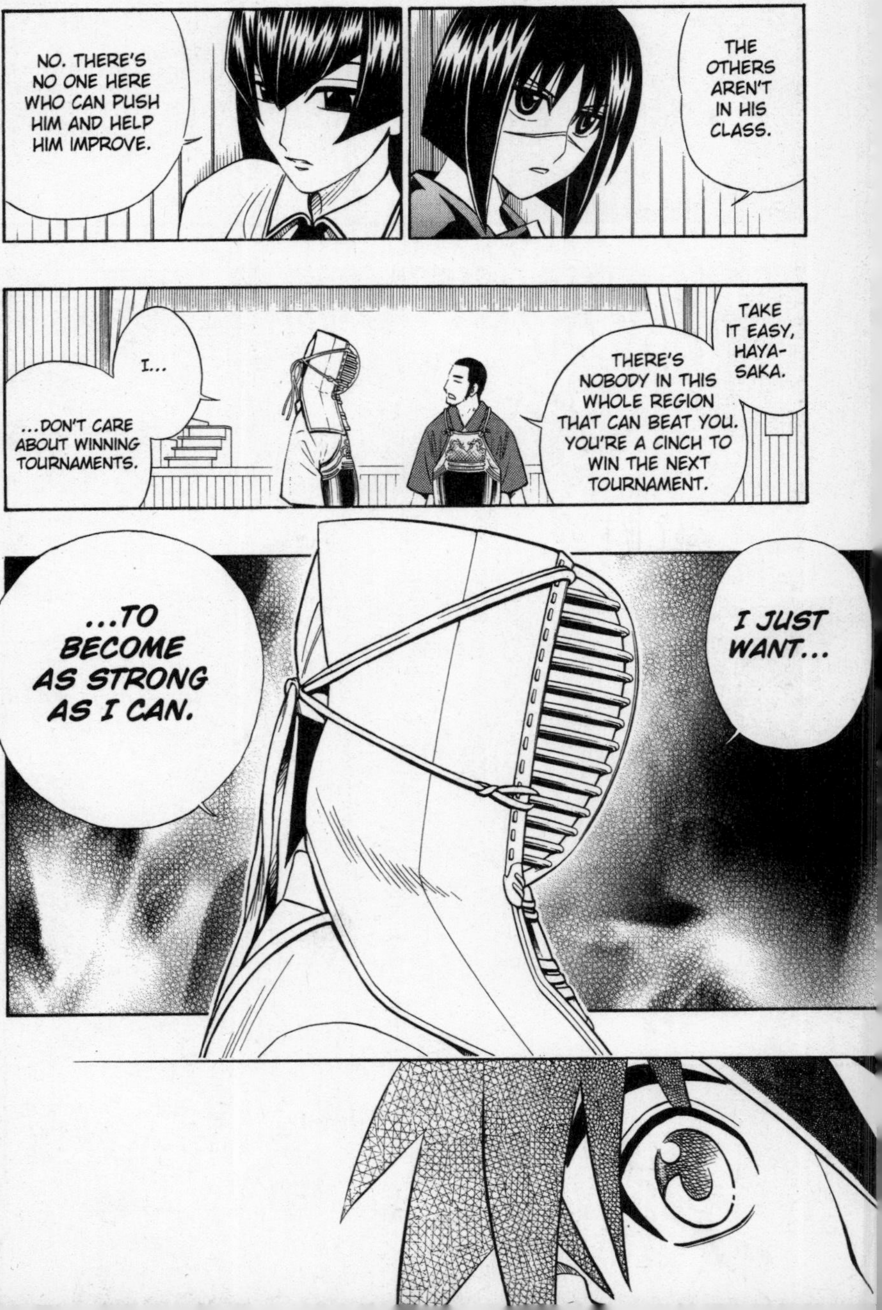
THE OTHERS AREN'T IN HIS CLASS.
NO. THERE'S NO ONE HERE WHO CAN PUSH HIM AND HELP HIM IMPROVE.
TAKE IT EASY, HAYA-SAKA.
THERE'S NOBODY IN THIS WHOLE REGION THAT CAN BEAT YOU. YOU'RE A CINCH TO WIN THE NEXT TOURNAMENT.
I...
...DON'T CARE ABOUT WINNING TOURNAMENTS.
I JUST WANT...
...TO BECOME AS STRONG AS I CAN.

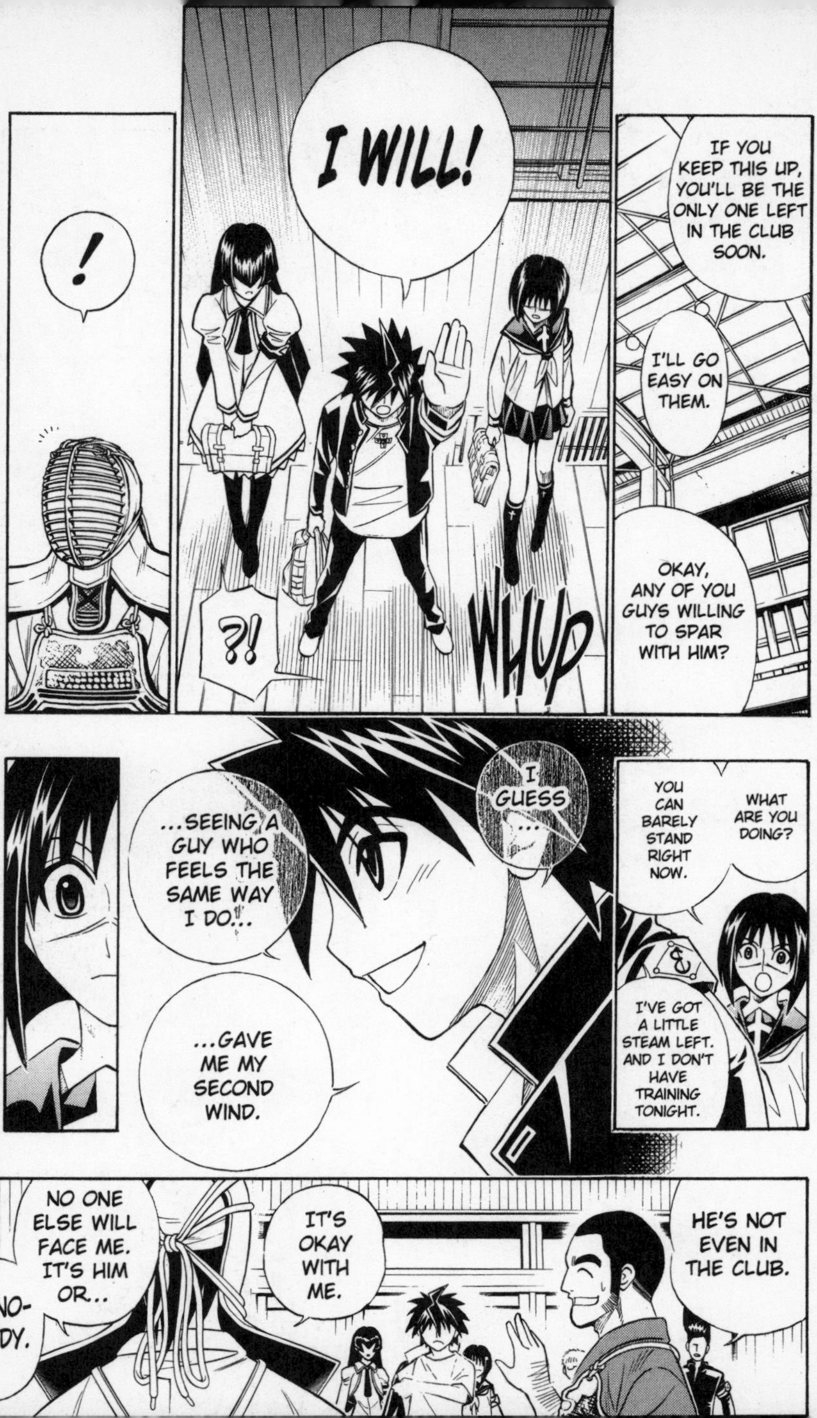
IF YOU KEEP THIS UP, YOU'LL BE THE ONLY ONE LEFT IN THE CLUB SOON.
I'LL GO EASY ON THEM.
OKAY, ANY OF YOU GUYS WILLING TO SPAR WITH HIM?
I WILL!
WHUP
?!
!
WHAT ARE YOU DOING?
YOU CAN BARELY STAND RIGHT NOW.
I'VE GOT A LITTLE STEAM LEFT. AND I DON'T HAVE TRAINING TONIGHT.
I GUESS...
...SEEING A GUY WHO FEELS THE SAME WAY I DO...
...GAVE ME MY SECOND WIND.
HE'S NOT EVEN IN THE CLUB.
IT'S OKAY WITH ME.
NO ONE ELSE WILL FACE ME. IT'S HIM OR...
...NO-BODY.

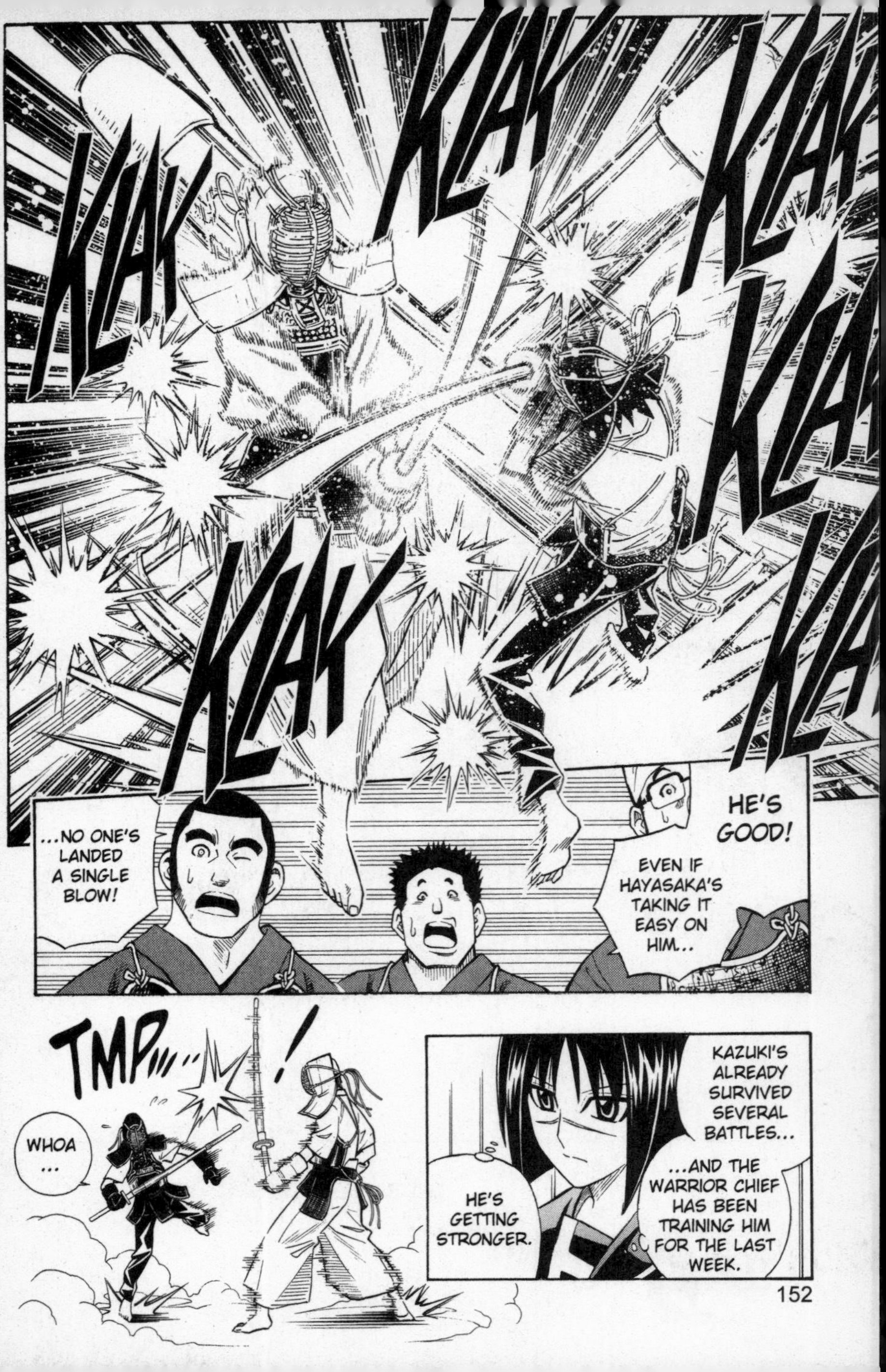
KLAK
KLAK
KLAK
HE'S GOOD!
EVEN IF HAYASAKA'S TAKING IT EASY ON HIM...
...NO ONE'S LANDED A SINGLE BLOW!
KAZUKI'S ALREADY SURVIVED SEVERAL BATTLES...
...AND THE WARRIOR CHIEF HAS BEEN TRAINING HIM FOR THE LAST WEEK.
HE'S GETTING STRONGER.
TMP...
!
WHOA...

READ THIS WAY

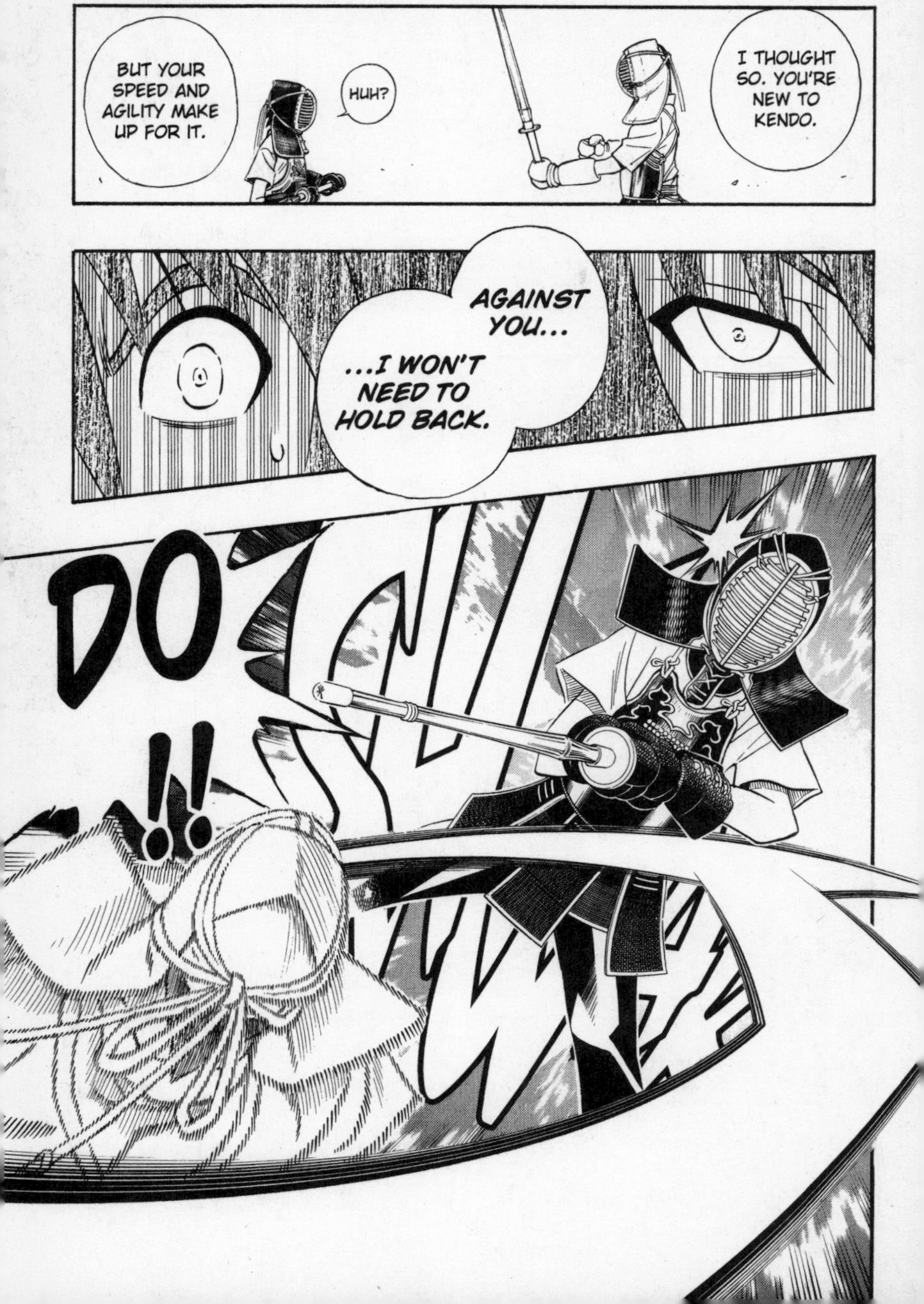
I THOUGHT SO. YOU'RE NEW TO KENDO.
HUH?
BUT YOUR SPEED AND AGILITY MAKE UP FOR IT.
AGAINST YOU...
...I WON'T NEED TO HOLD BACK.
DO!!

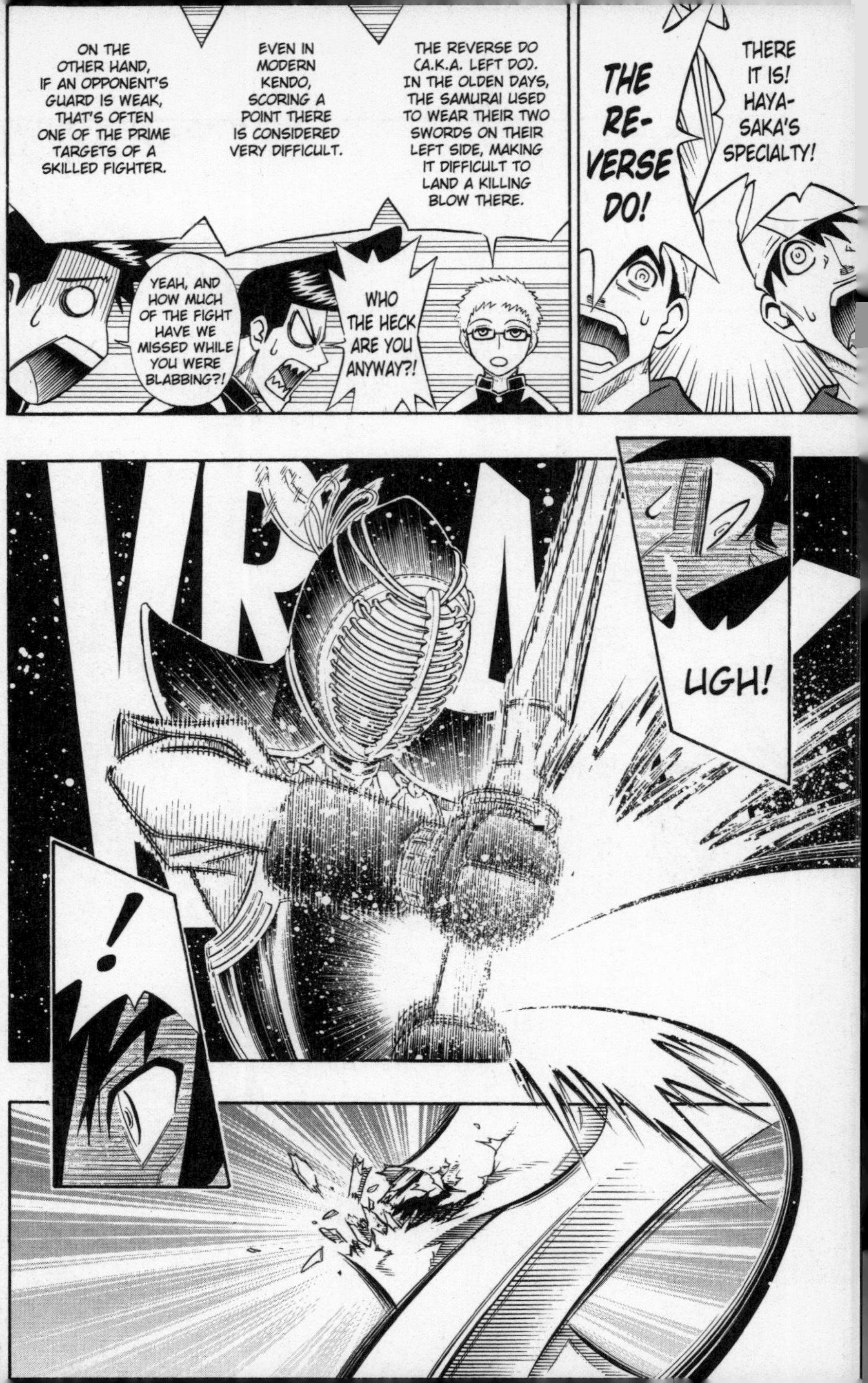
THERE IT IS! HAYASAKA'S SPECIALTY!
THE REVERSE DO!
THE REVERSE DO (A.K.A. LEFT DO). IN THE OLDEN DAYS, THE SAMURAI USED TO WEAR THEIR TWO SWORDS ON THEIR LEFT SIDE, MAKING IT DIFFICULT TO LAND A KILLING BLOW THERE.
EVEN IN MODERN KENDO, SCORING A POINT THERE IS CONSIDERED VERY DIFFICULT.
ON THE OTHER HAND, IF AN OPPONENT'S GUARD IS WEAK, THAT'S OFTEN ONE OF THE PRIME TARGETS OF A SKILLED FIGHTER.
WHO THE HECK ARE YOU ANYWAY?!
YEAH, AND HOW MUCH OF THE FIGHT HAVE WE MISSED WHILE YOU WERE BLABBING?!
UGH!
!

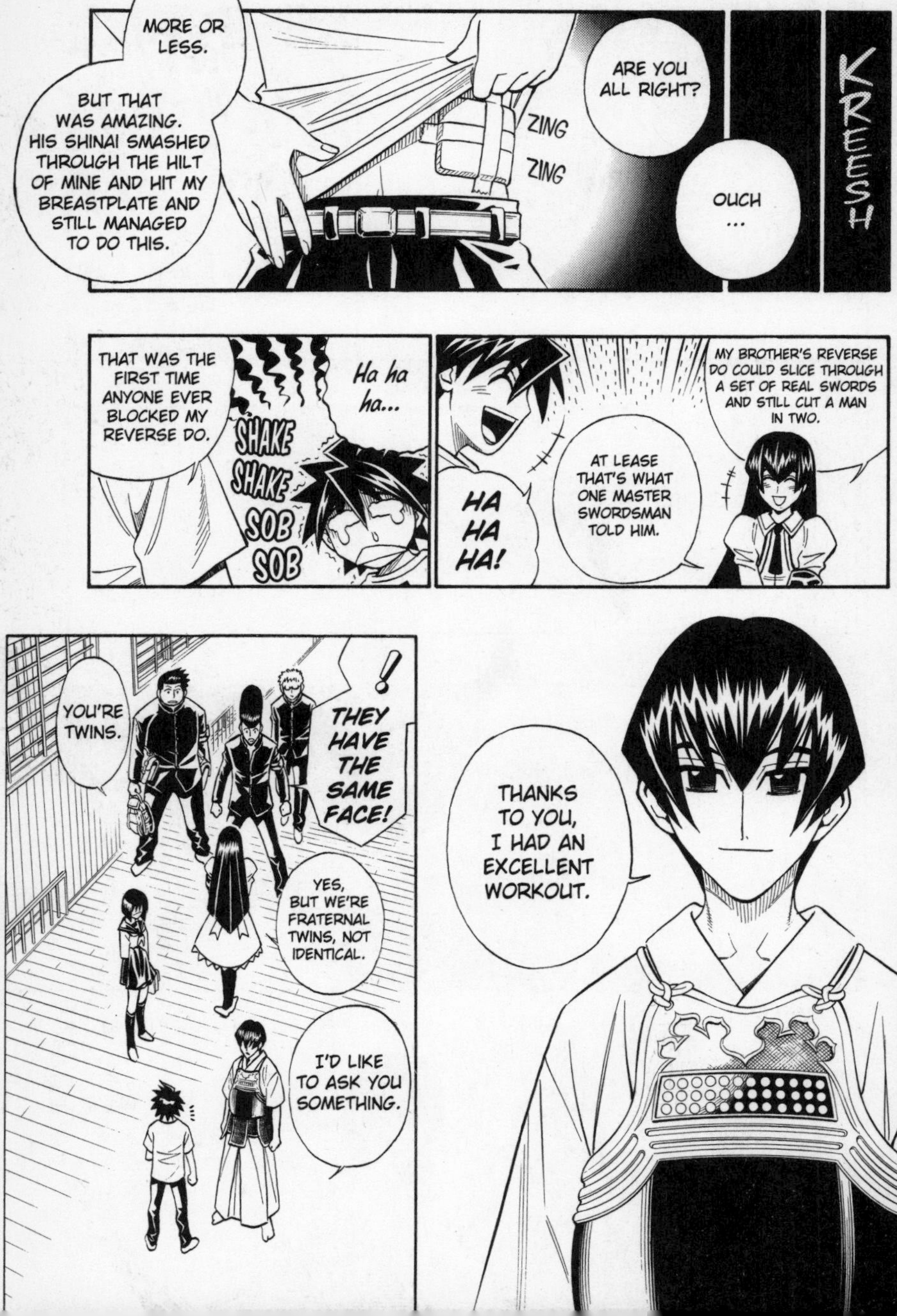
KRESH
OUCH ...
ARE YOU ALL RIGHT?
ZING ZING
MORE OR LESS.
BUT THAT WAS AMAZING. HIS SHINAI SMASHED THROUGH THE HILT OF MINE AND HIT MY BREASTPLATE AND STILL MANAGED TO DO THIS.
MY BROTHER'S REVERSE DO COULD SLICE THROUGH A SET OF REAL SWORDS AND STILL CUT A MAN IN TWO.
AT LEASE THAT'S WHAT ONE MASTER SWORDSMAN TOLD HIM.
HA HA HA!
Ha ha ha...
THAT WAS THE FIRST TIME ANYONE EVER BLOCKED MY REVERSE DO.
SHAKE SHAKE SOB SOB
THANKS TO YOU, I HAD AN EXCELLENT WORKOUT.
!
THEY HAVE THE SAME FACE!
YOU'RE TWINS.
YES, BUT WE'RE FRATERNAL TWINS, NOT IDENTICAL.
I'D LIKE TO ASK YOU SOMETHING.

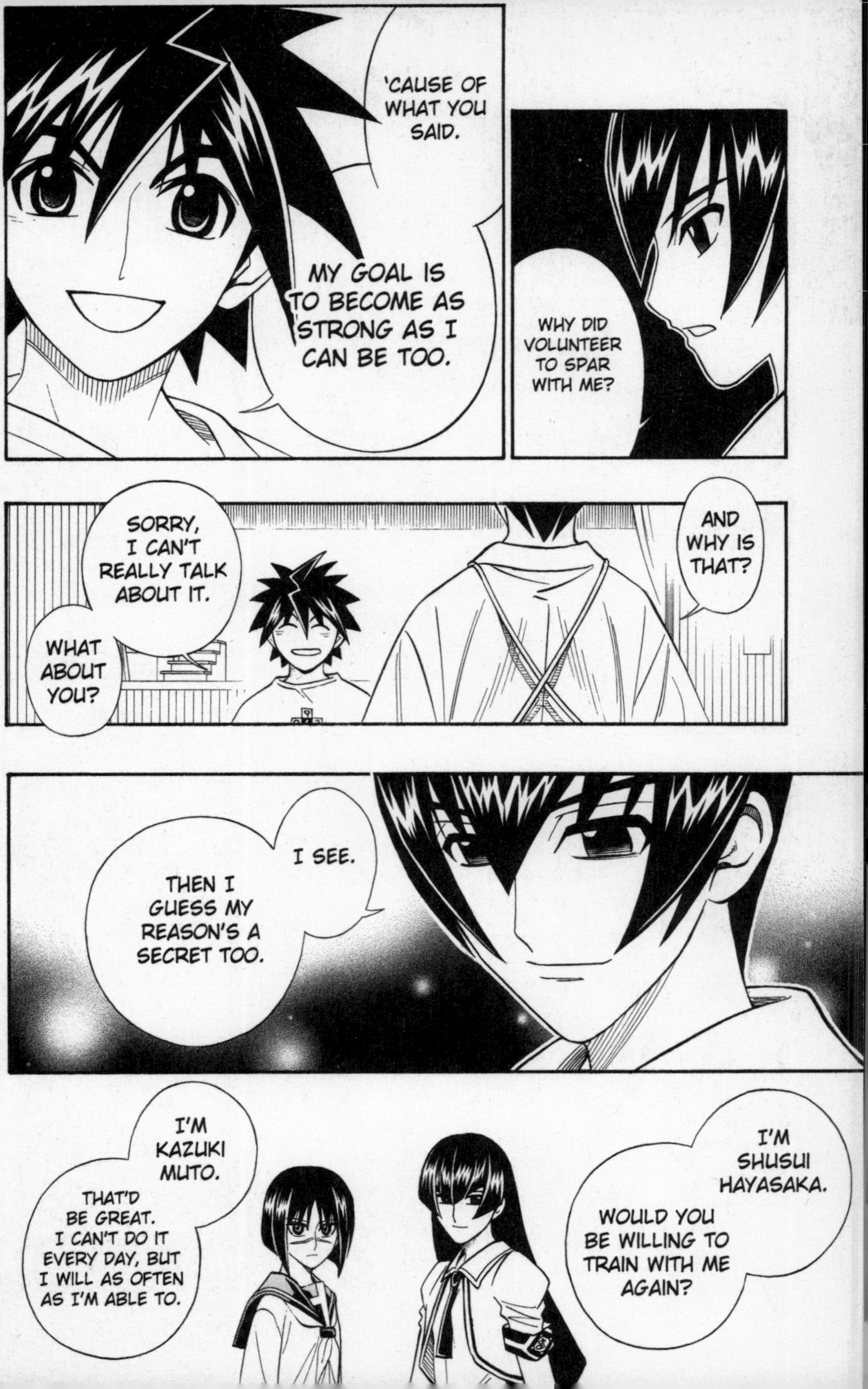
WHY DID VOLUNTEER TO SPAR WITH ME?
'CAUSE OF WHAT YOU SAID.
MY GOAL IS TO BECOME AS STRONG AS I CAN BE TOO.
AND WHY IS THAT?
SORRY, I CAN'T REALLY TALK ABOUT IT.
WHAT ABOUT YOU?
I SEE.
THEN I GUESS MY REASON'S A SECRET TOO.
I'M SHUSUI HAYASAKA.
WOULD YOU BE WILLING TO TRAIN WITH ME AGAIN?
I'M KAZUKI MUTO.
THAT'D BE GREAT. I CAN'T DO IT EVERY DAY, BUT I WILL AS OFTEN AS I'M ABLE TO.

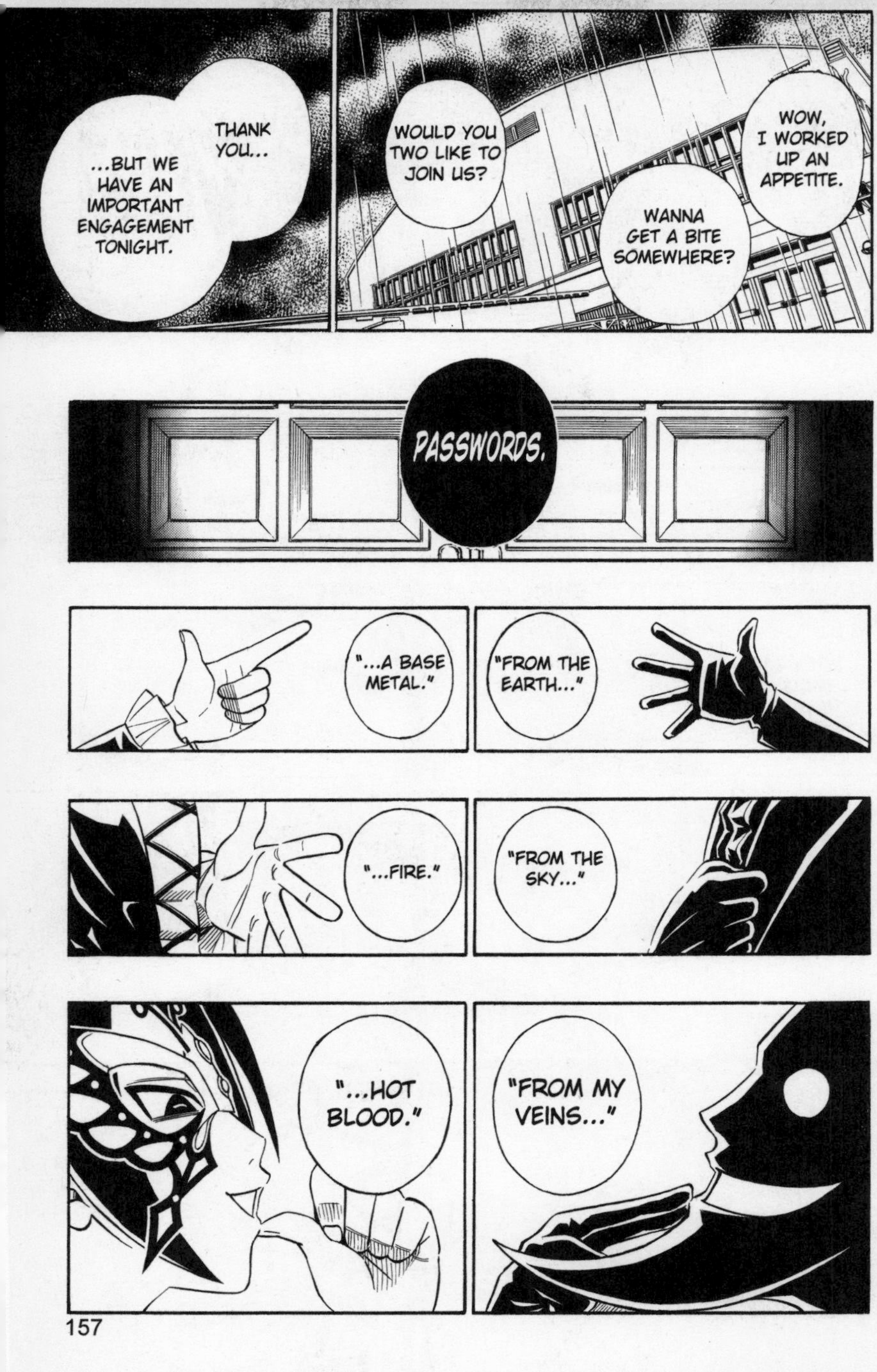
WOW, I WORKED UP AN APPETITE.
WANNA GET A BITE SOMEWHERE?
WOULD YOU TWO LIKE TO JOIN US?
THANK YOU...
...BUT WE HAVE AN IMPORTANT ENGAGEMENT TONIGHT.
PASSWORDS.
"FROM THE EARTH..."
"...A BASE METAL."
"FROM THE SKY..."
"...FIRE."
"FROM MY VEINS..."
"...HOT BLOOD."

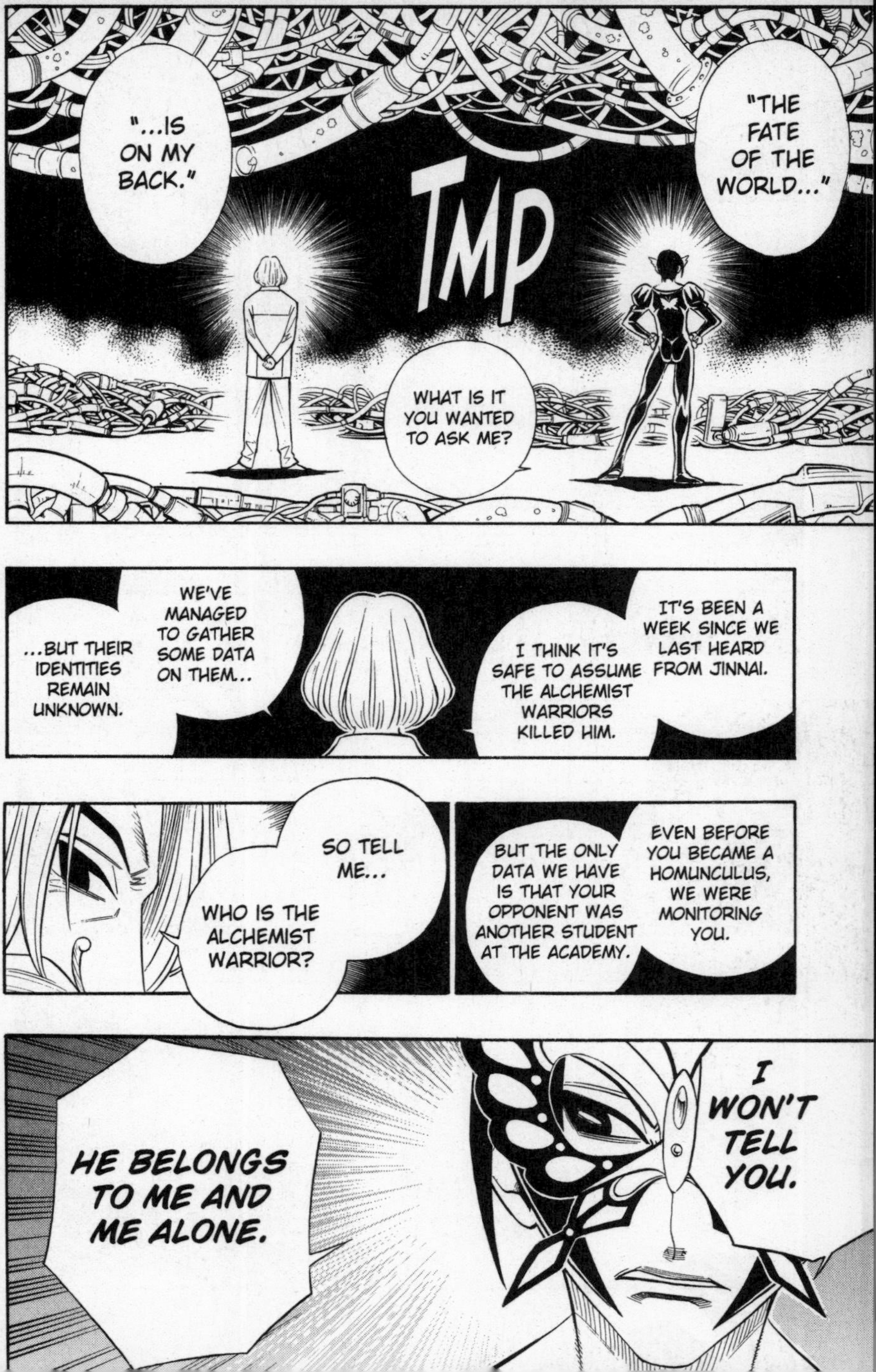
"THE FATE OF THE WORLD..."
"...IS ON MY BACK."
TMP
WHAT IS IT YOU WANTED TO ASK ME?
IT'S BEEN A WEEK SINCE WE LAST HEARD FROM JINNAI.
I THINK IT'S SAFE TO ASSUME THE ALCHEMIST WARRIORS KILLED HIM.
WE'VE MANAGED TO GATHER SOME DATA ON THEM...
...BUT THEIR IDENTITIES REMAIN UNKNOWN.
EVEN BEFORE YOU BECAME A HOMUNCULUS, WE WERE MONITORING YOU.
BUT THE ONLY DATA WE HAVE IS THAT YOUR OPPONENT WAS ANOTHER STUDENT AT THE ACADEMY.
SO TELL ME...
WHO IS THE ALCHEMIST WARRIOR?
I WON'T TELL YOU.
HE BELONGS TO ME AND ME ALONE.

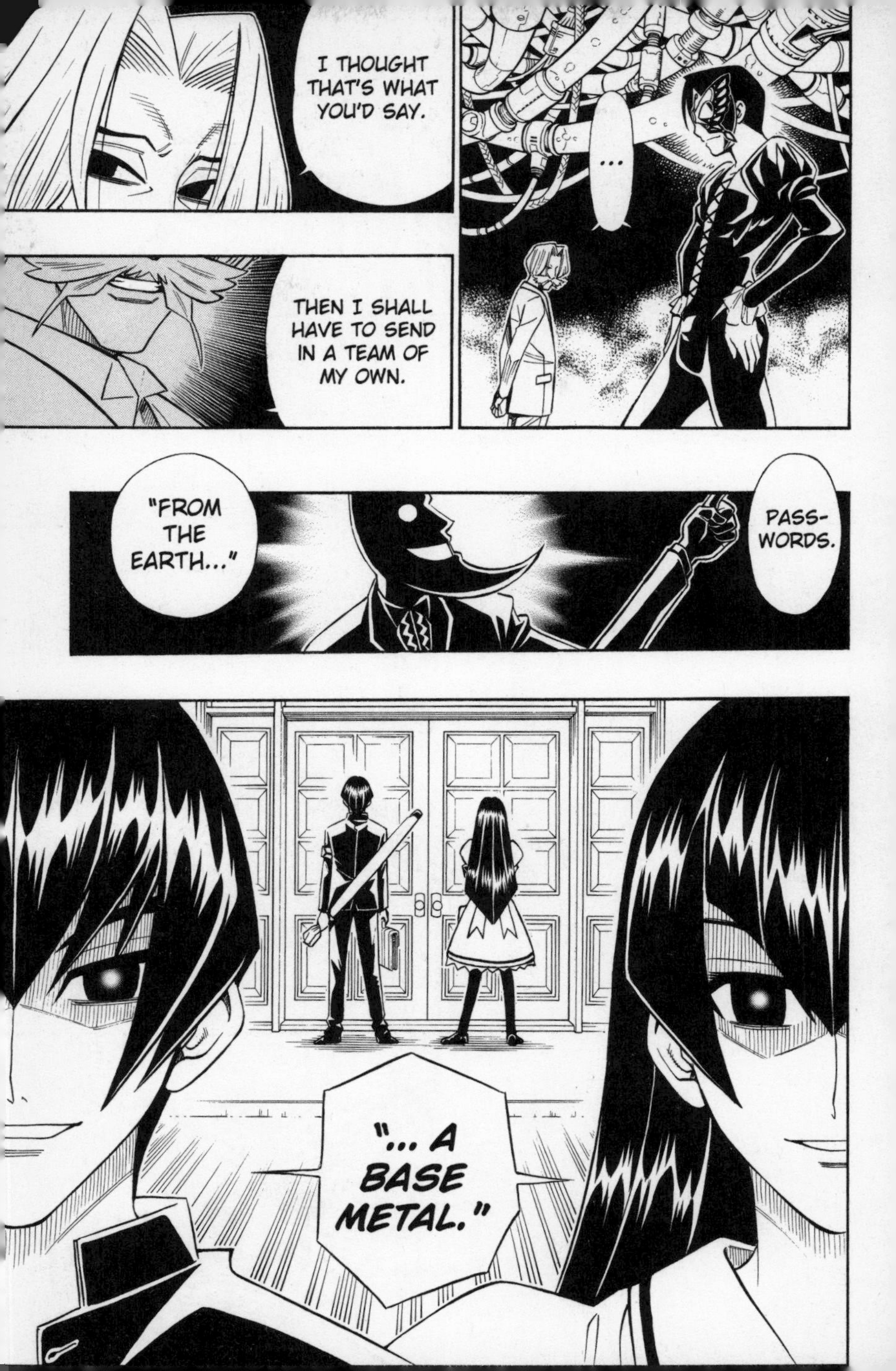
...
I THOUGHT THAT'S WHAT YOU'D SAY.
THEN I SHALL HAVE TO SEND IN A TEAM OF MY OWN.
PASS-WORDS.
"FROM THE EARTH..."
"... A BASE METAL."

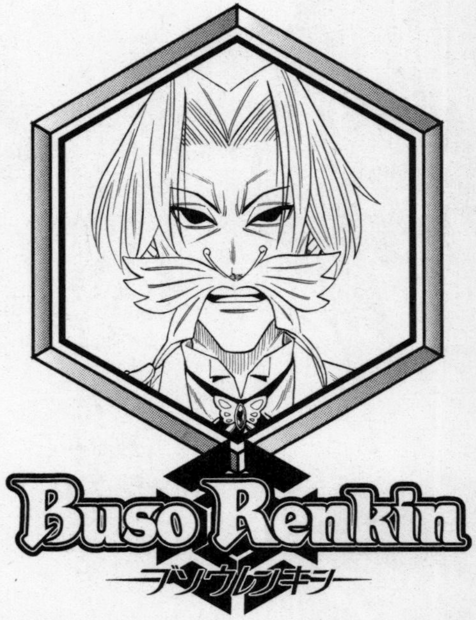

Buso Renkin

ブソウレンキン

CHAPTER 26: TRAINING DAY

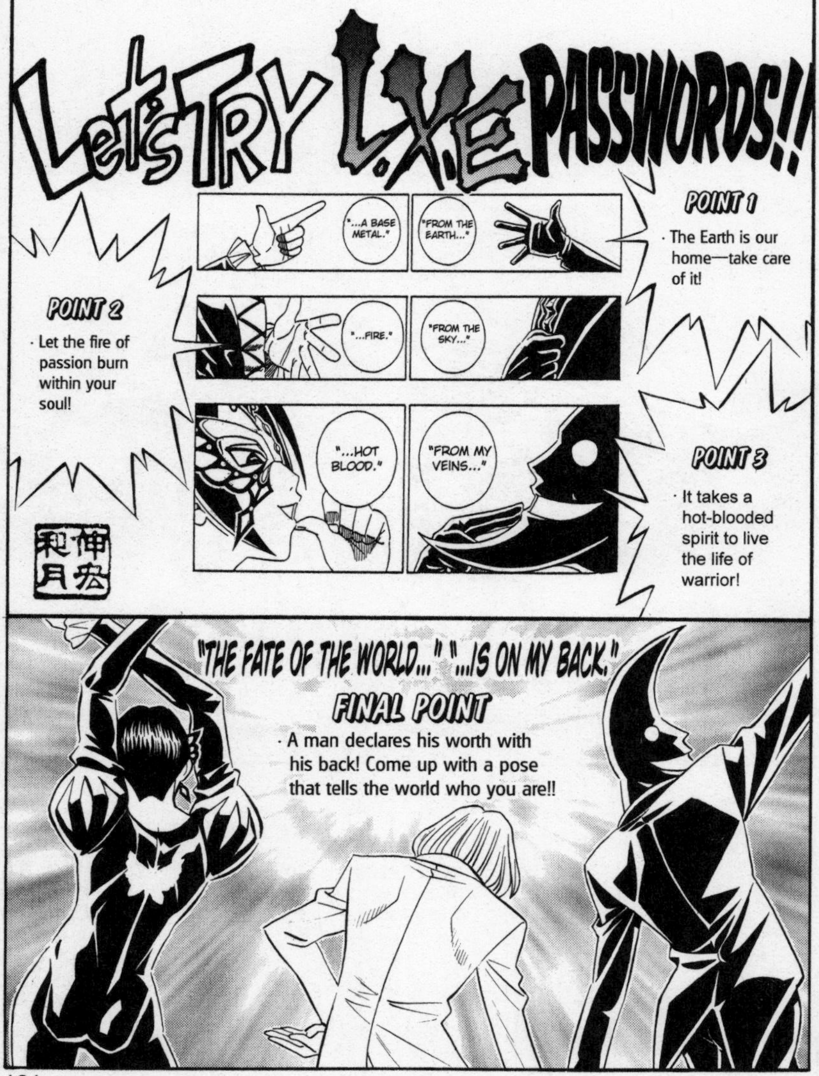
Let's TRY L.X.E PASSWORDS!!
"FROM THE EARTH..."
"...A BASE METAL."
POINT 1
· The Earth is our home—take care of it!
"FROM THE SKY..."
"...FIRE."
POINT 2
· Let the fire of passion burn within your soul!
"FROM MY VEINS..."
"...HOT BLOOD."
POINT 3
· It takes a hot-blooded spirit to live the life of warrior!
"THE FATE OF THE WORLD..." "...IS ON MY BACK."
FINAL POINT
· A man declares his worth with his back! Come up with a pose that tells the world who you are!!

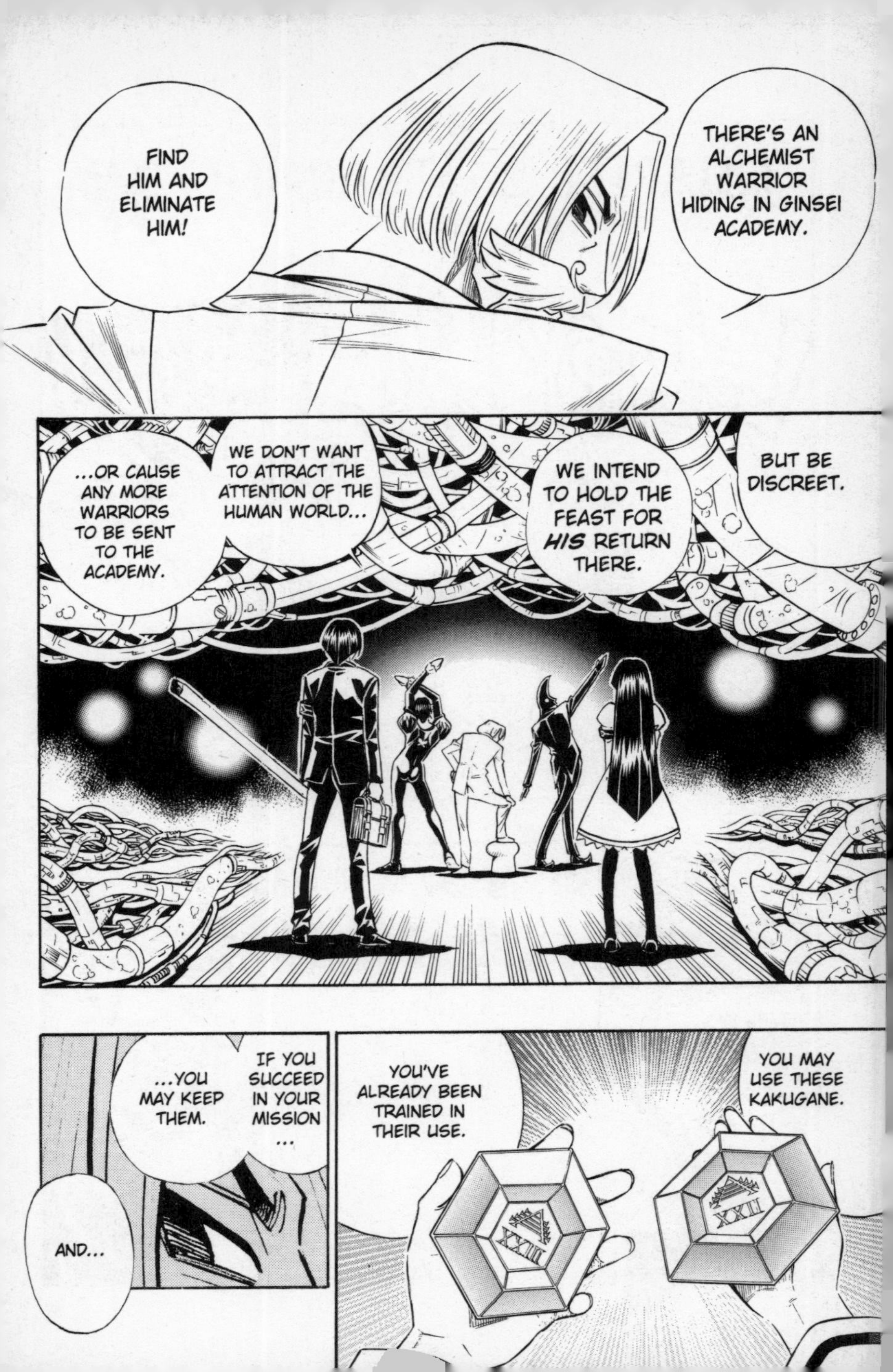
THERE'S AN ALCHEMIST WARRIOR HIDING IN GINSEI ACADEMY.
FIND HIM AND ELIMINATE HIM!
BUT BE DISCREET.
WE INTEND TO HOLD THE FEAST FOR *HIS* RETURN THERE.
WE DON'T WANT TO ATTRACT THE ATTENTION OF THE HUMAN WORLD...
...OR CAUSE ANY MORE WARRIORS TO BE SENT TO THE ACADEMY.
YOU MAY USE THESE KAKUGANE.
YOU'VE ALREADY BEEN TRAINED IN THEIR USE.
IF YOU SUCCEED IN YOUR MISSION ...
...YOU MAY KEEP THEM.
AND...

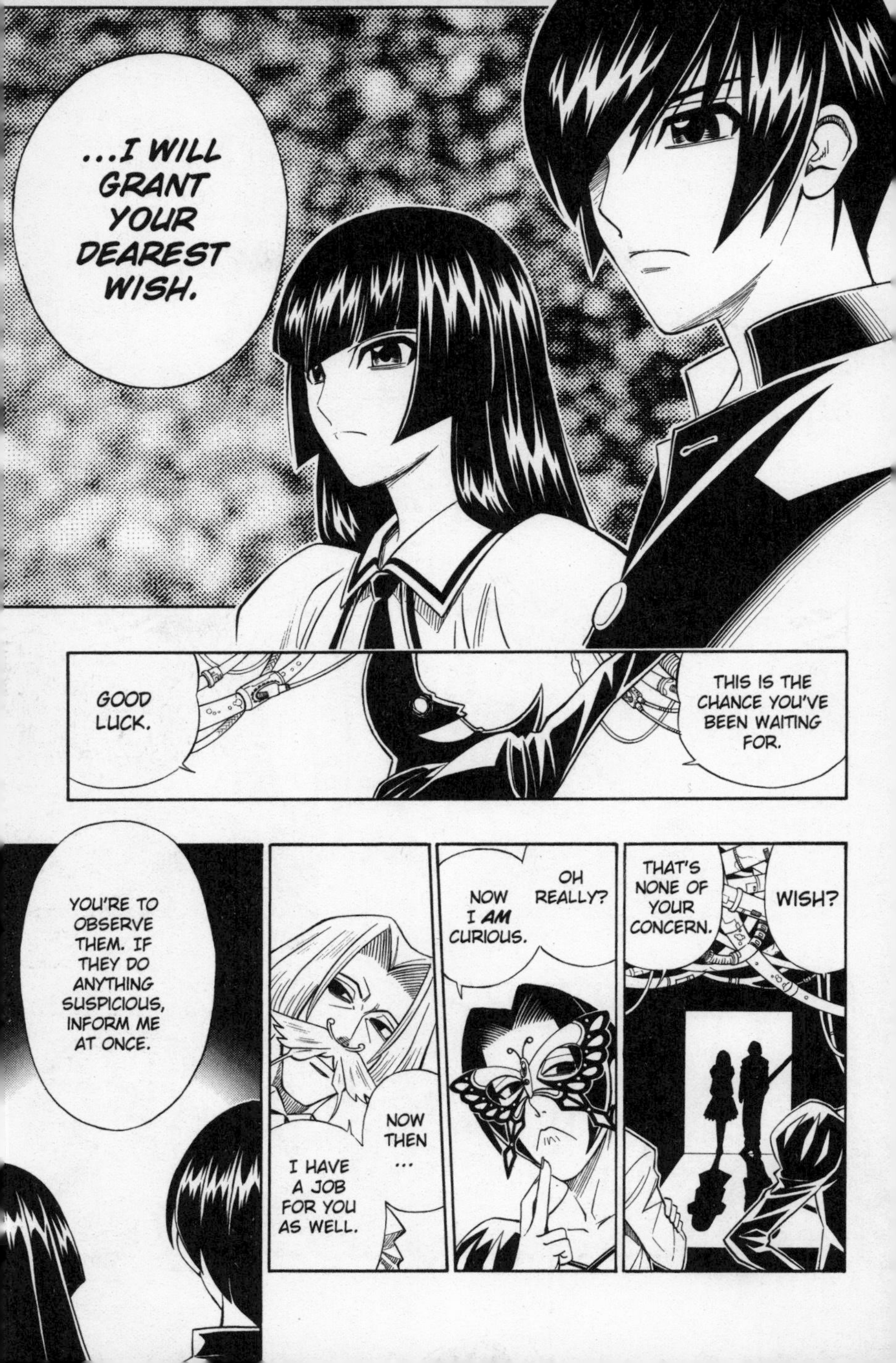
...I WILL GRANT YOUR DEAREST WISH.
THIS IS THE CHANCE YOU'VE BEEN WAITING FOR.
GOOD LUCK.
WISH?
THAT'S NONE OF YOUR CONCERN.
OH REALLY?
NOW I *AM* CURIOUS.
NOW THEN ...
I HAVE A JOB FOR YOU AS WELL.
YOU'RE TO OBSERVE THEM. IF THEY DO ANYTHING SUSPICIOUS, INFORM ME AT ONCE.

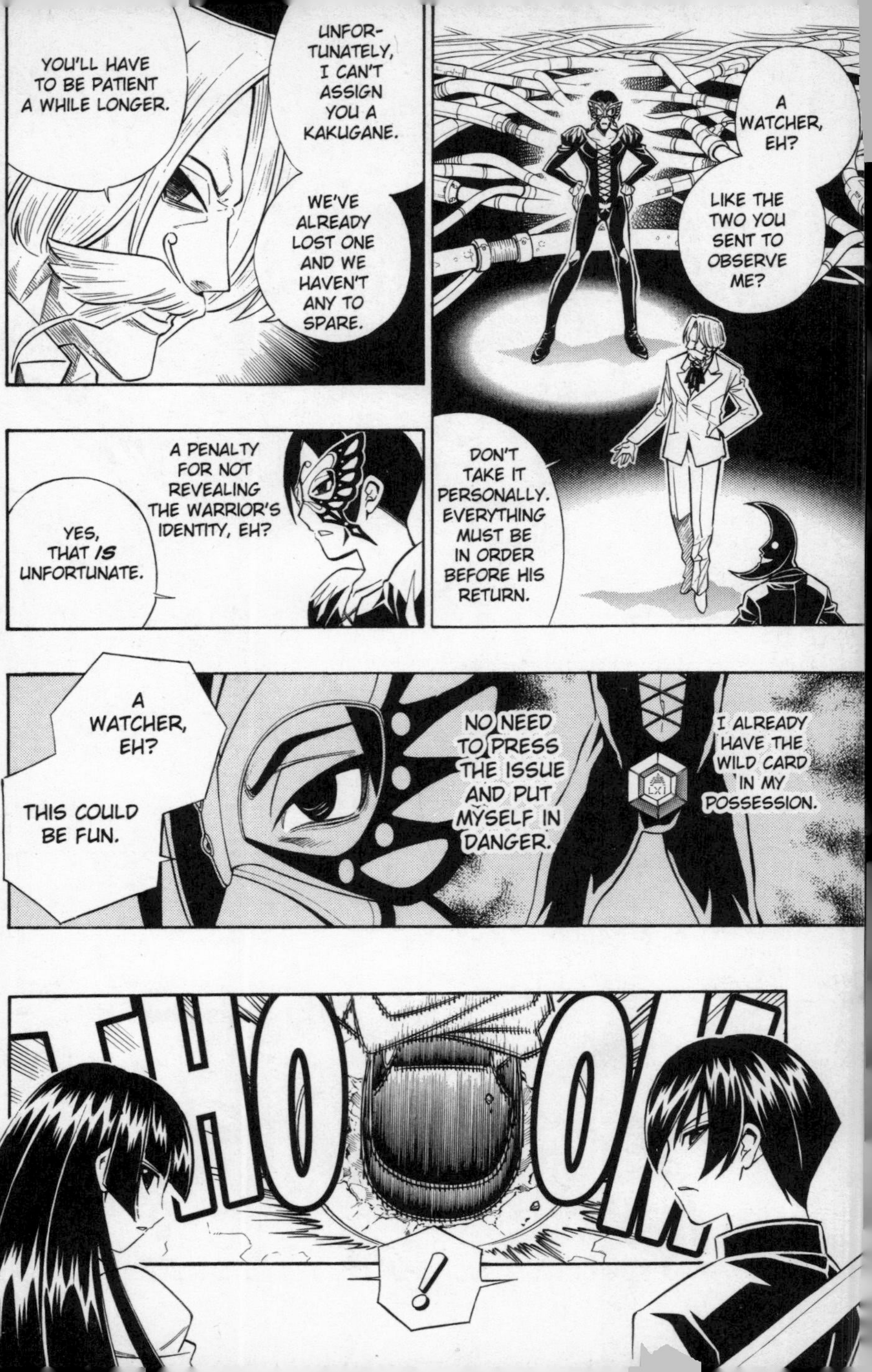
A WATCHER, EH?
LIKE THE TWO YOU SENT TO OBSERVE ME?
DON'T TAKE IT PERSONALLY. EVERYTHING MUST BE IN ORDER BEFORE HIS RETURN.
UNFORTUNATELY, I CAN'T ASSIGN YOU A KAKUGANE.
WE'VE ALREADY LOST ONE AND WE HAVEN'T ANY TO SPARE.
YOU'LL HAVE TO BE PATIENT A WHILE LONGER.
A PENALTY FOR NOT REVEALING THE WARRIOR'S IDENTITY, EH?
YES, THAT *IS* UNFORTUNATE.
I ALREADY HAVE THE WILD CARD IN MY POSSESSION.
NO NEED TO PRESS THE ISSUE AND PUT MYSELF IN DANGER.
A WATCHER, EH?
THIS COULD BE FUN.
WHOOM
!

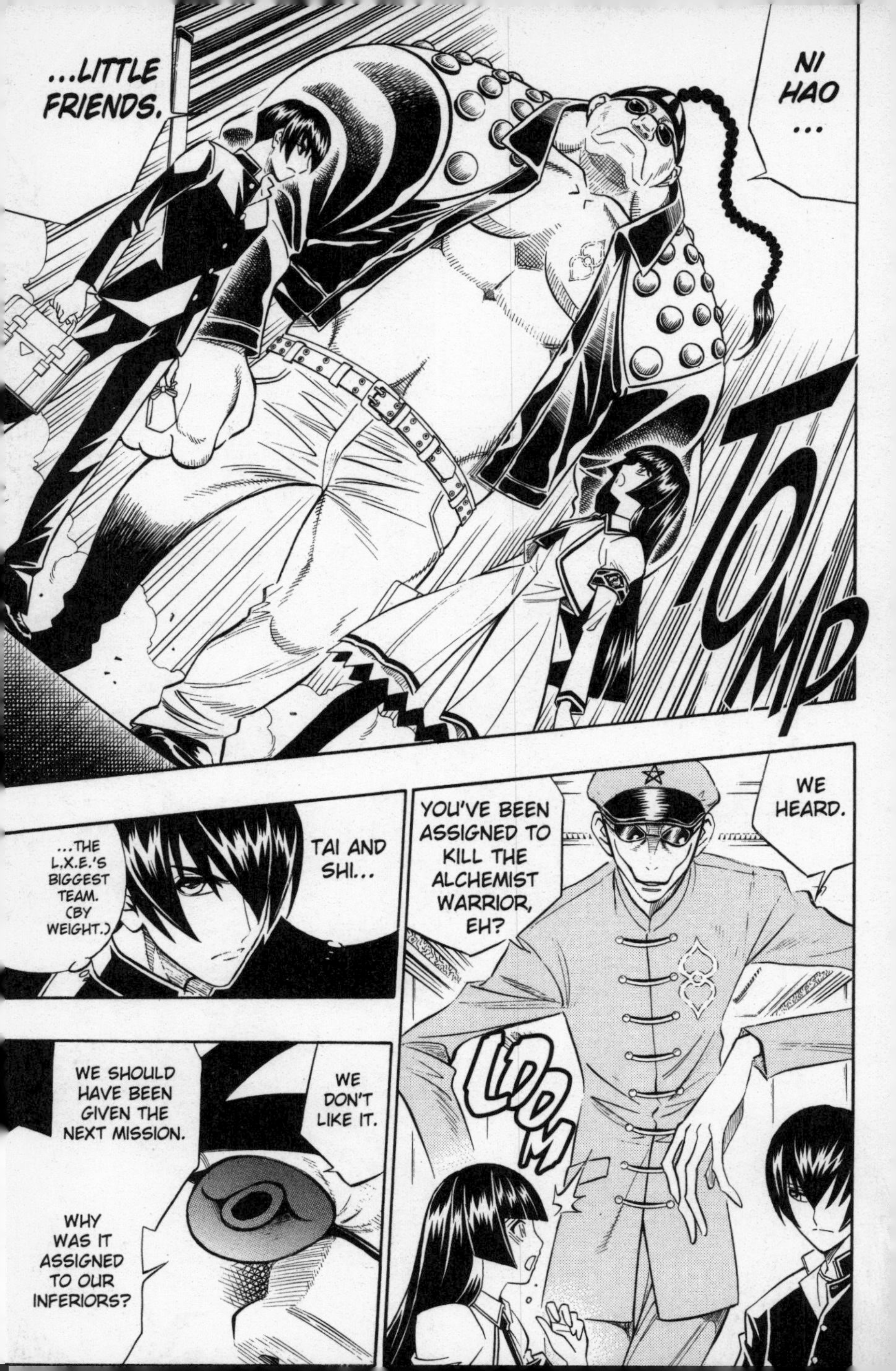
NI HAO ...
...LITTLE FRIENDS.
TOMP
WE HEARD.
YOU'VE BEEN ASSIGNED TO KILL THE ALCHEMIST WARRIOR, EH?
LOOM
TAI AND SHI...
...THE L.X.E.'S BIGGEST TEAM. (BY WEIGHT.)
WE DON'T LIKE IT.
WE SHOULD HAVE BEEN GIVEN THE NEXT MISSION.
WHY WAS IT ASSIGNED TO OUR INFERIORS?

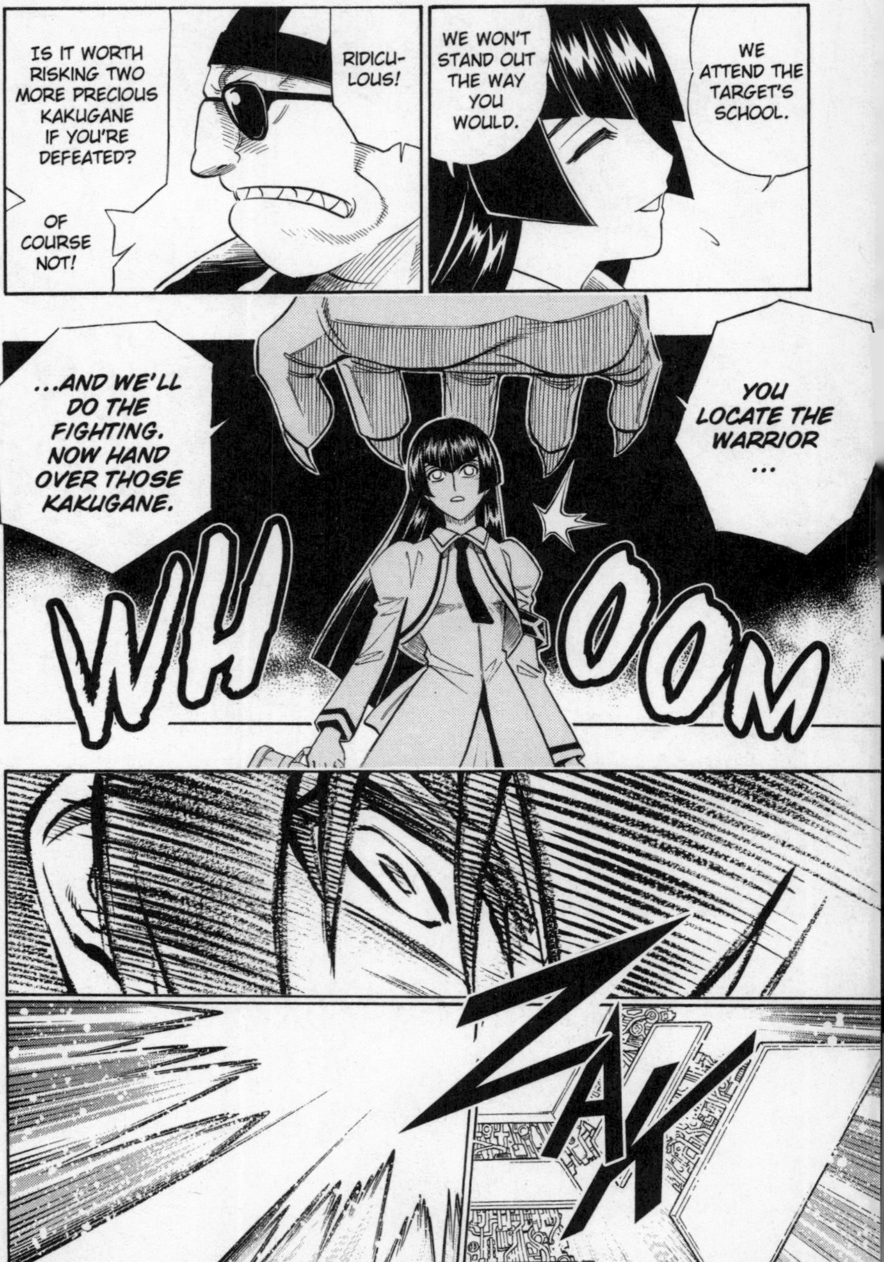
WE ATTEND THE TARGET'S SCHOOL.
WE WON'T STAND OUT THE WAY YOU WOULD.
RIDICU-LOUS!
IS IT WORTH RISKING TWO MORE PRECIOUS KAKUGANE IF YOU'RE DEFEATED?
OF COURSE NOT!
YOU LOCATE THE WARRIOR ...
...AND WE'LL DO THE FIGHTING. NOW HAND OVER THOSE KAKUGANE.
WHOOM
ZAK

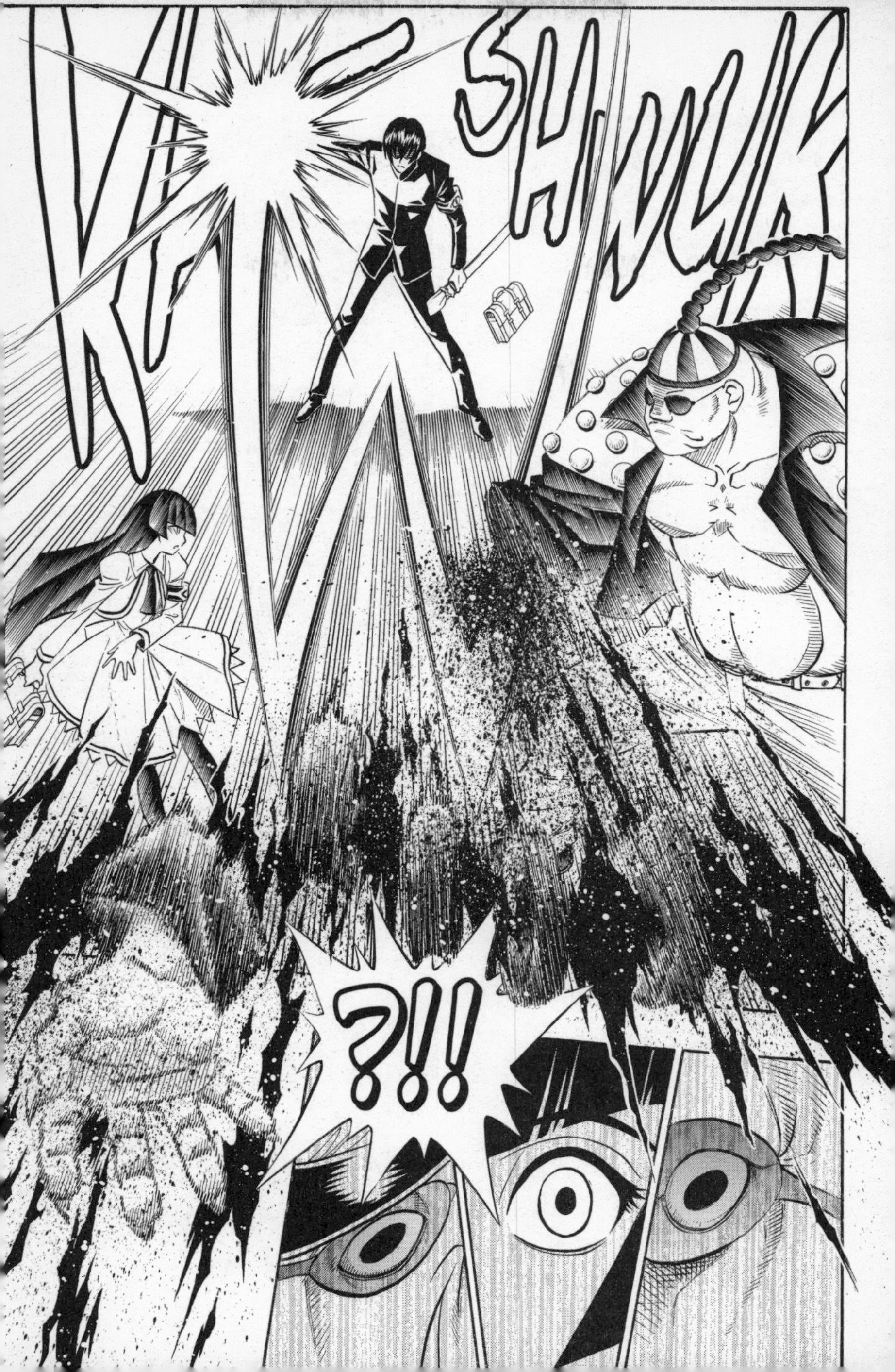
KA SHUNK
?!!

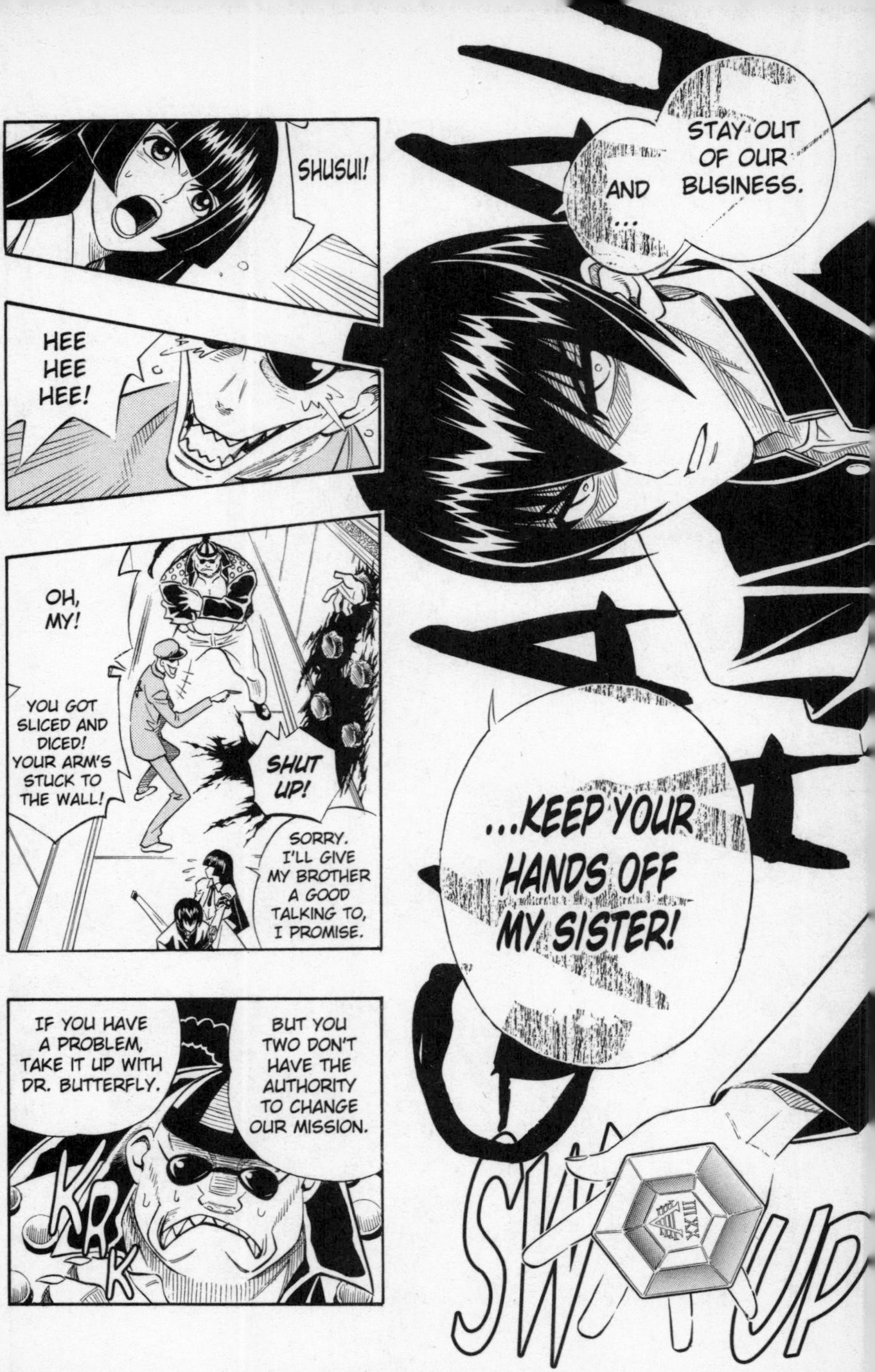
STAY OUT OF OUR BUSINESS.
AND...
...KEEP YOUR HANDS OFF MY SISTER!
SHUSUI!
HEE HEE HEE!
OH, MY!
YOU GOT SLICED AND DICED! YOUR ARM'S STUCK TO THE WALL!
SHUT UP!
SORRY. I'LL GIVE MY BROTHER A GOOD TALKING TO, I PROMISE.
BUT YOU TWO DON'T HAVE THE AUTHORITY TO CHANGE OUR MISSION.
IF YOU HAVE A PROBLEM, TAKE IT UP WITH DR. BUTTERFLY.
KRK

READ THIS WAY

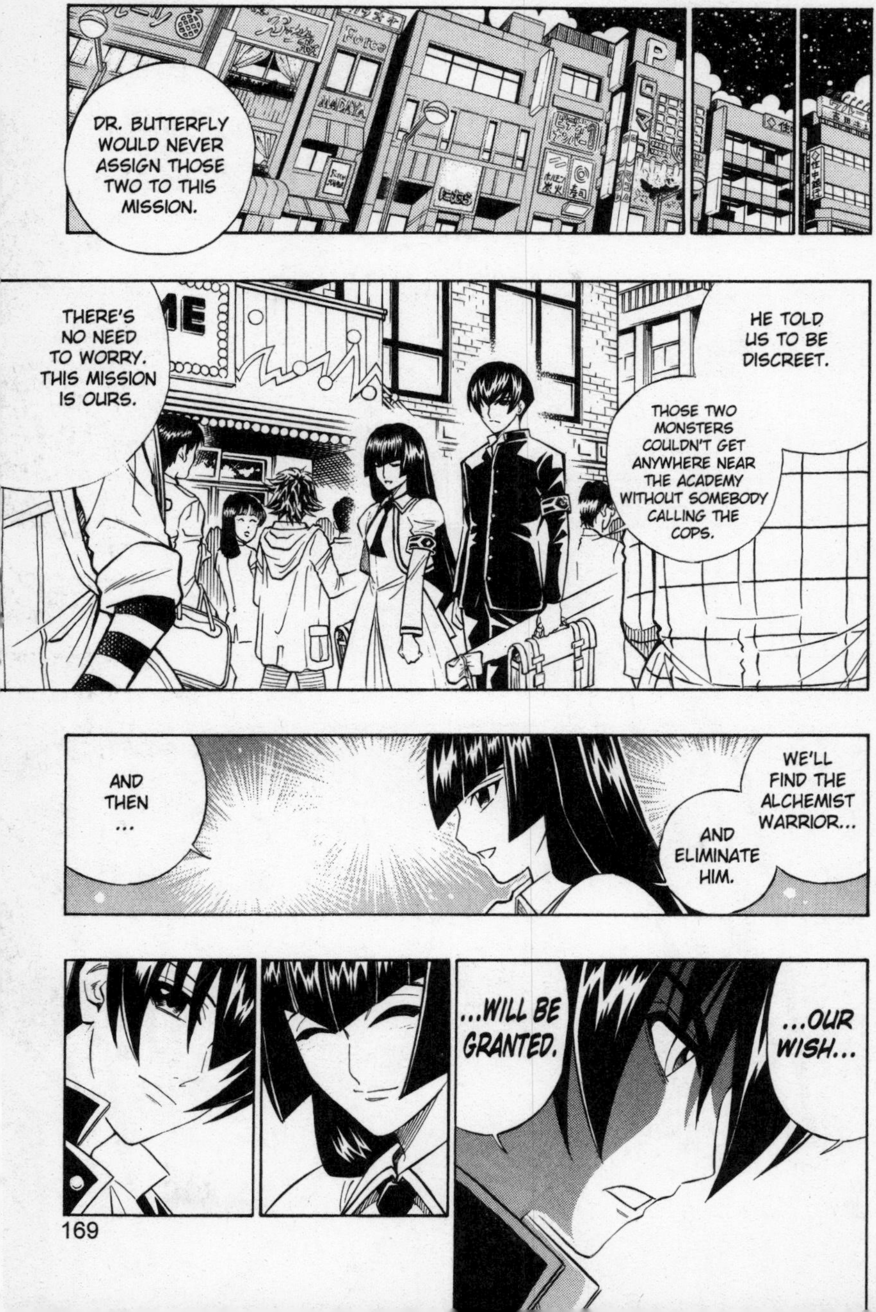
DR. BUTTERFLY WOULD NEVER ASSIGN THOSE TWO TO THIS MISSION.
HE TOLD US TO BE DISCREET.
THOSE TWO MONSTERS COULDN'T GET ANYWHERE NEAR THE ACADEMY WITHOUT SOMEBODY CALLING THE COPS.
THERE'S NO NEED TO WORRY. THIS MISSION IS OURS.
WE'LL FIND THE ALCHEMIST WARRIOR...
AND ELIMINATE HIM.
AND THEN ...
...OUR WISH...
...WILL BE GRANTED.

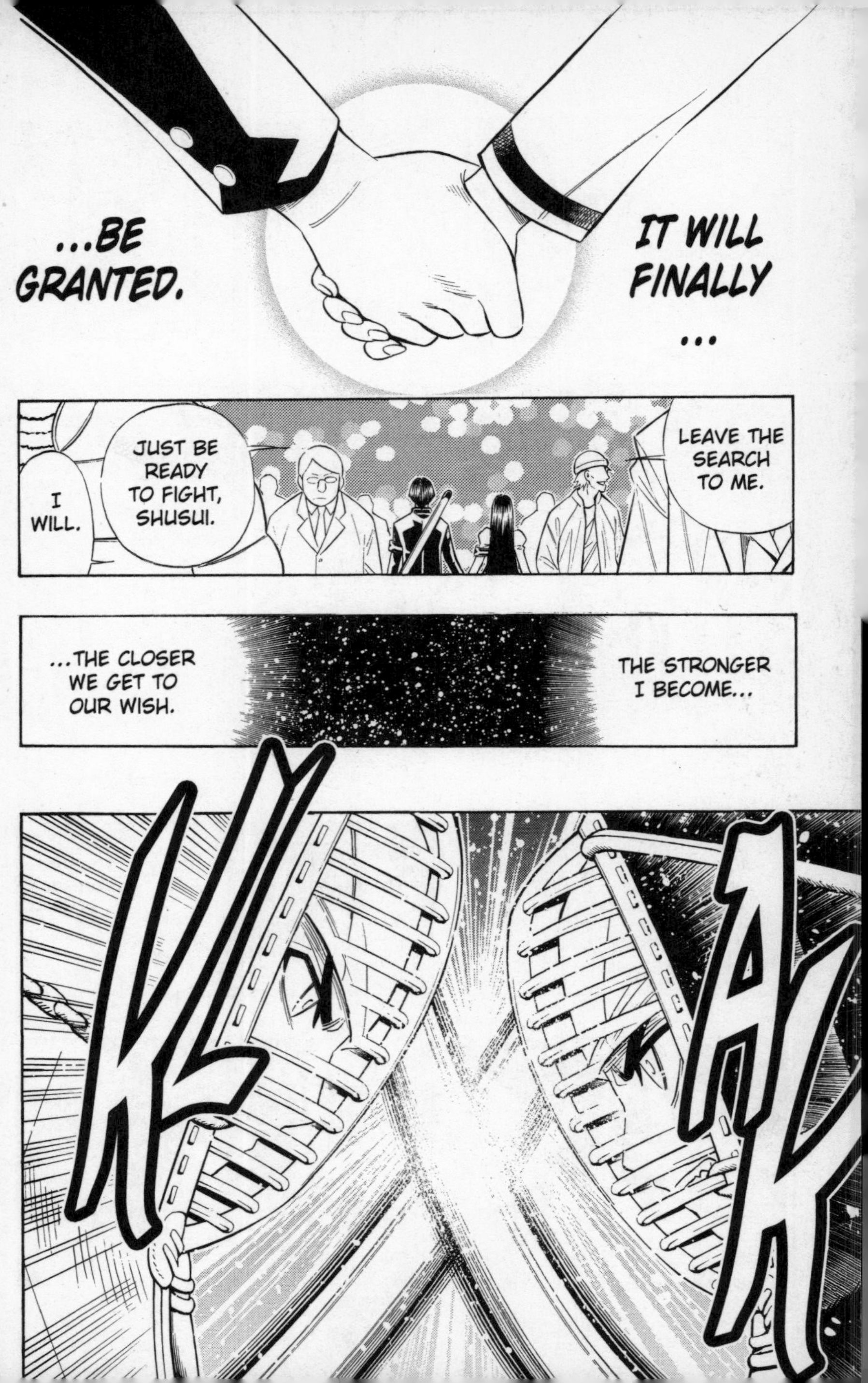
IT WILL FINALLY ...
...BE GRANTED.
LEAVE THE SEARCH TO ME.
JUST BE READY TO FIGHT, SHUSUI.
I WILL.
THE STRONGER I BECOME...
...THE CLOSER WE GET TO OUR WISH.
KLAK

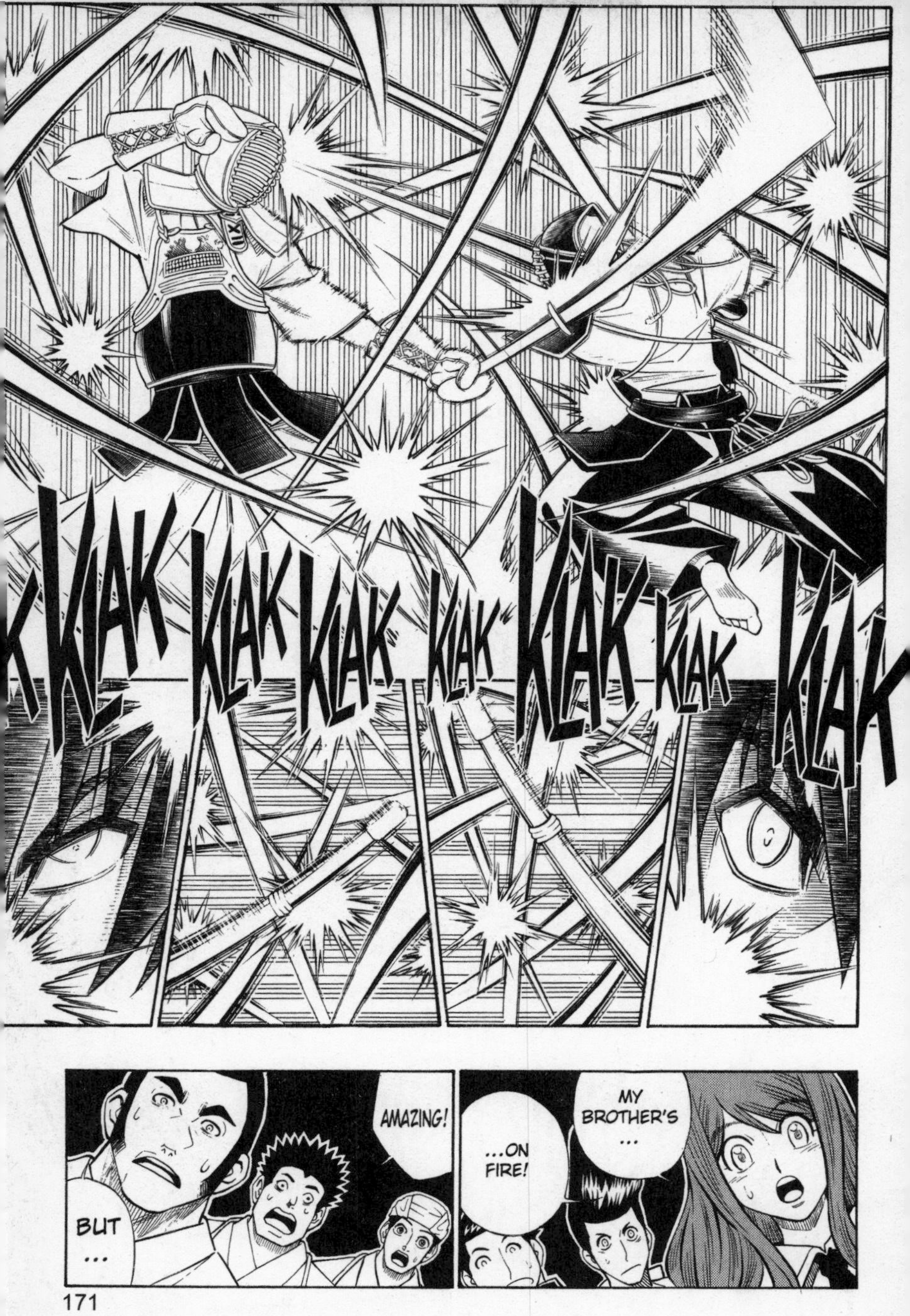
KLAK KLAK KLAK KLAK KLAK KLAK KLAK
MY BROTHER'S ...
...ON FIRE!
AMAZING!
BUT ...

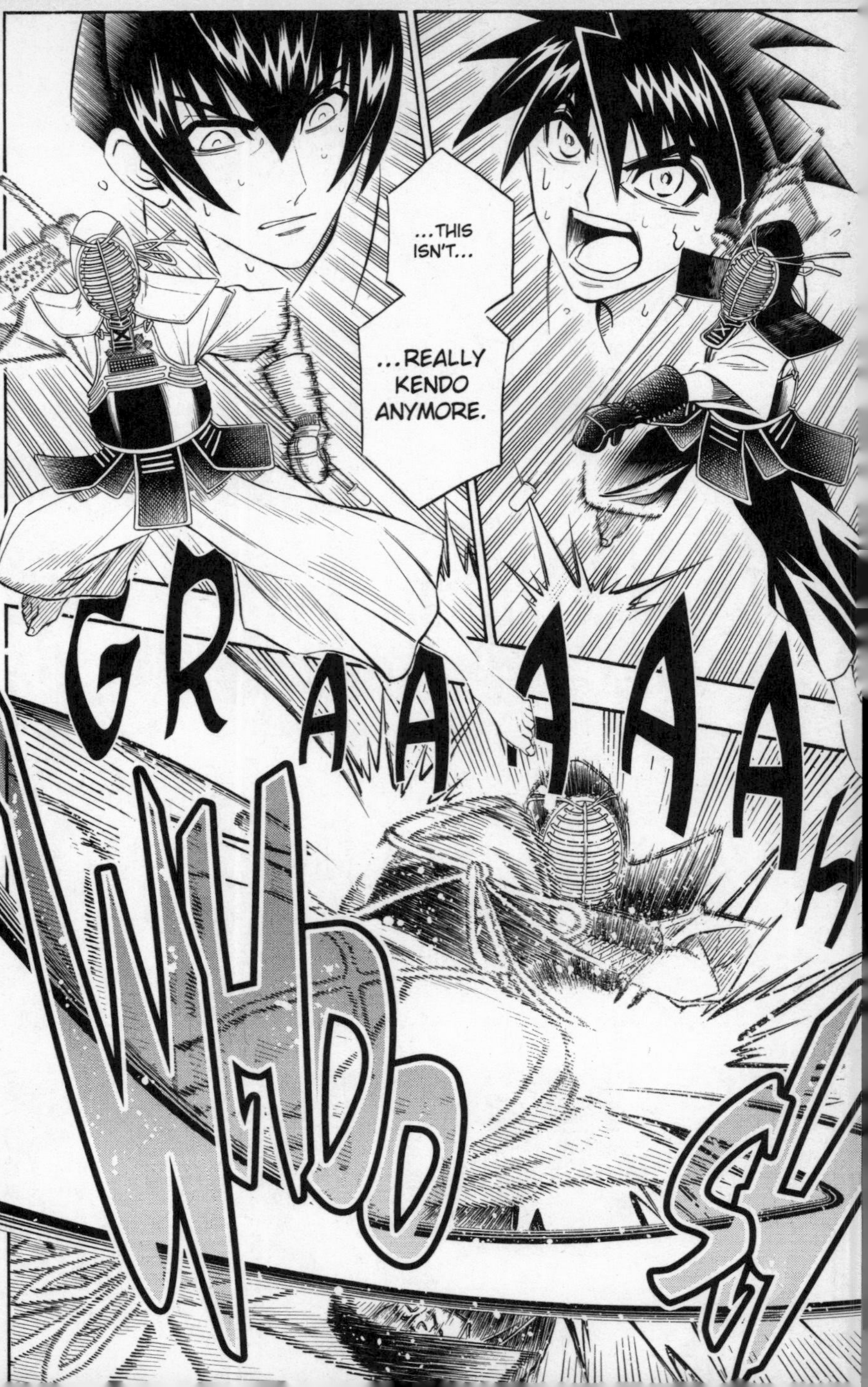
...THIS ISN'T...
...REALLY KENDO ANYMORE.
GRAAAAAH
WHOOSH

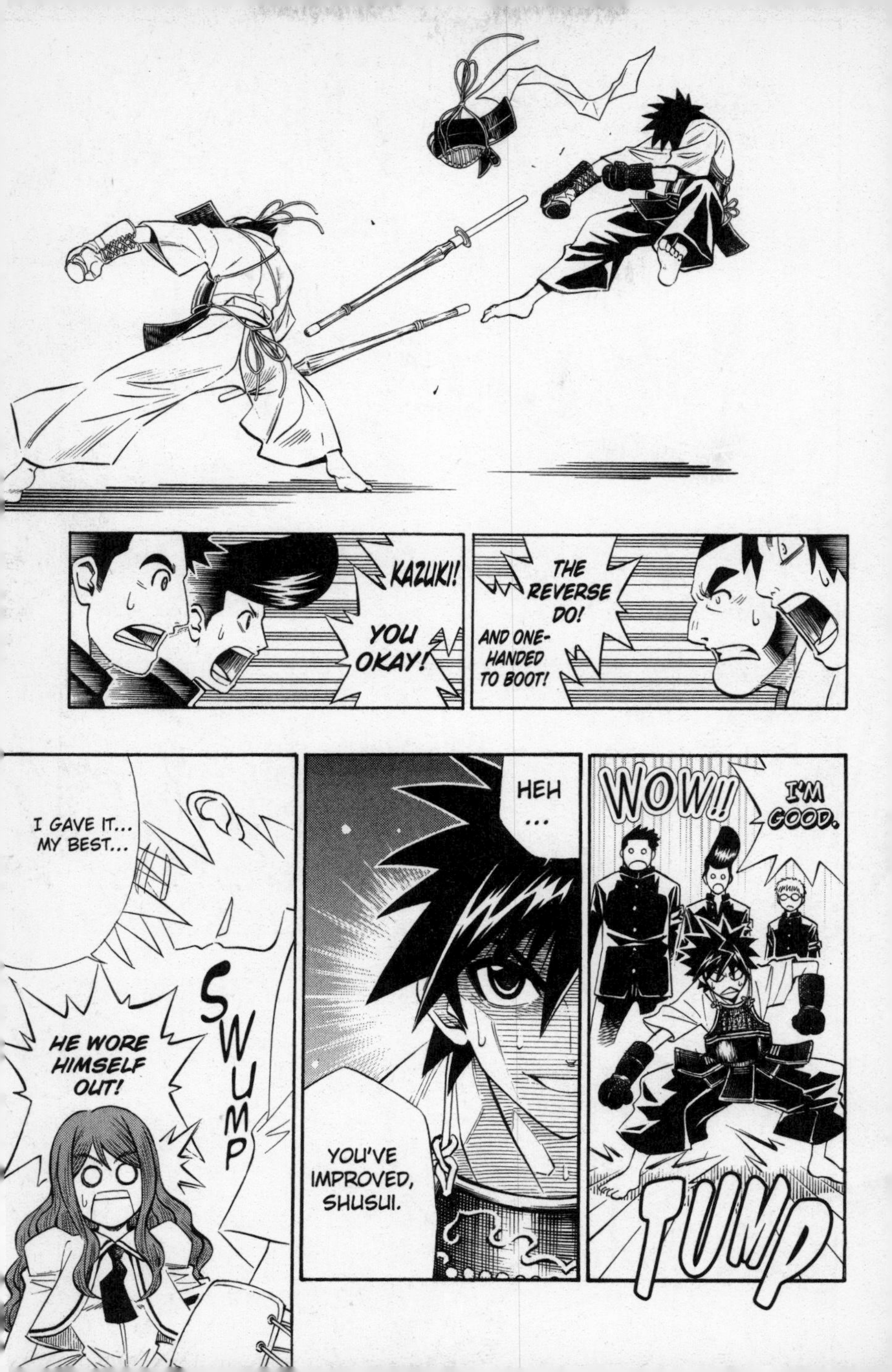
THE REVERSE DO!
AND ONE-HANDED TO BOOT!
KAZUKI!
YOU OKAY!
WOW!!
I'M GOOD.
TUMP
HEH ...
YOU'VE IMPROVED, SHUSUI.
I GAVE IT... MY BEST...
SWUMP
HE WORE HIMSELF OUT!

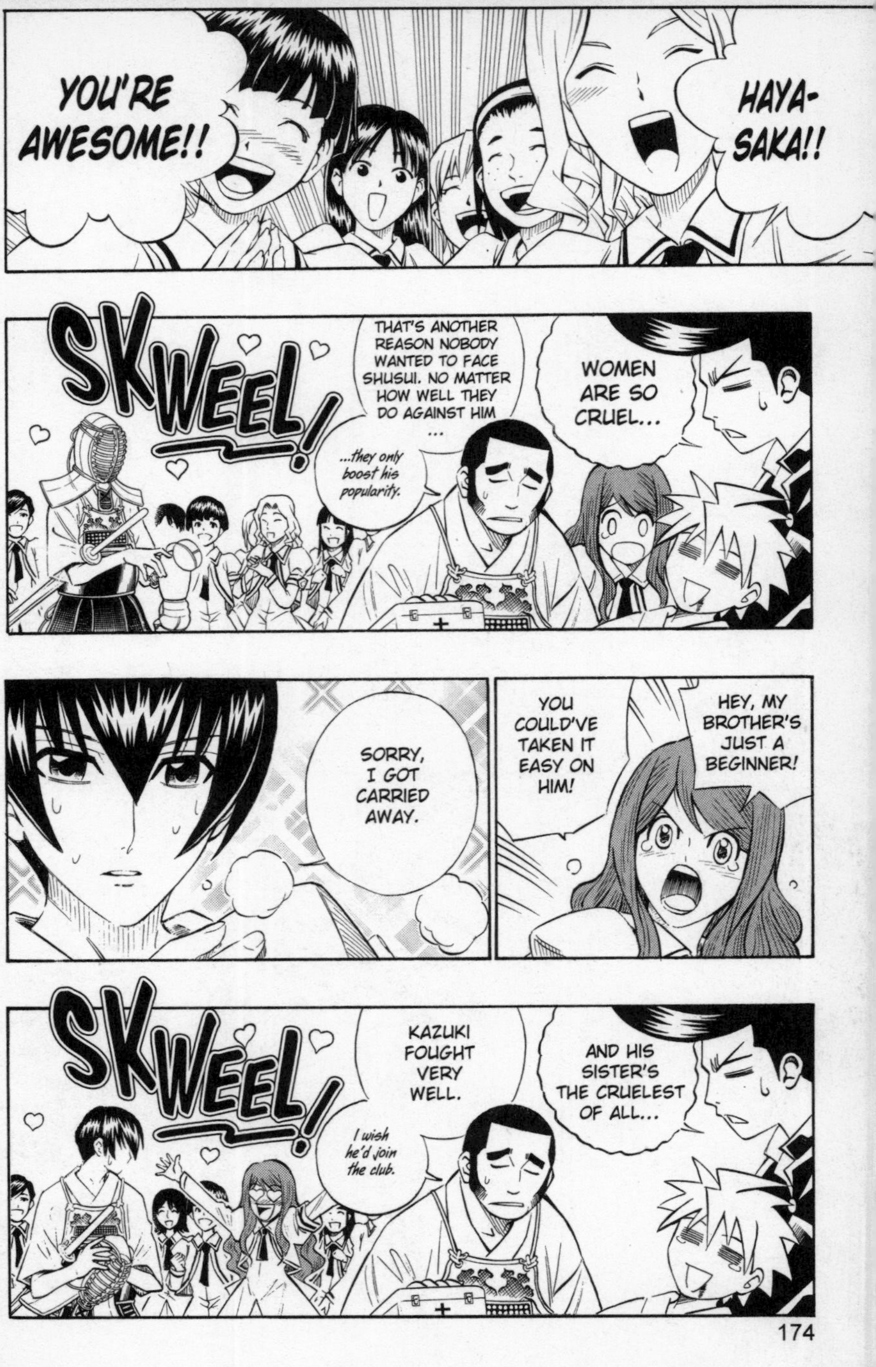
HAYA-SAKA!!
YOU'RE AWESOME!!
THAT'S ANOTHER REASON NOBODY WANTED TO FACE SHUSUI. NO MATTER HOW WELL THEY DO AGAINST HIM ...
...they only boost his popularity.
WOMEN ARE SO CRUEL...
SKWEEL!
HEY, MY BROTHER'S JUST A BEGINNER!
YOU COULD'VE TAKEN IT EASY ON HIM!
SORRY, I GOT CARRIED AWAY.
KAZUKI FOUGHT VERY WELL.
I wish he'd join the club.
AND HIS SISTER'S THE CRUELEST OF ALL...
SKWEEL!

READ THIS WAY

ARE YOU ALL RIGHT ...
...KAZUKI?
YEAH, JUST A LITTLE FRUSTRATED.
IT'S BEEN A WEEK AND I STILL CAN'T STOP HIS REVERSE DO.
ARE YOU KIDDING ME?!
YOU SHOULD BE PROUD TO BE DOING SO WELL AGAINST SHUSUI AFTER ONLY ONE WEEK!
Even if what you're doing isn't exactly Kendo.
TWITCH
TWITCH
YOU'RE INCREDIBLE!
REMARK-ABLE INDEED.
HMPH... HE'S STILL NO MATCH FOR MY POMPADOUR ATTACK!
THOSE GUYS ARE RIGHT, KAZUKI. YOU'RE IMPROVING FAST.
BUT SO AM I.
IT'S AS IF YOU AND I...
...WERE DESTINED TO FACE EACH OTHER.

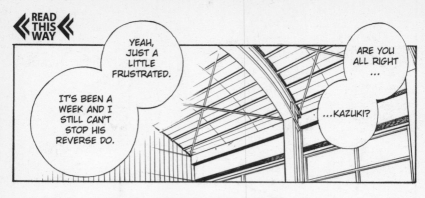

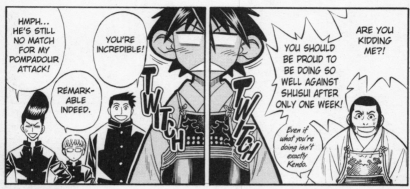

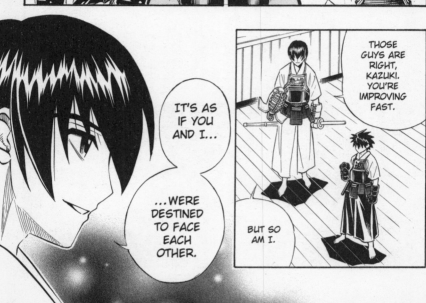

...

TUK

HE'S GETTING BASIC TRAINING AS AN ALCHEMIST WARRIOR...

...AND MORE BATTLE EXPERIENCE IN THESE KENDO MATCHES.

BUT MORE IMPORTANTLY...

I WANT TO BECOME AS STRONG AS I CAN BE!

...HE'S GOT THE DRIVE TO SEE IT ALL THROUGH.

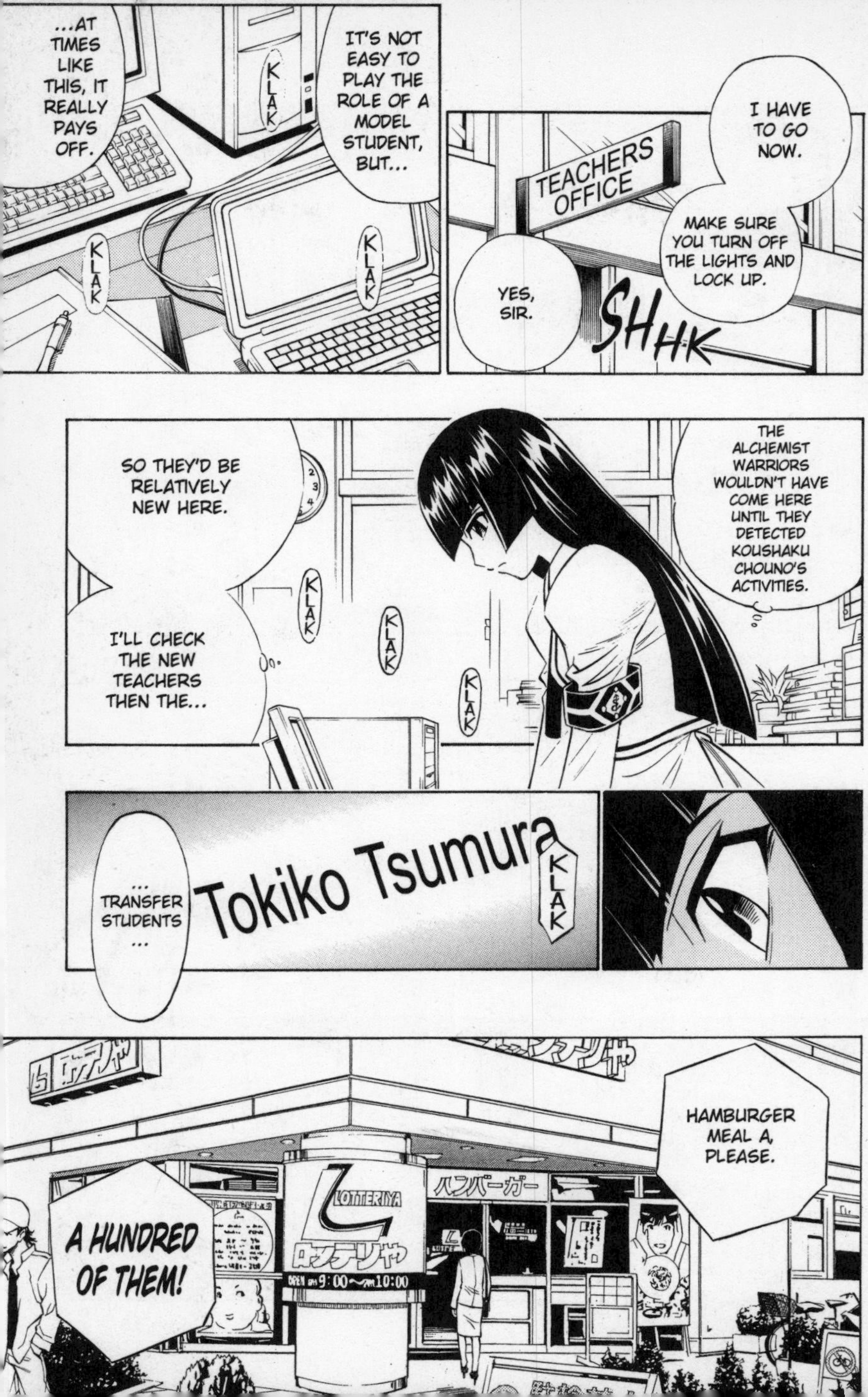
TEACHERS OFFICE
I HAVE TO GO NOW.
MAKE SURE YOU TURN OFF THE LIGHTS AND LOCK UP.
YES, SIR.
SHHK
IT'S NOT EASY TO PLAY THE ROLE OF A MODEL STUDENT, BUT...
...AT TIMES LIKE THIS, IT REALLY PAYS OFF.
KLAK
KLAK
KLAK
THE ALCHEMIST WARRIORS WOULDN'T HAVE COME HERE UNTIL THEY DETECTED KOUSHAKU CHOUNO'S ACTIVITIES.
SO THEY'D BE RELATIVELY NEW HERE.
I'LL CHECK THE NEW TEACHERS THEN THE...
KLAK
KLAK
KLAK
...TRANSFER STUDENTS...
Tokiko Tsumura
KLAK
HAMBURGER MEAL A, PLEASE.
A HUNDRED OF THEM!
LOTTERIYA
ロッテリヤ
ハンバーガー
OPEN 9:00〜10:00

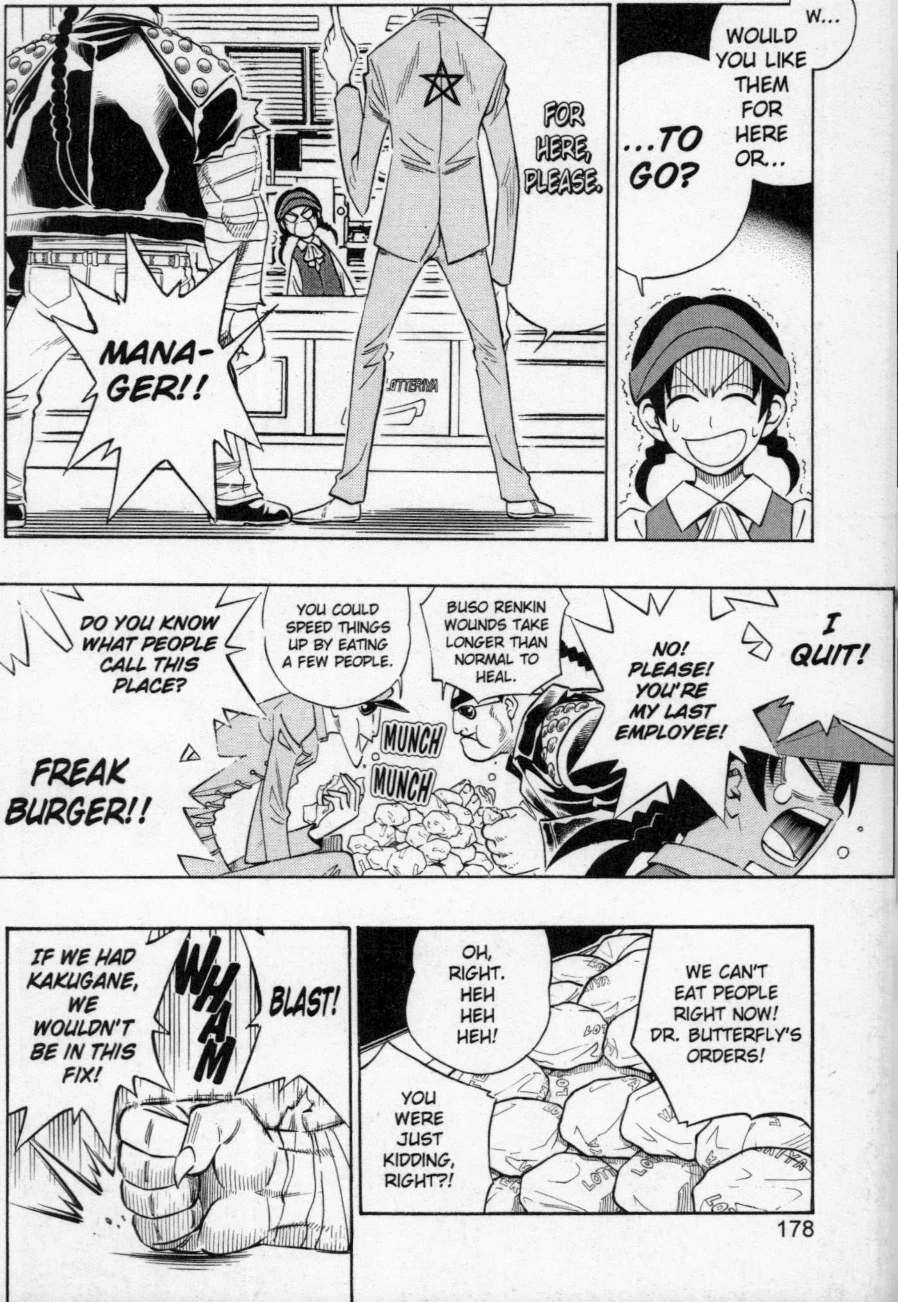
W... WOULD YOU LIKE THEM FOR HERE OR...
...TO GO?
FOR HERE, PLEASE.
MANA-GER!!
I QUIT!
NO! PLEASE! YOU'RE MY LAST EMPLOYEE!
BUSO RENKIN WOUNDS TAKE LONGER THAN NORMAL TO HEAL.
MUNCH
MUNCH
YOU COULD SPEED THINGS UP BY EATING A FEW PEOPLE.
DO YOU KNOW WHAT PEOPLE CALL THIS PLACE?
FREAK BURGER!!
WE CAN'T EAT PEOPLE RIGHT NOW! DR. BUTTERFLY'S ORDERS!
OH, RIGHT. HEH HEH HEH!
YOU WERE JUST KIDDING, RIGHT?!
BLAST!
WHAM
IF WE HAD KAKUGANE, WE WOULDN'T BE IN THIS FIX!

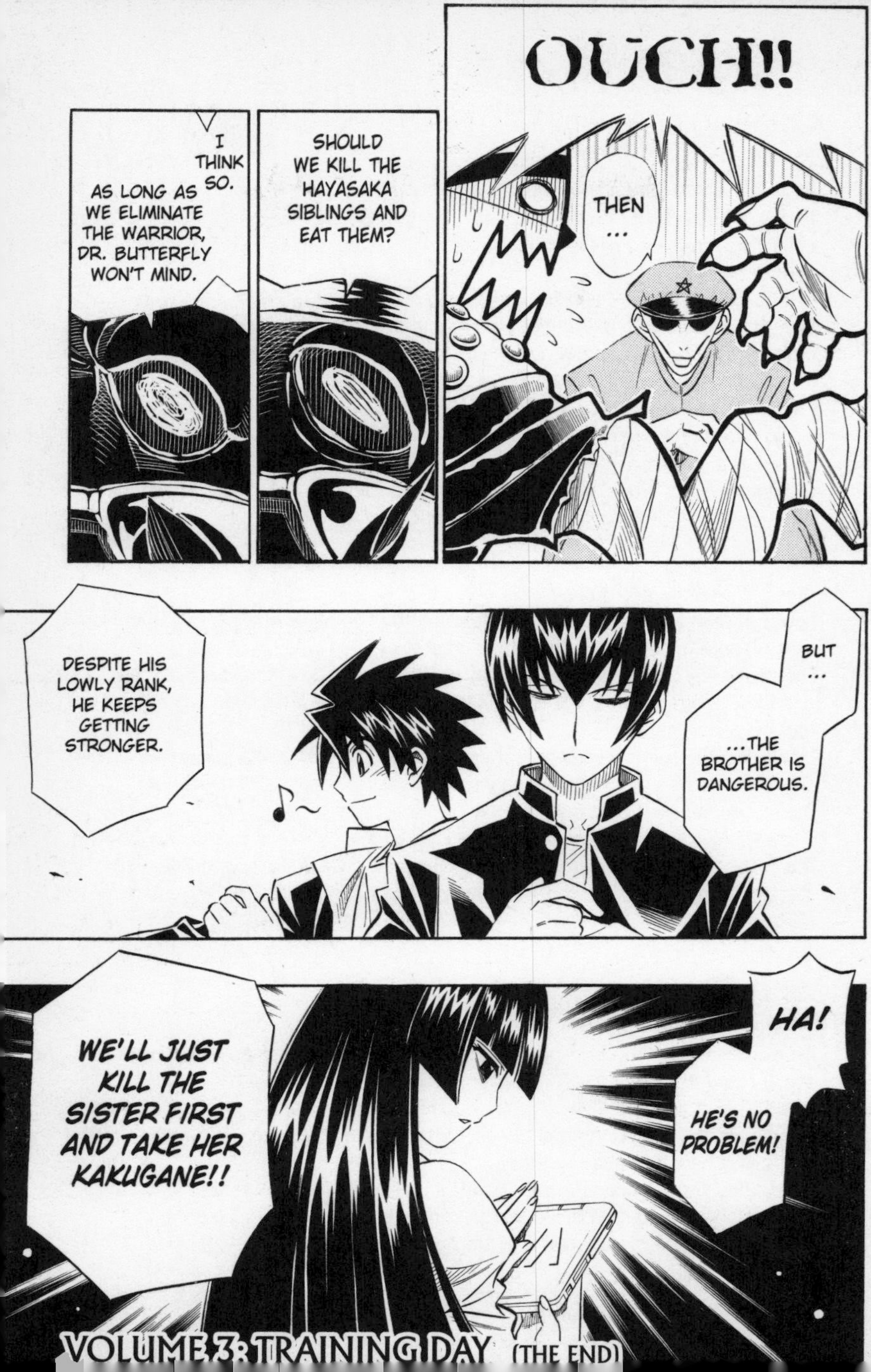
OUCH!!
THEN ...
SHOULD WE KILL THE HAYASAKA SIBLINGS AND EAT THEM?
I THINK SO.
AS LONG AS WE ELIMINATE THE WARRIOR, DR. BUTTERFLY WON'T MIND.
BUT ...
...THE BROTHER IS DANGEROUS.
DESPITE HIS LOWLY RANK, HE KEEPS GETTING STRONGER.
HA!
HE'S NO PROBLEM!
WE'LL JUST KILL THE SISTER FIRST AND TAKE HER KAKUGANE!!
VOLUME 3: TRAINING DAY (THE END)

Chapter 18: If You Doubt that You Are a Hypocrite
· There's a bit of drama in the snail family on the "Experiencing Technical Difficulties" card. One of the little ones is really a slug. I hope to tell that story if I get the chance.
· I tried to show Kazuki's conflicted feelings in this chapter. Actually, I'd like to have done more with it, but that would've gotten depressing, so I condensed it into one chapter. ("Make the mountains tall and the valleys between narrow" is the Shonen manga philosophy. Especially at Jump)
· Here the L.X.E. was introduced. The name comes from the American comic book series, *The League of Extraordinary Gentlemen* (L.X.G.). In the beginning, I considered making its members famous alchemists, but I was told that only alchemy fanatics would get it, so that idea was canned.

Chapter 19: Kazuki and Tokiko's Choice, Part 1
· I put Tokiko in a Ginsei Academy uniform on the title page as a gift to all the fans who wanted to see her in one. I have to say, it doesn't really suit her.
· The freaky pig, Buhiro, makes a casual appearance. I know that some readers don't like things like this, but please forgive this bit of humor. I couldn't help myself.
· I really like the comic exchange between Kazuki and Tokiko in this chapter. I can only write them when I feel my gray matter leaking out. It really makes me appreciate the skills of comedic comic artists.
· There's a hint about the big boss of the L.X.E. in this chapter. I wasn't sure how much to reveal, but by juxtaposing the speeches of Dr. Butterfly and Bravo, I managed to plant the desired information. I just hope the readers were able to pick up on it.

Chapter 20: Kazuki and Tokiko's Choice, Part 2
· Papillon makes his return in an elegant outfit. I really enjoyed drawing him like that. I could really feel my gray matter leaking out.
· Here I played with the idea so often found in American comics that heroes and villains are shocking to normal people by sticking my characters in a burger joint, and this is how it turned out. Hmm…
· Kazuki decides he's going to fight. Watsuki believes this is the true essence of the hero, but it's so hard to illustrate it convincingly. Even though it's the main theme of this series, I still find it hard to portray.

· The True Power of humanoid Homunculi is that they can use both conventional weapons and Buso Renkin. This was an idea that I had before the series started, but now I think it may have been a little overcomplicated.

Chapter 21: Kazuki and Tokiko's Choice, Part 3

· Kinjo's habit of saying "Hyahoo!" was pretty popular. I guess he was really happy to get his own Kakugane.
· The giant fist was another pre-series idea I had. Someone suggested that I make the battles funny, but I'll go into that another time.
· In the early stages, Bravo would yell "BRA-BRA-BRA-BRA-BRA-BRAA!" whenever he delivered a flurry of punches, but some people thought that was too much. Duh…
· I ran out of pages in this chapter so Kazuki didn't get to do much. I should have extended the story by another chapter.

Chapter 22: Night in the Dormitory

· I played with the timeline here and added flashbacks which made the story a little hard to follow. Sorry about that.
· Tokiko's tracksuit turned out well despite being hurriedly designed. I can't expect to get lucky like that every time so I need to do more research on teen fashions. But at my age, going to a bookstore to buy teen fashion mags is a little embarrassing.

Chapter 23: Warrior Tokiko

· The crowd scenes (students, pedestrians, and people in the backgrounds) were mostly drawn by assistants due to time constraints. Unfortunately, they had a hard time imitating my art style. I always thought my characters had a very simple anime look to them…
· When Rokumasu and the others were hypnotized, I decided they should retain elements of their regular personalities instead of turning into totally mindless zombies.
· I learned how to show Tokiko jumping around in her Valkyrie Skirt from drawing her battle with Washio. I'm glad the readers liked it so much.
· A bit of Tokiko's past was revealed. But who is this Nishiyama?
· Because this isn't an adult manga, I covered some of the more graphic gore with mosaics, but an editor suggested that I stop this because it makes them seem worse than they really are. What do I do now? [see page 114.5]

Chapter 24: Destroy All Enemies

· I exposed Tokiko's legs by having her track pants get ripped as a service to our readers…not. This was something I wanted to experiment with. After drawing Papillon for a while, I realized it was easier to draw defined bodies than bodies in loser clothes. When I first started as a manga artist, I hated drawing stuff like that. But I tested the theory and in fact, unclothed legs are easier to draw. As a result, Tokiko's battle with Papillon was easy.

· This is the debut of Ouka. Because I hadn't drawn her very much, her face didn't feel right to me.

Chapter 25: The Hayasaka Siblings

· My editor and I got into a heated debate about whether it was King Kamehameha or King Hamehameha who took the day off when it rained. I thought it was Kamehameha, so I went with that. Later I learned that it was Hamehameha, but it was too late to change it by then. So for Watsuki, the correct answer is Kamehameha!

· The kendo scenes were very popular in reader polls. Maybe they bring back memories.

· I learned that stuff about the Reverse Do from my kendo teacher in junior high. He was an amazing master with the rank of seventh-dan.

· This is the debut of Shusui. Again, not having drawn him much, his face didn't seem right.

· I put a lot of school activities into this chapter. There's the soccer scene, the kendo club, and the walk home. I wanted to show more of the academy. School scenes are rare in boys battle manga, so I wanted to do them to set myself apart.

Chapter 26: Training Day

· My editors told me not to play around in my storytelling, but I have to do what I'm inspired to do at the moment! I haven't gotten to the point were I can do totally serious manga. My goal is to create manga that readers will find fun and compelling!

· Return of the Freak Burger. Will the perils of the Burger Girl continue?

Hence…→   To be continued.

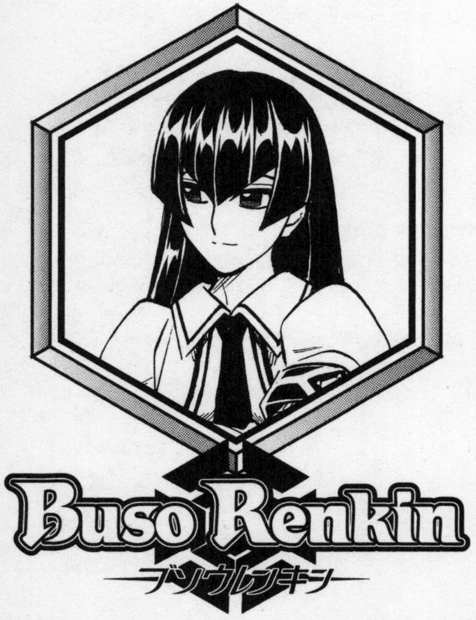

Buso Renkin

ブソウレンキン

Coming Next Volume

Kazuki and Tokiko are in for it
this time when they take on male
and female twin warriors from
the L.X.E.! During a fierce battle
Kazuki learns the tragic past of
the twins and realizes there are
more to his foes than he first
thought.

Available in February 2007!

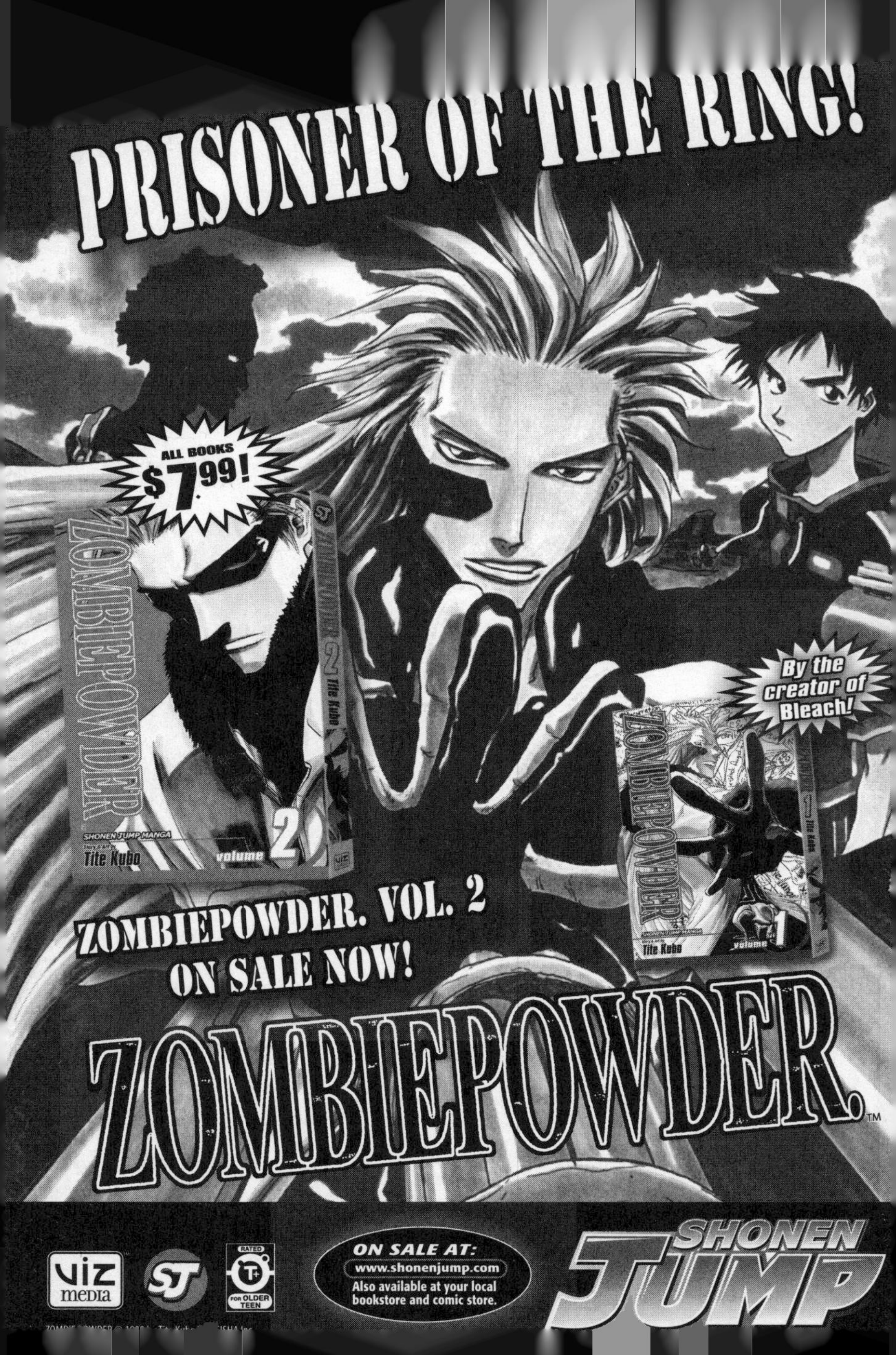

PRISONER OF THE RING!
ALL BOOKS $7.99!
ZOMBIEPOWDER 2 Tite Kubo
SHONEN JUMP MANGA
Tite Kubo
volume 2
By the creator of Bleach!
ZOMBIEPOWDER 1 Tite Kubo
SHONEN JUMP MANGA
Tite Kubo
volume 1
ZOMBIEPOWDER. VOL. 2
ON SALE NOW!
ZOMBIEPOWDER.™
viz media
SJ
RATED T+ FOR OLDER TEEN
ON SALE AT:
www.shonenjump.com
Also available at your local bookstore and comic store.
SHONEN JUMP

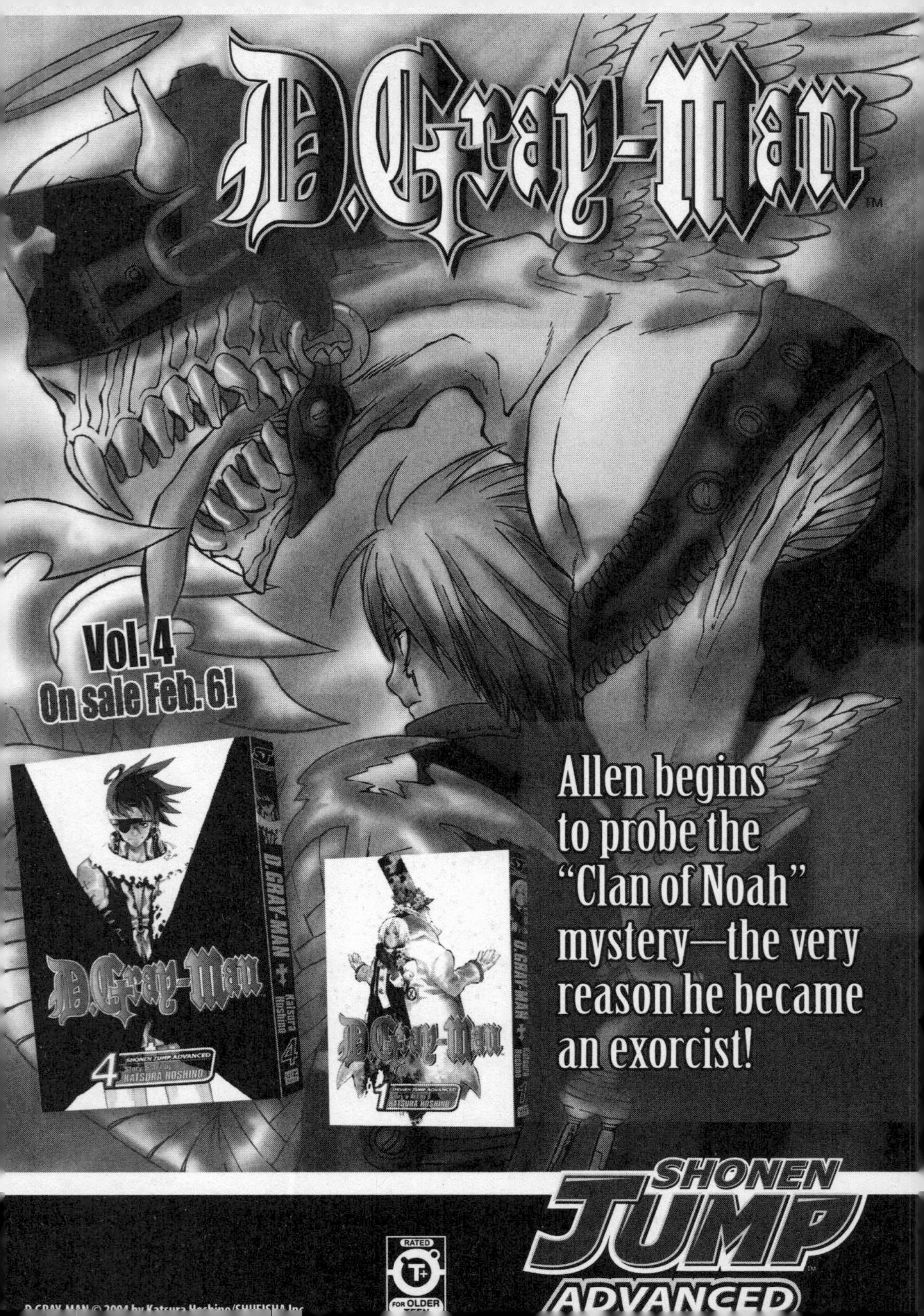
D.Gray-Man™
Vol. 4
On sale Feb. 6!
D.GRAY-MAN
D.Gray-Man
4 SHONEN JUMP ADVANCED
KATSURA HOSHINO
D.GRAY-MAN
1 SHONEN JUMP ADVANCED
KATSURA HOSHINO
Allen begins to probe the "Clan of Noah" mystery—the very reason he became an exorcist!
SHONEN JUMP ADVANCED
RATED T+ FOR OLDER TEEN
D.GRAY-MAN © 2004 by Katsura Hoshino/SHUEISHA Inc.

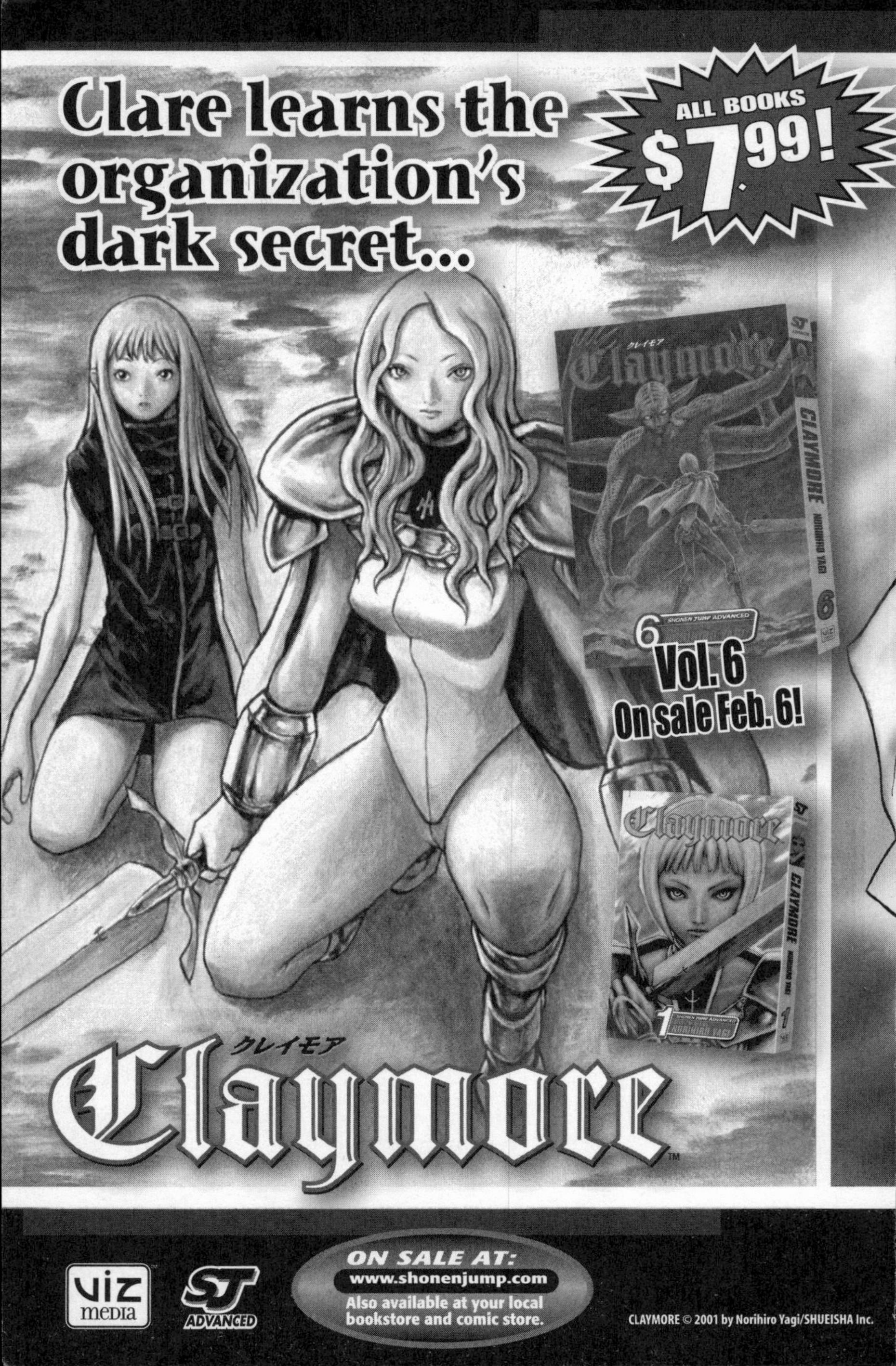
Clare learns the organization's dark secret...
ALL BOOKS $7.99!
Vol. 6
On sale Feb. 6!
クレイモア
Claymore™
viz media
SJ ADVANCED
ON SALE AT:
www.shonenjump.com
Also available at your local bookstore and comic store.
CLAYMORE © 2001 by Norihiro Yagi/SHUEISHA Inc.

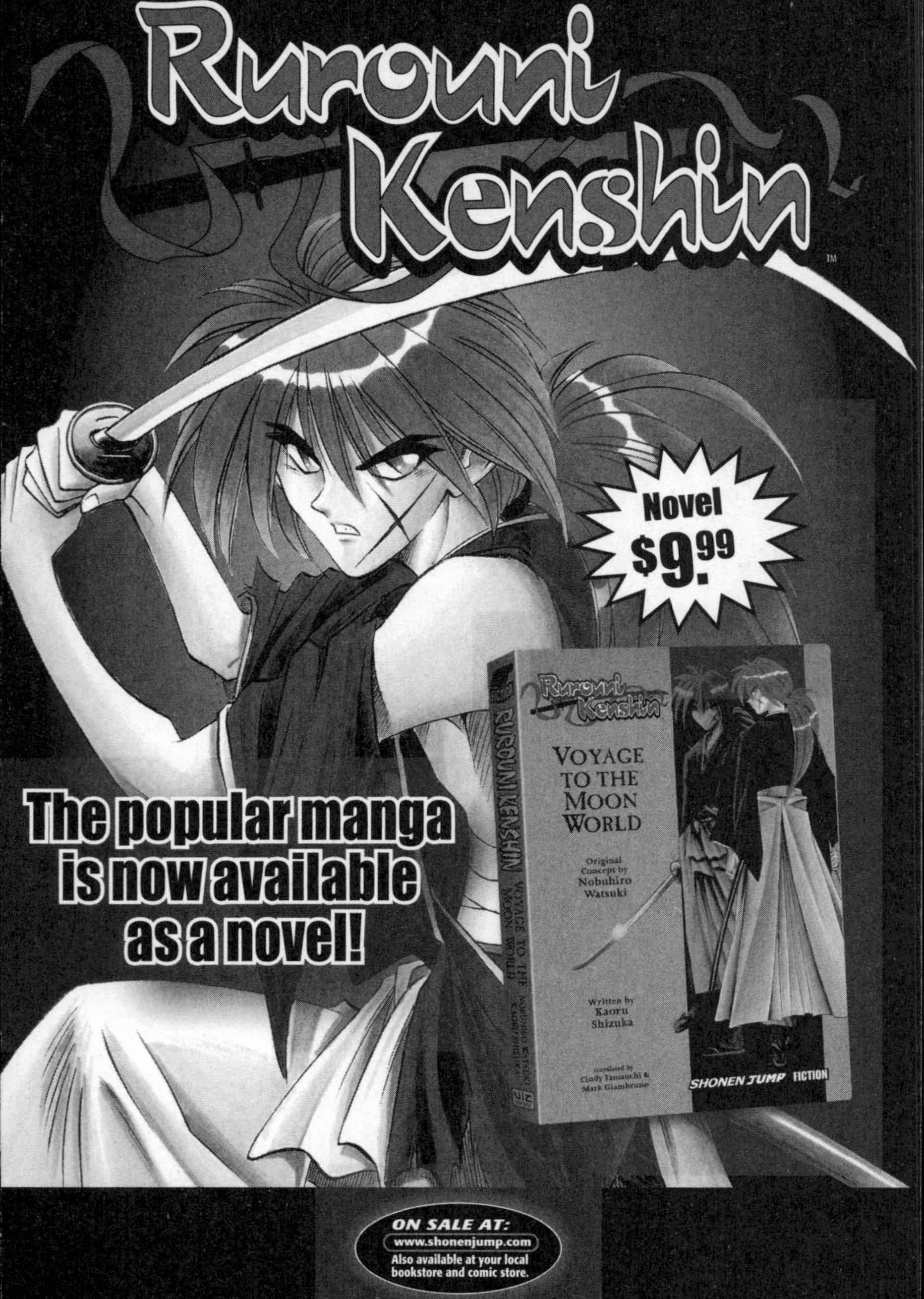
Rurouni Kenshin
TM
Novel
$9.99
Rurouni Kenshin
RUROUNI KENSHIN
VOYAGE TO THE MOON WORLD
Original Concept by Nobuhiro Watsuki
Written by Kaoru Shizuka
translated by Cindy Yamauchi & Mark Giambruno
SHONEN JUMP FICTION
The popular manga is now available as a novel!
ON SALE AT:
www.shonenjump.com
Also available at your local bookstore and comic store.

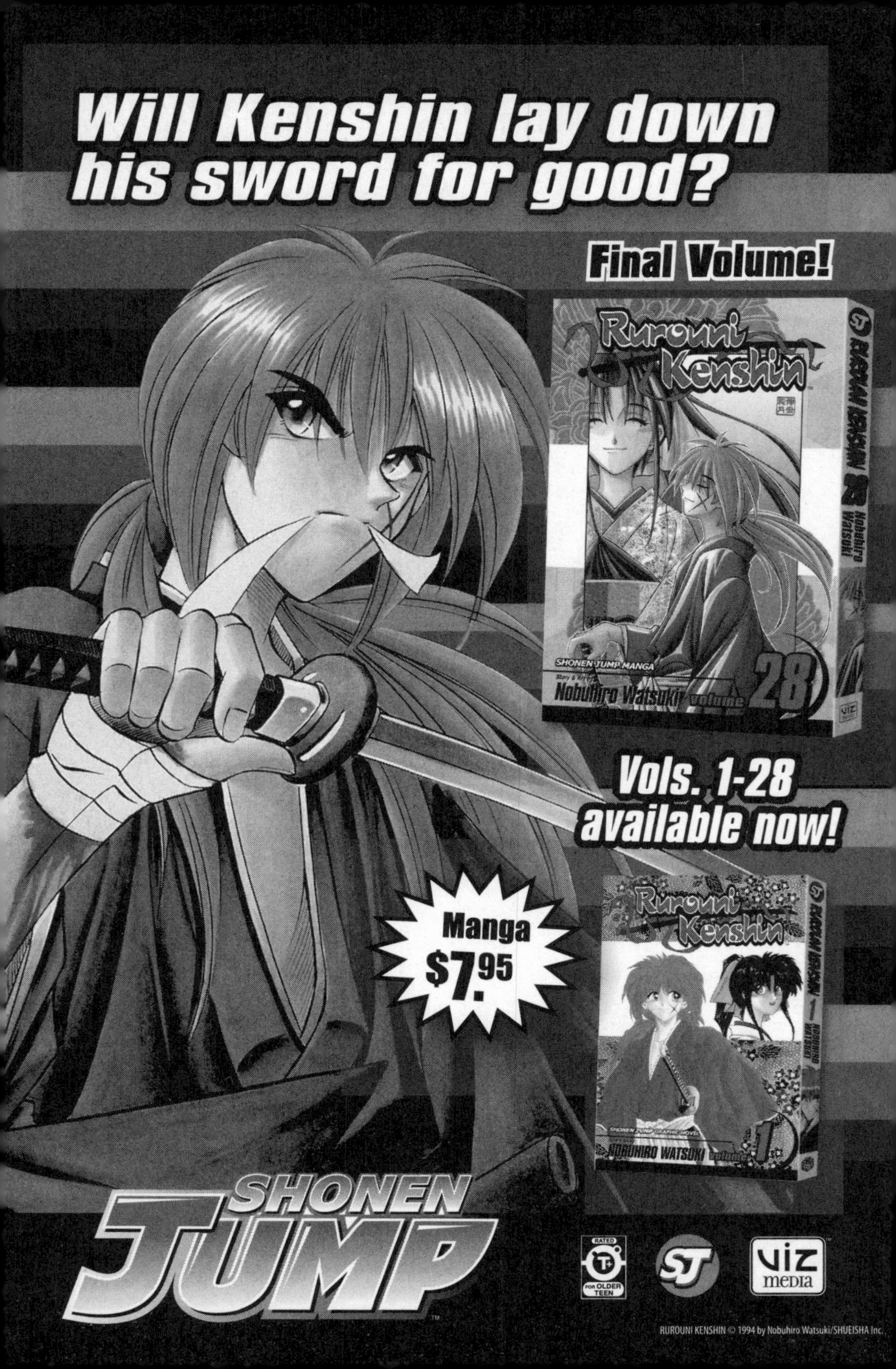
Will Kenshin lay down his sword for good?
Final Volume!
Vols. 1-28 available now!
Manga $7.95
SHONEN JUMP
RUROUNI KENSHIN © 1994 by Nobuhiro Watsuki/SHUEISHA Inc.

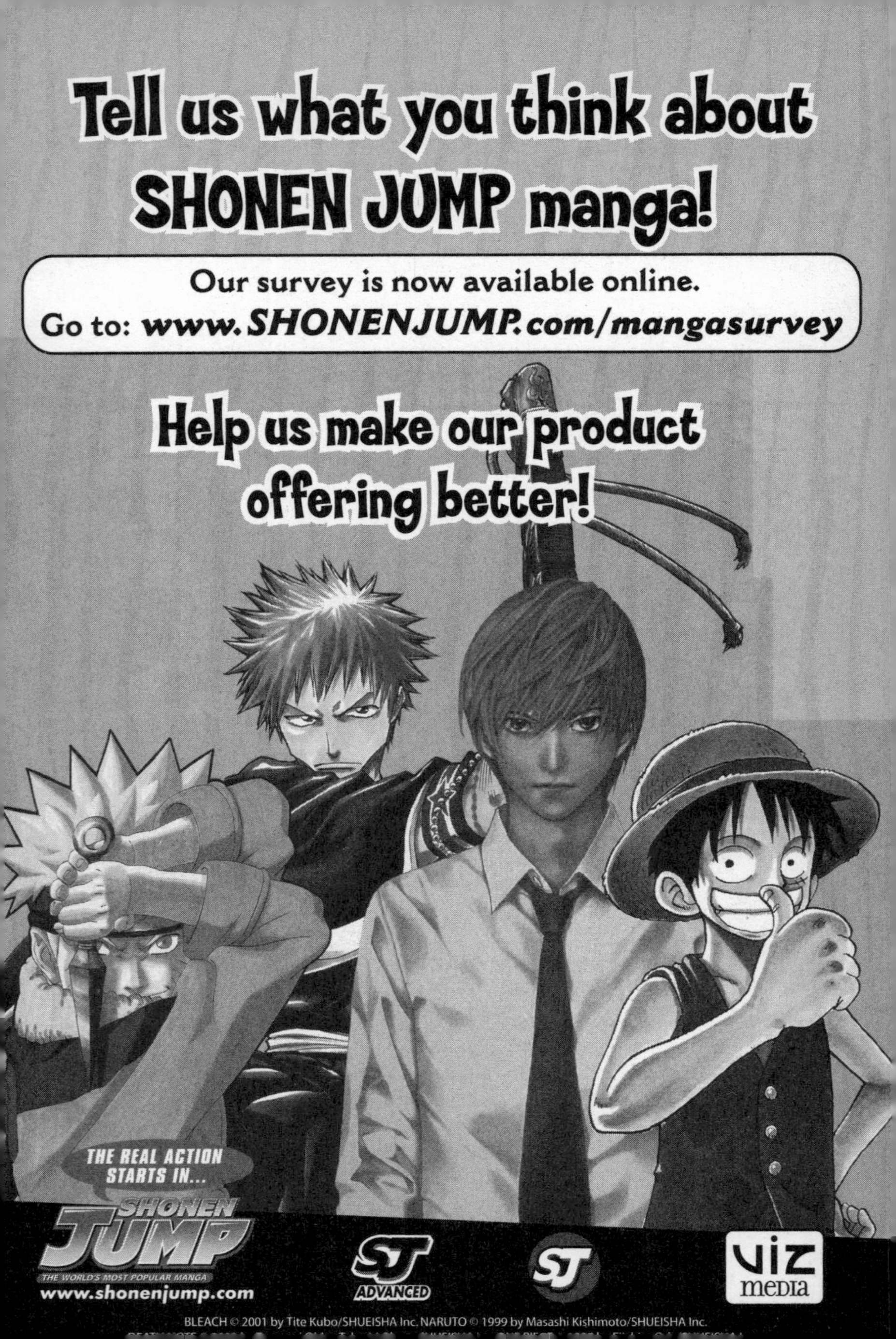